D0439305

Mozambique

Mary Fitzpatrick

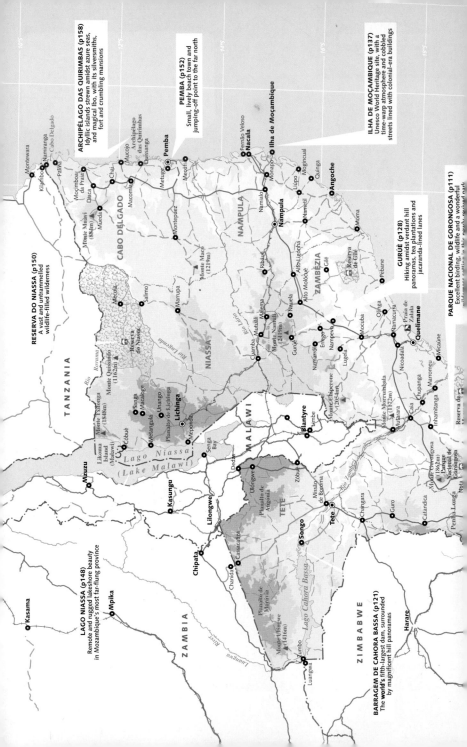

ARCHIPÉLAGO DAS QUIRIMBAS (p158)
Idyllic islands strewn amidst azure seas, and magical Ibo, with its silversmiths, fort and crumbling mansions

PEMBA (p152)
Small, lively beach town and jumping-off point to the far north

ILHA DE MOÇAMBIQUE (p137)
Unesco World Heritage site, with a time-warp atmosphere and cobbled streets lined with colonial-era buildings

RESERVA DO NIASSA (p150)
A vast and untrammelled wildlife-filled wilderness

GURUÉ (p128)
Hiking amidst verdant hill panoramas, tea plantations and jacaranda-lined lanes

PARQUE NACIONAL DE GORONGOSA (p111)
Excellent birding, wildlife and a wonderful

LAGO NIASSA (p148)
Remote and rugged lakeshore beauty in Mozambique's most far-flung province

BARRAGEM DE CAHORA BASSA (p121)
The world's fifth-largest dam, surrounded by magnificent hill panoramas

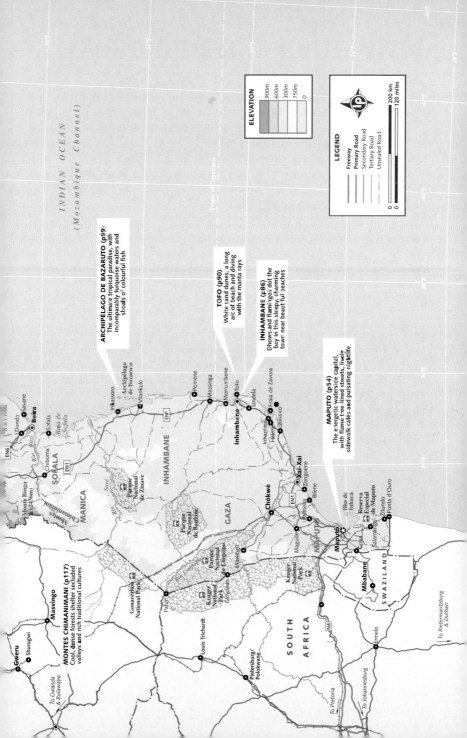

ARCHIPÉLAGO DE BAZARUTO (p99)
The ultimate tropical paradise, with incomparably turquoise waters and shoals of colourful fish

TOFO (p90)
White sand dunes, a long arc of beach and diving with the manta rays

INHAMBANE (p86)
Dhows and flamingos dot the bay in this sleepy, charming town near beautiful beaches

MAPUTO (p54)
The energetic waterside capital, with flame tree-lined streets, lively sidewalk cafés and pulsating nightlife

MONTES CHIMANIMANI (p117)
Cool, dense forests shelter secluded valleys and rich traditional cultures

INDIAN OCEAN
(Mozambique Channel)

ELEVATION
900m
600m
300m
150m
0

LEGEND
Freeway
Primary Road
Secondary Road
Tertiary Road
Unsealed Road

0 — 200 km
0 — 120 miles

Tropic of Capricorn

To Gwanda & Bulawayo
Gweru
Shungwi
Masvingo

Monte Binga (2436m)
Montes Chimanimani

MANICA

Dondo
Savane
Beira
Sofala
Baía de Sofala
Chiboma

SOFALA

Parque Nacional de Zinave

INHAMBANE

Rio Save

Inhassoro
Archipélago de Bazaruto
Vilankulc

Massinga
Morrumbene
Pomene
Tofo
Inhambane
Lindela
Inharrime
Helene
Praia de Zavora
Quissico

Parque Nacional de Banhine

GAZA

Gorongosa National Park
Pafuri
Louis Trichardt

Parque Nacional de Limpopo

Rio Limpopo

Massingir
Chókwè
Zongoene
Xai-Xai
Bilene

Kruger National Park
Giriyondo

Magude
Palmeira
Moamba
EN1

Pietersburg/Polokwane

SOUTH AFRICA

N4

Ermelo
To Johannesburg
To Pretoria

SWAZILAND
Mbabane

Ilha de Inhaca
Reserva Especial de Maputo
Salamanga
Zitundo
Ponta d'Ouro

Maputo
Boane

To Pietermaritzburg & Durban

Destination Mozambique

Mozambique, with its sublime 2500km coastline, magical offshore islands and fascinating cultures, is among the continent's best kept secrets. Although many of its attractions were long inaccessible due to a protracted guerrilla war, the dark times are now well in the past. Since the 1992 peace accords, the country has surged ahead and is now one of the continent's rising stars, with an upbeat atmosphere, overflowing markets and a tourism potential that's only beginning to be realised. Visit here now though, before word gets out, and don't spend too much time setting an agenda. Mozambique travel is about forgetting the Western time frame and immersing yourself in centuries-old rhythms.

Whether it's watching fishers haul in their nets, sitting captivated as a Makonde woodcarver plies his trade, or feeling the pulsating energy of a Chopi *timbila* performance, the highlights throughout are Mozambique's people and cultures. The past is preserved through a rich legacy of storytelling and folklore. Traditional religions flourish, as do traditional music and dance. In contrast to its more strait-laced neighbours – all former British colonies or protectorates – Mozambique's modern face reflects a unique blend of African, Arabic, Indian and Portuguese influences. Its cuisine is spicier, its music more tropical and its pace more laid-back.

Sail on a dhow past pristine white sands in the Archipélago das Quirimbas; laze under the palms on the Archipélago de Bazaruto, a quintessential tropical paradise; wander past stately colonial-era buildings and moss-covered ruins on Ilha de Moçambique; and explore the wild and remote Lago Niassa shoreline. In larger towns and resorts, you can enjoy as much comfort as you'd like. Elsewhere travel is rough and rugged, but throughout it offers the chance to experience Africa well away from established tourist circuits.

CRAIG PERSH

Culture & People

Fishermen and Nyanja women beachside at Lago Niassa (p148)

Woman in a protective *musiro* mask (p140), Ilha de Moçambique

OTHER HIGHLIGHTS

- Absorb the complex rhythms of a *timbila* performance (p83) on the outskirts of Quissico
- Take part in an informal soccer match (p69) on Maputo's stretch of beach

Trace the history of Mozambique's independence back to President Samora Machel (p25)

Islands & Beaches

PAUL BERNHARDT

Catch your breath at the sleepy coastal town of Vilankulo (p95)…

OLIVER STREWE

Wander through the silent Stone Town (p137) of Ilha de Moçambique

…before taking a dhow boat (p191) to the lush Archipélago de Bazaruto

TOM COCKREM

OTHER HIGHLIGHTS

- Discover the historical forts on the haunting Ilha do Ibo (p158)
- Soak in the sun and enjoy the party-time vibe at Tofo beach (p90)

Urban Charm

DAVID ELSE

Visit the imposing Catedral de Nossa Senhora de Fátima, (p133) Nampula

OTHER HIGHLIGHTS

- Walk off a seafood feast while admiring the colonial-style architecture of Beira (p106)
- Take time out in the jacaranda-lined streets of Lichinga (p146)

KEVIN WRIGHT

Catch a ride in a vintage *habana* car (p64) and explore Maputo's nightlife

Sample the spices at the Mercado Municipal (p62) in downtown Maputo

OLIVER STREWE

Wildlife & Wilderness

LAURA BR

Explore the vast and wild Parque Nacional de Gorongosa (p111)

Dive with the Giant Reef Rays at Ponta d'Ouro (p44)

TIM ROCK

PAUL BERNHARDT

Spot the exotic birds inhabiting
Archipélago de Bazaruto (p99)

OTHER HIGHLIGHTS

- Hike up the beautiful Monte Binga (p118), Mozambique's highest peak
- Go elephant-spotting in the country's largest protected area, Reserva do Niassa (p150)

Contents

Regional Map Contents

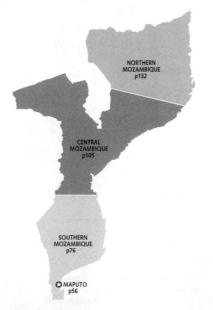

NORTHERN MOZAMBIQUE p132

CENTRAL MOZAMBIQUE p105

SOUTHERN MOZAMBIQUE p76

MAPUTO p56

The Author

MARY FITZPATRICK

Originally from Washington, DC, Mary set off after graduate studies for several years in Europe. Her fascination with languages and cultures soon led her further south to sub-Saharan Africa, where she has spent much of the past decade living and working, including almost four years in Mozambique. Mary has travelled extensively throughout the country, speaks Portuguese and Swahili, and has authored and co-authored numerous other guidebooks on Southern and East Africa and elsewhere on the continent. She calls Cairo home at the moment, travels south whenever she gets the chance and, when she's not in Mozambique, spends her free time dreaming of the Mozambican coastline.

My Favourite Trip

If I could set my own itinerary, I'd spend as much time as possible in northern Cabo Delgado province (p131) between Pemba and Palma, including island hopping in the Archipélago das Quirimbas (p158). Niassa province would be next on the list, exploring the Lago Niassa coastline (p148) and visiting the Reserva do Niassa (p150). Heading southwards, essential stops would include Ilha de Moçambique (p137), Parque Nacional de Gorongosa (p111), the Archipélago de Bazaruto (p99), Morrungulo (p94), Inhambane (p86) and Ponta Malongane (p77) before finishing up in and around Maputo (p54).

Reserva do Niassa
Palma
Lago Niassa
NIASSA
Archipélago das Quirimbas
Pemba
Ilha de Moçambique
CABO DELGADO
Parque Nacional de Gorongosa
Archipélago de Bazaruto
Morrungulo
Inhambane
Maputo
Ponta Malongane

Getting Started

Mozambique is a vast country – over three times the size of the UK – with internal flights that don't always coordinate and a still-adventurous road network, so you'll need to give some thought to which areas you'd like to visit. After narrowing down your main interests, there's little point in setting a rigid itinerary, as chances are you won't be able (nor want) to stick to it anyway.

In major cities and tourist areas along the coast, all budgets and travel styles are catered for. Here, you'll find an ever-expanding selection of midrange and upscale accommodation options, and good flight and bus connections, but expect prices to be generally higher than elsewhere in the region. Away from popular coastal destinations, travel is rough and rugged. It will be of appeal primarily to toughened backpackers who don't mind bumping around for hours on a bus over bad roads and staying in no-frills *pensões* (inexpensive hotels), and alternatively, to well-moneyed adventurers who can afford the necessary charter flights and hefty price tags to enjoy exclusive bush and island getaways.

WHEN TO GO

Mozambique is best visited during the cooler dry season from May to October/November. It's also possible to travel during the early part of the warmer, rainy season from November to January (though be prepared for high temperatures, especially in January). If possible, avoid the height of the rains – from about February to March/April – as many roads become impassable and flooding is common in the south and centre.

See Climate (p171) for more information

Apart from weather, another consideration is South African school holidays – although this is relevant mainly for southern coastal destinations. Around Easter, Christmas/New Year's and in August, Mozambique's southern coastal resorts become overrun with the vacationing neighbours and advance bookings are highly advisable.

For the best times for diving, see p43.

DON'T LEAVE HOME WITHOUT...

You can get most things you'll need in Maputo, except for specialised camping and sporting equipment, and certain toiletries, such as contact lens solution. Some essentials to bring from home:

- mosquito repellent and net
- torch
- shore-shoes for beach walking
- sunscreen and sunglasses
- travel alarm (to help you wake up in time to catch all those early morning buses)
- Visa card for accessing cash at ATMs
- bed sheet or lightweight sleep sack (for shoestring travellers)
- sturdy water bottle
- travel insurance including medical air evacuation to Johannesburg
- Portuguese phrasebook
- jerry cans for carrying extra fuel, if driving
- passport and a notarised copy
- a country map

COST-CUTTING TIPS

Some tips for saving money, whatever your budget:

- Focus on one area of the country to minimise long-haul transportation costs.
- Use public transport.
- Eat local food.
- Always ask about children's, midweek and low-season discounts.
- Keep your schedule flexible to take advantage of last-minute deals.
- Avoid peak season travel (eg Christmas–New Year's, Easter holidays) when prices are highest.
- Travel in a group (four is ideal) for any organised tours.
- Watch for flight-accommodation packages from Johannesburg, especially for the southern resorts and Pemba.

COSTS & MONEY

Mozambique has the well-deserved reputation of being expensive in comparison with its neighbours. Accommodation and internal flights will be your highest-cost items; fruits, produce and seafood bought at local markets, together with local road transport, are among the least costly categories.

For accommodation, especially at the budget and midrange levels, you'll need to hunt to find value for money (and you should expect to pay more than in South Africa), although there are an increasing number of places catering to backpackers in the south and the far north. Staying in basic lodging, eating local food and travelling with public transport, plan on spending from at least US$25 per day.

Midrange travel with some comforts will cost from US$50 to US$150 per day, excluding airfares. At the top end, plan on anywhere from US$150 to US$500 per day at some of the exclusive island lodges, excluding rental cars and flights.

TRAVEL LITERATURE

Kalashnikovs and Zombie Cucumbers: Travels in Mozambique by Nick Middleton – part travelogue and part historical overview – is a highly entertaining read covering everything from colonial times and the war to aid and development.

With Both Hands Waving: A Journey Through Mozambique by Justin Fox is another insightful and often humorous look at Mozambique in the early 1990s.

Empires of the Monsoon by Richard Seymour Hall – a scholarly yet readable book – covers a broad historical and geographical sweep, including Mozambique, and gives an excellent overview of the influences shaping coastal cultures.

Hunting Pirate Heaven by Kevin Rushby looks at the entire East African coast, including Mozambique. Although it's nominally about tracking pirate footsteps, it offers glimpses of local life as well.

A Complicated War: The Harrowing of Mozambique by William Finnegan examines the roots of Mozambique's civil war through a series of vivid close-ups on various areas of the country and is essential reading for anyone interested in gaining a deeper understanding of the country's postcolonial era.

HOW MUCH?

Plate of grilled prawns US$12

Single day dive US$40 to US$50

Short taxi ride US$2

Daytime dhow safari US$45

Maputo–Inhambane bus fare US$9

TOP TENS
THINGS TO DO IN MOZAMBIQUE

....If You Have Plenty of Money

- Treat yourself to a week in the Archipélago de Bazaruto (p99)
- Enjoy your own tropical paradise at one of the private island getaways in the Archipélago das Quirimbas (p158)
- Base yourself at Nkwichi Lodge on the shores of Lago Niassa, and explore the surrounding Mozambican bush (p148)
- Luxuriate in a sea-view room at Maputo's Hotel Polana (p66) and charter a vintage *habana* (p64) to take you around town
- Visit Reserva do Niassa (p150)

....If You're on a Shoestring Budget

- Visit magical Ilha de Moçambique (p137) – also add this to the list if you have plenty of money
- Spend a week chilling out at Praia de Tofo, a long arc of white sand near Inhambane (p90)
- Take the train between Cuamba and Nampula, and enjoy the passing scenes of rural Mozambican life (p132)
- Get a group together in Vilankulo for a dhow safari and snorkelling around the islands of the Archipélago de Bazaruto (p97)
- Travel overland to laid-back Pemba and relax on the beach for a few days before making your way to Pangane (p152)

MOZAMBICAN MUSIC

For an introduction to Mozambique's music scene, dip into some of the following:

- *Karimbo* (Mabulu)
- *Timbila Ta Venáncio* (Venáncio Mbande)
- *Timbila* (Eduardo Durão)
- *Katchume* (Kapa Dêch)
- *Afrikiti* (Stewart Sukuma)
- *Soul Marrabenta* (Mabulu)
- *Vana Va Ndota* (Ghorwane)
- *Tsuketani* (Kapa Dêch)
- *Dilon* (Dilon Djindji)
- *Automy Dzi Txintxile* (Léman)

CULTURAL EXPERIENCES

Whatever your budget, there's nothing better than immersion for getting to know local life. For starters, give the following a try:

- Spending the early morning or late afternoon sitting at a dhow port, watching the boats arrive with their catches
- Watching a Chopi *timbila* performance or some *mapiko* dancing
- Listening to church singing
- Browsing a small-town market
- Sailing in a dhow
- Sharing a plate of *xima* or *matapa* with locals
- Watching the sun rise over the Indian Ocean
- Walking around Ilha de Moçambique or Ilha do Ibo at dawn
- Spending an afternoon in a small village without a camera
- Watching Makonde carvers at work

INTERNET RESOURCES

African Studies Centre Mozambique Page (www.africa.upenn.edu/Country_Specific /Mozambique.html) Lots of links.

Kanimambo (www.kanimambo.com) In Portuguese, but with English listings and many links.

Lonely Planet (www.lonelyplanet.com) Travel tips, the Thorn Tree bulletin board and other links.

Mozambique Guide (www.mozguide.com) Especially helpful if you'll be visiting Mozambique with your own vehicle, with a chat site and updated information on routes and road conditions.

Mozambique Home Page (www.mozambique.mz) Mozambique's official website, with general information in Portuguese, news and links.

Mozambique News Agency (www.poptel.org.uk/mozambique-news/) Mozambique news in English.

Niassa Tourism (www.niassatourism.com) Good info and beautiful photos to lure you to oft-forgotten Niassa province.

Itineraries

CLASSIC ROUTES

THE SOUTHERN COAST
10 Days/Maputo to Vilankulo

Mozambique's superb beaches are what draw most visitors. For an easy coast-focused introduction, spend a few days getting oriented in **Maputo** (p54), and enjoying the city's sights and attractions. Take the bus north to **Inhambane** (p86) to take in the sunset over the bay, with the flamingos and dhows, before heading out the next day to the beaches at **Tofo** (p90) or **Barra** (p92). Divers should add two or three extra days to the itinerary (more for a certification course). Continue north to **Vilankulo** (p95) and finish up around the **Archipélago de Bazaruto** (p99), snorkelling or taking a dhow safari, before returning to Maputo by bus, or flying from Vilankulo directly out to Johannesburg.

Time permitting, recommended detours along the way include placid **Catembe** (p71) and the wild **Reserva Especial de Maputo** (p79) – both from Maputo (allow two extra nights total) or one of the other **beaches around Inhambane** (p88).

If driving a 4WD, consider entering Mozambique through South Africa's Kruger National Park and stopping at **Parque Nacional do Limpopo** (p84) before heading to the coast or alternatively, crossing via the Kosi Bay border post, and spending a few days at **Ponta d'Ouro** and **Ponta Malongane** (p77). Another possible coastal stop for self-drivers is one of the tranquil **beaches around Xai-Xai** (p83).

This classic 1000km journey takes in Maputo plus some of Mozambique's best beaches in an easy route that can be done by driving (mostly on sealed roads), flying or a bit of both in an air-road circuit in/out of Johannesburg (bus to/from Maputo, then fly between Vilankulo and Johannesburg). It's also easy to do in reverse, from north to south.

ROADS LESS TRAVELLED

GRAND TOUR
Two to Three Months/Maputo to Pemba

Except for the southern beaches, most of Mozambique is a 'road less travelled'. For a grand overland tour, start in the south, following the itinerary outlined under The Southern Coast (opposite), with stops in Maputo, Inhambane, Tofo or Barra, Vilankulo and the Archipélago de Bazaruto. From Vilankulo, continue by bus north to **Beira** (p106), with a day or two in this old port city before detouring inland for a couple of nights in **Parque Nacional de Gorongosa** (p111) and perhaps also in **Chimoio** (p113). The route continues north via **Quelimane** (p123), **Gurúè** (p128), **Nampula** (p132) and if you're interested in diving, **Nacala** (p47), to **Ilha de Moçambique** (p137), where it's easy to spend two or three days taking in the ambience and the sights. Continue northwards via bus to **Pemba** (p152). Follow a few days enjoying this sunny, low-key beach town with a visit to one of the nearby **bush camps or lodges around Pemba** (p157) or perhaps an excursion to **Montepuez** (p152) before heading off to the **Archipélago das Quirimbas** (p158). **Pangane** (p162) is the next stop – it can be reached by road, after returning to Pemba, or by dhow from the Archipélago das Quirimbas, depending which island you visit. From there, it's on to **Moçimboa da Praia** (p163) and then over the Rio Rovuma into Tanzania. Alternative routes include returning from the Archipélago das Quirimbas to Pemba, and flying directly to Maputo or South Africa from there, or branching westwards from Nampula (after visiting Ilha de Moçambique) to **Cuamba** (p144) and then to **Lichinga** (p146) and **Lago Niassa** (p148), and on to Malawi.

Allow as much time as possible for this 3700km-long adventure along the Mozambican coast (plus some inland detours). It's possible via public transport (though you may want to take a flight or two to break up some of the longer stretches) or as self-drive, and is just as good done from north to south.

TAILORED TRIPS

'BEST OF MOZAMBIQUE' SAMPLER

Mozambique's highlights are its beaches and islands, its cultures and people, and the adventure of it all. Here's a small sampling of some of the best the country has to offer in each area. For beaches and islands, there are too many to name, but among the finest stretches of sand are those at **Ponta d'Ouro** (p77), **Tofo** (p90), **Morrungulo** (p94), the **Archipélago de Bazaruto** (p99) and the **Archipélago das Quirimbas** (p158). The two archipelagos, together with **Ilha de Moçambique** (p137) – a Unesco World Heritage site – easily crown the list of island getaways.

Cultural highlights include **tufo dancing** (p32) on Ilha de Moçambique, masked **mapiko dancing** (p160) in the Cabo Delgado province, **Chopi timbila orchestras** (p83) around Quissico and a sampling of **Maputo's art museums** (p61) and its **nightlife** (p68). Start the latter with a performance by the **Companhia Nacional de Canto e Dança** (p68), and then charter a vintage **habana** (p64) to take you around on a city pub- and club-hopping tour.

For pure adventure, it's hard to beat Cabo Delgado and Niassa provinces, especially the coastal stretch from **Pangane** (p162) north to the Rio Rovuma; the **Reserva do Niassa** (p150); and the beautiful **Lago Niassa** (p148) shoreline between Cóbuè and Metangula, an ideal place to get an authentic taste of the African bush.

INLAND IDYLLS

The majority of Mozambique's finest attractions are along the coast, but there are some inland gems as well. If you're after greenery and something off-beat, don't miss the **Montes Chimanimani** (p117) and the **Penha Longa** (p117) area, with cool forests, villages and hiking – though you'll need to have plenty of time and be self-sufficient. The wilderness, birds and animals at **Parque Nacional de Gorongosa** (p111) are another highlight for nature lovers.

For anglers, or anyone after something different, spending a few days at **Lago Cahora Bassa** (p121) will likely fit the bill, with attractive hill scenery, a cool, refreshing climate and an impressive dam. **Gurúè** (p128), with its tea plantations, and the sacred **Monte Namúli** (p128) nearby, is another worthwhile stop.

The newly opened **Parque Nacional do Limpopo** (p84) is a convenient place to visit if you're arriving with your own vehicle from South Africa, and anyone interested in birding should consider the area south and east of **Caia** (p123), perhaps with a stop at **Monte Gorongosa** (p112) en route.

The train ride between **Nampula** (p132) and **Cuamba** (p144) cuts through often-striking, inselberg-studded landscapes and offers a great slice of Mozambican life. Topping the list are **Lago Niassa** (p148), with its unspoiled coastline and crystal clear waters, and the wild **Reserva do Niassa** (p150), one of the most remote areas of the country.

Snapshot

Orgulhosamente Moçambicana (Proudly Mozambican); *Deixe a malaria fora da rede* (Leave malaria outside of the net); *Vamos viver com Jeito* (double meaning – 'Let's live with care/flair', 'We'll live with Jeito [a condom brand]'). In many ways, Mozambique's mood can be read in its billboards.

FAST FACTS

Population: 19.7 million

Area: 801,590 sq km

HIV prevalence rate: 16%

Official language: Portuguese

Literacy rate: 48% (64% for males, 33% for females)

Life expectancy at birth: 40 years

Inflation: 7.8%

Elephants in Reserva do Niassa: about 12,000

Number of islands in the Archipélago das Quirimbas: 22 plus numerous islets

Dugongs around Archipélago de Bazaruto: less than 100

In 1992, following almost two decades of fighting, the country was in a shambles and schools and infrastructure were destroyed. No-one would have dreamed of pasting 'proudly Mozambican' – the bold advertising slogan used by mCel (Mozambique Cellular) – across a massive billboard atop Maputo's tallest building. Yet in the decade and a half that have passed since then, the country has moved forward light years. It has its first Olympic gold medal winner (Maria de Lurdes Mutola, the face accompanying the mCel slogan), close to one million people with cell phones, and a raft of new, modern high-rises and hotels in Maputo and other major towns. Tourism – which has been slowly on the incline for years – is finally beginning to boom as the world wakes up to the country's charms and as the country readies itself to receive visitors. There's a lively and fast-developing cultural scene, picking up where colonial-era oppressions and war caused things to leave off. The political arena is relatively stable, and the government is making at least nominal efforts to battle corruption – new president Armando Guebuza campaigned on an anticorruption ticket. And the economy, helped along by large infusions of external aid, is on a definite upswing.

Yet the picture isn't all rosy. While the macroeconomic statistics are indeed impressive, many people still struggle to eke out a living on an official monthly minimum wage of less than US$60. HIV/AIDS is another shadow. Despite a well-funded advertising effort to promote the use of Jeito condoms and general AIDS awareness, the government recently revised its estimate of the nationwide infection rate upwards to about 16%. Countrywide, up to 1.7 million people are living with HIV.

Malaria, a scourge throughout much of the continent, takes its toll in Mozambique and surpasses HIV/AIDS as the main cause of death. It also results in countless hours of lost work, decreased productivity and illness on the part of those who suffer with it but survive. On the political front, the investigation into the 2000 murder of journalist Carlos Cardoso drags on, fettered by entrenched interests and corruption at the highest levels.

Balancing out these differing faces of Mozambique, it's sometimes hard to see which one wins out. But if you took a poll, chances are that most Mozambicans would side with the optimistic view. Yes, there are problems with AIDS, education, jobs and more. But the future is bright, the mood is upbeat and these days it's likely that almost all Mozambicans, if asked, would smile and agree with the sentiment of being proudly Mozambican.

History

From Bantu-speaking farmers and fishers to Arabic traders, Goan merchants and adventuring Europeans, Mozambique has long been a crossroads of cultures.

IN THE BEGINNING

The first people to see Mozambique's Indian Ocean sunrises were small, scattered clans of nomads who were likely trekking through the bush as early as 10,000 years ago. They may have been distant cousins of the San – skilled hunter-gatherers who left rock paintings throughout southern Africa and who still live in the region today. However, Mozambique's early nomads left few traces and little is known about this era.

The real story begins about 3000 years ago, when Bantu-speaking peoples from the faraway Niger Delta in West Africa began moving slowly through the Congo basin in one of the greatest population migrations on the African continent. Over a period of centuries they journeyed into east and Southern Africa, reaching present-day Mozambique sometime around the 1st century AD, where they made their living farming, fishing and raising livestock.

EARLY KINGDOMS

Most of these early Mozambicans set themselves up in small chiefdoms, some of which gradually coalesced into larger states or kingdoms. In central Mozambique, the most organised of these states were those of the Karanga or Shona, who by the 11th century AD were grouped into a loose confederation with its centre at Great Zimbabwe, present-day Zimbabwe. Around 1450 Great Zimbabwe was mysteriously abandoned. However, the related Manyikeni chieftaincy, inland from Vilankulo, prospered as a trading centre until the 17th century (you can still visit the remains, see p84). Other Karanga kingdoms – most notably Manica, along the current Mozambique–Zimbabwe border – continued to thrive as late as the 19th century.

At about the same time that Great Zimbabwe began to decline, the renowned kingdom of Monomotapa emerged. This kingdom, named after the *mwene mutapa* (the title of the ruler), was based south and west of present-day Tete. From this pivotal point it controlled the lucrative gold trade between the Zambezi and Save rivers. It was tales of these legendary gold fields ruled over by Monomotapa that first attracted European interest in Mozambique. However – perhaps ironically – both the gold fields and Monomotapa's kingdom were smaller and less cohesive in reality than the Europeans believed.

In northern Mozambique, one of the most powerful groups was the Maravi (also known as the Malâwi), who exercised dominion over a large area extending from the Rio Zambezi into what is now southern Malawi and Zambia. Maravi rule was based on control of the ivory trade. At the height of its power in the late 17th century AD, it reached as far as Mogincual and Angoche on the coast, although the kingdom was plagued by weak central structure and infighting. In the far north near Lago Niassa and in present-day Niassa province, were various Yao chiefdoms. Their power gradually increased, until by the 17th and 18th centuries Yao commercial networks

'At about the same time that Great Zimbabwe began to decline, the renowned kingdom of Monomotapa emerged'

TIMELINE

from c100AD	from 8th century
Bantu-speakers begin arriving in present-day Mozambique	Sofala and other trading settlements are established along the coast

Malyn Newitt's *A History of Mozambique* is a detailed but superb analysis of Mozambican history from about 1500, and the definitive work on the country.

extended across Mozambique to the Indian Ocean, where they were the main trading partners with Arab ivory and slave merchants. Yet, like the Maravi, the Yao remained only loosely organised and decentralised.

In the northeast, in what are now Nampula and Zambézia provinces, were groupings of Makua-Lomwe peoples. Their largest political unit was the village, although some loosely confederated chiefdoms began to form around the 16th century.

Southern Mozambique, which was settled by the Nguni and various other groups, remained decentralised until the 19th century when consolidation under the powerful kingdom of Gaza gave it at least nominal political cohesion.

THE ARRIVAL OF THE ARABS

From around the 8th century AD, sailors from Arabia began to arrive along the East African coast. Trade flourished and intermarriage with the indigenous Bantu-speakers gave birth to Swahili language and culture. By the 9th century several settlements had been established – most notably Kilwa island, in present-day Tanzania, which soon became the hub of Arab trade networks throughout southeastern Africa.

Along the Mozambican coast, the most important trading post was at Sofala (p112), near present-day Beira, which by the 15th century was the main link connecting Kilwa with the old Shona kingdoms and the inland gold fields. Other early coastal ports and settlements included those at Ilha de Moçambique, Angoche, Quelimane and Ilha do Ibo, all ruled by local sultans. Today, the traces of this long history of eastward trade, carried out over the centuries on the winds of the monsoon, are still evident in the rich cultural melange found in Mozambique's coastal towns.

PORTUGUESE ADVENTURERS

In 1498 Vasco da Gama landed at Ilha de Moçambique en route to India. It is likely that another Portuguese explorer, the intrepid Pêro da Covilhã, had reached Sofala even earlier via an overland route, disguised as a Muslim merchant. Within a decade after da Gama's arrival, the Portuguese had established themselves on the island and gained control of numerous other Swahili-Arab trading posts – lured in part by their need for supply points on the sea route to the East and in part by their desire to control the gold trade with the interior.

Over the next 200 years, the Portuguese busily set up trading enclaves and forts along the coast, making Ilha de Moçambique the capital of what they called Portuguese East Africa. By the mid-16th century, ivory had replaced gold as the main trading commodity and by the late 18th century, slaves had been added to the list, with close to one million Africans sold into slavery through Mozambique's ports.

MOZAMBIQUE

No-one is quite sure where the name Mozambique (Moçambique in Portuguese) originated. According to tradition, it's derived from the name and title of the sultan on Ilha de Moçambique when the Portuguese arrived there in the late 15th century – Musa Mbiki (Musa bin Mbiki), or possibly Musa Malik.

---

late 15th century	1498
Rise of the kingdom of Monomotapa	Vasco da Gama lands on Ilha de Moçambique

The first major journey inland was made around 1511 by António Fernandes, who got as far as the kingdom of Monomotapa and returned with extensive information about river routes and trade conditions in the interior. Following Fernandes' trip, several other expeditions went inland. By the 1530s, the Portuguese had occupied settlements which had been established earlier by Arab traders in the Zambezi River Valley at Tete and Sena, and over the next century they became increasingly involved at the inland trading fairs (feiras), although the coast continued to be the focus of activity. Yet, both on the coast and inland, there was little cohesion to the Portuguese ventures and their influence in Mozambique remained weak and fragmented.

PORTUGAL'S POWER STRUGGLE

In the 17th century, the Portuguese attempted to strenghten their control by setting up prazos (enormous agricultural estates) on land granted by the Portuguese crown or by wresting control of it from local chiefs. This, however, did little more than consolidate power in the hands of individual prazeiros (holders of the land grants).

The next major effort by the Portuguese to consolidate their control came in the late 19th century with the establishment of charter companies, operated by private firms who were supposed to develop the land and natural resources within their boundaries. Major ones included the Zambezia Company (with a concession in present-day Tete and Zambézia provinces); the Mozambique Company (in Manica and Sofala provinces, and also under British control); and the Niassa Company (in present-day Cabo Delgado and Niassa provinces). In reality, these charter companies operated as independent fiefdoms, and did little to consolidate Portuguese control. They also were economic failures (only the Zambezia Company was profitable), and soon became notorious for labour abuses and for the cruel and appalling conditions under which the local populations within their boundaries were forced to live.

With the onset of the 'Scramble for Africa' in the 1880s, Portugal faced growing competition from Britain and the other colonial powers and was forced to strengthen its claims in the region. In 1891 a British-Portuguese treaty was signed, which set the boundaries of Portuguese East Africa and formalised Portuguese control in the area. Despite this, the country continued without cohesion. The Portuguese were only able to directly administer the area south of the Rio Save (which had attained some degree of political unity under the rulers of the Gaza kingdom) and Ilha de Moçambique. The rest of the centre and north remained under the control of prazeiros (charter companies).

'In 1891 a British-Portuguese treaty was signed, which set the boundaries of Portuguese East Africa and formalised Portuguese control in the area'

THE EARLY 20TH CENTURY

One of the most significant events in early 20th-century Mozambique was the large-scale labour migration from the southern provinces to South Africa and Rhodesia. This exodus was spurred by expansion of the Witwatersrand gold mines, and by passage of a new labour law in 1899 which formally divided the Mozambican population into nonindigenous (não indígenas or assimilados), who had full Portuguese citizenship rights, and indigenous (indígenas), who were subject to the provisions of colonial law and forced to work, to pay a poll tax and to adhere to pass laws. For an African to acquire nonindigenous status, it was necessary to demonstrate Portuguese 'culture'

from 17th century	1850s
Portuguese divide large areas of central Mozambique into vast agricultural estates (prazos)	Gaza kingdom reaches its height under Soshangane

and a level of education. For *indígenas* Mozambicans who were unable to get employment on European-run plantations in their home regions, the options were limited to accepting six months of annual labour at minimal pay on public works projects, leaving Mozambique to seek a better life in the surrounding colonies or accepting employment as contract labourers in South Africa.

The other major development defining early 20th-century Mozambique was the growing economic importance of the southern part of the country. As ties with South Africa strengthened, Lourenço Marques (as Maputo was then known) took on increasing importance as a major port and export channel and in the late 19th century the Portuguese transferred the capital here from Ilha de Moçambique.

In the late 1920s António Salazar came to power in Portugal. To maximise the benefits that Portugal could realise from its colonies, he sealed them off from non-Portuguese investment, terminated the leases of the various concession companies in the north, abolished the remaining *prazos* and consolidated Portuguese control over Mozambique. While some of his policies, including the introduction of agricultural schemes, resulted in economic growth, overall conditions for Mozambicans worsened considerably. There was not even a pretence of social investment in the African population and of the few schools and hospitals that did exist, most were in the cities and reserved for Portuguese, other whites and privileged African *assimilados*.

THE MUEDA MASSACRE

'Resentment at the 'massacre of Mueda' helped to politicise the local Makonde people and became one of the sparks kindling the independence struggle.'

Discontent with the situation grew and a nationalist consciousness gradually developed. This was nurtured by Mozambican exile groups and by the country's small group of educated elite, including nationalist intellectuals such as the poets Marcelino dos Santos, José Craveirinha and Noémia de Sousa.

In June 1960, at Mueda in northern Mozambique, an official meeting was held by villagers protesting peacefully about taxes. Portuguese troops opened fire on the crowd, killing large numbers of demonstrators. Resentment at the 'massacre of Mueda' helped to politicise the local Makonde people and became one of the sparks kindling the independence struggle. From this point onwards, the Mozambican liberation movement began to grow. External support came from several sources, but most notably from the government of Julius Nyerere in neighbouring Tanganyika (now Tanzania). In 1962, following a meeting of various political organisations working in exile for Mozambican independence, the Frente pela Libertação de Moçambique or Mozambique Liberation Front (Frelimo) was formed in Dar es Salaam (Tanzania). The first president of the organisation was Eduardo Chivambu Mondlane, a southern Mozambican educated in the USA, Portugal and South Africa who had spent several years working with the UN.

THE INDEPENDENCE STRUGGLE

Frelimo was plagued from the outset by internal divisions. However, under the leadership of the charismatic Mondlane and operating from bases in Tanzania, it succeeded in giving the liberation movement a structure and in defining a programme of political and military action to support its aim of complete independence for Mozambique. On 25 September 1964, Mondlane proclaimed the beginning of the armed struggle for national independence,

1962	1964
The Mozambican Liberation Front (Frelimo) is born	Eduardo Mondlane declares the beginning of the independence war

which Frelimo initiated by attacking a Portuguese base at Chai, in Cabo Delgado province.

By 1966 large areas of Cabo Delgado and Niassa provinces were liberated, but progress was slow. A setback for Frelimo came in 1969 when Mondlane was assassinated by a letter bomb delivered to him at his office in Dar es Salaam. He was succeeded as president by Frelimo's military commander and another southerner, Samora Moises Machel. Under Machel, Frelimo sought to extend its area of operations to the south. The Portuguese meanwhile attempted to eliminate rural support for Frelimo by implementing a scorched earth campaign and by resettling people in a series of fortified village complexes (aldeamentos) where they would be isolated from contact with Frelimo forces, and where they could receive social services (provided by the Portuguese in an effort to win support for the Portuguese cause). However, struggles within Portugal's colonial empire and increasing international criticism sapped the government's resources. The final blow for Portugal came in 1974 with the overthrow of the Salazar regime. In 1974 at a ceremony in Lusaka (Zambia), the Portuguese government agreed to hand over power to Frelimo and a transitional government was established. On 25 June 1975, the independent People's Republic of Mozambique was proclaimed with the wartime commander Samora Machel as president and Joaquim Chissano, a founding member of Frelimo's intellectual elite, as prime minister.

Since 1995 Mozambique has been part of the Commonwealth of Nations, to which all its neighbours belong. It is the first member not to have been ruled by Britain at some point.

INDEPENDENCE – THE EARLY YEARS

The Portuguese pulled out virtually overnight, leaving the country in a state of chaos with few skilled professionals and virtually no infrastructure. Frelimo, which found itself suddenly faced with the task of running the country, threw itself headlong into a policy of radical social change. Ties were established with the USSR and East Germany and private land ownership was replaced with state farms and peasant cooperatives. Meanwhile, schools, banks and insurance companies were nationalised and private practice in medicine and law was abolished in an attempt to disperse skilled labour. Education assumed a high priority and literacy programmes were launched with the aim of teaching 100,000 people each year to read and write. Much assistance

---

WHAT'S IN A NAME?

Spend enough time in Mozambique and you'll soon start to notice that many street names are the same. Here's a quick guide to the figures and events behind them.

Eduardo Mondlane Founding president of Frelimo, and leader of the independence movement
Samora Machel Successor of Mondlane as Frelimo president, and first president of independent Mozambique
Josina Machel A prominent freedom fighter, married to Samora Machel; Mozambican Women's Day (7 April) was inaugurated in her honour, on the anniversary of her death
Julius Nyerere First president of Tanzania (then Tanganyika) and major supporter of the Mozambican independence movement
Kwame Nkrumah Ghanaian president, founding member of the Organisation for African Unity and leader of the Pan-African movement
25 de Junho Mozambican independence day (1975)
25 de Setembro Start of the independence war in 1964
Amilcar Cabral Freedom fighter and revolutionary leader in Guinea-Bissau

---

1975	1980s
Mozambique gains independence, with Samora Machel as president	Externally supported Renamo destabilisation tactics ravage the country

was received from foreign volunteers, notably from Sweden. Maoist-style 'barefoot doctors' provided basic health services such as vaccinations and taught hygiene and sanitation.

However, Frelimo's socialist programme proved unrealistic and by 1983 the country was almost bankrupt. Money was valueless and shops were empty. While collectivisation of agriculture had worked in some areas, in many others it was a disaster. The crisis was compounded by a three-year drought and by South African and Rhodesian efforts to destabilise Mozambique – largely because the oppositional African National Congress (ANC) and Zimbabwe African People's Union (ZAPU), both of which were fighting for majority rule, had bases there.

Onto this scene came the Resistência Nacional de Moçambique or Mozambique National Resistance (Renamo). This ragtag group had been established in the mid-1970s by Rhodesia (now Zimbabwe) as part of its destabilisation policy. It was kept alive in later years with backing from the South African military and certain sectors in the West.

RAVAGES OF WAR

Renamo, which had been created by external forces rather than by internal political motives, had no ideology of its own beyond the wholesale destruction of social and communications infrastructure within Mozambique and destabilisation of the government. Many commentators have pointed out that the war which went on to ravage the country for the next 17 years was thus not a 'civil' war, but one between Mozambique's Frelimo government and Renamo's external backers.

Recruitment was sometimes voluntary but frequently by force. Roads, bridges, railways, schools and clinics were destroyed. Villagers were rounded up and anyone with skills – teachers, medical workers etc – was shot. Atrocities were committed on a massive and horrific scale.

Ironically, part of the problem stemmed from the Frelimo re-education camps that were established after independence. Their inmates included political opponents as well as common criminals and they were notorious for their human rights abuses. Rather than establishing respect for state authority, the camps provided a fertile recruitment ground for Renamo.

The drought and famine of 1983 crippled the country. Faced with this dire situation and the reality of a failed socialist experiment, Frelimo opened Mozambique to the West in return for Western aid.

In 1984 South Africa and Mozambique signed the Nkomati Accord, under which South Africa undertook to withdraw its support of Renamo, and Mozambique agreed to expel the ANC and open the country to South African investment. While Mozambique abided by the agreement, South Africa exploited the situation to the full and Renamo activity did not diminish.

Samora Machel died in a plane crash in 1986 under questionable circumstances, and his place was taken by the more moderate Joaquim Chissano. The war between the Frelimo government and the Renamo rebels continued but by the late 1980s, political change was sweeping through the region. The collapse of the USSR altered the political balance, and the new president of South Africa, FW de Klerk, made it more difficult for right-wing factions to supply Renamo.

For a well-researched look at the roots of civil war in Mozambique and Angola, including the role of apartheid-era South Africa in continuing the conflicts, read William Minter's *Apartheid's Contras*.

And Still They Dance by Stephanie Urdang is an intriguing analysis of women's roles in the wars and struggles for change.

1992	1994
Peace comes to Mozambique	First multiparty elections

CHIEFS & PROVINCES

Before independence, most villages were led by traditional leaders (*régulos*, often inherited positions). Beginning in the late 1970s, the Frelimo government displaced these leaders, installing local government administrators (*secretários*) in their place. Population displacement during the war further weakened traditional authority structures. More recently, many traditional leaders have been reinstated and both structures often coexist, with power divided between the chief and the government-appointed administrator, and many communities organised around a council of elders, headed by a chief.

Mozambique's 10 provinces (each with a governor and some autonomy) and their capitals: Maputo (Maputo), Gaza (Xai-Xai), Inhambane (Inhambane), Sofala (Beira), Manica (Chimoio), Tete (Tete), Zambézia (Quelimane), Nampula (Nampula), Niassa (Lichinga) and Cabo Delgado (Pemba). Maputo city is sometimes considered an 11th province.

PEACE AT LAST

By the early 1990s, Frelimo had disavowed its Marxist ideology, announcing that Mozambique would switch to a market economy, with privatisation of state enterprises and multiparty elections. After protracted negotiations in Rome, a ceasefire was arranged, followed by a formal peace agreement in October 1992 and a successful UN-monitored disarmament and demobilisation campaign.

Since the signing of the peace accords, Mozambique has been remarkably successful in moving beyond war and in transforming military conflict into political competition. In October 1994, the country held its first multiparty elections. With close to 90% of the electorate participating, Renamo won a surprising 38% of the vote, compared with 44% for Frelimo, and majorities in five provinces. The results were attributable in part to ethnic considerations and in part to Frelimo's inability to overcome widespread grassroots antipathy. In the second national elections, held in December 1999, Renamo made an even stronger showing, winning in six out of 11 provinces. However, unlike the first elections, which earned Mozambique widespread acclaim as an African model of democracy and reconciliation, the 1999 balloting sparked protracted discord. Renamo accused Frelimo of irregularities in counting the votes and boycotted the presidential inauguration, sparking a wave of rioting and violence.

There are many small political parties, but none with parliamentary seats. Political allegiance tends to be regional – Renamo is strong in the centre, Frelimo in the north and south.

MOZAMBIQUE TODAY

Since then, things have settled down. In December 2004, prominent businessman and long-time Frelimo insider Armando Guebuza was elected with a solid majority to succeed Chissano, who had earlier announced his intent to step down. With a long-running banking and corruption scandal dominating the headlines, Frelimo is now working to polish its public image, while Renamo is still striving to prove itself as a viable political party. Progress has been interrupted by natural calamities, including severe flooding in 2000 and 2001. Yet Mozambique has a remarkable ability to rebound in the face of adversity and most observers count the country among the continent's rising stars.

Moçambique para todos (http://macua.blogs.com) has an excellent survey of Mozambique's current events, in Portuguese, with English translations available.

1995	**2005**
Mozambique becomes a member of the British Commonwealth	Cornerstone is laid for 'Unity Bridge' linking Mozambique and Tanzania across the Rio Rovuma

The Culture

THE NATIONAL PSYCHE

You don't need to travel long in Mozambique before hearing the word *paciência* (patience). It's the great Mozambican virtue and most Mozambicans have it in abundance, with each other and with outsiders. You'll be expected to display some in return, especially in dealings with officialdom, and Western-style impatience is always counterproductive. While at times frustrating to a pressured, Western mentality, it is this same low-key, warm Mozambican way that soon gets hold of most visitors to the country and keeps them here much longer than they had originally planned. But don't let the languid, tropical pace sway you completely: underlying it is a rock-hard determination that has carried Mozambique from complete devastation following two decades of war to near the top of the list of the continent's success stories.

Another prominent feature of modern-day Mozambique is its cultural diversity. To casual observers, the country may look like one long beach backed by faceless bush, yet it is remarkably decentralised in comparison with many of its neighbours, with each province boasting its own unique history, cultures and traditions. There has long been an undercurrent of north–south differences, with geographically remote northerners often feeling neglected by powerhouse Maputo, where proximity to South Africa and good road links have pushed economic development along at a rapid pace. Yet this has remained low-level and tribal rivalries don't play a major role in contemporary Mozambican life. Religious frictions are also minimal, with Christians and Muslims living side by side in a relatively easy coexistence.

AIDS continues to cut its dark swathe through Mozambican society. Infection rates are highest in the south and centre, where they exceed 20% in some areas, and about 20,000 children die annually of AIDS-related causes. Public discussion has opened up dramatically in recent years, spurred in part by former first lady Graça Machel, who was one of the first to break the taboo with her 1999 announcement that her brother-in-law (and brother of former president Samora Machel) had died of AIDS-related complications. There are prominent public advertising campaigns in major towns and lots of work being done at the local level, especially through theatre groups and peer chat sessions at schools, to break down the stigmas. Yet discussion still remains muted in many areas and deaths are commonly explained away as 'tuberculosis' or with silence.

LIFESTYLE

Much of Mozambique moves to centuries-old rhythms of the harvest and the monsoon. About 80% of Mozambicans are involved at least parttime in subsistence agriculture, tending small plots with cassava, maize and other crops. You'll see these *machambas* (farm plots) wherever you travel, along with large stands of cashew trees (especially in the north), mangoes and – in the central highlands around Gurúè – tea plantations. Along the coast, fishing is a major source of livelihood. The small ports are fascinating to watch at dawn and in the late afternoon when the boats come in with their catches. At the national level, commercial fishing – especially the prawns for which Mozambique is famous – accounts for about one-fourth of merchandise exports.

Despite the occasional setbacks of seasonal flooding, which gained Mozambique worldwide attention in 2000 and 2001, tourism has become an

Samora Machel's famous rallying cry, *'A luta continua'* ('The struggle continues'), inspired Mozambicans in the early independence years, and still stirs up national pride.

increasingly important source of income, as the world discovers the country's charms. This is particularly evident in Maputo, where top-end hotels are rapidly multiplying, and in the far north, where there has been extensive investment in the luxury travel market.

On the personal level, despite the tourism boom and encouraging economic news, much of daily life is shaped by the struggle to make ends meet. Annual per capita income is about US$300 (compared with about US$26,000 in the UK) and most Mozambicans strive to earn a living in the expansive and lively informal sector as traders, street vendors and subsistence farmers.

Mozambique's main social security system and welfare net is the community and extended family, and family obligations are taken seriously. If one family member is lucky enough to have a good job, it is expected that their good fortune will filter down to even distant relatives. Another example is seen with funerals, which are always attended by all those concerned, even if this necessitates long journeys and time away from work. It's expected that friends, acquaintances and other family members will make a small donation – either monetary or in-kind (such as a bag of rice) – to the family of the deceased to help them cover expenses and get by in the months ahead.

Funerals themselves are generally lengthy affairs and are preceded by a period of mourning at the family homestead, where friends and acquaintances go to pay their last respects and offer condolences. It's common for widows and other members of the immediate family to wear black for up to a year after the death in remembrance.

Customs surrounding engagements and weddings are similarly oriented to encompass the entire family, and payment of *lobola* (bride price) by the family of the husband to the family of the wife is common. For more on the status of women, see p181.

SOCIAL ETIQUETTE

Most Mozambicans are fairly easy-going towards foreigners. However, keeping a few basics in mind will help to smooth your interactions.

- Always greet others and inquire about their wellbeing prior to launching into questions or conversation. It's also usual to greet people when entering or leaving a room.

- When shaking someone's hand, the custom in many areas is to touch your left hand to your right elbow.

- Ask permission before photographing people, especially in remote areas, and follow through if you promise to send a copy of the photo.

- In traditional Mozambican culture, elders and those in positions of authority are treated with deference and respect. It smoothes things considerably to follow suit.

- When visiting villages, ask to see the chief to announce your presence and request permission before setting up camp or wandering around. You will rarely be refused.

- When receiving a gift, it's polite in many areas to accept it with both hands, sometimes with a slight bow or, alternatively, with the right hand while touching the left hand to the right elbow. When only one hand is used to give or receive, make it the right.

- Spoken thanks are not as common as in the West, so don't be upset if you are not verbally thanked for a gift.

- Shorts and sleeveless tops are fine at beach resorts. In traditional communities, you'll have an easier time with more conservative garb. Long trousers or a skirt (for women) and a top with some sort of sleeve are appropriate anywhere.

POPULATION

Sparsely populated Mozambique (about 19 million inhabitants) has a population density averaging only about 24 people per sq km – well below all of its neighbours except Zambia. About half of the population is concentrated in the centre and north, especially in Zambézia and Nampula provinces, which – with about 40% of the total – are the most densely populated provinces in the country. Over 70% of the total population lives in rural areas. Settlement in the south of the country is primarily along the coastal belt, with only scattered villages in the dry interior. Niassa province – the Siberia of the southern hemisphere – is the least densely populated province, with about seven inhabitants per sq km. Mozambique's population growth rate is estimated at about 1.4%, tempered by an AIDS infection rate that is officially estimated at about 16% countrywide, but exceeds 20% in some areas such as the Tete and Beira corridors.

There are 16 main ethnic groups or tribes. The largest is the Makua, who inhabit the provinces of Cabo Delgado, Niassa, Nampula and parts of Zambézia and comprise about 25% of the total population (although the designation 'Makua' was externally determined and actually includes many distinct subgroups). Other major groups include the Makonde in Cabo Delgado; the Sena in Sofala, Manica and Tete; and the Ronga and Shangaan, who dominate the southern provinces of Gaza and Maputo. You'll likely also encounter Lomwe and Chuabo (Zambézia); Yao and Nyanja (Niassa); Mwani (Cabo Delgado); Nyungwe (Tete); and Tswa and Chopi (Inhambane).

Patrilineal systems predominate in southern Mozambique and in the Islamic coastal areas of the far north (among the Mwani, for example), while in the centre and in northern inland areas many tribes are matrilineal, including the Lomwe, Makonde, Makua and Nyanja. Some groups in the Rio Zambézi valley, such as the Chuabo, Sena and Nyungwe, incorporate elements of both systems in their traditions.

About 1% of Mozambique's population is of Portuguese extraction, most of whom are at least second generation and consider themselves Mozambicans first. There are also small numbers of other European and Asian residents. Life expectancy is about 40 years.

As expected with such ethnic diversity, there is also a rich array of languages. For more, see p204, which also includes an introduction to Portuguese pronunciation and a glossary of words and phrases.

Among many matrilineal peoples, clan members are believed to descend from a common female ancestor. Family name and important decisions are determined through the mother or through her brother or other male relatives.

SPORT

Soccer (football) is the main spectator sport. Local games always draw large and enthusiastic crowds – the whole village may turn out in rural areas – and the nationally known teams such as Maxaquene, Costa do Sol and Ferroviário de Maputo inspire fierce loyalty on the part of their fans.

Second to soccer is basketball, which also draws crowds – especially women's basketball, with the famed Clarisse Machanguana (now back in Mozambique after a pro-career in the USA) leading the way.

The track and field scene is dominated by the internationally acclaimed 800m runner, Maria de Lurdes Mutola (the 'Maputo Express'), who has won numerous world cup titles and in 2000 became Mozambique's first Olympic gold medallist.

MEDIA

Mozambique has a lively media, which includes the government-aligned *Notícias* (the most widely circulated daily) and a number of independent publications. Its growth since state press controls were loosened in the early

TRADITIONAL HEALERS

Feeling under the weather? If you follow what most Mozambicans would do, you'll head straight for the nearest *curandeiro* (traditional healer). Traditional medicine is widely practised in Mozambique – often as the only remedy and sometimes in combination with Western medical treatment. As a result, *curandeiros* are respected and highly sought-after. They are also often relatively well paid, frequently in kind rather than in cash. In some rural areas far from health clinics or a hospital, the *curandeiro* may be the only provider of medical assistance.

Individual *curandeiros* have various powers, so selection of the proper one is important. After clamping down on *curandeiros* following independence, the government now permits them to practice, although it attempts to regulate the system. A national association of *curandeiros* has been formed (Associação dos Médicos Tradicionais de Moçambique, or Ametramo), with centres in each of the provincial capitals. Officially, each *curandeiro* must be registered at the provincial level, although unlicensed practice remains widespread.

The practice of traditional medicine is closely intertwined with traditional religions, and in addition to *curandeiros*, you may encounter *profetas* (spirit mediums or diviners) and *feticeiros* (witch doctors). All three power areas can be vested in one person, or they can be different individuals. While *curandeiros* and *profetas* are commonly recognised, the identity of a *feticeiro* is usually not known. Most larger markets have a traditional remedies section selling bird claws, dried leaves and plants, and the like. Diviners often carry a small sack of bones (generally matching male and female parts of the same species) which facilitate communication with the ancestors.

1990s was spearheaded largely by Carlos Cardoso. Cardoso, one-time head of the state news agency, *Agência de Informação de Moçambique* (AIM), was Mozambique's leading investigative journalist and founder of the independent *Mediafax*, a publication once described by the *New York Times* as the vanguard of free press in Africa. Cardoso's murder in November 2000, in connection with his investigation into a massive banking scandal in which high-ranking government circles were implicated, sent shock waves through the press world in Mozambique and abroad. Since then, the ongoing efforts of his convicted assassin, Anibal Antonio dos Santos Junior ('Anibalzinho'), to escape from prison continue to garner headlines and shadows still linger over open reporting in Mozambique.

For background on the Cardoso case, see www.cpj.org/Briefings/2002/Cardoso_nov02/cardoso_nov02.html.

RELIGION

About 35% of Mozambicans are Christians, about 25% to 30% are Muslims, and the remainder are adherents of traditional religions. Among Christians, the major denomination is Roman Catholicism. However, membership in evangelical Protestant churches is growing rapidly, particularly in the south. One church you're also likely to come in contact with is the local Zionist church, whose members are often seen on the beach along Maputo's Avenida Marginal in the early morning carrying out initiation rituals. Muslims are found primarily in the northern provinces of Nampula, Cabo Delgado and Niassa, with the highest concentrations on the coast and along old trading routes.

Traditional religions based on animist beliefs remain widespread, and traditional beliefs are often incorporated into the practice of Christianity. In most areas, there are strong beliefs concerning the powers which the spirits of the ancestors have over the destiny of living persons. There is also often identification of different levels of deities. In the south, for example, most groups identify an all-powerful God as well as various lesser spirits who receive prayers and influence events. In connection with these beliefs, there are many sacred sites, such as forests, rivers, lakes and mountains, which play important roles in the lives of local communities.

THE GENDER GAP

The gender gap in Mozambican education has been narrowing at the primary level over the past decade, thanks to strong government priority placed on increasing enrolment levels across the board. However, at the secondary level, the gap has widened. Only about one-third of students at the upper secondary school level, and only about one-fourth of tertiary level students, are girls. Maputo city is the only place in the country where there is a negligible gender gap at all levels.

Comparatively lower enrolment rates and higher drop-out rates countrywide among girls are due in part to cultural attitudes. There is a traditional preference for sons and a pervasive expectation that girls will take on chores at home. Early marriages and early pregnancies are another factor. HIV/AIDS is also a major contributor. As the number of AIDS orphans rises – there are currently an estimated 470,000 in Mozambique – girls are required to stay home to take care of ill family members or younger siblings. For more on the status of women in general, see p181.

EDUCATION

The Mozambican educational scene shows a mixed picture. On the one side, there is an ever-increasing number of university graduates and, thanks to a major government campaign, primary school enrolment levels have increased to a nationwide average of almost 70%. On the other side, dropout rates are high, and less than 5% of the population goes on to complete secondary school. One factor is financial constraints, with annual fees (about US$60 per year) posing formidable sums for many rural families. Uneven school distribution is another, as many zones are still without adequate facilities, despite a massive postwar school rebuilding programme.

Other issues include low levels of teacher training and morale. Close to 40% of teachers at the primary level are inadequately trained and salaries are often low, missed or delayed. High teacher-to-pupil ratios (sometimes as high as one primary-level teacher for 80 or more pupils) means that in many classrooms little learning is occurring. AIDS is also an increasingly serious problem. The Ministry of Education predicts that within the next decade, about 17% of teachers in the country will die of AIDS across all educational levels.

One person can make a difference. For an inspiring story of one woman's accomplishments in helping more Mozambican children to have the chance for an education and future, see www .asemworld.org.eng/.

ARTS

During the colonial era, indigenous artistic expression in Mozambique was generally suppressed, especially if it was deemed to display overly strong nationalist leanings. Those traditions that were permitted to continue were often trivialised by the colonial administration and relegated to the realm of folklore.

With independence, the situation changed. The new Frelimo government made promotion of indigenous culture one of its priorities, and actively supported international artistic exchanges. The start of the civil war brought this heady period for the arts to an abrupt halt. Fortunately things are again on the upswing. Since the signing of the peace accords, Mozambique's rich artistic traditions have been at the forefront, and today – despite an influx of Western influences – are thriving.

Dance

Mozambicans are superb dancers, and experiencing their rhythm and movement – whether in a Maputo nightclub or at a traditional dance performance in the provinces – is a chance not to be missed.

Dance, music and singing accompany almost every major occasion. Many dances tell a story, and often offer political and social commentary as well.

Others are specific to particular events. Most dances involve some sort of costume, which frequently includes rattles tied to the legs. Masked dancing is not as common in Mozambique as in some areas of Africa and is done primarily by the Makonde in northern Mozambique (see p160) and the Chewa-Nyanja in Tete province, who are known for their Nyau masks.

On Ilha de Moçambique and along the northern coast, you're likely to see *tufo*, a dance of Arabic origin. It is generally performed only by women, all usually wearing matching *capulanas* (Mozambican sarongs) and scarves, and accompanied by special drums (some more like tambourines) known as *taware*. *Tufo* was traditionally danced to celebrate Islamic feast days and other special events. A similar dance, usually performed to celebrate the Islamic feast of Maulidi, is also found in Zanzibar and around Kilwa, in Tanzania.

Other dances found in the north, particularly around Moçimboa da Praia, include *muáli*, a dance of initiation; *batuque*, sometimes performed at circumcision ceremonies; and *rumba*.

In the south, one of the best known dances, particularly in Maputo, is *makwaela*, characterised by a cappella singing accompanied by foot percussion. It developed in South Africa among mine-workers who were often forced to practise their dance steps without disturbing their white guards. The lyrics focused traditionally on the hardships and dreams of daily life. It was Mozambique's Grupo Makwaela dos TPM that, together with South Africa's Ladysmith Black Mambazo, helped internationalise *makwaela*.

In Tete and Manica provinces, a common dance is *nyanga*, which involves a dancer who simultaneously sings and plays the panpipes (which are also known as *nyanga*).

The best place to get information on traditional dance performances is at the *casa de cultura* ('house of culture' or cultural centre), found in every provincial capital. These exist primarily to promote traditional culture among young Mozambicans by offering music and dance lessons and similar training. However, you can often see rehearsals and performances of local song and dance groups here, and staff can be a good source of information on cultural events in the province.

Literature

Mozambique has a rich body of literature, written almost exclusively in Portuguese. However, a number of major works (including all titles in this section cited in English) have been translated. Despite the harshness of the colonial era, the Portuguese language is not viewed with animosity, but rather as playing a unifying role for Mozambique's various ethnic groups. It takes on a unique richness in the context of Mozambican literature, where it has given voice to the country's aspirations for independence and expression to its national identity.

During the colonial era, local literature generally focused on nationalist themes. Two of the most famous poets of this period were Rui de Noronha and Noémia de Sousa. De Sousa in particular focused on affirmation of Mozambican nationalism through definition of racial identity.

In the late 1940s José Craveirinha (1922–2003) began to write poetry focusing on the social reality of the Mozambican people and calling for resistance and rebellion – which eventually led to his arrest. Today, he is honoured as Mozambique's greatest poet, and his work, including 'Poem of the Future Citizen', is recognised worldwide. A contemporary of Craveirinha's was another nationalist called Luis Bernardo Honwana, famous for short stories such as 'We Killed Mangey Dog' and 'Dina'.

As the armed struggle for independence gained strength, Frelimo freedom fighters began to write poems reflecting their life in the forest, their marches

In addition to his poetry and political activism, José Craveirinha is credited with discovering and encouraging Maria de Lurdes Mutola (see p30) to become a runner when she was still an unknown soccer player.

and the ambushes. One of the finest of these guerrilla poets was Marcelino dos Santos. Others included Sergio Vieira and Jorge Rebelo.

With Mozambican independence in 1975, writers and poets felt able to produce literature without interference. The new-found freedom was soon shattered by Frelimo's war against the Renamo rebels, but new writers emerged, including Mia Couto, whose works include *Voices Made Night*, *Every Man is a Race* and *Under the Frangipani*. Other writers from this period include Ungulani Ba Ka Khossa, Heliodoro Baptista and Eduardo White. More recent is Farida Karodia, whose *A Shattering of Silence* describes a young girl's journey through Mozambique following the death of her family.

Lilia Momple, born on Ilha de Moçambique in 1935, has long been a major voice in contemporary literary circles. Her works include *Neighbours – The Story of a Murder* and *The Eyes of the Green Cobra*. Other contemporary woman writers include journalist and activist Lina Magaia, who is known for her *Dumba-Nengue – Run for Your Life: Peasant Tales of Tragedy in Mozambique*, and Paulina Chiziane, who authored *Niketche – A Story of Polygamy*, and whose *Balada de Amor ao Vento* (Love Dance for the Wind, 1990) was the first novel to be published by a Mozambican woman.

A significant development was the establishment of the Mozambique Writers' Association in 1982, which has been active both in publishing new material and in advancing the spread of indigenous literature throughout the country. Its prestigious José Craveirinha prize was recently awarded to Mia Couto and Paulina Chiziane.

Music
TRADITIONAL
Traditional music is alive and well in Mozambique, particularly in villages and rural areas. Some musical instruments you are likely to see include:

mbila A marimba or xylophone common in central and southern Mozambique (the plural is *timbila*), that can range from less than 1m to several metres in length. The keys are made of wood, under which are resonance chambers made from gourds and covered by animal membrane.

For an excellent survey of Mozambique music, see www.mozambique -music.com.

nyanga The *nyanga* (panpipe) is found around Tete city and in southern Tete province. It is made of hollow cane tubes joined together by cord. *Nyanga* is also the name given to the dance which is traditionally done to the accompaniment of panpipes.

pankwe A small guitarlike instrument made of a hollow gourd and wooden stem with six or seven strings. It is found primarily in Nampula, as well as in parts of Niassa and Cabo Delgado provinces.

tchakare This is another stringed instrument found in northern Mozambique. It has only one string, which is played with a bow similar to a hunting bow.

xikitsi This flat, hollow instrument is made with reeds and filled with stones or grain kernels, and is found throughout southern Mozambique. The *xikitsi* is played by shaking it back and forth with the hands while simultaneously using the thumbs to beat a rhythm, and is commonly used as accompaniment for vocal groups.

The *timbila* orchestras of the Chopi people in southern Mozambique are one of the best-known musical traditions in the country; for more, see p83.

MODERN
Modern music flourishes in the cities and the live music scene in Maputo is excellent. *Marrabenta* is considered Mozambique's national music. It developed in the 1950s in the suburbs of Maputo (then Lourenço Marques) and has a light, upbeat style and distinctive beat inspired by the traditional rural *majika* rhythms of Gaza and Maputo provinces. It is often accompanied by a dance of the same name. Initially, *marrabenta* was played with acoustic guitars, traditional drums and other percussion instruments, with a lead

singer and a female chorus. Later, electric guitars and other modern instruments were introduced. One of *marrabenta*'s best known proponents was Orchestra Marrabenta, formed in the 1980s by members of another popular band, Grupo RM, together with dancers from Mozambique's National Company of Song and Dance. When Orchestra Marrabenta split in 1989, several members formed Ghorwane (www.ghorwane.com), who perform frequently in Maputo; check their website for upcoming events.

There are numerous new generation bands. One of the best known is Kapa Dêch (pronounced 'kapa dezh'), a group of musicians who have taken traditional beats and built popular melodies around them using a keyboard and other modern instruments. Another is Mabulu, a band that combines classic *marrabenta* rhythms (in the venerable persons of the late Lisboa Matavel together with Dilon Djindji) with hip-hop. They recorded their top-selling first release, *Karimbo*, in 2000 when much of the southern part of the country was under water in severe flooding, followed by *Soul Marrabenta*.

Other acclaimed musicians include Chico António, who plays sophisticated, traditionally based music with conga drums, flute, and bass, electric and acoustic guitars; Léman, a trumpet player and former member of Orchestra Marrabenta, whose music combines traditional beats with contemporary inspiration; José Mucavele, an acoustic guitarist who plays a mixture of traditional and contemporary rhythms; Roberto Chidsondso; and Elvira Viegas. Fany Mpfumo, now deceased, was one of Mozambique's best known *marrabenta* musicians and still features on popular cassettes. For a listing of CDs to get you introduced to the scene, see p14.

AK-47s, land mines and other weapons are turned into art – for more on Arms into Art, see www .africaserver.nl/nucleo /eng.

Sculpture & Painting

Mozambique is well known for its woodcarvings, particularly for the sandalwood carvings found in the south and the ebony carvings of the Makonde. The country's most famous sculptor is the late Alberto Chissano, whose work received wide international acclaim and inspired many younger artists. The main centre of Makonde carving is in Cabo Delgado province, particularly around Mueda on the Makonde Plateau, with carving communities also around Pemba, and in Nampula province. While some pieces have traditional themes, many Makonde artists have developed contemporary styles. One of the leading members of the new generation of Makonde sculptors is Nkatunga, whose work portrays different aspects of rural life. Others carvers include Miguel Valíngue, and Makamo, who is known for his sandalwood carvings that combine Makonde influences with southern stylistic elements from his native Gaza.

The most famous painter in the country is Malangatana. Other internationally famous artists include: Bertina Lopes, whose work reflects her

Malangatana, edited by Júlio Navarro, is a beautiful collection of reproductions of many of the famous painter's works, plus a bit of background text as well.

MALANGATANA

Malangatana Valente Ngwenya – known universally as 'Malangatana' – is one of Mozambique's and Africa's greatest artists. Although best known for his paintings, Malangatana has also worked in various other media, including murals, sculptures and ceramics. His style is characterised by its dramatic figures and flamboyant yet restrained use of colour, and by its highly symbolic social and political commentary on everything from colonialism and war to peacetime rebuilding and the universality of the human experience.

In addition to his artwork, which is displayed in galleries worldwide, Malangatana has left his mark across a broad swath of Mozambican cultural life. This has included playing founding roles in the establishment of the Museu Nacional de Arte (p61) and the Núcleo de Arte (p61) and setting up the Centro Cultural de Matalana (p73).

For an overview of
Mozambique's art scene,
see www.arte.org.mz.

research into African images, colours, designs and themes; Roberto Chichorro, known for his paintings dealing with childhood memories; and Samate, one of Mozambique's earliest painters. Naguib, Victor Sousa and Idasse are among the best-known artists in the newer generation. All of these painters and sculptors have exhibits in the Museu Nacional de Arte (p61) in Maputo.

Ricardo Rangel, who is known for his black-and-white stills, is widely regarded as Mozambique's most famous photographer (plus co-owner of Chez Rangel, one of Maputo's best night spots – see p68).

Cinema

Mozambique's tiny film industry is distinguished primarily by its short but powerful documentaries on current social issues. One of the most esteemed directors is Licínio Azevedo. His *Disobedience* (2001), which tells the tale of a woman accused of causing her husband's suicide, was given a citation at the Zanzibar International Film Festival. Azevedo's *Time of the Leopards* is another classic, based on stories from Mozambique's independence war.

Another prominent director is Gabriel Mondlane. His credits include codirecting *A Miner's Tale* (2001), the story of a Mozambican migrant worker in the South African gold mines and the scourge of AIDS that he brings back to his rural community.

For a historical perspective, watch for Margarida Cardoso's *Kuxa Kanema – The Birth of Cinema* (2003) – a fascinating chronicle of the birth and rise of Mozambique cinema in the heady postindependence days under the direction of Samora Machel, and then its downfall a decade later with Machel's death.

Environment

THE LAND

Mozambique is a vast land spread out over about 800,000 sq km. To the east, it is edged by a spectacular coastline that winds for about 2500km, from Ponta d'Ouro in the south to the Rio Rovuma in the north. To the north and west it shares its borders with six other countries, including Malawi, which almost slices it in half.

Unlike most of its seaside neighbours, Mozambique has extensive coastal lowlands, which form a broad plain 100km to 200km wide in the south and leave the country vulnerable to seasonal flooding. In the north, this plain narrows and the terrain rises to mountains and plateaus on the borders with Zimbabwe, Zambia and Malawi.

One of the most notable geographical features in southern Mozambique is the chain of shallow, coastal barrier lakes strung between Ponta d'Ouro and the Archipélago de Bazaruto. In central Mozambique, the predominant geographical feature is the long Rio Zambezi valley and its wide delta plains. In many areas of the north, particularly in Nampula and Niassa provinces, towering granite outcrops or inselbergs dominate the landscape.

Two of Southern Africa's largest rivers – the Zambezi and Limpopo – cut giant swathes through the country on their way to the sea. Other major rivers are the Rio Save, dividing southern and central Mozambique, and the Rio Rovuma, which forms the border with Tanzania.

Mozambique's highest peak is Monte Binga (2436m) in the Montes Chimanimani on the Zimbabwe border.

The Zambezi is Africa's fourth largest river, after the Nile, Zaïre and Niger rivers.

WILDLIFE
Animals

Mozambique doesn't have the animal herds that you'll see in neighbouring Tanzania, Zambia or South Africa, and most of its large animal populations were decimated during the war. Yet there's still plenty left, with over 200 different types of mammals wandering around the interior. Challenging access, dense vegetation and skittishness on the part of the animals make spotting in most areas difficult; as it stands, the country will likely be of appeal as a safari destination primarily to a small circle of well-moneyed adventurers. Watch close for developments though, as work is going full force in reviving Mozambique's parks and reserves, especially Reserva do Niassa and Parque Nacional de Gorongosa, and the wildness and relatively low visitor numbers mean that anyone who does venture this way on safari is likely to come away satisfied.

MOZAMBIQUE'S COASTAL LAKES

Apart from Madagascar, Mozambique is the only country in East Africa with major coastal barrier lakes or lagoons. The lakes are separated from the sea by well-developed longshore dune systems, and most aren't more than 5m deep. Among the most important are Lagoa Uembje (Uembje Lagoon) at Bilene, Lago Inhampavala (Lake Inhampavala) north of Xai-Xai, Lago Quissico (Lake Quissico) just east of Quissico town and Lago Poelela (Lake Poelela), about 30km north of Quissico and traversed by the EN1.

With the exception of Uembje, none of the lakes have links with the sea and their brackish waters are rich with marine and bird life. This includes numerous freshwater fish species, white storks, little egrets and pink flamingos. At Lake Quissico alone, between 50 and 60 bird species have been recorded.

The largest wildlife concentrations are found in the Reserva do Niassa in Mozambique's far north, which is home to large herds of elephants, buffaloes and zebras. Modest populations of elephants, hippos and several other large mammals also make their home in Parque Nacional de Gorongosa. With the creation of the **Parque Internacional do Grande Limpopo** (www.greatlimpopopark.com), work is underway to encourage wildlife populations in the south to rebound, and wildlife restocking is already underway in the Mozambique section of the park (Parque Nacional do Limpopo, see later in this chapter), although everything is still in the early stages.

Mozambique is officially home to 170 reptile and 40 amphibian species, although the actual numbers are almost certainly much higher. In the Chimanimani area alone, 60 reptile species (including the endemic flat rock lizard and 34 species of snake) have been identified. More visible are the crocodiles, which you'll likely either see or hear about if you spend time near any of the country's rivers.

Mozambique's rich insect biodiversity includes an endemic dragonfly *(Ceriagrion mourae)* and the malaria-carrying *anopheles* mosquito. Endemic mammal subspecies include the blue Niassa wildebeest and a subspecies of Burchell's zebra, both of which are found only in northern Mozambique.

BIRDS

Mozambique makes up for its lack of easily accessible large mammal populations with an abundance of colourful birds. If you have an adventurous bent and don't mind the lack of facilities, it's an ornithologist's paradise.

Of the approximately 900 bird species that have been identified in the Southern Africa region, close to 600 have been recorded in Mozambique. Among these are numerous aquatic species, which make their homes in the country's extensive southern wetlands. On Ilha de Inhaca alone, 300 bird species, including seven species of albatross, have been recorded. Rare and unique species (most of which are found in isolated montane habitats such as the Montes Chimanimani, Monte Gorongosa and Monte Namúli) include the dappled mountain robin, the chirinda apalis, Swynnerton's forest robin, the oliveheaded weaver and the greenheaded oriole. Other rare species include the Cape vulture, the east coast akalat and the longbilled apalis; see p168.

MARINE LIFE

Until its terrestrial parks become more accessible, Mozambique's highest profile wildlife attractions are those swimming around under the sea. The

Ornithologists should look for *Birds of the Niassa Reserve* (Vincent Parker), *Birds of the Maputo Special Reserve* (V Parker & F de Boer), plus Vincent Parker's *Atlas of the Birds of Sul do Save, Southern Mozambique*.

Mozambique hosts five of the world's seven turtle species. Yet, their situation is precarious due to consumption of turtles and their eggs, and the popularity of shells and other turtle products for souvenirs and medicines.

ELEPHANTS OF THE SEA

The dugong, whose closest terrestrial relative is believed to be the elephant, is a lumbering marine mammal that favours the tropical coastal waters of the Indian and western Pacific oceans. They may live up to 70 years, sometimes reach up to 3m in length, and can tip the scales at 170kg. To maintain their rotund figures, dugong spend their days lazing in the shallows and feeding on sea grasses and algae.

Dugong are prized for their meat and fat and their large size and gentle manner make them easy prey for hunters. They also frequently become trapped in fishing nets and are then killed for their meat. Today they are classified as endangered.

Dugong have been sighted in many areas along the Mozambican coastline, including around Baía de Inhambane, Angoche, Ilha de Moçambique, Nacala and the Archipélago das Quirimbas. However, the largest population – which is also considered to be the largest population in East Africa – is found in the waters of the Archipélago de Bazaruto. Dugong numbers here plummeted to fewer than 100 but seem to be stabilising, thanks to the protection given to them by Parque Nacional de Bazaruto.

MANGROVES

In addition to being famous for its beautiful beaches, the Mozambican coast is also notable for its extensive mangrove swamps, especially in the centre and north of the country. These play an essential role in coastal ecosystems by curbing erosion, enriching surrounding waters with nutrients, and providing resources for local communities. The wood of mangroves is resistant to insects, and is prized for building houses, beds and fishing traps. Around Pemba, an infusion of the bark of one species of mangrove is used for dyeing fishing nets.

Despite their usefulness, Mozambique's mangroves have come under attack. Large stands are cleared for the establishment of solar salt pans and shrimp aquaculture ponds. Others are cut for charcoal production and firewood.

country's coastal waters host populations of dolphins, including spinner, bottlenose, humpback and striped dolphins, and Ponta d'Ouro is one of the best places in the region for swimming with these graceful creatures. Mozambique's waters are also renowned as the home of the ungainly and elusive dugong (see boxed text), as well as loggerhead, leatherback, green, hawksbill and olive Ridley turtles.

The Mozambican coast also serves as a winter breeding ground for the humpback whale, which occurs primarily in the country's southern waters between Ponta d'Ouro and Inhambane. Between July and October, it's also common to see whales in the north, offshore from Pemba.

For more on the best times and places for spotting some of this marine life, see p47.

ENDANGERED SPECIES

Mozambique's once abundant wildlife herds have been exploited since at least the 16th century, when there are records of thriving trade in ivory and tortoise shell. In more recent times, the war and poaching have taken their toll. Today, large mammals believed to be extinct or on the verge of extinction in the country include the black rhino, white rhino, giraffe, tsessebe, roan antelope and the African wild dog. The blue Niassa wildebeest is found in the Reserva do Niassa but is thought to be endangered. One snake species, the African rock python, is also believed to be endangered.

The dugong is probably the best known among endangered marine species, while marine turtles are considered threatened. Endangered birds include thyolo alethes and wattled cranes.

Plants

Mozambique is bursting at the seams with colourful and varied flora. This is most obvious in the array of lavender jacarandas, brilliant red flamboyants, and other flowering trees that you'll see lining the streets of Maputo and other provincial capitals. Along the coast are endless stands of coconut palms, especially in Inhambane and Zambézia provinces, while in drier inland areas, such as around Tete, the landscape is dotted with enormous baobabs – a tree whose rootlike branches make it look as if it were standing on its head.

Large tracts of central and north-central Mozambique are covered by miombo or light woodland, characterised by broadleaf deciduous *brachystegia* trees. Mopane woodland derives its name from the tall, multistemmed mopane tree, which grows well in soils with a high clay content. It is predominant in southern inland areas between Rio Limpopo and Rio Save, and in the upper Zambezi River Valley.

New plant species are being discovered in Mozambique all the time, with close to 6000 recorded thus far. Of these, an estimated 250 are thought to be found nowhere else in the world. The Maputaland Centre of Plant Diversity, straddling the border with South Africa south of Maputo, is considered one of the most important areas of the country in terms of plant diversity and has been classified as a site of global botanical significance. The Montes Chimanimani along the Zimbabwe border are also notable for their diversity of plants, with at least 45 endemic species. Other important highland areas include Monte Namúli, the Gorongosa Massif and Monte Chiperone in western Zambézia province.

NATIONAL PARKS & RESERVES

Mozambique has six national parks: Gorongosa, Zinave, Banhine and Limpopo in the interior; Parque Nacional de Bazaruto offshore; and Parque Nacional das Quirimbas, encompassing both coastal and inland areas in Cabo Delgado province.

Bazaruto is the most accessible, and the most visited. In addition to its tropical island setting, it's famed for its offshore coral reefs and fish and the fact that it hosts the largest remaining dugong population in the region. Various islands within the boundaries of Parque Nacional das Quirimbas can now also be easily (albeit rather expensively) visited and diving can be arranged with all the island lodges both here and on Bazaruto.

Gorongosa is easy to visit if you have access to your own vehicle. For now, the park is primarily of interest to birders and anyone just wanting to experience the bush rather than as a safari destination, although its tourism and wildlife are beginning to make a comeback, thanks to the involvement of the US-based Carr Foundation (see p111).

Parque Nacional de Limpopo is now open to visitors; see p84. Zinave and Banhine are not yet officially open, and have no visitor infrastructure. Both will ultimately be incorporated into a 'transfrontier conservation area' surrounding Parque Internacional do Grande Limpopo, which will link Mozambique's Limpopo park with South Africa's Kruger National Park and Gonarezhou National Park in Zimbabwe. For all parks, those under 12 years

The Parque Internacional do Grande Limpopo is part of the larger Peace Parks Foundation initiative that envisions a series of transfrontier conservation areas throughout Southern Africa; see www .peaceparks.org.

MAJOR NATIONAL PARKS & RESERVES

Park	Features	Activities	Best time to visit
Parque Nacional das Quirimbas (p158)	islands, sea, mangroves & coastal forest: corals, marine turtles, coconut crabs, dugongs & more	diving & snorkelling	year-round
Parque Nacional de Bazaruto (p99)	islands & sea: corals, dolphins, dugongs, marine turtles, flamingos & more	diving, snorkelling, birding	year-round
Parque Nacional de Gorongosa (p111)	grasslands, coastal plain, rainforest & lakeshore: birds, waterbucks, impalas, occasionally hippos, lions & elephants	birding, hiking, vehicle safaris	Apr/May-Nov
Parque Nacional do Limpopo (p84)	rivers & bush, farmland: occasional elephants, plus smaller wildlife & birds	short vehicle safaris, birding	May-Dec
Reserva Especial de Maputo (p79)	woodlands, grasslands, dry forest, coast: elephants, birdlife	camping & limited vehicle safaris	May-Dec
Reserva do Niassa (p150)	miombo woodland, savannas, wetlands, rivers & riparian forests: elephants, antelopes, buffaloes, zebras & more	walking & vehicle safaris	May-Dec

---

SACRED FORESTS

A good example of the contributions that local traditions can make to biodiversity conservation is seen in western Manica province around the beautiful foothills of the Montes Chimanimani. Communities here recognise various types of sacred areas. One is the *dzimbahwe* (chief's compound), where each chiefdom has its own spot, generally in a densely forested area, and access is strictly limited. Another is the *gwasha*, a forest area used by chiefs, elders and spirit mediums for rainmaking and other ceremonies. Both the *dzimbahwe* and the *gwasha* are treated with great respect and no development, wood cutting or harvesting are permitted. Hunting is under the control of the chiefs, as is the gathering of medicinal and other plants.

---

of age are admitted free and those between 13 and 20 years are eligible for the child rate.

In addition to Reserva do Niassa, Mozambique's wildlife reserves include Marromeu, Pomene, Maputo and Gilé, plus numerous controlled hunting areas and forest reserves.

The government has also approved development of several 'transboundary natural resources management areas', including one which is to form part of Parque Internacional do Grande Limpopo. The goal is to try to create an environment favourable for both local residents and the local wildlife, without regard to national boundaries.

A new protected area is in the process of being declared around the Archipélagos das Ilhas Primeiras e Segundas, offshore between Angoche and Pebane. It will protect one of Mozambique's largest green turtle nesting sites. The area is also known for its whales, coral reefs and prolific birdlife, and is a major breeding ground for sooty terns.

ENVIRONMENTAL ISSUES

From rampaging elephants destroying farmers' crops and massive flooding to the plundering of natural resources by unscrupulous timber harvesters and commercial fishing operators, Mozambique's challenges to preserving its exceptional ecosystems reads like a high adventure novel. Fortunately the country and its natural resources have come increasingly into the international spotlight over the past decade; WWF (Worldwide Fund for Nature) and other organisations are working with the Mozambican government to make large strides in protecting the country's wealth.

Some of the most exciting progress is the protection of Mozambique's marine resources. Highlights here include the recent creation of Parque Nacional das Quirimbas, the creation and recent extension of Parque Nacional de Bazaruto, and ongoing efforts to declare a new protected marine area around the Archipélago das Ilhas Primeiras e Segundas. In the Archipélago das Quirimbas, the area's new protected status has already brought noticeable improvement in the previously rapidly declining fish populations in inshore fishing areas. On the Ilhas Primeiras e Segundas, local fishermen are already working with the WWF to protect sooty tern and green turtle breeding grounds, with a focus on minimising sale and consumption of eggs and products.

On the terrestrial side, as conservation measures and antipoaching efforts have begun to show successes, and populations of elephants and other wildlife increase, instances of human–elephant conflict are increasing. This is particularly a problem in the far north of the country, where elephants eat and destroy crops in large areas of Niassa province, as well as in coastal sections of Parque Nacional das Quirimbas and elsewhere in the region. Thus far, the main way of combating this has been to lay

In 2006, Rolling Stones guitarist Ronnie Wood joined forces with The CarbonNeutral Company to plant a new forest in Mozambique's Parque de Nacional Gorongosa. Fans were offered the chance to buy their very own tree in Ronnie Wood Wood, in return for a certificate of ownership designed by the rocker-cum-artist.

Reserva do Niassa is Mozambique's largest protected area. The Niassa-Selous corridor, spanning the Mozambique–Tanzania border, is the world's largest elephant range.

RESPONSIBLE TOURISM

With the increase in tourism in Mozambique, popular coastal resorts are beginning to show the effects of degradation. Some things you can do to prevent the situation from worsening:

▪ Don't drive on the beaches. (It's bad for the environment, and illegal in Mozambique.)

▪ Support the local economy whenever possible – shop at local markets, patronise local establishments and buy local crafts, preferably directly from those who make them.

▪ Pack up your litter from beaches and campsites.

▪ Save natural resources. Water especially is a precious resource throughout much of the country. Try not to waste it in hotels, and in rural areas try to avoid spilling or wasting water from communal pumps. Ask permission before drawing water from a community well.

▪ Look for opportunities to interact with local communities.

▪ Reciprocation of kindness is fine, but indiscriminate distribution of gifts from outside is never appropriate. Donations to recognised projects are more sustainable and have a better chance of reaching those who need them most.

▪ Don't buy items made from ivory, skin, shells, turtles, coral, etc.

▪ Respect local culture and customs.

Also check out the website of the **UK-based Tourism Concern** (www.tourismconcern.org.uk) for some additional steps you can take to minimise your impact.

For more on what's happening environmentally in Mozambique, check out WWF-Mozambique at www.wwf.org.mz.

electric fencing in community areas. However, the fences are expensive and difficult to maintain and it is not possible to use them in all affected areas. More sustainable techniques are also gradually being introduced to complement the fences, including encouraging cultivation of Mozambique's famous *piri-piri* (chilli peppers), clearing of small buffer zones between crop areas and the bush and roping off crop areas with strings soaked in a mixture of oil and chilli peppers.

Illegal timber practices are more complicated to combat, with entrenched interests at every level. An illustration of the challenges is seen in northern and central Mozambique, where tropical hardwoods are felled with little or no regulation. The inspectors who are supposed to patrol forest areas and control logging activities are poorly paid, with little incentive and inadequate resources to do their job. Bribery is commonplace and controls are weak or nonexistent. Reports indicate that even if companies get a logging permit they often operate outside the areas assigned to them. In addition to environmental damage, the widespread practice of exporting unprocessed logs (rather than processing the timber in Mozambique, with the attendant local economic gain) means local communities receive little benefit from timber resources. There is often neither replanting nor sustainable harvesting (ie taking one tree in every 10 in a cyclical pattern) and the potential for farming on the cleared forest is limited, as soils are unsuitable or too thin.

The Endangered Wildlife Trust (www.ewt.org .za) is also active in Mozambique through its partner, the Fundação Natureza em Perigo.

While lasting improvements in the protection and management of Mozambique's timber and other natural resources will only be possible as the country's overall economic situation progresses, there are several bright spots in the picture, including a network of smaller-scale projects focused on sustainable development and community resource management. For one example of what is being done in the timber area, see p108.

Diving

Travelling around Southern Africa and trying to decide whether to come to Mozambique for the diving? The answer is: come! Although word is slowly leaking out, the country still remains largely unknown and underrated as a diving destination. It's hard to believe when you consider the length of its coastline, the almost-pristine condition of many offshore reefs and the chance of landing coveted sightings of dolphins, whale sharks, manta rays or even dugongs. Quality equipment, instruction and certification are readily available in all of the main coastal areas, including Ponta d'Ouro, Ilha de Inhaca, Tofo, Vilankulo, the Archipélago de Bazaruto, Ilha de Moçambique, Nacala, Pemba and the Archipélago das Quirimbas. Prices are comparable to elsewhere in East Africa, though somewhat higher than in South Africa. Rounding off the picture are an almost complete lack of overdevelopment and commercialism, the natural beauty of the Mozambican coast, seasonal humpback whale sightings, excellent fish diversity and a fine and generally untouched array of hard and soft corals, especially in the north. You'll also have most areas almost to yourself – a treat if you've been fighting for space in more popular dive destinations – plus, in some areas, the adventure of exploring relatively unknown sites.

INFORMATION
Conditions & Seasons

While Mozambique is considered a year-round diving destination, conditions and visibility can vary significantly. The best months are generally April/May to July and again in November/December (August to October can get quite windy). The worst months are generally February and March, when rains are heavy, and some resorts only operate with skeleton staff, though all this varies as you move up the coast. Visibility tends to be best in late autumn and winter (April through October), when water temperatures are between 22° and 25°C. In summer, the water temperature rises to 28° or 29°C.

All ability levels are catered for, with dive sites ranging from shallow snorkelling reefs close to shore, to deeper dives, with depths varying from about 7m to more than 35m. Most dives are done from rubber inflatable boats powered by 2x85HP+ motors, or a similar configuration. An exception to this is diving with some of the top-end resorts on the Bazaruto and Quirimbas archipelagos, and in Nacala, where refitted dhows or yachts are common.

Depending on the location and season, most divers are content with a full 3mm wetsuit, though some operators use 5mm suits as standard.

Dive Training & Certification

While some travellers get their certification in South Africa and then come to Mozambique to actually dive, quality dive instruction and certification (generally PADI, although a few places also offer NAUI) is available at all of the coastal dive resorts surveyed on p44. For operator listings and contact details see the regional chapters.

Prices for dives and instruction are fairly uniform, though some of the best deals are available up north, and throughout there are often discounts in the low season. Rates average between US$40 and US$50 per dive, including equipment and boat travel, and decrease the more dives you do. With your own equipment, expect to pay from about US$25 to US$35 per dive. Four-day open-water certification courses cost from about US$300 to

For general background information on diving in the region, it's well worth hunting up a copy of *Lonely Planet's Diving & Snorkelling South Africa*, which also includes a section on southern Mozambique.

DIVING SAFETY

Some things to keep in mind before starting your diving:

▪ Possess a current diving certification card from a recognised scuba diving instructional agency (and don't forget to bring it with you, together with your log book).

▪ Be sure you are healthy and feel comfortable diving.

▪ Obtain reliable information about physical and environmental conditions at the dive site (eg from a reputable local dive operation).

▪ Dive only at sites within your realm of experience; if available, engage the services of a competent, professionally trained dive instructor or dive master.

▪ Be aware that underwater conditions vary significantly from one region, or even site, to another and that seasonal changes can significantly alter any site and dive conditions.

▪ Ask about local laws, regulation and etiquette regarding local marine life and the environment.

US$450 and should generally be booked in advance, especially during peak seasons and in the south.

If your main reason for coming to Mozambique is to dive, it's worth considering booking a dive-accommodation package. Most of the resort-based operators listed in the regional chapters offer these and they can also be arranged with some of the operators listed on p190. For liveaboard arrangements around the Bazaruto and Quirimbas archipelagos, see www.divethebig5.com/html/liveaboard.html. Pemba Beach Resort Hotel (p156) arranges liveaboards in the Archipélago das Quirimbas on its luxury yacht, MY *Fantastique*, and dhow-based liveaboard arrangements are possible in Nacala; see p47.

Dive Operators & Dive Tours

Most operators are resort-based, with reliable rental equipment, secure washing and drying facilities and South African staff who are familiar with the local terrain and conditions. When choosing, quality should be the main consideration. Take into account the operator's experience and qualifications; knowledgeability and competence of staff; and the condition of equipment and frequency of maintenance. Try to assess whether the overall attitude is serious and professional, and – ask about safety precautions – radios, oxygen, emergency evacuation procedures, boat reliability and back-up engines, first-aid kits, safety flares and life jackets. On longer dives, do you get an energising meal, or just tea and biscuits? An advantage of operators offering PADI courses is that you'll have the flexibility to go elsewhere in the country (or world) and have what you've already done recognised at other PADI dive centres.

PRINCIPAL DIVE SITES
Southern Mozambique

Most dive sites are in the south, where there is a wide choice of operators.

PONTA D'OURO & PONTA MALONGANE

This stretch of coast is a popular destination for divers venturing over from South Africa, and gets crowded during the April and December South African school holidays (see p175), when certification courses should definitely be booked in advance. Visibility is generally better than at sites just over the border, coral growth is prolific at some sites and, with luck, it's possible to dive amongst sharks (primarily hammerheads and Zambezis), plus potato bass and dolphins (there's also an onsite dolphin tour operator, p77). Most sites are within a short boat ride from shore and there's a good reef wall at the southern end of the point for snorkelling. Most diving is based out of informal dive camps catering to budget travellers and dive–accommodation deals are available. For more upmarket diving, contact Ponta Mamoli (p79).

ILHA DE INHACA
Diving from Ilha de Inhaca is tide-dependent and conditions are variable, though on good days you can expect to see a variety of sharks, manta rays, potato bass and more. Bottlenose and humpback dolphins are also sometimes seen, and occasionally dugongs. August and September should be avoided, as it's often too windy to go out.

Until recently, diving has been a one-operator show (no certification courses), but several new developments are planned for the near future so this may change.

Snorkelling features high on the list at Inhaca, with the best snorkelling in the sheltered waters around Cabo Santa Maria, off Inhaca's southernmost tip. For more see p72.

For some detailed descriptions of diving sites in southern Mozambique, check out www.diversityscuba.com, www.devoceandiving .com and www.barra diveresorts.com.

TOFO & BARRA
It was diving that put Tofo (p90) on the map, and it's still one of the most popular places in Mozambique to dive and get certified. There's a selection of operators and a lively dive subculture. Corals aren't as plentiful as to the south or north but this is compensated for by the likelihood of manta and whale shark sightings, and the relative proximity to the world-class Manta Reef, plus Amazon and other choice sites.

RESPONSIBLE DIVING

As Mozambique's popularity as a tourist and diving destination grows, pressure on dive sites is increasing. Following are some tips for helping preserve the ecology and beauty of the reefs:

- Don't use anchors on reefs and take care not to ground boats on coral.
- Avoid touching living marine organisms or dragging equipment across the reef. If you must hold on to the reef, only touch exposed rock or dead coral.
- Be conscious of your fins. Even without contact, the surge from heavy fin-strokes near the reef can damage delicate organisms. Take care not to kick up clouds of sand, which can smother delicate reef organisms.
- Practise and maintain proper buoyancy control. Major damage can be done by divers descending too fast and colliding with the reef.
- Take care in underwater caves. Spend as little time in them as possible as your air bubbles may get caught within the roof, leaving previously submerged organisms high and dry. Take turns to inspect the interior of a small cave.
- Resist the temptation to collect or buy corals or shells (which is not only ecologically damaging, but also illegal).
- Take home all rubbish. Plastics in particular are a serious threat to marine life.
- Don't feed fish, as this disturbs their normal eating habits and encourages aggressive behaviour.
- Minimise your disturbance of marine animals, including dolphins and turtles.

Dive conditions and facilities at Barra (p92) are similar, although Barra has somewhat more upmarket accommodation offerings and you'll need to travel a bit further to get to several of the best sites.

Several of the resorts south of Tofo in the Inhambane area (see Around Inhambane, p88) have inhouse dive operators and this is another possible base for diving in this area. While it's convenient to Manta Reef (and to wonderful snorkelling at Pandane reef just offshore), you'll have to travel a bit to the other main sites.

For more detail on regional reefs and marine life, try A Field Guide to the Seashores of Eastern Africa & the Western Indian Ocean Islands by Matthew Richmond, Coral Reefs of the Indian Ocean – Their Ecology and Conservation by TR McClanahan et al and Marine Life of the Pacific & Indian Oceans by Gerald Allen.

VILANKULO & ARCHIPÉLAGO DE BAZARUTO

There is wonderful diving and snorkelling around the islands of the Archipélago de Bazaruto, though it tends to be slightly pricier than further south and most sites are well offshore. Among the draws are Two Mile Reef, two miles northeast of Ilha de Benguera (about an hour in a speedboat from Vilankulo), which is considered the best in the area and has a variety of sites. On the inside of the reef is the sheltered Aquarium, which is also ideal for snorkelling. Dolphins and dugongs are highlights, as are seasonal humpback whales. Santa Carolina, which is the only rock island of the archipelago, offers excellent snorkelling. Magaruque island is also a snorkelling destination, with plenty of fish on the reef just off its western shore. The main drawback is relatively long boat rides to most sites, especially if you're based in Vilankulo. Budget and midrange travellers should arrange things in Vilankulo. Most of the top-end resorts on the islands also have dive operators. For more, see p97.

Northern Mozambique

The north is Mozambique's adventurous frontier, not only for travel, but also for diving. Pemba has long had a low-key but quality dive scene that's now beginning to gain more attention. The newest developments are in the Archipélago das Quirimbas and surrounding areas which are considered to have some of the best unexplored diving to be found anywhere.

ILHA DE MOÇAMBIQUE

The main attraction of diving here is having Ilha de Moçambique (p137) as a backdrop. Other draws include wall dives off nearby Goa and Sena islands, a 16th-century wreck, sea turtles, dolphins, seasonal humpback whales (August/September to November), sea kayaking and the chance to

---

MOZAMBIQUE'S CORALS

Corals are found only between the latitudes of 30° north and 30° south, and although scattered coral communities extend along the Mozambican coast into South Africa, the reefs near Mozambique's Ilha de Inhaca are considered to be the southernmost of the African mainland.

In addition to being fascinating to explore, coral reefs are among the most productive and diverse of the earth's ecosystems. About 25% of the world's fish species depend on reefs during at least some stage of their life cycle. Reefs also protect the coast from damaging wave action and erosion, and contribute to the formation of islands and sandy beaches.

Despite some areas of damage, Mozambique's reefs – including extensive fringing reef systems in the north, and the southern reefs dotting the southern coast at intervals between the Archipélago de Bazaruto and Ilha de Inhaca – are considered to be in generally very good condition and are mostly unexplored; a notable exception are those off Ilha de Inhaca which have been extensively studied. Studies are also underway of the northern reefs around the Archipélago das Quirimbas, with early reports indicating that these may be some of the richest reefs along this side of the continent.

WATCHING WHALES & MORE

The likelihood of seeing whale sharks, humpback whales, dolphins, manta rays and dugongs is one of the highlights of diving the Mozambique coast. Whale sharks – the world's largest fish – are most prolific in the south during the summer months from about November to March/April, although they are occasionally seen at other times of year as well.

Humpback whales migrate up the southeast African coastline from Antarctica to mate and calve, reaching Mozambican waters around June. Between July and September/October, it's common to see them offshore along the length of the country.

Dolphins can be seen year round, although the winter months of June through August tend to be particularly good. Mantas can also be seen year round, and are almost guaranteed around Tofo and Barra and the nearby Manta Reef. Green and other sea turtles are a highlight of the north. Dugongs are usually sighted around the Archipélago de Bazaruto – see p38.

---

combine diving with a dhow safari (September to November only, see p140). As there's only one island-based dive operator, confirm your timing with them before setting plans.

NACALA

Nacala's single – but very clued in and recommended – dive operator (Bay Diving, see p144) has put the enormous, blue Nacala Bay on the map in diving circles. If you have an adventurous bent and are after something different, consider diving at Nacala – it's cutting edge, personalised and well away from standard tourism loops. Diving can be arranged from a customised dhow (which can also be chartered for liveaboard arrangements). There's an array of sights within relatively close reach and night dives are organised from shore.

There are good overviews of northern Mozambique dive sites on several resort websites, including www .quilalea.com, www .pembabeachresort.com and www.medjumbe resort.com.

PEMBA

Pemba has a low-key, agreeable and good value dive scene, with rewarding dive sites, a relaxed, beachside ambience and professional, personalised operators catering to all ends of the market. There are a range of sites, suitable for all levels and diveable year-round.

The diving begins about 500m offshore from Praia de Wimbi, where the coastal shelf drops off steeply, offering a spectacular wall dive. Once you've had your fill here, there are other sites nearby and the Archipélago das Quirimbas is within easy reach.

ARCHIPÉLAGO DAS QUIRIMBAS

This is Mozambique's newest diving destination and largely unexplored. Most diving here is top-end and based at the island resorts, though it's also possible to arrange packages with Pemba-based operators. Highlights include the protected marine sanctuary around Quilaluia island (which has a PADI dive centre) and the famed Lazarus bank, which is one of the most exciting new destinations in the country. Vamizi (certified divers only) and Rongui islands both have lovely coral gardens close to shore, as does Quilaluia. If you're island-based, there is a range of close-in sites to chose from, and fine snorkelling close to shore on Vamizi and Quilaluia.

Food & Drink

Mozambique has some of the best cuisine in Southern Africa, blending African, Indian and Portuguese influences. It's especially noted for its seafood, including excellent *camarões* (prawns) and *lagosta* (crayfish), and the ubiquitous *peixe grelhada* – grilled catch of the day. Even local dishes, especially along the coast, have a pizzazz that sets them off from those in neighbouring countries, with liberal use of coconut milk and *piri-piri* (hot pepper) to liven up what might otherwise come off as bland. Meat lovers have their day too, with a good selection of high-quality meats from nearby South Africa.

Whatever the meal may be, it's hard to beat the coastal backdrop – what wouldn't taste good while dining with your feet in the sand, the stars overhead and the waves lapping softly nearby – and the warm and lively local hospitality.

Hoje Temos...Receitas de Moçambique, edited by Marielle Rowan, has recipes for Mozambican dishes in English and Portuguese.

STAPLES & SPECIALITIES

Local dishes generally consist of a maize- or cassava-based staple (called *xima* or *upshwa*) or rice, served with a sauce of beans, vegetables or fish, and in rural areas, this type of food – together with grilled chicken and chips, which is found almost everywhere – will be the main option. Specialities to watch for include *matapa* (cassava leaves cooked in a peanut sauce, often with prawns or other additions, and rumoured to be one of President Armando Guebuza's favourite dishes) in the south, and *galinha á Zambeziana* (chicken with a sauce of lime juice, garlic, pepper and *piri-piri*) in Quelimane and Zambézia provinces. *Caril* (curry) dishes are also common, as are *chamusas* (samosas – triangular wedges of fried pastry, filled with meat or vegetables) and other snacks. Avocado salads – often with tomatoes – are another treat. Grilled chicken is either plain with salt or liberally seasoned with *piri-piri*.

For more recipes for Mozambican cuisine, check www.macua .org/receitas/receitas.htm or www.receitasemenus .net (follow the links to Cozinha Moçambicana).

Along the coast and at most restaurants, the highlight is the excellent and reasonably priced seafood. In addition to grilled prawns, lobster and crayfish, *lulas* (calamari) are also popular, usually served grilled or fried. Inland, around Lago Niassa, the most popular fish is *chambo*.

Throughout the country, bakeries sell delicious, fresh and piping hot bread rolls every morning.

IS THERE FISH ON THE MENU?

Long gone are the old war days when dining out in Mozambique meant bringing your own food to the restaurant. But eating out can still be something of an experience, especially when it comes to figuring out the rationale behind menu cards. Menu cards in Mozambique are often grand affairs – with long listings of *entradas* (entrées), *pratos principais* (main courses) and *sobremesas* (desserts). They get your mouth watering and hold out the promise of a fancy three-course meal with all the trimmings. Yet when it gets down to placing your order, what's actually available is often much more limited – although it can take a while to find this out. You'll ask the waiter for *cordon bleu*, as advertised on the menu. He will duly write down the order, head to the kitchen and then reappear several minutes later to tell you that *cordon bleu* 'acabou' (is 'finished'). Perhaps the process will be repeated again and then again until finally *you* get the hang of it and ask what *is* available. The answer will almost always be *peixe grelhada* (grilled fish) – most likely not the barracuda or other speciality described in glowing terms on the menu but (usually) just as good.

DRINKS

Mozambicans enjoy their drinks, and beer *(cerveja)* is available almost everywhere, though outside major cities you'll need to hunt to find it cold. Local brands include Manica and Laurentina, and are sold by the bottle *(garafa)* or can *(lata)*. Dois M (2M) – the national lager – is produced jointly by Mozambique and South African Breweries. South African beers are also easy to come by, including Castle, Black Label, Lion and Amstel, as are Namibian beers, such as Windhoek Lager. Portuguese wine *(vinho)* is sold in hotels and in supermarkets in larger towns, and South African wines are easy to find in Maputo and other cities.

The most common local brews (called *nipa* in some areas of the north) are made from the fruit of the cashew as well as *mandioca* (cassava), mango and sugar cane – they are generally rather lethal and to be avoided, at least in larger quantities. Palm wine *(sura)*, which is slightly tamer, is common in southern Mozambique, particularly in the area south and west of Maputo, where it is manufactured and then sold over the border in South Africa. The best places for trying local brew are at weddings or other local celebrations, where they are almost always served.

Bottled water *(água mineral)* is available in all larger towns. In villages and rural areas, it can be harder to find, so it's worth carrying a filter if you'll be travelling extensively away from main towns.

Soft drinks *(refrescos* or 'sodas')* are available almost everywhere. In cities and larger towns, you usually have the choice of local brand soft drinks (for example, *cola nacional*) or the more expensive international brand. Good imported nonsweetened fruit juices from South Africa, sold in long-life cartons, are available in all larger towns.

According to tradition, *ukanhi,* a southern Mozambique traditional brew made from the fruit of the *canhoeiro* tree, should never be sold.

WHERE TO EAT & DRINK

Most towns have a *café, pastelaria* or *salão de cha* where you can get coffee or a pastry, and inexpensive snacks and light meals such as omelettes, *pregos* (thin steak sandwiches) or burgers. Many of these places also offer more substantial meals (averaging under US$4), such as chicken and chips and similar fare. Bread is often served, though you may be charged extra for this.

Larger towns and provincial capitals will have at least one fancier restaurant and generally several. Prices and menu offerings at these places are remarkably uniform throughout the country, ranging from about US$6 to US$10 for meals such as grilled fish or chicken with rice or potatoes (either fried, *batatas fritas*, or boiled, *batatas cozidas)*. Most of these midrange restaurants also offer generally very good Portuguese-style soups, such as *caldão verde* (made with greens and often flavoured with sausage), with bread, and sometimes will have a small dessert menu that will include *salada de fruta* (fruit salad – made almost everywhere with banana, papaya and mango in season) and perhaps a few other choices. In addition, Maputo, Beira and larger towns have an array of restaurants offering a good selection of other cuisines. In villages and rural areas, sometimes the only choice are *barracas* (small food stalls).

Larger towns have wonderful sidewalk cafés where you can enjoy delicious *bolos* (cakes) or light meals, plus *café espresso* or *chá* (tea), while watching the passing scene.

If a hotel or restaurant tells you meals or particular dishes are available *por encomenda*, it means that you'll need to make a special order. The best thing to do is to call or stop by in the morning for a meal that evening.

Most restaurants are open daily for lunch and dinner. A few stay open straight through, but more standard are lunch hours from about 11am or noon to about 3pm, and dinner from about 6.30pm until 10pm. The smaller the town, the earlier its eating establishments will close down. Bookings are almost never necessary and are generally not possible anyway. Mozambique's restaurants are not known for their speedy service and waits of up to an hour (or more, especially when away from major centres) are common. If you're in a rush, stop by the restaurant several hours before you want to eat and put in an order. For info on tipping, see p177.

Quick Eats

Everywhere in Mozambique – from cities to the smallest villages – you'll find *barracas*, often along the roadside or at markets, where you can get a plate of local food such as *xima* and sauce for about US$1 or less. If the *barraca* seems to do a good business (with fast food turnover), the surroundings are reasonably clean and the food is well-heated and freshly prepared, you should have no trouble eating at these places and they offer fine insights into local life.

For self-caterers, it's easy anywhere along the coast or around Lago Niassa to make arrangements with local fishermen for a fresh catch, which you can then arrange to have cooked up at your hotel. The best times to look are early morning and late afternoon when the boats come in with their catch. If you plan on shopping frequently at fish markets, it's a good idea to carry your own pocket-sized weighing scale and a plastic bag for the fish.

Markets in all larger towns sell an abundance of fresh tropical fruits – papayas, mangoes, bananas, pineapples, tangerines, oranges and litchis are among the highlights – and a reasonably good selection of vegetables, plus rice and other grains – all inexpensive.

Maputo, Beira and larger towns have well-stocked supermarkets selling imported goods at high prices. South African products are widely available through Shoprite, a South African supermarket chain which has stores in Maputo, Beira, Chimoio and Nampula.

> Mozambique is renowned for its prawns, and annual prawn export revenues exceed US$90 million.

VEGETARIANS & VEGANS

Vegetarians who eat seafood will have no problems in Mozambique. Otherwise, you will need to be more creative, as many sauces contain meat or seafood. Bean dishes *(feijão)* are available, although not as widely as in other parts of the region, and those served at Brazilian and Portuguese restaurants often include pork or other meat. Nuts – especially peanuts *(amendoins)* and cashews *(castanhas de caju)* – are easy to find on the streets and in markets. For lacto-ovo vegetarians, boiled eggs are available everywhere. Supermarkets in the larger towns usually stock long-life cheese. Yogurt is available in most provincial capitals, though it is often the sweetened, long-life variety rather than the real thing.

There is a large Indian population along the coast and Indian shop owners can often point you in the direction of a good vegetarian meal.

DINING MOZAMBICAN STYLE

An invitation to share a family meal in Mozambique is a real treat. Before eating, it's usual that a bowl of water is passed around for washing hands. The usual procedure is to hold your hands over the bowl while your hostess pours water over them. Sometimes soap is provided, as is a towel for drying off.

A maize- or cassava-based staple or rice will be the centre of most meals. You'll often be offered utensils, but if everyone else is eating with their hands, it's good to do the same. It's a bit of an art and it may seem awkward at first but will start to feel more natural after a few tries. The usual procedure is to take a bit of the staple with the right hand, roll it into a small ball with the fingers, dip it into the sauce and eat it, trying to avoid letting the sauce drip down your arm.

While containers of water or home-brew may be passed around from person to person, it is not customary to share coffee, tea or bottled soft drinks. Following the meal, the water and wash basin are brought around again for the hands.

DOS & DON'TS

■ If you receive an invitation to eat and aren't hungry, it's OK to explain that you have just eaten, but still try to share a few bites of the meal in recognition of the bond with your hosts.

■ Try to leave a small amount on your plate at the end of the meal to show your hosts that you have been satisfied.

■ For the same reason, don't take the last bit of food from the communal bowl or serving plate – your hosts may end the evening worrying that they haven't provided enough.

■ Don't handle or eat food with the left hand; it's also generally considered impolite to give someone something with the left hand.

■ If everyone else is eating with their hands, try to do the same, even if cutlery is also provided.

■ Defer to your host for any customs that you are not sure about.

HABITS & CUSTOMS

Meals connected with any sort of social occasion are usually drawn-out affairs for which the women of the household will have spent several days preparing. Local style is to eat with the (right) hand from communal dishes in the centre of the table. Sodas are the usual meal accompaniment. If water is on the table, it will generally be unpurified.

Three meals a day is the norm, although breakfast is frequently nothing more than tea or coffee and a piece of bread. Coffee is often made with a heavily sweetened mixture of Nescafé or an unappealing chicory blend and Nido milk powder, except in cafés and restaurants where the real thing is available. The main meal is usually eaten at midday.

Street snacks and meals-on-the-run are common. European-style restaurant dining – while readily available in major cities – is not really a part of local Mozambican culture, except among the small elite class, although sidewalk cafés are popular across a broad spectrum. Also common are gatherings at home, or perhaps at a rented hall, to celebrate special occasions, with the meal as the focal point.

EAT YOUR WORDS

Want to know *matapa* from *mariscos?* Get behind the cuisine scene, by getting to know the language. For pronunciation guidelines see p204.

Useful Phrases

I'm (a) vegetarian.
Eu sou vegetariano/a. (m/f)   e·oo soh ve·zhe·ta·ree·*a*·noo/a

I don't eat meat.
Não como carne.   nowng *ko*·moo *kaar*·ne

I'll have a beer, please.
Vou tomar uma cerveja.   vo too·*mar oo*·ma ser·ve·*zha*

What would you recommend?
O que é que recomenda?   oo ke e ke rre·koo·*meng*·da

... without/with chilli peppers ...
... sem/com piri-piri ...   seng/kong *pee*·ree *pee*·ree

That was delicious!
Isto estava delicioso!   eesh·too *shtaa*·va de·lee·see·o·zoo

The bill, please.
A conta, se faz favor.   a *kong*·ta, se faz fa·*vorr*

I'd like (a/the) ..., please.
Queria ..., por favor.   ke·*ree*·a ..., poor fa·*vorr*

local speciality
uma especialidade local   *oo*·ma shpe·see·a·lee·*daa*·de loo·*kaal*
menu (in English)
um menu (em inglês)   oong me·*noo* (eng eeng·*lesh*)

I'm allergic to ...
Eu sou alérgico/a (m/f)   e·oo soh a·*ler*·zhee·koo/a
  nuts
  oleaginosas   o·lee·a·zhee·*no*·zash
  peanuts
  amendoins   a·meng·doo·*eengsh*
  seafood
  marisco   ma·*reesh*·koo
  shellfish
  crustáceos   kroosh·*taa*·se·oosh

Food & Drink Glossary
FOOD

arroz	a·*rrosh*	rice
batatas	ba·*taa*·tash	potatoes
batatas fritas	ba·*taa*·tash *free*·tash	chips/fries
bife	*bee*·fe	steak
camarão	ka·ma·*rowng*	prawn
caril	ka·*reel*	curry
carne	*kaar*·ne	meat
chamusa	sha·*moo*·sa	meat- or vegetable-filled fried dough triangle; also samosa
feijão	fay·*zhowng*	beans
frango/galinha	frang·goo/ga·*lee*·nya	chicken
fruta	*froo*·ta	fruit
lagosta	la·*gosh*·ta	crayfish/lobster
legumes	le·*goo*·mesh	vegetables
lulas	*loo*·lash	squid (calamari)
mandioca	man·dee·*o*·ka	cassava/manioc
ovos	*o*·voosh	eggs
ovos mexidos	*o*·voosh me·*shee*·doosh	scrambled eggs
pão	powng	bread
peixe	*pay*·she	fish
prego no pão	*pre*·goo noo powng	steak sandwich
sopa	*so*·pa	soup

DRINKS

agua ...	aa·*gwa* ...	... water
fervida	fer·*vee*·da	boiled (OK to drink)
mineral	mee·ne·*raal*	mineral
quente	*keng*·te	hot
(chávena de) chá ...	(shaa·ve·na de) shaa ...	(cup of) tea ...
(chávena de) café ...	(shaa·ve·na de) ka·fe ...	(cup of) coffee ...
com (leite)	kong (lay·te)	with (milk)
sem (açúcar)	seng (a·soo·kar)	without (sugar)
um copa de ...	oong ko·poo de ...	a glass of ...
cerveja	ser·ve·zha	beer
leite	lay·te	milk
sumo de laranja	soo·moo de la·rang·zha	orange juice
refresco	rre·fresh·co	soft drink

CONDIMENTS

açucar	a-*soo*-kar	sugar
piri-piri	*pee*-ree-*pee*-ree	chilli pepper
sal	saal	salt

OTHER

almoço	aal-*mo*-soo	lunch
barraca	ba-*rra*-ka	street food stall
conta	*kong*-ta	bill
cozido/a (m/f)	koo-*zee*-doo/a	boiled
grelhado/a (m/f)	gre-*lyaa*-doo/a	grilled
jantar	zhang-*taar*	supper
mata bicho (slang, literally, 'kill the beast')	*ma*-ta *bee*-shoo	breakfast
menu	me-*noo*	menu (a set meal)
mercado	mer-*kaa*-doo	market
pequeno almoço	pe-*ke*-noo aal-*mo*-soo	breakfast
quiosque	kee-*osh*-ke	snack bar
recibo	rre-*see*-boo	receipt
restaurante	res-tow-*rang*-te	restaurant

Maputo

Maputo

With its Mediterranean-style architecture, waterside setting and wide avenues lined by jacaranda and flame trees, Maputo is easily one of Africa's most attractive capitals. It's also the most developed place in Mozambique by far, with a wide selection of hotels and restaurants, well-stocked supermarkets, shady sidewalk cafés and a lively cultural scene.

The heart of the city is the bustling, low-lying baixa (busy port and commercial area). Here, Portuguese-era buildings with their graceful balconies and wrought-iron balustrades jostle for space with ungainly Marxist-style apartment blocks. *Galabiyya*-garbed men gather in doorways for a chat, Indian traders carry on brisk business in the narrow side-streets and women wrapped in colourful *capulanas* (sarongs) sell everything from seafood to spices at the massive Mercado Municipal.

A few kilometres away, along the seaside Avenida Marginal, life takes a more leisurely pace. Fishermen stand along the roadside with the day's catch, hoping to lure custom from the constant parade of passing vehicles; banana vendors loll on their carts in the shade, with Radio Moçambique piping out eternally upbeat rhythms in the background; and local soccer teams vie for victory in impromptu matches in the sand.

Maputo is pricier than elsewhere in the country – especially for imported goods brought in on the toll road linking Johannesburg and the South African economy with Maputo's port and the sea. Yet, there's enough selection to make it a good destination no matter what your budget. Getting to know the city is a highlight of visiting Mozambique and essential to understanding the country. Don't miss spending time here before heading north.

HIGHLIGHTS

- Catch some culture at one of Maputo's many **museums** (p61)
- Dine out in style, sampling a different **restaurant** (p66) every night
- Shop for souvenirs and browse for bargains at the city's colourful **markets** (p69)
- Experience the pulsating pace of the capital's thriving **nightlife** (p68)
- Enjoy the laid-back ambience of **Ilha de Inhaca** (p72), take in the sea air at **Praia de Macaneta** (p73) or sample upcountry life in quiet **Catembe** (p71)

HISTORY

Long before Europeans discovered Maputo's charms, the local Ronga people were living here, making their living by fishing, whale hunting and farming, with a bit of local trading thrown in to make ends meet.

In 1545 Portuguese navigator Lourenço Marques happened upon Baía de Delagoa, now known as Baía de Maputo (Maputo Bay), in his journey up the Southern African coastline. His reports attracted other traders who established temporary settlements offshore on Inhaca and Xefina Grande islands as bases for ivory trading forays to the mainland. Yet Portuguese attention was soon diverted northwards and they all but abandoned their activities in the south.

Lourenço Marques – as the area eventually became known – took on a new glow in the mid-19th century, with the discovery of diamonds and gold in the nearby Transvaal Republic. Around 1898 it replaced Ilha de Moçambique as the capital of Portuguese East Africa. A new rail link with the Transvaal in 1894 and expansion of the port fuelled the city's growth. In the 1950s and 1960s, 'LM' became a favoured playground for Portuguese holiday makers, and for apartheid-era South Africans who came over the border in droves seeking prawns, prostitutes and beaches. With Mozambican independence in 1975, the city's original residents reasserted themselves and in 1976 President Samora Machel changed the name to Maputo, honouring an early chief who had resisted Portuguese colonialism.

ORIENTATION

Maputo sits on a low escarpment overlooking Baía de Maputo, with the long avenues of its upper-lying residential sections spilling down into the baixa.

Many businesses, the train station, banks, post and telephone offices and some budget accommodation are in the baixa, on or near Av 25 de Setembro, while embassies and most better hotels are in the city's more staid upper section, especially around the Sommerschield diplomatic and residential quarter. Maputo's tallest building and a good landmark is known as 'trinta e trés andares' (33 Storey Building), in the baixa on the corner of Avs 25 de Setembro and Rua da Imprensa. At the northernmost end of the Marginal and about 7km from the centre is Bairro Triunfo and the Costa do Sol area, with a small beach and several places to stay and eat.

About 10km west of Maputo is the large suburb of Matola, site of the Chissano Museum (p61), and home to many industries.

Maps

The *Planta de Endereçamento do Centro da Cidade de Maputo* (1997), put out by Conselho Municipal in collaboration with Coopération Française, is somewhat dated but still the best city map; look for it at hotel bookshops. There's a larger version of the same map in book form (*Guia das Vias 1997*) which includes the city's outskirts.

MAPUTO IN...

Two Days

After breakfast at your hotel or a sidewalk café, get an early start on some of the **Walking Tour** (p63) sights, with a detour from the **Mercado Municipal** (p62) to buy some textiles at the nearby **shops** (p69). Once finished the morning's sight-seeing, hire a **laranjinha** (p64) for a ride along Av Marginal to **Restaurante Costa do Sol** (p66) for lunch with sea breezes.

The **Museu Nacional de Arte** (p61) is an essential afternoon stop, before resting up for an evening at **Chez Rangel** (p68), or a pub- and club-hopping tour in a **habana** (p64).

Spend day two visiting more museums – the **Núcleo de Arte** (p61), **Museu Chissano** (p61) and **Malangatana's house and studio** (p61) are highlights – and **craft shopping** (p69). For dinner, treat yourself to a seafood grill buffet at **Hotel Polana** (p67) or enjoy the local cuisine and ambience at **Feira Popular** (p67) before heading out for another night on the town.

Four Days

Follow the two-day itinerary. On day three, take the ferry to **Catembe** (p71) and lunch at **Restaurante Marisol** (p71). On day four go to **Inhaca** (p72) for relaxation on the beach on Ilha dos Portuguêses or snorkelling around Cabo Santa Maria.

GREATER MAPUTO

INFORMATION		Maputo Backpackers...................**6** D2		ENTERTAINMENT 🎭	
ATM.....................................**1** C3		Residencial Belsol........................**7** D2		Costa do Sol Stadium & Matchiki-Tchiki	
Irish Embassy...........................**2** C3		Residencial Kaya Kwanga...........**8** C3		Complex...................................**12** C3	
SIGHTS & ACTIVITIES		EATING 🍴		SHOPPING 🛍	
Mercado de Xipamanine (Xipamanine		Shoprite...................................**9** B3		Shanty Craft...............................**13** D2	
Market).................................**3** A3		Super Mares.............................**10** D2			
Mercado do Peixe (Fish Market)........**4** C3				TRANSPORT	
		DRINKING 🍷		Junta Transport Stand.................**14** A2	
SLEEPING 🏠		Coconuts Live & Complexo			
Kurhula Parque Self-Catering Chalets..**5** D2		Mini-Golfe............................**11** C3			

INFORMATION
Cultural Centres
British Council (Map pp58–9; ☎ 21-310921, 21-321577; www.britishcouncil.org/mozambique; 226 Rua John Issa) Near the UK high commission.

Centro Cultural Franco-Moçambicano (Map pp58–9; ☎ 21-320787; www.ccfmoz.com; Praça da Independência; ⌚ 2-6pm Mon, 9am-6pm Tue-Fri, 9am-noon Sat) An excellent place with art exhibitions, music and dance performances, films, theatre and more.

Centro Cultural Português (Instituto Camões; Map pp58–9; ☎ 21-493892; www.instituto-camoes .pt/ccp/ccpmaputo.htm; 720 Av Julius Nyerere) Art and photography exhibits; opposite the South African high commission.

Centro de Estudos Brasileiros (Map pp58–9; ☎ 21-306840, 21-306774; cnr Av Karl Marx & Av 25 de Setem-

bro) Exhibitions of Lusophone artists, and Portuguese language courses.

Emergency
For emergency medical treatment, see opposite.

If you are the victim of a crime and need to get a police report as reference for your insurance company, these can be obtained with time and patience at the police station nearest the site of the crime. Useful police stations include those on Av Kim Il Sung, 1½ blocks south of Av Kenneth Kaunda; near the corner of Avs Mao Tse Tung and Amilcar Cabral; and on Av Julius Nyerere, three blocks south of Av 24 de Julho. Some insurance companies will accept a report from your embassy.

Official emergency numbers include **Central Police Station** (☎ 21-325031, 119), **Fire** (☎ 197, 198) and **Hospital Central** (☎ 21-325000/9), but it's generally better to seek help from your hotel or embassy.

Internet Access

Mundo's Internet Café (Map pp58–9; Av Julius Nyerere; per hr US$2; ☒ 8am-10.30pm Mon-Sat, 10am-10.30pm Sun; ☒) Next to Mundo's restaurant.

Net Cabo (Map pp58–9; Tigre Centre, 1st fl, Av Ho Chi Min; per hr US$1.80; ☒ 9am-7.30pm Mon-Sat) One block uphill from the cathedral.

Pizza House Internet Café (Map pp58–9; Av Mao Tse Tung; per hr US$1.60; ☒ 8am-10pm Mon-Fri, 10am-10pm Sat & Sun) Upstairs at Pizza House restaurant.

Teledata (Map pp58–9; Av 24 de Julho; per hr US$1.20; ☒ 7.30pm-8pm Mon-Fri, 9am-6pm Sat) One block west of Av Vladimir Lenine, and diagonally opposite Africa Bar.

Medical Services

Clínica 222 (Map pp58–9; ☎ 82-0002220, 21-312222, 21-313000; cnr Av 24 de Julho & Rua Augusto Cardoso; ☒ 24hr) Similar to Clínica de Sommerschield, but cash only.

Clínica de Sommerschield (Map pp58–9; ☎ 82-3056240, 21-493924/6; 52 Rua Pereira do Lago; ☒ 24hr) Just off Av Kim Il Sung; has a lab and a doctor on call. Advance payment required (meticais, rand, dollars or Visa card)

Farmácia Apotheka (Map pp58-9; ☎ 21-495633; Polana Shopping Centre, 1st fl, cnr Avs 24 de Julho & Julius Nyerere; ☒ 9am-9pm Mon-Sat, 10am-8pm Sun)

Farmácia Calêndula (Map pp58–9; ☎ 21-497606; 222 Av Mao Tse Tung; ☒ 8am-8pm Mon-Sat, 9am-1pm Sun) Just up from Av Julius Nyerere.

Farmácia Capital (Map pp58–9) Main (☎ 82-3014055; Franca Centro Comercial, Ground fl, cnr Avs 24 de Julho & Amilcar Cabral; ☒ 24 hr) Branch (Av Mao Tse Tung ☎ 82-3014056; ☒ 7.30am-8pm Mon-Sat) The Mao Tse Tung branch is just up from Pizza House restaurant.

Money

There are 24-hour ATMs all over town, including one on Av Marginal, and at:

BIM Expresso (Map pp58–9; cnr Avs Mao Tse Tung & Tomás Nduda)

BIM Headquarters (Map pp58–9; cnr Avs Karl Marx & 25 de Setembro)

Polana Shopping Centre (Map pp58–9; cnr Avs Julius Nyerere & 24 de Julho)

Standard Bank (Map pp58–9) Headquarters (Praça 25 de Junho) Branch (Hotel Polana) Also changes travellers cheques with a minimum US$35 commission, original purchase receipt required.

For changing cash, in addition to the banks, there are *casas de câmbio* (foreign exchange bureaus) along Av Julius Nyerere southeast of the Hotel Polana, Hotel Pestana Rovuma on Rua de Sé and on Av Mao Tse Tung around Av Tomás Nduda. Out of hours try **Cotacambios** (Airport ☒ 6am-9.30pm Mon-Thu, 6am-10pm Fri, 7am-10pm Sat, 11.30am-10.30pm Sun; City Centre Polana Shopping Centre, ground fl, cnr Avs 24 de Julho & Julius Nyerere; ☒ 9am-9pm Mon Sat, 10am 10pm Sun).

Post

Main post office (CTT; Map pp58-9; Av 25 de Setembro; ☒ 8am-6pm Mon-Sat, 9am-noon Sun) With poste restante.

Telephone

Telecomunicações de Moçambique (TDM; Map pp58-9) Branch (Ground fl, 33 Storey Bldg, Rua da Imprensa; ☒ 8am-10pm) Branch (Hotel Pestana Rovuma) International calls.

Tourist Information

Bureau de Informação Pública (Public Information Bureau, or BIP; Map pp58-9; ☎ 21-491106, 21-491226; cnr Avs Eduardo Mondlane & Francisco Magumbwe; ☒ 7.30am-3.30pm Mon-Fri, 9am-noon Sat) A dated and dusty selection of books on Mozambique, most in Portuguese; sometimes also city maps.

Fundo Nacional de Turismo (Futur; Map pp58–9; www.futur.org.mz; 1203 Av 25 de Setembro) Colourful listings brochures covering Maputo and all of Mozambique's provinces.

Travel Agencies

Dana Tours (Map pp58-9; ☎ 21-497483, 21-495514; info@danatours.net; 729 Av Mao Tse Tung) An excellent agency that specialises in the coast and can sort you out for destinations throughout Mozambique (plus a few in Swaziland and South Africa). Midrange and up with occasional budget offerings. Their sister operator, Dana Agency (☎ 21-484300; travel@dana.co.mz) in the same compound, does domestic and international flight bookings.

Mextur (Map pp58-9; ☎ 21-428427/9; mextur@emilmoz.com; 1233 Av 25 de Setembro) Domestic flight and travel arrangements.

Mozambique Adviser (Map pp58-9; ☎ 21-309477; www.adviser.co.mz) Bookings desk in the lobby of Hotel Polana; southern Mozambique travel arrangements, car rentals and boats to Inhaca.

Nau Tours (Map pp58-9; ☎ 21-380034; www.nautours.co.mz) A good contact for lower-budget trips to Catembe, Reserva Especial de Maputo and Ponta d'Ouro, plus boats to Inhaca and Cabo Santa Maria.

MAPUTO

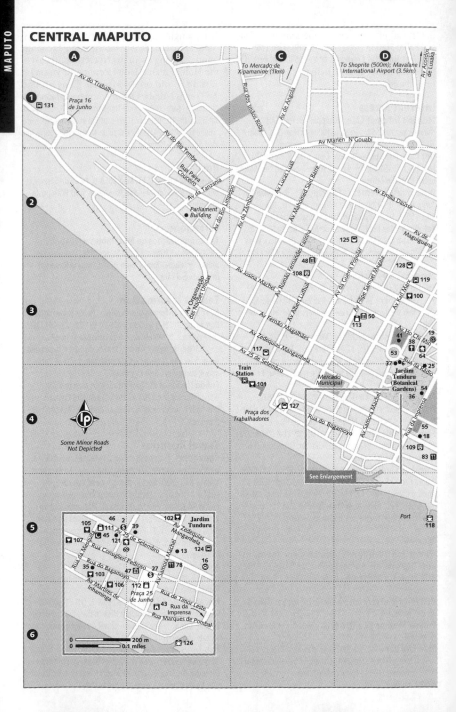

CENTRAL MAPUTO

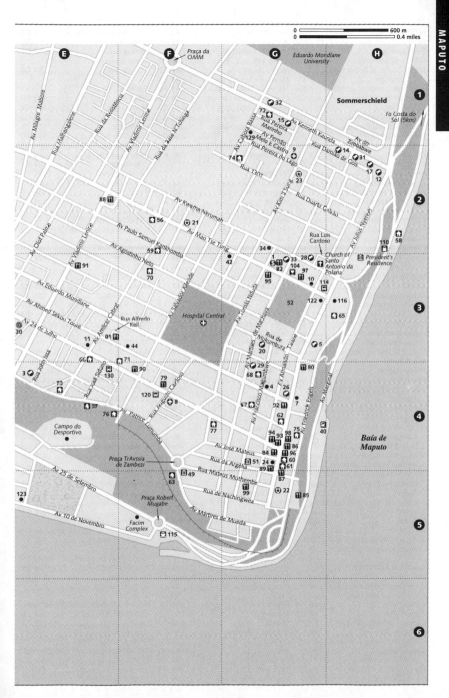

MAPUTO

DANGERS & ANNOYANCES

Although most visitors enjoy their visits in Maputo without mishap, be vigilant when out and about whether during the day or night, and take the precautions mentioned on p172. Also see the boxed text on p173. In particular, try to avoid carrying a bag, wearing expensive jewellery or having any external trappings of wealth when walking around town – don't give a potential thief any reason to think that you might have something of value. At night, always take a taxi and, day or night, avoid putting yourself in isolated situations. Areas of the city to avoid include the isolated stretches of the Marginal between Praça Robert Mugabe and the Holiday Inn, and the two access roads leading down to the Marginal from Av Friedrich Engels. Also avoid the area below the escarpment just south of Av Patrice Lumumba. If you get stopped by the police, always insist on going to the nearest station (*esquadrão*).

There are several restricted areas that are off-limits to pedestrians, where photos are also prohibited. These include the eastern footpath (sidewalk) on Av Julius Nyerere in front of the president's residence, and the Ponta Vermelha zone in the city's southeastern corner.

On a more prosaic note, Maputo now has traffic lights, but they don't always work, so be careful when cruising through an intersection on green.

SIGHTS

The heart of old Maputo is in the baixa, which is where most of the sights are, though there are also some wonderful museums in the outlying suburbs.

Museu Nacional de Arte

Half a block west of Av Karl Marx, the **Museu Nacional de Arte** (National Art Museum; Map pp58-9; http://musart.tvcabo.co.mz; 1233 Av Ho Chi Min; admission free; 2-6pm Tue-Sun), has an excellent collection of paintings and sculptures by Mozambique's finest contemporary artists, including Malangatana and Chissano.

Núcleo de Arte

This long-standing **artists' cooperative** (Map pp58-9; ☎ 21-492523; www.africaserver.nl/nucleo; 194 Rua da Argélia; closed Sun) is a focal point among Mozambican artistic circles. It has frequent exhibitions featuring the work of up-and-coming

artists (some of which is for sale), including pieces made in the 'Guns into Art' project (check their website for more). There's also a pottery area, and a garden where you can talk with the artists and watch them at work. It's in a dilapidated colonial-era house near the Hospital Central.

Casa e Museu Malangatana

It's possible to visit the **Casa e Museu Malangatana** (House and Studio of Malangatana; ☎ 21-465286, 21-465681; Rua de Camões, Bairro do Aeroporto; 8am-5pm Mon-Fri, 8am-noon Sat), dedicated to Mozambique's most renowned painter. It is filled with dozens of his own paintings as well as several sculptures of Alberto Chissano. Call ahead to arrange an appointment. The house is located several kilometres outside the city centre; ask directions when arranging the visit.

Museu Chissano

Works of the renowned sculptor Alberto Chissano are displayed in his family's residence at the **Museu Chissano** (Rua Torre de Vale, Bairro Sial, Matola; admission US$2; 9am-noon & 3-5pm Tue-Sun) together with the works of other sculptors and painters. It's outside Maputo in the Matola suburb in an area called Bairro Sial: take Av 24 de Julho towards Matola. Approaching Matola, watch for some grey warehouses on the left side of the roadway, and turn right onto a small tarmac road branching off the main road roughly opposite the warehouses. Follow this for 1.2km and then turn right again. Continue about 1km past the police station. Take the first left after the police station and continue 100m to the T-junction; the Chissano Museum is in the large white house in front of you to the right. Taxis charge from around US$25 return, including waiting time.

Train Station

Maputo's imposing **train station** (Caminho dos Ferros de Moçambique or CFM; Map pp58-9; Praça dos Trabalhadores) is one of the city's landmark buildings. The dome was designed by an associate of Alexandre Gustav Eiffel (of Eiffel Tower fame), although Eiffel himself never set foot in Mozambique. Also impressive are the wrought-iron lattice work, pillars and verandas gracing the exterior. Inside are some old steam engines, and the Chez Rangel Jazz Café (see p68), one of the city's best night spots. Although the station is still in use, trains run infrequently and it's often deserted.

Praça de Independência

This wide plaza is rimmed on one side by the soaring white spire of the **Catedral de Nossa Senhora da Conceição** (Map pp58–9) and on the other by the hulking, neoclassical **Conselho Municipal** (City Hall; Map pp58–9). Just off the square is the **Casa de Ferro** (Iron House; Map pp58–9), which was designed by Eiffel in the late 19th century as the governor's residence, though its metal-plated exterior proved unsuitable for tropical conditions.

Markets

The **Mercado Municipal** (Municipal Market; Map pp58–9; Av 25 de Setembro), with its long rows of vendors, tables piled high with produce, fresh fish and colourful spices, and stalls overflowing with everything from brooms to plastic buckets, is Maputo's main market, and well worth a stroll. Get there early in the morning when everything is still fresh, and before the crowds. The much smaller and lively **Mercado de Peixe** (Fish Market; Map p56), just off Av Marginal, sells a good sampling of what lies underneath the nearby waters; choose what you'd like and get it grilled up on little charcoal burners nearby.

Fortaleza

The old **fort** (Map pp58–9; Praça 25 de Junho; admission free; ☺ 8am-5pm) was built by the Portuguese in the mid-19th century near the site of an earlier fort. Inside is a garden and a small museum with remnants from the era of early Portuguese forays to the area.

STOLEN GOODS & BIRD CLAWS

Not exactly a tourist attraction, but a Maputo institution nonetheless, is the enormous and chaotic **Mercado de Xipamanine** (Xipamanine Market, Map p56). The market, which sprawls over the length of several football fields beyond the termination of Av Eduardo Mondlane, is the place to go to buy everything from used appliance parts to mattresses and sofas. More interesting is the enormous selection of traditional medicines and remedies, including an array of animal pelts, bird claws and more. Xipamanine is also notorious as the hub of the local underworld, with an impressive assortment of stolen items for resale.

Museu de História Natural

The recently renovated **Museu de História Natural** (Map pp58–9; ☎ 21-490879; www.museu.org.mz; Praça Travessa de Zambezi; admission US$2; ☺ 9am-11.30pm & 2-4pm Tue-Sun) near Hotel Cardoso is worth a stop to see its Manueline architecture and its garden with a mural by Malangatana. Inside are some moderately interesting taxidermy specimens, and what is probably the region's only collection of elephant foetuses.

Museu da Revolução

The sombre **Museum of the Revolution** (☎ 21-400348; Av 24 de Julho; admission US$0.60; ☺ 9am-noon & 2-6pm Mon-Fri, 2-6pm Sat, 3-6pm Sun) documents Mozambique's independence struggle. Exhibits are in Portuguese, but with many photos, and provide a good feel for events that have shaped the country's recent history.

Museu da Moeda

Housed in a yellow building on the corner of Rua Consiglieri Pedroso, the **Museu da Moeda** (Map pp58–9; Praça 25 de Junho; admission US$0.20; ☺ 9am-noon & 2-4.30pm Tue-Sat, 2-5pm Sun) dates from 1860. Inside are exhibits of local currency, ranging from early barter tokens to modern-day bills. At the time of writing, it's temporarily closed for renovations.

Praça dos Heróis Moçambicanos

The large Plaza of the Mozambican Heroes, along Av Acordos de Lusaka near the airport (Map p56), is notable for its 95m-long mural commemorating the revolution. The star-shaped white marble structure in its centre holds the remains of Mozambique's revolutionary and postindependence heroes, including Eduardo Mondlane and Samora Machel, as well as those of national poet José Craveirinha. Photographs are prohibited. Except on 3 February, when it's open to the public, you'll need to get permission to visit (including to walk across the praça) from the BIP (p57).

ACTIVITIES
Running

Maputo hosts numerous road races, including a half-marathon and a mini-triathlon; watch ads in *Notícias* and on embassy bulletin boards. For work-outs, there's a track at **Parque dos Continuadores** (Map pp58–9; Av Mao Tse Tung), near Av Julius Nyerere, and a local **Hash House Harriers** (http://groups.msn.com/maputohashhouseharriersgroup; Aeroclube, Av Kwame Nkrumah; meets 3.45pm Sat).

Swimming & Boating

For lap swimming, try the 25m pool at **Clube Naval** (Map pp58-9; ☎ 21-492690, 21-494881; www .clubenaval.com; admission US$4; ☺ from 7am Mon-Fri). The pool at Hotel Polana (see p64) is also 25m at its widest, though only open to hotel guests. Swimming at the beach along Av Marginal is possible though inadvisable due to considerations of cleanliness and occasional rumours of sharks.

The best contact for boat rentals and fishing charters is Clube Naval, which is also the best place to launch a boat if you bring your own.

Tennis

There are frequent tournaments at the courts at the botanical gardens (Jardim Tunduru, corner Rua da Imprensa and Rua da Rádio), where short- and long-term memberships can be arranged. Clube Naval has courts open to its members, and several of the top-end hotels have courts for their guests.

LANGUAGE COURSES

The following offer Portuguese language classes:

Centro de Estudos Brasileiros (Map pp58-9; ☎ 21-306840, 21-306774; cnr Avs Karl Marx & 25 de Setembro)
Instituto das Línguas (Map pp58-9; ☎ 21-325684, 21-305473; marketing.il@tvcabo.co.mz; 1260 Av Ahmed Sekou Touré)

The main African languages spoken in Maputo are Shangana and the closely related Ronga. There's no formal instruction, but tutors can be easily arranged; ask around for reliable teachers at the language schools listed here, at your embassy, or at local businesses and offices.

WALKING TOUR

Central Maputo is compact and easily explored on foot. For descriptions of most of the sights in this tour, see p61. A good place to start is at Praça 25 de Junho, with the old **fortaleza** on its eastern side. Diagonally opposite is the **Museu da Moeda**.

Leave Praça 25 de Junho to the west via Rua Consiglieri Pedroso which, together with Rua do Bagamoyo one block south, forms the heart of the oldest area of the city. The second cross street you'll reach is Rua da Mesquita, where the new **Jumma Masjid** stands on the site of what was once Maputo's oldest mosque.

Continue south along Rua da Mesquita to Rua do Bagamoyo and the building housing the national archives, **Archivo do Património Cultural**. Turning west on Rua do Bagamoyo brings you soon to Praça dos Trabalhadores, with its large WWI monument and Maputo's impressive **train station**.

Head north one block to Av 25 de Setembro and then east to the **Mercado Municipal**. Continue east along Av 25 de Setembro for 1½ blocks, and then north along Av Samora Machel for three blocks to **Praça da Independência** and the large, white **Catedral de Nossa Senhora da Conceição**. Next to the cathedral to the west is the **Conselho Municipal** building, which was completed around 1945. One block north of Praça da Independência and two blocks west of City Hall is the **Museu Nacional de Arte** – well worth a detour.

From the museum, return to Praça da Independência. On the praça's southeastern edge is the beautifully restored building housing the **Centro Cultural Franco-Moçambicano**. On the small street just south of the cultural centre is the **Casa de Ferro**. Opposite are Maputo's overgrown **botanical gardens**, known as Jardim Tunduru, which were laid out in 1885 by the English landscaper Thomas Honney. The tennis courts on the garden grounds serve as headquarters of the Mozambican Tennis Federation, and you can often see some of the country's best players practising. At the main entrance to the botanical gardens on Av Samora Machel is a large statue of Machel, Mozambique's first president. Exit the gardens to the north on Rua da Rádio, where Rádio Moçambique is located, and then head one block east to Av Vladimir Lenine. The attractive building on the opposite corner houses the **British High Commission**. Go south on Av Vladimir Lenine (which turns into Rua da Imprensa here), passing the **Supreme Court** building on your left. The second cross street you reach is Av 25 de Setembro, with **Café Continental** (cnr Avs 25 de Setembro & Samora Machel) – an ideal spot to end the walk.

TOURS

The best way to see the sights is to charter a *laranjinha* or *habana* (see p64).

The Mozambique Adviser desk at Hotel Polana arranges reasonably priced half- and full-day city tours, pub crawls ('Maputo by Night') and other excursions.

TREAT YOURSELF

In keeping with its Afro-Latino rhythms, Maputo now boasts its own fleet of *habanas* – sleek 1950s vintage cars imported from Cuba, complete with fedora-sporting drivers and period tunes on the sound system. The vehicles are in mint condition, with huge, comfortable seats and are an excellent way to see the sights or cruise around town on day or night-time city tours. They can also be chartered for airport pickups, or evenings on the town pub- and club-hopping – guided or not, as you like.

The same company has a fleet of brightly coloured and well-maintained *laranjinhas* – Maputo's version of Cuba's cocos taxis – that are ideal for daytime sightseeing or for a leisurely ride along Av Marginal to lunch at Restaurante Costa do Sol. The *laranjinhas* have meters, with prices roughly equivalent to city taxi prices, or about US$30 per hour; habana charters are about US$45 per hour. Contact **Laranjinhas Turismo e Taxis Lda** (☎ 21-491071/5, ext 2618, 82-410 0001; egrafica@virconn.com) at Hotel Cardoso for bookings of both (they can also help you plan your Maputo itinerary). You can also catch *laranjinhas* at their stands in front of Hotel Polana or Holiday Inn.

SLEEPING
Maputo has a wide accommodation selection, with something for all tastes. If you want to be in the thick of things, choose somewhere in or near the baixa. For sea breezes and more tranquillity, head to the upper part of town in and around Sommerschield, or to Av Marginal and Costa do Sol.

Budget
The closest camping grounds are about 35km north of Maputo at Marracuene and Macaneta. Maputo has three good backpackers, all with English-speaking staff and heaps of information on what to do in and around Maputo. All can also help with airport pickups and transfers to the bus depots for early morning buses north.

Maputo Backpackers (Map p56 ☎ 21-451213, 82-467 2230; Quarta Av, Bairro Triunfo; dm US$8-10, d/tw US$32/35, tr without/with bathroom US$49/55) This cosy place is near Costa do Sol and just in from Av Marginal. The spotless rooms all have fans, and if the house isn't too crowded, cooking is permitted. Chapas to/from town stop nearby.

Base Backpackers (Map pp58-9; ☎ 21-302723; thebasebp@tvcabo.co.mz; 545 Av Patrice Lumumba; dm/d US$8/20) Popular and often full, with a convenient location on the edge of the baixa, a mixture of dorm rooms and doubles, a kitchen, and a backyard bar, terrace and braai area with views to the port in the distance.

Fatima's Backpackers (Map pp58-9; ☎ 21-302994, 82-414 5730; www.mozambiquebackpackers.com; 1317 Av Mao Tse Tung; camping per person US$5, dm US$6-12, d without/with bathroom US$24/32) Located in the upper part of town, Maputo's longest-running backpackers has a helpful owner, an outdoor

kitchen and bar area, and rooms plus dorm beds in a house next door.

Other than the backpackers, good, safe shoestring accommodation in Maputo is scarce, and most people opt to pay a bit more for one of the places hovering between budget and midrange. These include:

Hotel Santa Cruz (Map pp58-9; ☎ 21-303004; www .teledata.mz/hotelsantacruz; 1417 Av 24 de Julho; s/d US$28/32, with bathroom US$32/38) The most basic of the bunch, in a nondescript high-rise near the corner of Av Amilcar Cabral, with reasonable rooms and some plants in the courtyards to brighten things up. Not optimal for solo women travellers.

Hotel Costa do Sol (Map p56; ☎ 21-450115; rcs@teledata.mz; Av Marginal; s/d with bathroom US$31/47) Above Restaurante Costa do Sol, with clean, straightforward rooms with fan, and the beach just across the road. Continental breakfast included.

Hotel África II (Map pp58-9; ☎ 21-488729; hotel .africa@tvcabo.co.mz; 322 Av Julius Nyerere; s/d US$40/50, with bathroom US$50/65; 🔌 🖳) A good-value place that could just as easily be midrange, with straightforward rooms in a convenient central location. Prices include continental breakfast.

Hotel África I (Map pp58-9; ☎ 21-488729; hotel .africa@tvcabo.co; Av Paulo Samuel Kankhomba; s/d US$50/65) Under the same management as Hotel África II and of similar standard.

Residencial Belsol (Map p56; ☎ 21-451245; Segunda Av; r with bathroom US$40) Good-value rooms and a restaurant (meals US$7 to US$10). It's just off Av Marginal, chapas drop you off at the turnoff.

Midrange
Pensão Martins (Map pp58-9; ☎ 21-324926, 21-324930; morgest@tvcabo.co.mz; 1098 Av 24 de Julho; s/d/ste US$40/45/60; 🔌 🖳 🖳) This is a low-key

place with a convenient, central location, a predominately male clientele and 22 rather spartan rooms with TV and minifridge, that are decent value for the doubles. There's an outdoor restaurant. Continental breakfast is included.

Hoyo-Hoyo Residencial (Map pp58-9; ☎ 21-490701; promotour@tvcabo.co.mz; 837 Av Francisco Magumbwe; s/d US$38/45; **P** 🏊) This solid, no-frills hotel lacks pizzazz but its 36 rooms are comfortable, serviceable and fairly priced, with TV and breakfast included. The inhouse restaurant, Petiscos (meals from US$5), is known for its delicious Goan cuisine.

Kurhula Parque Self-Catering Chalets (Map p56; ☎ 21-450115; rcs@teledata.mz; Av Marginal; 4-person chalet US$90; **P**) Under the same management as Hotel Costa do Sol, and just next door, is serviced self-catering chalets – each with a double bed and a loft with two twin beds – set behind a fence on the inland side of the beach road.

Residencial Palmeiras (Map pp58-9; ☎ 21-300199; carlos.pereira@tvcabo.co.mz; 948 Av Patrice Lumumba; s without bathroom US$35, s/d US$40/55; **P** 🏊) A converted residence with a handful of quiet, clean and comfortable rooms – all but one with private bathroom, and all with TV – near the British High Commission. Continental breakfast included.

Residencial Villa Itália (Map pp58-9; ☎ 21-497298; vitalia@vlrconn.com; 635 Av Friedrich Engels; s/d/ste US$55/65/75) This large colonial-era house has a popular restaurant downstairs, a homey ambience and a few spacious, spotless rooms on the upper level. Breakfast included.

Mozaika (Map pp58-9; ☎ 21-303939, 21-303965; www .mozaika.co.mz; 769 Av Agostinho Neto; s/d from US$60/70, apt US$140; **P** 🏊 🏊) In a convenient, central location one block west of the Hospital Central, Mozaika has small but well-appointed rooms – each decorated with its own theme, and all set around a garden courtyard with a small pool. There's a self-catering apartment and a bar, though no restaurant. Breakfast included.

Villa das Mangas (Map pp58-9; ☎ 21-497507; villadasmangas@tvcabo.co.mz; 401 Av 24 de Julho; s/d from US$60/75; 🏊 🏊) The bright Villa das Mangas offers small rooms with TV around a garden with a tiny pool in the centre, and a sleek restaurant (meals from US$9) and bar attached.

Ibis (Map pp58-9; ☎ 21-352200; www.accorhotels .com; 1743 Av 25 de Setembro; r US$49; **P** 🏊) The good-value Ibis is centrally located in the

baixa, with small, spiffy rooms at very reasonable prices, plus a restaurant, business facilities and disabled access.

Residencial Kaya Kwanga (Map p56; ☎ 21-492706/7; www.kayakwanga.co.mz; Av Marginal; s/d US$60/75; **P** 🏊 🏊 🏊) This sprawling place has chalet-style rooms with TV set around a large, grassy compound en route to Costa do Sol. There's a restaurant and conference facilities, and prices include breakfast.

Hotel África Prestige (Map pp58-9; ☎ 21-488729; hotel.africa@tvcabo.co.mz; Av Julius Nyerere; r with bathroom US$80; 🏊) Next door to Hotel África II and under the same management is this unsigned place, in a refurbished green and white house with polished wood décor and rooms with ceiling fan, minifridge and TV. Continental breakfast included.

Hotel Terminus (Map pp58-9; ☎ 21-491333; www .terminus.co.mz; cnr Avs Francisco Magumbwe & Ahmed Sekou Touré; s/d from US$60/100; **P** 🏊 🏊 🏊) This three-star establishment has small but well-appointed rooms with TV, plus good service and facilities, a business centre, a tiny pool and a restaurant. It's popular with business travellers – and one of the better business traveller choices outside the Top End listings – and often fully booked. Breakfast included.

There are several private residences in the Sommerschield area offering B&B-style accommodation. Most are of similar quality, with nicely furnished rooms, usually with air-con, TV and telephone, and most also with private bathroom. They include **Residencial Augustijn** (Map pp58-9; ☎ 21-493693; t.theunissen@tvcabo.co.mz; 204 Rua Pereira Marinho; s/d US$50/55) and the larger, hotel-style **Residencial Sundown** (Map pp58-9; ☎ 21-497543; www .hotelmaputo.com; 107 Rua 1301; s/d with full breakfast from US$55/65; 🏊 🏊), with pleasant rooms and wireless internet access. Breakfast is included and meals can be arranged.

Top End

Except as noted, rates at all of the top end places include a full buffet breakfast.

Hotel Cardoso (Map pp58-9; ☎ 21-491071; www .hotelcardoso.co.mz; 707 Av Mártires de Mueda; s/d US$135/150, with sea view from US$160/175; 🏊) Opposite the Natural History Museum, and on the cliff top overlooking the bay and port, this 130-room hotel is a Maputo classic, with good service, a business centre and a bar with sunset views over the water.

Hotel Pestana Rovuma (Map pp58-9; ☎ 21-305000; www.pestana.com; 114 Rua da Sé; s/d from US$115/150; ⬚ ⬚ ⬚) Centrally located just off Praça da Independência and opposite the cathedral, the 200-room Pestana Rovuma is another venerable Maputo establishment, with a long history, well-appointed rooms, a small gym, a business centre and a selection of upscale shops and boutiques downstairs. It's run by the Pestana Group, and offers attractively priced package excursions from Johannesburg that include their sister hotels on Ilha de Inhaca and in the Archipélago de Bazaruto.

Hotel Avenida (Map pp58-9; ☎ 21-492000; www.hotelavenida.co.mz; 627 Av Julius Nyerere; s/d from US$160/175; ⬚ ⬚ ⬚ ⬚) This five-star high-rise in a busy location in the upper part of town offers good dining, efficient service, a business centre and sleek rooms with all the amenities. Prices include use of the health club and sauna.

Hotel Polana (Map pp58-9; ☎ 21-491001; www.polana-hotel.com; 1380 Av Julius Nyerere; s/d from US$150/168, ste from US$450; ⬚ ⬚ ⬚) In a prime location on the cliff top with views over the sea, the Polana is Maputo's classiest hotel, and one of the most genteel hotels in the region. It has rooms in the elegant main building or in the newer 'Polana Mar' section closer to the water. There's a beautiful pool set in expansive grounds filled with rustling palms and flowering trees, a business centre, a casino and a restaurant with daily breakfast and weekend dinner buffets. Ask about package deals from Johannesburg. If you're thinking of splurging in Maputo, this is one of the best places to do it.

Other recommendations:

Holiday Inn (Map pp58-9; ☎ 21-495050; www.ichotelsgroup.com/h/d/hi/1/en/hd/mpmto; Av Marginal; r from US$150/165; ⬚ ⬚ ⬚ ⬚) The only upper-end hotel set directly on the water (though there's no swimming). Rooms and services are on a par with those of other Holiday Inns in the region, and there's a small gym and a waterside restaurant.

Girassol Bahia Hotel (Map pp58-9; ☎ 21-360360, 21-360350; www.girassolhoteis.co.mz; 737 Av Patrice Lumumba; s/d US$125/135; ⬚) One of the newer arrivals on the scene, the four-star Girassol offers reliable rooms and service at reasonable prices.

EATING
Restaurants

Maputo has an excellent restaurant selection and it would be easy to go for several weeks trying a new place each evening.

Mundo's (Map pp58-9; ☎ 21-494080; cnr Avs Julius Nyerere & Eduardo Mondlane; meals US$5-9; ⬚ 7am-1am) Burritos, burgers, pizzas and other hearty fare – all served up in large portions on wooden tables set around a streetside veranda and cooled by a misting system in the summer months. Mundo's also has all-day breakfast and a play area for children.

Mimmo's (Map pp58-9) Branch (☎ 21-309491; cnr Avs 24 de Julho & Salvador Allende; meals US$5-7) Branch (☎ 21-313492; cnr Avs Vladimir Lenin & Maguiguana; ⬚) This bustling streetside pizzeria offers a wide selection of pasta, seafood and meat grills and curries. Its newer, slicker sister restaurant is also called Mimmo's and has indoor dining.

Restaurante El Greco (Map pp58-9; ☎ 21-491898; Av Julius Nyerere; pizzas & meals US$4-8; ⬚ 9am-10pm Tue-Sun; ⬚) The long-standing El Greco's has an extensive menu featuring pizzas, pastas and seafood and meat grills, and a steady flow of old-timers clientele.

Restaurante Costa do Sol (Map p56; ☎ 21-450038, 21-450115; rcs@teledata.mz; Av Marginal; meals from US$5; ⬚ 11am-10.30pm Sun-Thu, 11am-midnight Fri & Sat) A Maputo institution, this large, breezy place just in from the beach draws the crowds on weekend afternoons. There's seating on the large beach-facing porch or indoors, an array of fresh seafood dishes and grills. It's located 5km north of the centre at the northern end of Av Marginal.

Vintage India (Map pp58-9; ☎ 21-486430; 450 Av Julius Nyerere; ⬚ lunch & dinner) The rather drab interior of this place is compensated for by tasty curries and Mughlai cuisine, plus a good-value lunchtime buffet (US$6).

Dock's (Map pp58-9; ☎ 21-493204; docks.naval@intra.co.mz; Av Marginal; meals US$3-10; ⬚ 9am-2am) At Clube Naval, with good seafood grills and burgers, and breezy, waterside seating. There's live music on most Thursday (jazz, advance reservations required) and Friday evenings, and a late-night bar. The US$0.60 compound entry is deducted from your meal bill.

Manjar Os Deuses (Map pp58-9; ☎ 21-496834; Av Julius Nyerere; meals from US$10; ⬚ lunch & dinner Sun-Fri, from 6pm Sat) Not quite 'food of the gods', but nevertheless quite nice, with tasty cuisine (featuring dishes from Portugal's Alentejo and Algarve regions) served in a pleasant, wood-toned ambience.

Villa Itália (Map pp58-9; ☎ 21-497298; vitalia@virconn.com; 635 Av Friedrich Engels; meals from US$6; ⬚ Tue-Sun) This popular restaurant is an amenable spot to spend a quiet evening chatting over dinner, with shaded outdoor garden seating, or indoors in a spacious, refurbished house. It's also one Maputo's best bets for Italian food, with well-prepared pasta dishes, pizzas, salads and seafood.

Hotel Polana (Map pp58-9; ☎ 21-491001; www .polana-hotel.com; 1380 Av Julius Nyerere; meals from US$10, dinner buffet US$30) Offers á la carte dining, plus sumptuous weekend dinner buffets accompanied by a Cuban-style salsa band. Saturday evenings feature an excellent seafood grill, piled high with crayfish, prawns and other delicacies.

Feira Popular (Map pp58-9; Av 25 de Setembro; admission US$0.60; ☺ lunch & dinner; P) Another Maputo institution, where you can mix and mingle with the crowds as you wander amid dozens of small bars and restaurants set inside a large, walled compound. **O Escorpião** (☎ 21-302180, 21-304377; meals from US$6), with a mix of traditional and Portuguese dishes, and **Coqueiro** (meals from US$3.50) specialising in Zambézian cuisine, are two of the best known. Taxis wait outside until the early hours.

Other recommendations:

Jardim dos Mariscos (Map pp58-9; Av Friedrich Engels; snacks & meals from US$3) A good daytime spot for children, with an eatery serving pizzas and an array of standard fare, plus a large playground and lawn.

Xhova's Inter-Thai Restaurant (Map pp58-9; Rua Mateus Muthembe; ☺ Tue-Sat lunch & dinner, Sun lunch) Temporarily closed for annual vacation when we passed through, but the Thai cuisine is rumoured to be delicious.

Micasa (Map pp58-9; cnr Av Julius Nyerere & Rua da Argélia; ☺ 9.30am-3pm & 6pm-10pm Mon-Fri, Sat 6pm-10pm) A classy, subdued ambience, with candles, water goblets and linen cloths on the closely spaced tables, and nicely prepared seafood, meat and pasta dishes.

Las Brassas Restaurant & Cigar Bar (Map pp58-9; ☎ 84-313 1111; Av Julius Nyerere; meals US$5-6; ☺ lunch & dinner) A good place for Portuguese cuisine, with a suitably dark and smoky Old World ambience and an array of seafood and meat dishes.

Cafés

The café tradition is one of the nicer things left behind in Maputo by the Portuguese, and the city's cafés have become somewhat of an institution. Most of the older ones have a staid feel to them, and the faded ambience and worn furnishings that you'd expect from places that have been around for decades, while the newer ones tend to be young and lively. All serve a selection of tasty *bolos* (cakes) and

light meals, plus *café espresso* and *chá* (tea), and make good spots for a break while walking around town.

Café Continental (Map pp58-9; ☎ 21-302005; cnr Avs 25 de Setembro & Av Samora Machel; pastries & light meals from US$1.50) The *grande dame* of the city was undoubtedly once grander than it is now – with a down-at-the-heel feel and the original furnishings long since gone – but it makes a good spot to watch the passing scene.

Hotel Polana Tea Room (Map pp58-9; ☎ 21-491001; Hotel Polana, Av Julius Nyerere; pastries & light meals from US$2-15; ☺ 8am-10pm; ⊠) The most genteel of the city's cafés, where you can settle back in plush chairs while sampling an array of delectable pastries and home-made ice cream. They also have a good-value lunchtime salad buffet.

Other recommendations:

Náutilus Pastelaria (Map pp58-9; cnr Avs Julius Nyerere & 24 de Julho; light meals US$2-5; ☺ 6am-9pm; ⊠) Crêpes, sandwiches and light meals in a glassed-in dining area from where you can watch the passing street scene.

Vasilis Bakery & Coffee Bar (Map pp58-9; Av Mao Tse Tung) A lively, popular place just up from Av Julius Nyerere.

Estoríl (Map pp58-9; Av Mao Tse Tung) Reliable and bourgeoisie.

Café Milano (Map pp58-9, Av 24 de Julho) Just off Rua Augusto Cardoso, with a large, slightly hectic streetside eating area offering falafel, shawarma and other Lebanese snacks and light meals plus the usual array of standards.

Quick Eats

Piri-Piri Chicken (Map pp58-9; Av 24 de Julho; chicken to takeaway/eat-in US$6.50/8) A Maputo classic, with grilled chicken – with or without *piri-piri* (spicy chilli sauce) – to take away or eat here.

Pizza House (Map pp58-9; ☎ 21-485257; 601/607 Av Mao Tse Tung; pizzas & light meals US$2-5; ☺ 6.30am-10.30pm) Indoor and outdoor seating, plus pastries, sandwiches, burgers, grilled chicken and other light meals and a small convenience store. Upstairs is an internet café.

Esplanada Kalú (Map pp58-9; ☎ 21-303174; Rua Alfredo Keil; meals from US$3; ☺ 9am-midnight) Good for Maputo flavour, with pick-and-choose salads and grilled meat on skewers, all halal. It's just off Av 24 de Julho.

Mercado Janeta (Map pp58-9; cnr Avs Vladimir Lenine & Mao Tse Tung; meals US$0.50) Close to the pulse of the city, with stalls serving up plates of *xima* (the maize-based staple) and sauce.

Gianni Sorvetaria (Map pp58-9; Polana Shopping Centre; cnr Avs Julius Nyerere & 24 de Julho; 🕙 10am-9pm; 🔀) We think the home-made ice cream at the Hotel Polana Tea Room is the best, but this comes close.

Self-Catering

Supermarkets in Maputo are on the pricey side, but well-stocked, with a wide selection of imports from South Africa. Luscious papayas, mangoes and other excellent tropical fruits and vegetables are available at Maputo's markets and from streetside vendors.

Deli-cious Deli (Map pp58-9; Polana Shopping Centre; cnr Avs Julius Nyerere & 24 de Julho) Deli meats and cheeses, sandwiches, wine and other imported items.

Deli 968 (Map pp58-9; 🕿 21-488855; 978 Av Julius Nyerere) Similar but smaller.

Mahomed & Co Supermercado (Map pp58-9; Polana Shopping Centre, cnr Avs Julius Nyerere & 24 de Julho; 🕙 10am-8pm) Small, but conveniently located.

Shoprite (Map p56; Av Acordos de Lusaka; 🕙 9am-8pm Mon-Sat, 9am-1pm Sun) Large selection.

Super Mares (Map p56; Av Marginal) Upmarket and well-stocked.

DRINKING & ENTERTAINMENT
Pubs & Clubs

Maputo's thriving nightlife scene includes a large and frequently changing selection of cafés, pubs, bars and clubs. Thursday through Saturday are the main nights, with things only getting going after 11pm; check *Notícias* or posters around town for specials. Cover charges at most places range from US$2 to US$10.

Chez Rangel (Map pp58-9; 🕙 evenings only, Wed-Sat) This jazz café at the train station is one of Maputo's best night spots, with intimate surroundings and the atmospheric architecture of the train station as a backdrop. There's live music on Saturdays (admission US$12), and otherwise your choice of a large collection of old jazz gramophone records. An ideal spot to sip a *caipirinha* while taking in afro-jazz beats.

África Bar (Map pp58-9; 🕿 21-314821; 2182 Av 24 de Julho; admission US$2; 🕙 from 5pm Wed-Sun) Next to Ciné África, this sleek, hip spot is a good place to start or finish the evening, and draws the expat crowds, especially on Thursday (jazz night, admission free).

Coconuts Live (Map p56; 🕿 21-322217; Complexo Mini-Golfe, Av Marginal; disco admission US$8; 🕙 Fri & Sat) A weekend disco catering to a younger, less formal crowd, plus a popular chill-out **lounge** (admission free; 🕙 Wed-Sun).

Dock's (Map pp58-9; 🕿 21-493204; docks.naval@intra .co.mz; Av Marginal; meals US$3-10; 🕙 9am-2am) The late-night waterside bar here is especially popular on Fridays (happy hour from 11pm), and when the weather is warm.

The main collection of pubs is along and around the seedy and rather dicey Rua do Bagamoyo (go in a group, and without valuables); current favourites include **Gypsy's Bar** (Map pp58–9) and the nearby **Maxim's** (Map pp58–9).

If **Mambo Kaffé** (Map pp58-9; 73 Travessa da Palmeira) reopens (it was closed when we passed through), it's definitely worth checking out, with overflow crowds and live salsa music on weekends. It's just off Rua do Bagamoyo.

Also recommended:

Gil Vicente (Map pp58-9; 🕿 21-308768; Av Samora Machel; 🕙 from about 10pm Thu-Sat) A popular café and late-night bar, especially on Thursday (jazz night).

Sinatra's (Map pp58-9; cnr Av Mártires de Inhaminga & Travessa do Varieta; 🕙 from 9pm Mon-Sat) A great little place with live Brazilian-Mozambican fusion music and cuisine to match.

Sixty Levels (Map pp58-9; 7th fl, 343 Rua Consiglieri Pedroso; 🕙 Wed-Sat) A good late-night bar catering to a somewhat older crowd, with views over the city and dancing.

Complexo Sheik (Map pp58-9; cnr Avs Julius Nyerere & Mao Tse Tung; admission US$8; 🕙 10pm-5am Thu-Sat) Dancing with the elite set until dawn; upstairs is a restaurant.

Hotel Terminus Pool Bar (Map pp58-9; 🕿 21-491333; cnr Avs Francisco Magumbwe & Ahmed Sekou Touré) Good for a quiet drink, or if you want to stick close to your hotel.

Livingstone's Bar & Restaurant (Map pp58-9; Av Mao Tse Tung; 🕙 10am-11pm Mon-Thu, 10am-dawn Fri & Sat) A dark, British-toned pub that also serves meals.

Traditional Music & Dance

The best ways to find out what's on are by reading *Notícias* newspaper and watching the posters hung around town. Also check with the Centro Cultural Franco-Moçambicano for upcoming music and dance performances.

Companhia Nacional de Canto e Dança (National Company of Song & Dance; Map pp58-9; 🕿 21-400913; www .cncd.org.mz; Casa de Cultura, 1719 Av Albert Luthuli) Mozambique's renowned Companhia Nacional de Canto e Dança is based at the Casa de Cultura, near the intersection with Av Ho Chi Min. Rehearsals are often open to the public, and you can get schedules of upcoming performances.

Theatre

Teatro Avenida (Map pp58-9; ☎ 21-326501; teatro avenida@tvcabo.co.mz; 1179 Av 25 de Setembro) Teatro Avenida is home to Maputo's best-known theatre group, Mutumbela Gogo. Plays are in Portuguese. Also watch for M'Beu, a theatre group for high-school students, formed under the auspices of Mutumbela Gogo.

Sport

Football (soccer) is the national passion. You can watch or join informal weekend matches along the northern end of Av Marginal, or on any empty field. To see a game, head to Costa do Sol stadium (p56) on weekend afternoons.

SHOPPING

Maputo has a wide selection of reasonably priced crafts.

Craft market (Map pp58-9; Praça 25 do Junho; ☉ about 8am-1pm Sat) A good place to start is the Saturday morning craft market, with an array of woodcarvings and other items, some of which are of quite decent quality. In the upper part of town, try the craft vendors (Av Julius Nyerere) who spread their woodcarvings and other wares daily in front of Hotel Polana; hard bargaining is required.

MozArte (Map pp58-9; ☎ 21-312723; Av Filipe Samuel Magaia; ☉ 8am-noon & 2.30-5.30pm Mon-Fri, 9am-1pm Sat) Just around the corner from Museu Nacional de Arte, with artists' workshops and a selection of crafts in the adjoining shop.

Artedif (Map pp58-9; ☎ 21-495510; Av Marginal; ☉ 9am-2.30pm Tue, 9am-3.30pm Wed-Mon) This co-operative for disabled people is about 400m south of Holiday Inn. Crafts sold here are slightly more expensive than those at the street markets, but tend to be of higher quality. Prices are fixed.

Shanty Craft (Map p56; ☎ 21-450111, 21-450305; Segunda Av, Bairro Triunfo; ☉ 10am-5pm Mon-Sat) An excellent stop for high-quality souvenirs and gifts, with a large selection of crafts from around the country.

For *capulanas* (the colourful cloths that women wear around their waist) and other textiles, try **Casa Elefante** (Av 25 de Setembro) or some of the other nearby shops opposite the Mercado Municipal. This is also a good place to look for a tailor (*alfaiataria*).

For books and music, try the following:

Publicações Europa-América Livraria (Map pp58-9; Av José Mateus) A modest selection of English-language books and magazines.

Rádio Moçambique (Map pp58-9; Rua da Rádio) Cassettes and CDs.

Sensações (Map pp58-9; cnr Avs Julius Nyerere & Eduardo Mondlane) A few cassettes and CDs, and sometimes English-language magazines; next to Mundo's restaurant.

GETTING THERE & AWAY

Air

For domestic and international flights to/from Maputo, see p183.

Airline offices in Maputo include:

Air Corridor (Map pp58-9; ☎ 21-311582, 21-311585; 33 Storey Bldg, cnr Av 25 de Setembro & Rua da Imprensa)

Kenya Airways (Map pp58-9; ☎ 21-320337/8; aquarium@tvcabo.co.mz; 171 Av Karl Marx) At Aquarium Travel.

LAM (Map pp58-9) Central Reservations (☎ 21-4680000, 21-326001, 21-465801; www.lam.co.mz; cnr Avs 25 de Setembro & Karl Marx) Sales Office (☎ 21-490590; cnr Avs Julius Nyerere & Mao Tse Tung)

Moçambique Expresso (Mex; ☎ 21-466008; mex@mex.co.mz; Maputo airport) Can also be contacted via LAM.

South African Airways (Map pp58-9; ☎ 21-495483, 21-495484, 21-498097; www.flysaa.com; Av Fernão Melo e Castro, Sommerschield)

Swazi Express (☎ in South Africa 031 408 1115; www .swaziexpress.com; Maputo airport)

TAP Air Portugal (Map pp58-9; ☎ 21 303927/8, 21-431006/7; www.tap-airportugal.pt; Hotel Pestana Rovuma)

TransAirways (☎ 21-465108; fax 21-465011; transairways@virconn.com; Maputo airport)

Bus

Most of the main bus depots (listed following) are outside the city centre, so time your travels to avoid arriving at night. For upcountry fares and journey times, see the town headings.

Benfica (Map p56; Av de Moçambique) Chapas to Marracuene and other points close to Maputo.

Fábrica de Cerveja Laurentina (Map pp58-9; cnr Avs 25 de Setembro & Albert Luthuli) Chapas to Swaziland, South Africa, Namaacha, Boane and Goba depart from behind the beer factory.

'Junta' (Map p56; Av de Moçambique) Maputo's main long-distance bus depot is about 7km from the centre, just past Lhanguene cemetery. Nothing is organised – you'll need to ask where to find your bus – and most departures are about 5am. Coming into Maputo, some buses finish at Junta while others continue into the city and drop passengers at Ponto Final (corner Avs Eduardo Mondlane and Guerra Popular), from where it's about US$2 in a taxi to the central area.

Panthera Azul (Map pp58-9; ☎ 21-302077/83; www
.pantherazul.com; 273 Av Zedequias Manganhela) Weekly
bus to Beira (US$44, 18 hours), departing at 5am Tuesday
from its office.

Transportes Oliveiras (Map pp58-9; ☎ 21-405108, 21-
400475; Av 24 de Julho) The place to go to catch the ailing
Oliveiras buses to Inhambane (departing at 6am and 11am).
It's about 4km from the centre, just beyond Praça 16 de
Junho (about US$6 in a taxi). Via public transport, take any
chapa heading to Matola or Boane and ask the driver to drop
you at Oliveiras. Coming into Maputo, some Oliveiras buses
continue along Av 24 de Julho past Mimmo's (see p66), stopping near the Museum of Natural History. Oliveiras also runs
nonexpress buses to Xai-Xai, Maxixe and Vilankulo.

Departure and ticketing points for express
buses to Johannesburg include the following
(see p187 for times and prices):

Greyhound (Map pp58-9; ☎ 21-355700; www.grey
hound.co.za; 1242 Av Karl Marx) At Cotur Travel & Tours.

InterCape Mainliner (Map pp58-9; ☎ 21-431006;
www.intercape.co.za; 899 Av 24 de Julho) At Tropical Air
Travel.

Panthera Azul (Map pp58-9; ☎ 21-302077/83; www
.pantherazul.com; 273 Av Zedequias Manganhela) Behind
the main post office.

Translux (Map pp58-9; ☎ 21-303825, 21-303829;
www.translux.co.za; 1249 Av 24 de Julho) At Simara Travel
& Tours.

Train
Slow trains (most economy class only) connect Maputo with:

Chicualacuala (on the Zimbabwe border) Departing at
1pm on Wednesday from Maputo and at noon on Thursday
from Chicualacuala (2nd/economy class US$8/4, 19 hours).

Chokwé Departing Maputo at 9.55am on Saturday, and
from Chokwé about 4pm on Sunday (about US$0.80, 11
hours).

Marracuene Departing Maputo daily at 3.15am and
5.45pm, and from Marracuene at 4.45am and 7.30pm
(about US$0.20, 1½ hours).

Matola Departing morning and evenings in each direction
(US$0.20, 1½ hours).

Ressano-Garcia Departing Maputo at 7.45am daily, and
Ressano Garcia at 12.10pm (US$0.60, four to five hours).

GETTING AROUND
To/From the Airport
Maputo's Mavalane International Airport is
6km northwest of the city centre (US$8 to
US$10 in a taxi).

Via public transport, take bus 18, which
runs between the Natural History Museum
and the airport.

Boat
For boat charters to Inhaca, Ilha dos Portuguêses, Cabo Santa Maria (just south of Inhaca)
or Xefina Grande, and for fishing charters, see
the companies listed under Getting There &
Away in the Ilha de Inhaca section, p73.

Bus & Chapa
City buses, which are operated by Transportes
Públicas de Maputo (TPM), are numbered and
usually have destinations displayed in the window. All rides within the centre cost US$0.15.

Chapas go everywhere and cost US$0.20,
plus extra for large baggage. Some have sign-
boards, though for most you'll need to listen to
the destination called out by the driver's assist-
ant. To get to Junta, look for a chapa going to
'Jardim'. When coming back from Junta into
town, look for a chapa heading to 'Museu'.

Useful transport stands include:

Museu de História Natural (Map pp58–9) Chapas to
the airport and Junta.

Ponto Final (Map pp58–9; cnr Avs Eduardo Mondlane
& Guerra Popular) Terminus for some of the upcountry
buses, and for chapas running along Av Eduardo
Mondlane.

Praça dos Trabalhadores (Map pp58–9) Chapas to
Costa do Sol; chapas to Costa do Sol also depart from the
corner of Avs Mao Tse Tung and Julius Nyerere.

Ronil (Map pp58–9; cnr Avs Eduardo Mondlane & Karl
Marx) Chapas to Junta, Benfica and Matola.

Car
For general information on prices and rentals,
see p193. Car crime is rife in Maputo – park in
guarded lots when possible, or tip the young
boys on the street to watch your vehicle. Also
see p172.

Avis (Map pp58–9 ☎ 21-465497/8, 21-494473; www
.avis.co.za/main.asp?id=508; intersection Avs Julius Nyerere & Mao Tse Tung) Two branches: diagonally opposite
Hotel Polana, and at the airport.

Europcar (Map pp58–9 ☎ 21-497338, 21-466172, 82-
302 8330; europcar@virconn.com; 1418 Av Julius Nyerere)
Next to Hotel Polana and at the airport.

Hertz (Map pp58–9 ☎ 21-494982, 21-303171/3; hertz
.reservations@tropical.co.mz) At Hotel Polana, and at the
airport.

Imperial (☎ 82-300 5180, 21-494459, 21-315345;
www.imperialcarrental.co.za) At the airport.

Taxi
There are taxi ranks at Hotel Polana (☎ 21-
493255 to call a cab), across the street from
Hotel Pestana Rovuma, and at Hotel Cardoso.

Taxis also park near the train station and at the Mercado Municipal.

Some taxis have meters; otherwise, you will need to negotiate a price. Town trips start at US$2. From Costa do Sol to Junta costs about US$12.

AROUND MAPUTO

Maputo offers a good array of excursion – most along the coast, and all easily visited as day trips.

CATEMBE

Catembe, a bucolic town on the south side of Baía de Maputo, offers a taste of upcountry for those who won't have a chance to leave the capital. Head here for a day or overnight, munch on prawns, enjoy the views of Maputo's skyline from across the bay and get into local rhythms.

Catembe Gallery Hotel (☎ 21-380050; www.catembe.net; ste/tr US$95, apt US$300; ☒) has pleasant rooms with small balconies overlooking the bay and a handful of suites boasting Jacuzzis

and original paintings by local artists. There's also two serviced, family-style apartments with kitchens and the popular **Restaurante Marisol** (meals from US$5), known for its prawns, Mozambican cuisine, delicious home-made pasta and cheeses, make-your-own-pizzas and live music on Sundays. Next door and under the same management is **Pensão Catembe** (dm/r US$15/50), with dorm beds and doubles sharing facilities. Staff organise good value trips to Reserva Especial de Maputo, Inhaca and other destinations. It's about 4km north of the ferry dock; call first and staff will come and collect you.

Other places to try for a meal include **Esplanada-Bar Retiro de Catembe** (meals from US$4), about 400m down to the right on the beach when leaving the ferry pier, and the long-standing local hangout, **Diogo's** (meals from US$3), about 300m down the beach to the left of the ferry pier, with grilled prawns.

Getting There & Away

A large and struggling ferry runs daily between Maputo and Catembe from the dock near the Ministry of Finances (per person day/evening US$0.15/0.20, per vehicle US$6, 20 minutes). The first boat from Maputo departs at 5am, then 6am, 7am, 8.30am and thereafter every few hours or so until 10pm. From Catembe, the first departure is at 5.30am, then 6.30am, 7.30am and 9am, afternoon and evening departures from Catembe are at 1.30pm, 3.30pm, 5pm, 6pm, 7.30pm, 9.30pm, 10.45pm and 11.30pm (final boat, sometimes leaves earlier). Smaller passenger-only boats (US$0.20) also run throughout the day between about 7am and 7pm.

ILHA DE XEFINA GRANDE

Ilha de Xefina Grande, about 5km offshore from Costa do Sol, has a long and murky history as a Portuguese trading base, prison and war garrison. Now there's nothing left of its tumultuous past other than some old cannons and the remnants of a fort, and attractive, usually deserted beaches. Swimming, snorkelling and picnicking are the main diversions. There are no facilities and not much shade so bring everything you'll need with you, including water.

Motorboat charters can be arranged through any Maputo travel agency, or with the boat operators (listed under Ilha de Inhaca, following), from about US$35 per person,

AROUND MAPUTO

0 —————— 40 km
0 —————— 20 miles

To Bilene (100km);
Xai-Xai (150km)

Rio Nkomati
Kruger National Park
EN1

Komatipoort
Ressano Garcia

EN1

Moamba
Matalana
Rio Nkomati
INDIAN OCEAN
Marracuene

SOUTH AFRICA
EN4
Montes Libombos

Praia de Macaneta

Matola
Ilha de Xefina Grande
Ilha dos Portuguêses

Namaacha
Boane
MAPUTO
Ilha de Inhaca

Lomahasha
MR3
Catembe
Baía de Maputo
Cabo Santa Maria

Rio Umbeluzi

Goba
Barragem dos Pequenos Libombos
Península de Machangula

Bela Vista

SWAZILAND
Rio Tembe
Lago Maundo

Salamanga
Reserva Especial de Maputo

Rio Maputo
Lago Xingute
Lago Piti

To Ponta d'Ouro (20km);
South Africa (30km)
Zitundo

with a minimum of four people. Local boats from the fishing village 3km beyond Restaurante Costa do Sol at the northern end of the Marginal will take you over less expensively but much more slowly.

ILHA DE INHACA

Just 7000 years ago – almost like yesterday in geological terms – Inhaca was part of the Mozambican mainland. Today, this wayward chunk of Mozambican coastline lies about 40km offshore from Maputo, and is a popular weekend getaway. It's also an important marine research centre, known in particular for its offshore coral reefs. The reefs are among the most southerly in the world and since 1976, parts of the island and surrounding waters have been designated a reserve to protect them and local marine life. About 3km northwest of Inhaca is the tiny, uninhabited **Ilha dos Portuguêses** (Portuguese Island), a beautiful white patch of sand surrounded by clear waters. It was formerly a leper colony and is now part of the Inhaca marine reserve system.

The majority of Inhaca's residents belong to a subgroup of the Tembe-Tsonga and speak a dialect of Ronga distinct from (but mutually intelligible with) that found on the mainland.

Telecomunicações de Moçambique (7.30am-12.30pm & 2.30pm-7.30pm Mon-Fri, Sat 7.30am-noon), between Pestana Inhaca Lodge and Restaurante Lucas, has domestic and international calls.

Sights & Activities

The best beaches are on the island's northeastern edge past the lighthouse, and on Ilha dos Portuguêses. The closest good beach to the ferry pier is about 2km south, along the bay. On Inhaca's southwestern edge is a marine biology research station and a small **museum** (21-760009, 21-760013; admission US$3; 8.30-11.30am & 2-3.30pm Mon-Fri, from 9.30am Sat, Sun & holidays) with specimens of local fauna. Transport can be arranged through Pestana Inhaca Lodge or Restaurante Lucas. Otherwise, it's a 50-minute walk to the marine research station, and double that to the lighthouse.

Birding opportunities abound, with about 300 species recorded on Inhaca. This is a remarkable figure, considering that the island measures only about 72 sq km in area. Among others, watch for great-winged and white-chinned petrels, mangrove kingfishers, crab plovers and greater frigate birds.

The **woodcarvers** based at Pestana Inhaca Lodge work with light-coloured wood, which is then painted, or darkened with a mixture of finely powdered charcoal and water, followed by a layer of shoe polish.

Just south of Inhaca, across a narrow channel at the tip of Machangula Peninsula, is beautiful **Cabo Santa Maria**, with quiet beaches and crystal-clear waters ideal for snorkelling. The area, which is also known for its pelicans and flamingos, is usually visited by boat from Inhaca or direct from Maputo, although there's also an overland route through the Reserva Especial de Maputo and a self-catering camp; see p79.

DIVING & WATER SPORTS

Gone Fishin' (gonefishin@mailbox.co.za) operates out of Pestana Inhaca Lodge, and offers diving instruction and equipment rental, plus snorkelling, windsurfing and sea kayaking.

A new dive centre is scheduled to open shortly at Inhaca Azul. Follow the Inhaca links at www.exotictravelgroup .com for more information.

Sleeping & Eating

Marine Biology Research Station (21-760009, 21-760013; fax 21-492176; r per person US$15) Just in from the water on the island's southwestern edge, these no-frills rooms have shared facilities and cold-water showers. Primarily for students and researchers but is open to the public on a space-available basis. There is a kitchen, and a cook can be arranged, but you will need to bring your own food. Book rooms at least five days in advance.

Pestana Inhaca Lodge (21-305000; www.pestana.com; s/d/f with half board US$125/218/250;) Set in expansive, shaded gardens just north of the ferry pier on the island's western side, this four-star establishment is Ilha de Inhaca's main hotel. The brightly painted rooms have been recently upgraded, and offer billowy mosquito nets, fan and air-con and nicely modernised bathrooms. The family rooms (most of which are wheelchair-friendly) have one double bed, a sofa bed that can take two children, and a small veranda. Once you move past the hustle at the pier, it makes a relaxing retreat (go midweek or in the off-season for more quiet). There's a saltwater swimming pool, a restaurant (lunchtime buffet US$16) and favourably priced package deals from Johannesburg (also in combination with sister hotels in Maputo and on the Archipélago de Bazaruto).

Several new accommodation options on the island should be opening soon. For updates, check with **Inhaca Development** (inhacalodge@gomail.co.za), and with **Inhaca Azul** (☎ 21-402007; www.exotictravelgroup.com/in hacazul_lodge.htm; s US$80, 2 or more persons US$150), which already has a handful of self-catering chalets (up to eight people) just in from the beach north of Pestana Inhaca Lodge. Also see Ponta Torres Camp (p79).

Restaurante Lucas (☎ 21-760007; meals US$5-8, 1-/2-person seafood platter US$18/26, lobster/prawns about US$17; ☒ from 7am) This long-standing local-style restaurant is the main place to eat. It's pricey, but the seafood grills are delicious, and the ambience is laid back. Order in advance if you're in a rush or if you fancy a particular dish. It's located next to Pestana Inhaca Lodge.

Getting There & Away
AIR
There are daily flights to/from Maputo on **TransAirways** (☎ 21-465108, fax 21-465011; transairways@virconn.com) for US$50 return. Flights are in the afternoon in each direction, except Saturday, when they're in the morning.

BOAT
For speedboat charters to Inhaca (US$35 to US$50 per person, minimum four people) and Cabo Santa Maria, contact **Desemar** (☎ 82-301 8070, 82-309 7920; sergio302003@yahoo.com), which runs the fast and smooth MV Závora, or Nau Tours (p57). The ride takes about one hour, and can be rough during the windy months of August and September. All boats drop you at the beach in front of Pestana Inhaca Lodge; departures in Maputo are from next to Escola Náutica (Av Marginal). If you're travelling on your own and need a group to join for the boat charter, book through the tours desk in the lobby of Hotel Polana.

Alternatively, the **Vodacom ferry** (www.in haca.co.mz) departs from Maputo's Porto da Pesca (off Rua Marques de Pombal) at 8am on Tuesday, Thursday, Friday, Saturday and Sunday (US$16 one-way, two hours). Departures from Inhaca are at about 3pm on the same days. The less-reliable Nyaleti departs from the Catembe ferry pier at 7am on Tuesday, Thursday, Saturday and Sunday (1st/2nd class US$6/3.20 one-way, two to three hours), returning about 3pm (in theory) the same day.

Charter speedboats usually stop at Ilha dos Portuguêses en route to Inhaca. Otherwise, transport is easy to arrange with local fishermen on the beach in front of Pestana Inhaca Lodge, and at low tide it's sometimes possible to walk from Inhaca.

Getting Around
Car hire with driver can be arranged at Restaurante Lucas from about US$80 per day.

MARRACUENE & PRAIA DE MACANETA
Macaneta is the closest open-ocean beach to Maputo, with stiff sea breezes and long stretches of dune-fringed coast. It's on a narrow peninsula divided from the mainland by the Rio Nkomati, and is reached via Marracuene, 35km north of Maputo along the EN1. Marracuene was a getaway for wealthy Maputo residents during colonial days and the scene of some heavy fighting in the 1980s during the war. Today, it's a small riverside town with a sleepy, faded charm, its main street lined with bougainvilleas and old Portuguese villas in various states of repair.

Sights & Activities
Just north of Marracuene is Matalana village, birthplace of renowned artist Malangatana, and site of his **Centro Cultural de Matalana**. When finished, it is intended to be a local cultural hub, with an arts and crafts centre, arts training for children, an open-air theatre and more, all now in varying stages of completion.

GWAZA MUTHINI

Each year in February, Marracuene fills up with visitors commemorating those who died resisting colonial rule in the 1895 Battle of Marracuene, known locally as Gwaza Muthini. At the heart of the festivities is the killing of a hippo from the Rio Nkomati and the *kuphalha* ceremony, or invocation of the ancestors, although the hippo hasn't been very forthcoming in recent times and a goat is usually roasted instead. Gwaza Muthini also marks the beginning of the season for *ukanhi* – a traditional brew made from *canhu*, the fruit of the *canhoeiro* tree found throughout Maputo and Gaza provinces, and considered sacred in much of the region.

MAPUTO

At Macaneta, the main activity is swimming. Currents can be strong, so take care when plunging in, and with children.

Sleeping & Eating

MARRACUENE

Marracuene Lodge (☎ 21-494529; marracuene@teledata
.mz; camping per person US$8; r per person with/without half board US$55/39; ☒) This agreeable place is in a tranquil setting along the Rio Nkomati about 4km south of Marracuene, and reached via a signposted road (4WD) from the EN1. It has good camping with hot-water ablutions, plus a couple of two- and six-person self-catering chalets and a restaurant. Boat transfers to Macaneta beach are included in half-board rates, and otherwise cost US$16 per person. Birding is good, and boats can be hired for river trips.

Casa Lisa (☎ 82-304 1990; buckland@teledata.mz; camping per person US$5, chalets per person US$22-28) Just west of the EN1 about 18km north of Marracuene (watch for the signpost), this is a convenient overnight stop if you're driving between South Africa and points north and want to avoid sleeping in Maputo. On offer: simple three- and four-person chalets, most with bathroom, plus camping, a restaurant (breakfast and dinner only, no self-catering) and a bar.

MACANETA

Jay's Beach Camp (☎ 82-3001430, fax 82-3301430; camping per adult/child US$12.50/6.25, 2-/4-/6-person chalets US$62/94/125; ☒) The relaxed Jay's is a long-popular spot, with large, grassy grounds backed by sand dunes and coastal vegetation, camping with ablutions, no-frills chalets and a braai area. Day guests are welcome and children under 12 camp for free. Just over the dunes is a long, surf-pounded beach. It's 12km from the ferry and signposted (4WD only). Day use of compound per vehicle is US$4.

Macaneta Lodge (Complexo Turístico de Macaneta; ☎ 82-3229920; macanetalodge@tdm.co.mz; 2-/4-person bungalows with bathrooms US$70/140; ☒) The long-standing Macaneta Lodge is popular with day visitors who come to enjoy the seafood grills and the beach. Accommodation is in straightforward and recently renovated but rather soulless chalets. There's a good restaurant (meals from US$5), a small conference centre and a discotheque sometimes on weekends.

Motapa Estuary Lodge (☎ in South Africa 015-7933816; info@transfrontiers.com; 8-person lodge with/without full board US$586/312; ☒) This lovely place is in a tranquil setting on the Rio Nkomati, with four rustic double bungalows, a restaurant and bar, and the chance for fishing, canoe trips and birding. There's a river cruiser and transport to the long beach just north of Jay's Beach Camp can be arranged, as can ferry collections for those without their own 4WD. Follow signs to Jay's, but where the road splits, leave the right fork to Jay's and branch left along the unsignposted track for Motapa. The camp is generally rented out in its entirety and advance bookings are essential; overnight visitors only.

Getting There & Away

Via public transport, take any northbound chapa from Benfica (US$1.20, one hour) to the Marracuene turnoff, from where it's a 10-minute walk to the Rio Nkomati ferry (round-trip per vehicle US$6.50, five minutes, until about 6pm). Once on the other side, follow the road for about 5km to a junction of sorts, from where most of the Macaneta places are about 5km to 8km further (4WD essential).

For Matalana, continue north on the EN1 past Marracuene for about 7km to the Matalana junction, following signs first for the police training centre, and then for Centro Cultural de Matalana.

BARRAGEM DOS PEQUENOS LIBOMBOS

Barragem dos Pequenos Libombos (Pequenos Libombos Dam) lies in the hills about 45km southwest of Maputo and supplies the capital's water. The countryside is tranquil, the river has crocodiles and it makes an amenable day getaway if you have your own vehicle. The nearby Montes Libombos (Libombos Mountains) offer wide views and the area is good for cycling. **Complexo Turístico Pequenos Lebombos** (☎ 21-306729; d/q from US$35/75; ℗ ☒) at the dam has small self-catering cottages set around large lawns, with a pool (per adult/child US$5/2.50) and a restaurant (meals from US$5).

Getting There & Away

Chapas from Maputo to Goba drop you at the dam entrance (US$1, 1½ hours). Driving, head out on Av 24 de Julho to the Matola road, continue through Matola to Boane, go left and continue about 7km to the dam entrance. Alternatively, follow the signposted road linking the main road west of Boane with Goba.

Southern Mozambique

For over 500 years, visitors have been marvelling at the beauty of the southern Mozambican coastline. For the early Portuguese explorers, its white sands and sheltered bays served as a gateway to the fabled gold fields of the interior, and as convenient staging points on the long sea journey to the Orient. In more recent times, a steady stream of holiday-makers have been lured by promises of heaping plates of giant prawns and grilled *lagosta* (crayfish); languid days cooled by gentle Indian Ocean breezes; sultry nights enlivened by pulsating *marrabenta* rhythms; and the best diving and game fishing to be found in the region.

Today, Mozambique's southern coast is the most developed part of the country for tourism. And this popularity is well justified. From Ponta d'Ouro, with its pounding surf and windswept dunes, to the serene lagoons and shallow coastal lakes between Bilene and Závora, and the legendary beaches of Tofo and Barra, it boasts some of the most stunningly beautiful stretches of sand on the continent. In addition to the beaches, southern Mozambique has a wealth of cultural highlights as well, if you have the time to seek them out. These include the famed *timbila* (marimba) orchestras of the Chopi people and a rich body of traditional lore, much of which focuses on the old kingdom of Gaza.

Tourism infrastructure is fast expanding and caters to all budgets. Transport links – especially with nearby South Africa – are good, with sealed major roads and a reliable bus network. If you want an easy introduction to Mozambique, the south is a good place to start.

HIGHLIGHTS

- Plunge into the **Archipélago de Bazaruto**'s (p99) turquoise waters amidst shoals of colourful fish

- Stroll along charming **Inhambane**'s (p86) waterfront promenade, watching dhows silhouetted against the setting sun

- Drift off to sleep, lulled by the sounds of the sea at **Ponta d'Ouro** or **Ponta Malongane** (p77)

- Wander along the white, palm-fringed sands lining **Tofo** (p90) and nearby beaches and dive with the manta rays

- Marvel at the intricate rhythms and masterful techniques of a **Chopi timbila orchestra** (p83)

Archipélago de Bazaruto

Inhambane ★★ Tofo

★ Ponta d'Ouro & Ponta Malongane

SOUTHERN MOZAMBIQUE

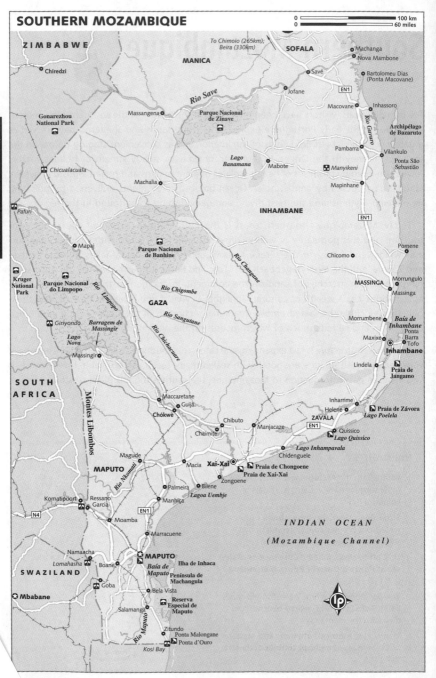

SOUTHERN MOZAMBIQUE

0   100 km
0   60 miles

ZIMBABWE

To Chimoio (265km);
Beira (330km)

SOFALA

Machanga
Nova Mambone

MANICA

Chiredzi

Savé

EN1

Bartolomeu Dias
(Ponta Macovane)

Rio Save

Jofane

Macovane   Inhassoro

Massangena

Parque Nacional
de Zinave

Gonarezhou
National Park

**Archipélago
de Bazaruto**

Pambarra   Vilankulo

Chicualacuala

Lago
Banamana   Mabote

Manyikeni   Ponta São
Sebastião

Machalia

Mapinhane

INHAMBANE

EN1

Pafuri

Pomene

Mapai

Parque Nacional
de Banhine

Chicomo

**Kruger
National
Park**

Parque Nacional
do Limpopo

Rio Chigombe

GAZA

Rio Sangutane

MASSINGA   Morrungulo
Massinga

Giriyondo   Barragem de
Massingir

Morrumbene   **Baía de
Inhambane**
Ponta
Barra
Tofo
Inhambane

Rio Chichacuare

Maxixe

Lago
Nova

Massingir

Lindela   **Praia de
Jangamo**

**SOUTH
AFRICA**

Maccaretane

Guijá

Inharrime

Praia de Závora
Lago Poelela

Chókwè   Chibuto   Manjacaze

ZAVALA
EN1

Helene

Chaimite   Quissico
Lago Quissico

Magude

Lago Inhampavala
Chidenguele

MAPUTO   Macia   **Xai-Xai**   **Praia de Chongoene**
Praia de Xai-Xai

Komatipoort   Ressano
Garcia   Palmeira   Bilene   Zongoene

Lagoa Uembje

Moamba   Manhiça

EN1

Namaacha

Marracuene

INDIAN OCEAN

(Mozambique Channel)

Lomahasha   Boane

SWAZILAND   Goba

MAPUTO   Ilha de Inhaca
*Baía de
Maputo*   Península de
Machangula

Mbabane

Bela Vista

Salamanga   **Reserva
Especial de
Maputo**

Zitundo
Ponta Malongane
Ponta d'Ouro

Kosi Bay

WARNING!

Southern Mozambique's beaches are spectacular, but don't let the beauty lull you into forgetting common sense safety precautions. See p172 for general tips. Women especially should avoid isolating situations, particularly at the mainland beaches around Tofo and Vilankulo. Enjoy the coastline but always stay within sight of your hotel or the crowds. Don't go jogging or walking on the beach alone.

National Parks & Reserves

Southern Mozambique's main park protects the Archipélago de Bazaruto (see p99). For more on other protected areas, see p84 and p40.

Getting There & Away

There are good air and road links between southern Mozambique, South Africa and Swaziland; see p183.

PONTA D'OURO & PONTA MALONGANE

The sleepy colonial-era town of Ponta d'Ouro has boomed in popularity in recent years and is the first Mozambique stop on many Southern Africa overland itineraries. Its best asset is its excellent beach – long, wide and surf-pounded. Offshore waters host abundant sea life, including dolphins and whale sharks and – from July to October – whales. Thanks to Ponta d'Ouro's proximity to South Africa, it fills up completely on holiday weekends.

About 5km north is the quieter and even more beautiful Ponta Malongane, with a seemingly endless stretch of windswept coastline fringed by high, vegetated dunes and patches of coastal forest.

There are no internet cafés, banks or ATMs; South African rands are accepted everywhere.

Activities
DIVING

For general information on diving, see p43. Dive operators are listed below in the Sleeping section. There's a dive equipment shop under Fishmonger Barracas.

DOLPHIN TOURS

Dolphins frequent the waters offshore from Ponta d'Ouro, and catching a glimpse of these beautiful creatures can be a wonderful experience. However, they're wild, which means sightings can't be guaranteed – let them come to you, if they wish, and don't go off in wild pursuit or try to touch them.

Dolphin Encountours (below) runs the best tours. Most are done as part of a three-night package from Johannesburg, priced from about US$422 per person. They include a short marine ecology course plus accommodation with half board, transfers to/from the Kosi Bay border post and – weather permitting – daily dolphin excursions. Walk-ins are accommodated on a space-available basis. Between June and August it's chilly in the boats, so bring a windbreaker.

Sleeping
PONTA D'OURO
Budget

Tandje Beach Resort (☎ in South Africa 011-678 0972; fax 011 678 0970; camping per person US$13, 2-/4-/6-person chalets US$47/112/180, per vehicle US$0.40) This large, seaside camping ground at the southern end of Ponta d'Ouro has shaded camping and somewhat tatty self-catering chalets with shared ablutions.

It's also the base for a handful of dive camps, which is where most budget travellers stay. All offer simple tented and/or reed hut accommodation, sharing ablutions with the camping ground, as well as diving courses and equipment rental. Most also offer both catered and self-catering options. The camps include the following:

Dolphin Encountours (☎ 82-920 8952, in South Africa 011-462 8103; www.dolphin-encountours.co.za; per person with half board in reed/wooden huts US$44/55) The best setup, with a choice of wooden huts with mosquito nets or simpler reed huts, and some hammocks for lounging. It's not actually a dive camp, but the base for Dolphin Encountours' dolphin tours.

Simply Scuba (☎ in South Africa 011-678 0972; www.simplyscuba.co.za; per person sharing from US$22) A cluster of high-domed tents and a communal kitchen.

Scuba Adventures (☎ 21-650026; www.scubatravel.co.za; per person sharing tent/hut US$23/27) More tents and reed huts, with the main office at Fishmonger Barracas.

The Whaler (☎ in South Africa 011-213 0213; www.thewhaler.co.za; s/d hut from US$29/42) Reed huts and a kitchen area.

Other recommendations:
Campismo Ninho (☎ in South Africa 082-788 8742; debby.viljoen@metso.net; camping per person US$11)

Basic camping in a great setting up a steep dune from the beach, with a bar and much more quiet than you'll find at other local camping grounds. It's a few kilometres north of Ponta d'Ouro, en route to Ponta Malongane.

Planet Scuba (☎ 82-809 7971; www.planetscuba .co.za; per person with half board US$55) On the hillside to the right about 300m before reaching Tandje Beach Resort, with rooms with net, fan and shared bathroom, plus diving and meals. Bring your own towels.

Midrange & Top End

Devocean Diving (☎ in South Africa 082-332 9029, 9am-4pm Mon-Fri only; www.devoceandiving.com; tents per person from US$55, r per person with full board from US$66, 8-person self-catering house US$495) About 400m from the sea along the main road into town, this is basically a dive camp but more pampered. Accommodation is in rooms in the main house or in furnished safari-style tents set around a small garden, with two self-catering houses nearby. Management was changing as we passed through, so check for updates.

Café del Mar (☎ 21-650048; cafedelmarponta@tropical .co.mz; r per person with half board US$59) This restaurant also has rooms, in spiffy reed chalets closely spaced around a small garden. All have net, fan and shared bathrooms with hot water. It's perched on a hilltop in the town centre about 200m in from the beach – look for the unmissable orange building. If you're after quiet, midweek is best; on weekends the bar has music until dawn.

Motel do Mar (☎ 21-650000; www.pontadoouro.co.za; 4-person chalets with/without sea view US$105/85) In a good seaside location (though not all rooms manage to have full sea views), this motel is a throwback to colonial days. It has a restaurant that does seafood grills, a 1960s ambience and blocks of faded 3-storey self-catering chalets, each with two twin-bedded rooms.

Bugan Villa Sol (☎ 82-310 4360, 84-752 0973; bougain villasol@gmail.com; per person from US$70; 🖭) New, and a welcome addition to Ponta d'Ouro's diving-dominated accommodation scene, this cosy B&B-style guesthouse makes a good weekend retreat for anyone wanting a break. There are three double rooms plus two larger family-style self-catering apartments, all impeccably decorated and set around well-tended gardens. There are also braai facilities and the beach is just a five-minute walk away. Prices include breakfast. The guesthouse is signposted from the entrance to town.

Praia de Ouro Sul (☎ in South Africa 082-871 2791; www.praiadeourosul.co.za; 4-person tents US$156, 6-person

chalets US$344) This beautiful place has luxurious logwood chalets on a high, vegetated dune with commanding views over the sea. Each comes with a fully equipped American-style kitchen, veranda and ceiling fans. There are also some safari-style tents tucked away amidst the trees on a forested hillside, each with refrigerator and nearby braai area, and a restaurant serving brunch and dinner. It's about 5km south of Ponta d'Ouro village and signposted from town.

Other recommendations:

Lar do Ouro (☎ 21-650038; info@pontadooura.com; s/d with half board US$98/141; 🖭) A homy B&B-style place with rooms (with nets) in white terracotta-roofed cottages and tasty meals. It's about a 15-minute walk from the beach; follow the well-signposted road leading to Praia de Ouro Sul, watching for Lar do Ouro's signboard to your right.

Kaya Kweru (☎ 21-650065; www.u-can.co.za; 2-person cottage US$62-94, 4-person cottage US$78-125; 🖭) About 200m north of the town centre and an option if you crave a dive-camp ambience but want more facilities. Accommodation is in rows of closely spaced stone-and-thatch cottages with bathrooms, all set in a featureless compound just in from the beach. There's also a restaurant, an open-air bar facing the sea and a full range of activities.

PONTA MALONGANE

Ponta Malongane is quieter and more spread out than Ponta d'Ouro, without a town, and with an excellent beach. You'll need your own transport here.

Budget

Ponta Malongane (☎ in South Africa 013-741 1975; www .malongane.co.za; camping per person US$13, dive-camp tents from US$16, rondavel/log hut d from US$24/25) This long-running, laid-back place is based at the sprawling and shaded Parque de Malongane. It has various accommodation options, including camping, simple two-person rondavels and small, rustic twin-bedded log cabins. There's also a restaurant, and a large self-catering area. Ask about dive-accommodation deals.

Midrange

Tartaruga Marítima Luxury Camp (☎ in South Africa 083-309 3469; www.tartaruga.co.za; s/d US$95/147; 🖭) About 2km further north, Tartaruga is a lovely and tranquil retreat, with spacious, comfortable safari-style tents tucked away in the coastal forest behind the dunes and just a few minute's walk from a wonderful stretch of beach. There's no restaurant but there's a raised lounge-bar and self-catering braai area with views over the open ocean.

Ponta Mamoli(☎ in South Africa 83 444 6346; www .pontamamoli.com; s/d chalets with half board US$176/281; 🖭) Cosy and pleasant two- and four-person log cabin–style chalets, a restaurant, a bar with good views, a braai area and a small pool surrounded by a large sun deck overlooking the sea. It's ideal for a pampered getaway, set on a quiet and deserted stretch of coastline 11km north of Ponta Malongane, and signposted. Diving, fishing and horseback riding can be arranged.

Eating

The following are all located in Ponta d'Ouro; the only dining options for Ponta Malongane are the restaurants at Ponta Mamoli and Ponta Malongane.

Café del Mar (☎ 21-650048; meals US$3-6; 🕑 lunch & dinner Wed-Mon) Café del Mar has the best food in town, featuring crêpes and other French fare, plus a bar with live music most weekends.

Scandals (meals US$1.50 5; 🕑 breakfast, lunch & dinner) This amenable divers' hangout just outside Tandje Beach Resort has all-day breakfasts, omelettes and light meals.

Fishmonger Barracas (☎ 21-650026; meals from US$5; 🕑 breakfast, lunch & dinner) A popular rooftop gathering spot in front of Café del Mar, with filling breakfasts, seafood platters and other hearty fare.

A Florestinha do Índico (meals US$5-8; 🕑 lunch & dinner) Several doors south of Fishmonger Barracas, with seating under thatched umbrellas scattered around a shady lawn, plus a selection of grills and other standards.

Other recommendations:

Bar Babalaza (meals from US$3; 🕑 lunch & dinner) Next to A Florestinha do Índico, with grilled fish, hamburgers, and more.

Bula Bula (meals US$5; 🕑 lunch & dinner) Next to Fishmonger Barracas, with burgers, pizzas and pub food.

For self-caterers, there's a tiny, pricey grocery store next to Fishmonger Barracas; almost everyone brings supplies from South Africa.

Getting There & Away

Ponta d'Ouro is 120km south of Maputo. The road is in decent shape for the first 60km, but soft, deep sand and slow going thereafter. Allow about 3½ hours in a private vehicle (4WD only).

Chapas depart Maputo's Catembe ferry pier at 8am on Tuesday and Friday (US$5, five hours). Departures from Ponta d'Ouro are at 8am Wednesday and Saturday. Otherwise, take the ferry (p71) to Catembe, where you can find transport to Salamanga (US$2.50, two hours) or Zitundo (US$4.50, four hours), two villages en route. From Zitundo, there's sporadic transport to Ponta d'Ouro (US$1, 30 minutes), which is 20km further south.

Kosi Bay border post is 11km south of Ponta d'Ouro along a sandy track (4WD), but there's no public transport. Coming from South Africa, there's a guarded lot at the border where you can leave your vehicle in the shade for US$5 per day. All the hotels do pick-ups from the border from about US$10 per person, minimum two. Allow about five hours for the drive to/from Durban (South Africa).

There's no public transport to Ponta Malongane, though chapas between Maputo and Ponta d'Ouro stop at the signposted turn-off, about 5km before Ponta Malongane. To get between Ponta d'Ouro and Ponta Malongane, you can walk along the beach at low tide or go via the road.

RESERVA ESPECIAL DE MAPUTO

En route to Ponta d'Ouro and just two hours from the capital is the 90 sq km **Reserva Especial de Maputo** (Maputo Special Reserve; admission per adult/child/vehicle US$8/2/8), which runs along a spectacularly beautiful and completely isolated stretch of coastline. It was gazetted in 1969 to protect the local elephant population (about 350 in the late 1970s), plus several turtle species. Until recently it was known as the Maputo Elephant Reserve. The elephants, who suffered from the effects of the war and poaching, are estimated to number only about 180 today – most quite skittish and seldom seen but planned restocking should improve chances of sightings. There are also small populations of antelope, hippo and smaller animals. The main attractions are the pristine wilderness feel of the place – it offers a true bush adventure close to the capital – and its birds. Over 300 different types of birds have been identified, including fish eagles and many wetland species. The coastline here is also an important nesting area for loggerhead and leatherback turtles; peak breeding season is November to January.

The heart of the reserve is Ponta Miliban-galala, about 35km from the main gate along the sea. While there are few spots that can rival the beauty of the coastline here, the bush road in from the gate is also highly interesting, as it passes through the reserve's rich diversity of habitats, including woodlands, grasslands and dry forests.

Although rehabilitation is scheduled, in conjunction with the planned extension of the reserve, and its ultimate merger with South Africa's Tembe Elephant Park, there are currently no facilities, apart from a basic beachside **camping ground** (camping per person US$6) at Ponta Milibangalala. You'll need to be completely self-sufficient, including with food and water (water suitable for washing is sometimes available at the main entrance). There's also an area at the main entrance next to the reserve office where you can pitch a tent, though almost everyone goes further in to camp along the beach.

About 4km north of the reserve along the main road (and 8km south of Salamanga village) is **Tsakane ka Madjadjane** – a community development project where you can experience local life, take nature walks, learn about honey-making and get a meal or simple overnight accommodation.

Continuing north within the reserve, past its northern boundary and on to the tip of the Península de Machangula, brings one to **Ponta Torres Camp** (☎ 82-252 4670, in South Africa 083-460 9492; www.africaafrica.co.za/Pontatorres.htm; per person US$38), a self-catering place targeted at anglers and birders in a beautiful setting on Cabo Santa Maria. It offers rustic safari-style tents (minimum four persons) with bathrooms and cooking facilities. Bring food and drink with you, though a few basics (including beer) are available from the nearby village. A 4WD is essential and you'll need to pay vehicle and entry fees for the reserve.

Getting There & Away

Tour operators organising visits to the reserve include **Dana Tours** (☎ 21-497483, 21-495514; info@danatours.net; 729 Av Mao Tse Tung) and **Nau Tours** (☎ 21-380034; www.nautours.co.mz). **Catembe Gallery Hotel** (☎ 21-380050; www.catembe.net) runs good-value all-inclusive day trips for US$85 (US$130 including a night in one of their luxury rooms). If you have your own transport (4WD), look out for the main entrance (known as '*campeamento principal*') marked

with a rusty signboard about 65km from Catembe along the Ponta d'Ouro road. From the turnoff, it's 3km to the park gate, and then about 35km further through the reserve to the coast. There's a second entrance further along the Ponta d'Ouro road, marked with a barely legible signpost, from where it's about 22km into the reserve.

Nau Tours organises visits to Tsakane ka Madjadjane.

NAMAACHA

Cool Namaacha lies on the border with Swaziland, about 70km west of Maputo. Its streets are lined by lavender, jacaranda and bright orange flame trees, and thanks to its favourable climate, it's the source of many of the flowers for sale on Maputo's street corners. The ornate colonial-era church is the main building of interest. At Namaacha's eastern edge is a rusty sign marking the way down to a small **cascata** (waterfall), 3.6km north of the main road and a good picnic spot.

Located on the main road in the town centre, **Hotel Libombos** (☎ 21-960102, 21-960099; d/ste US$52/70; ⛵) has comfortable rooms, some with views over the hills. There's a **restaurant** (meals about US$10) and a casino.

Behind the church, **Xisaka** (☎ 21-960330; s/d/ste weekend US$39/55/70, midweek US$50/80/102; ⛵ 🖥 🛏) has pleasant rooms with TV, a restaurant and conference facilities.

Chapas run throughout the day to/from Maputo (US$2, 1½ hours), departing Namaacha from the border, and stopping in front of the market on the main road.

BILENE

Despite a raft of new resort developments in the beach-facing areas, this small resort town seems stuck in a permanent time warp, with a collection of faded 1950s Portuguese-era holiday cottages and an old-timers' feel.

Bilene isn't on the open ocean, but rather spread along the edge of the wide and tranquil Lagoa Uembje (Uembje Lagoon), which is separated from the sea by a narrow, sandy spit. Thanks to its sheltered waters and its position as the first resort area north of Maputo, it's a popular destination with vacationing South African families, and on holiday weekends you'll be tripping over motorboats, windsurfing boards and quad bikes. If you're based in Maputo with a car at your disposal, it makes an enjoyable getaway but if you're touring and want some sand, head further north to the beaches around Inhambane or south to Ponta d'Ouro.

Unlike most of Mozambique's other coastal lakes and lagoons, Uembje gets influxes of fresh water via a narrow channel to the sea, so conditions vary with the seasons. In general the winter months are best, with breezes and waves.

In the 19th century, the area around Bilene served as capital for the Gaza chief, Soshangane. During colonial days, Bilene was known as São Martinho and the saint's feast on 4 November is still celebrated, often with processions, singing and dancing in the upper part of town away from the beach.

Sleeping

Complexo Palmeiras (☎ 281-59019; www.palmeiras.itgo.com; camping per site US$12, plus per person US$5, 4-person chalets with bathroom US$45) At the northern edge of town on the beach, the long-standing Palmeiras is very popular with South African families. It has good camping with hot-water ablutions, basic reed huts lined up in the sand, a few no frills chalets, a restaurant and a braai area. Go left along the beachfront road for about 1km.

Praia do Sol (☎ 82-3193040; www.pdsol.co.za; per person with half board US$86) About 4km south of town along the beach, this place has a collection of spacious two-, four- and five-person A-frame chalets overlooking the lagoon, plus some double rooms; all come with bathroom and nets. There's a restaurant (no self-catering), a bar and diving, canoeing, snorkelling and quad-bikes, plus boat trips across the lagoon to the ocean. Turn right onto the beachfront road and continue for about 3km, staying right at the fork.

Girassol Bilene Lodge (☎ 282-59071; www.girassolhoteis.co.za; per person half board US$85; ⬛) The Girassol (formerly Mahelane) is a pleasant change of pace, on the eastern banks of the lagoon and just over the dunes from the open sea, with four- and six-person chalets scattered around the hillside overlooking the lagoon and a restaurant. There's also swimming over the dunes in the sea. Access is via a short boat ride across the lagoon; in Bilene, leave your car at the guarded lot opposite the Petromoc petrol station, and follow the path from there to the beach to get the boat. Diving, fishing and other water sports can be organised.

Other recommendations:

Humula Complexo Turístico (☎ 282-59020, 21-314576; www.humulahotel.com; d US$50, ste from US$60, 4-person chalet from US$120; ⬛ ⬛) Set amidst manicured lawns in the town centre and away from the beach, with doubles, plus modern self-catering chalets (all with kitchenette and sitting area) and a restaurant. Breakfast costs extra.

Pousada São Martinho (☎ 281-59058, 82-722 2390; d US$20, 4-person chalets US$80-100; ⬛) No-frills rooms, plus pink block-style chalets set around a fenced compound, each with a tiny porch and a small living room. It's along the main road, just up from the beachfront road.

Eating & Drinking

Most of Bilene's eateries are clustered along or just off the beachfront road. They include **Estrela do Mar** (meals from US$2); **Complexo Aquarius** (☎ 281-59000; meals US$3-5), which also has air-con rooms, plus some cooped-up birds; the basic **Tchin-Tchin** (meals US$1-3), with grilled chicken and chips to take-away; and **Pavilhão Tamar** (meals about US$3), which also has a weekend disco (entry US$0.80). Just up from the main road next to the petrol station is **Café O Bilas** (pizzas from US$3), with pizzas and upstairs seating. Except as noted, seafood grills and Portuguese cuisine are the order of the day. Most places are open daily for lunch and dinner.

Getting There & Away

Bilene is 140km north of Maputo and 35km off the main road. A direct chapa departs Maputo's Xipamanine market at about 7am. Otherwise, go to Junta and have any northbound transport drop you at the Macia junction, from where pick-ups run throughout the day to/from Bilene (US$0.50, 30 minutes).

Leaving Bilene, a direct 30-seater bus to Maputo departs daily at 6am (and sometimes again at 1pm) from the town centre near the market (US$3.60, four to five hours). Otherwise take a chapa (from the roundabout at the entrance to Bilene, about 2km from the beach) to Macia and get onward transport from there.

Driving, the road to Bilene is tarmac throughout. Boat charters across the lagoon can be arranged with Praia do Sol or Complexo Palmeiras or more cheaply with local fishermen (from about $10 round-trip).

XAI-XAI

Xai-Xai (pronounced 'shy-shy', and known during colonial times as João Belo) is a long town, stretching for several kilometres along the EN1. It's of little interest to travellers, but its beach (Praia do Xai-Xai or 'Xai-Xai Beach', about 10km from the town centre),

SOUTHERN MOZAMBIQUE

THE GAZA KINGDOM

Gaza province is now famous for its beaches and coastal lakes, but as recently as the mid-19th century it was renowned as the seat of the kingdom of Gaza, one of the most influential in Mozambican history. At the height of its power around the 1850s, it stretched from south of the Rio Limpopo northwards to the Zambezi and westwards into present-day Zimbabwe, Swaziland and South Africa.

One of Gaza's most famous chiefs was Soshangane, who ruled most of southern Mozambique from his base at Chaimite. Soshangane died in 1858 and was succeeded by his son, Umzila, who in turn was succeeded by his son, Ngungunhane. Ngungunhane's first priority was to defend the Gaza kingdom from ever-increasing European encroachment. While outwardly acknowledging Portuguese sovereignty, he allowed raiding parties to attack Portuguese settlements and struck numerous deals with the British, playing off the two colonial powers against each other.

By the mid-1890s, the tides began to turn. In 1895 Ngungunhane was captured by the Portuguese, and spent the remainder of his life in exile in the Azores. He died in 1906, and the mighty Gaza kingdom came to an end.

with invigorating sea breezes, is an agreeable overnight stop if you're driving to/from points further north.

The capital of Gaza province, Xai-Xai was developed in the early 20th century as a satellite port to Maputo, although its economic significance never approached that of the national capital. Running just south of Xai-Xai is the 'great, grey-green greasy' Rio Limpopo (Limpopo River) of Rudyard Kipling fame. It's Mozambique's second largest waterway, with a catchment area of more than 390,000 sq km, and drains parts of Botswana, South Africa and Zimbabwe as it makes its way to the sea. Despite its size, water levels vary dramatically throughout the year, leaving some sections as just small streams during the dry winter months. The wetlands around the Limpopo's lower reaches are rewarding birding areas, and are most accessible near Zongoene.

Information

There are ATMs at **BIM Expresso** (EN1) near Kaya Ka Hina; at Standard Bank, one block behind Kaya Ka Hina; and at the BP petrol station at the northern end of town. For internet access try **Teledata** (per min US$0.04; ☑ 7.30am-10pm), diagonally opposite Standard Bank.

Sleeping & Eating

Kaya Ka Hina (☎ 282-22391; EN1; s/d US$15/19, with air-con & bathroom from US$24/26; ✖) This is the best deal if you need to stay in the town centre, with clean, no-frills rooms and a restaurant (meals US$2 to US$5). It's about 100m north of the *praça* transport stand.

Xai-Xai Camping & Caravan Park (☎ 282-35022; Praia do Xai-Xai; camping per site US$5, 2-person bungalows from US$22, 4-person self-catering house US$55) Xai-Xai Camping (ask for the 'campismo') is shaded and well located on the edge of the sand, though facilities are rundown. In addition to camping there are a few basic bungalows with shared bathroom, a self-catering house and a slow restaurant. It's just north of Complexo Halley.

Complexo Halley (☎ 282-35003, 282-35014; Praia do Xai-Xai; d with sea view US$36, ste from US$40; ✖) This long-standing beachfront hotel is the first place you reach coming down the access road from town and is the best choice. It has stiff sea breezes, a seaside esplanade, a restaurant (meals from US$2.50) and pleasant rooms (ask for one that's sea facing), all with bathroom and some with air-con and TV. On Friday evenings there's a disco at the hotel; on Saturdays it's across the road at the esplanade.

Getting There & Away

Buses between Xai-Xai and Maputo depart daily in each direction about 6am and 1pm (US$5, three to four hours, 200km) from the Oliveiras depot along the main road opposite Banco Austral. However, it's usually faster to try to get a seat on one of the north–south buses. To do this, take a chapa to the bridge control post (*pontinha*) at the southernmost end of town, where all traffic needs to stop.

Chapas, including to Macia (for Bilene) depart from the praça transport stand near the old Pôr do Sol complex on the main road at the southern end of town.

The beach is 8km off the main road. Chapas (US$0.20) depart from the praça, or you can catch them anywhere along the main road. They run at least to the roundabout about 700m uphill from the beach and sometimes further.

AROUND XAI-XAI

The lagoon studded coast north and south of Xai-Xai has a string of attractive beaches – all quiet, except during South African school holidays. It's a fine destination if you have your own vehicle and are interested in birding or just enjoying the tranquil waterscapes.

Sleeping

SOUTH OF XAI-XAI

Protea Zongoene Lodge (☎ 82-402 6791, in South Africa 012-346 8868; www.zongoene.com; camping per site US$8 plus per person US$14, 4-person self-catering house from US$195, s/d with half board US$161/258) This luxurious South African–run place is set near a good section of sand just south of the mouth of the Rio Limpopo. Accommodation is in spacious 'pool chalets', or more rustic cabins set just in from the beach amid vegetation and low dunes. There's also camping, a self-catering house,

a restaurant and the usual array of activities including fishing, snorkelling and boating. The turnoff is about 15km south of Xai-Xai at Chicumbane, from where it's about 35km further down a sandy track that can be negotiated by 2WD during the dry months.

NORTH OF XAI-XAI

Chongoene Holiday Resort (☎ 82-837 9700, in South Africa 012-997 7786; camping per person US$10, 6-person chalet per person US$23) About 8km north of the Xai-Xai Camping & Caravan Park along the beach (or about 12km north of Xai-Xai town via the main road), this still-in-process place is the reincarnation of the old colonial era Hotel Chongoene. It has camping, several rustic self-catering cottages and a restaurant, with more facilities planned.

Paraíso de Chidenguele (☎ in South Africa 082-550 7559; www.chidbeachresort.com; 4-/6-/8-person chalets US$155/208/258, 'overnight rooms' per person US$36) A low-key self-catering resort about 70km north of Xai-Xai and 5km off the main road. It's set on a narrow strip of heavily vegetated coast bordered by several shallow coastal lakes, the largest of which is Lago Inhampavala. There are straightforward self-catering thatch-and-wood

---

CHOPI TIMBILA ORCHESTRAS

The intricate rhythms and pulsating beat of Chopi *timbila* music are among Southern Africa's most impressive musical traditions. The music is played on *timbila* (singular: *mbila*) – a type of marimba or xylophone made of long rows of wooden slats carved from the slow-growing sneezewood tree. In age-old rites of passage, young Chopi boys would go into the bush to plant sneezewood *(mwenje)* saplings, which would then be harvested for *timbila* construction years later when their grandsons came of age.

At the heart of *timbila* music is the *mgodo* (performance), which involves an orchestra of up to 20 or more instruments of varying sizes and ranges of pitch, singers and dancers, rattle or shaker players and a single composition with movements similar to those of a Western-style classical symphony. Rhythms are complex, often demanding that the players master different beats simultaneously with each hand, and the lyrics are full of humour and sarcasm, dealing with social issues or community events.

Following a decline during the immediate postindependence and war years, *timbila* music is now experiencing a renaissance, due in part to the efforts of Venâncio Mbande, a master composer, player and *timbila* craftsman *par excellence*. Like many other Chopi, Mbande left Mozambique at a young age to seek work in the South African mines but kept the art of *timbila* alive and ultimately formed his own orchestra. In the mid-1990s Mbande returned to his home near Quissico, where he began teaching *timbila* music and craftsmanship. His orchestra, Timbila ta Venâncio, has received international acclaim. Numerous other orchestras have since been formed around Zavala district and Quissico is a centre for training young players.

Rehearsals of Venâncio Mbande's orchestra, which are free and open to the public, are held on most Sundays (weather permitting) at Mbande's unassuming house in Helene village – about 25km north of Quissico and just east of the EN1, marked by a small yellow signpost. The annual *timbila* festival in Quissico is usually held sometime between June and August.

GAZA'S NATIONAL PARKS

Although it took a severe blow during the war years, the wildlife which used to roam the interior of Gaza province is slowly making a comeback.

PARQUE NACIONAL DO LIMPOPO

Together with South Africa's Kruger National Park and Zimbabwe's Gonarezhou National Park, **Parque Nacional do Limpopo** (Limpopo National Park; ☎ 21-713000; entry per adult/child US$8/2) forms part of the Parque Internacional do Grande Limpopo (p40). Gonarezhou connections are still in the future, but Kruger and Limpopo are now linked via the Giriyondo border post, west of Massingir.

Limpopo's most interesting area is the so-called 'sanctuary' – a 30,000 hectare tract along the Kruger border where wildlife translocation efforts are focused. However, sightings are still hit and miss, and it's quite possible to drive through the park without seeing large animals. The only officially open roads are those connecting Giriyondo with Massingir, plus several smaller wildlife-viewing loops. There are people living within the park boundaries so it's likely that you'll also see some of these communities and their livestock on the park's eastern fringes.

Most visitors use Limpopo as a transit corridor between Kruger and the coast. There's also a four-day 4x4 'eco trail' (US$594 per vehicle) starting at Kruger's Punda Maria camp and continuing south through Limpopo park to the Komatipoort border post (book through www.dolimpopo .com, or www.sanparks.org). Additional offerings: the four-day Massingir Hiking Trail (US$406 plus accommodation and meal costs) from Barragem de Massingir (Massingir Dam) west along the Rio Machampane, and similarly priced three-night wilderness trails from Machampane Wilderness Camp (for details and bookings, see www.dolimpopo.com).

Sleeping

Campismo Aguia Pesqueira (camping per person US$4, tent rental per day US$4) This good park-run camping ground has camping along the edge of the escarpment overlooking Barragem de Massingir in the distance plus cold-water ablutions and a few tents for rent. It's about 20km inside the park gate and about 50km from Giriyondo border post. Bring all supplies with you.

Covane Community Lodge (covane2006@yahoo.com.br; camping per person US$8, tent tr US$18, bungalow d US$28, 5-person chalet US$64) On a rise overlooking Lago Nova and Barragem de Massingir, this good place is about 20km from the main park entrance. It's run by the local Canhane community with support from the Swiss aid agency, Helvetas, and offers camping plus rustic but pleasant accommodation in traditional houses or larger chalets. There are also tasty local meals and impressive sunset views over the water. In addition to trips into the park (from US$8 per person), staff can organise village tours, visits to a traditional healer and boat trips on the lake. Chapas run daily from Maputo's Junta to Massingir town (US$7), from where you can arrange a free pick-up to Covane with lodge staff.

chalets (the larger ones have lofts) plus some simple twin-bedded rooms, a bar and meals with advance notice. Snorkelling and fishing are possible with your own equipment. When driving through nearby Chidenguele town, stop for a look at the impressive cathedral.

Nhambavale Lodge (☎ in South Africa 082-326 6350; www.nhambavale.co.za; camping per person US$14, chalet d US$64) This relaxing lodge just north of Paraíso de Chidenguele is in a sheltered setting on Lago Inhampavala, and an easy 2km from the sea. In addition to good camping, it offers cosy, fully serviced stone chalets and is ideal for birding.

Also recommended:

Sunset Beach (☎ 82-057 5960; www.sunsetbeache .com; 6-person chalets US$225, 3-person rondavels US$90) At the southern edge of Chidenguele beach, with white stone-and-thatch self-catering chalets and smaller rondavels plus a restaurant. Low-key and pleasant.

Nascer do Sol (☎ 282-64500; www.nascer.co.za; camping per person US$16, chalets per person US$30-60) About 45km north of Xai-Xai and about 10km off the main road (4WD) amidst low dunes, with rustic, wooden self-catering chalets overlooking the sea and in varying sizes – accommodating from two to 10 persons – plus camping with hot water and a good restaurant.

Machampane Wilderness Camp (www.dolimpopo.com; s or d tent with full board US$285) Limpopo park's first luxury camp, with five spacious, attractive and well-located safari tents directly overlooking the Machampane River in the sanctuary area, about 20km from Giriyondo border post. Guided day and overnight walks can be arranged, as can vehicle safaris (all at extra cost).

Getting There & Away

The Giriyondo border post is about 70km west of Massingir. The main park entrance on the Mozambique side is **Massingir Gate** (🕒6am-6pm), about 5km from Massingir town on the opposite side of the impressive dam wall (currently being rehabilitated). There's another gate well north of Massingir near Mapai (accessed from South Africa via the Pafuri border post), and while it's not yet officially open, we've heard of several people transiting here.

If entering Limpopo from South Africa, you'll also need to pay Kruger park entry fees, and Kruger's gate quota system (see www.sanparks.org) applies. Only 4WDs are permitted to cross. The road is in good shape for the first 30km or so from Giriyondo but deteriorates thereafter.

From Massingir Gate, it's easy to continue eastwards via Macarretane and Chokwé to the EN1 at Macia, and then north to Xai-Xai and beyond. From Mapai, it's possible to continue on to Vilankulo along a rough route via Machalla, Mabote and Mapinhane (the junction with the EN1, about 55km southwest of Vilankulo); the Rio Limpopo near Mapai is unbridged, and only crossable during the dry season. About 30km before reaching Mapinhane, and signposted to the north of the road, are the overgrown ruins of **Manyikeni** – once the seat of a major trading centre and chieftaincy which was occupied between the 13th and 17th centuries, and which had links to Great Zimbabwe. At the moment the site is quite neglected, although it has been proposed for inclusion as a Unesco World Heritage site.

There's no petrol for sale in or near Limpopo; the closest tanking up stations on the Mozambique side are in Xai-Xai and (less reliably) at Manjacaze or Chibuto. Travelling via Mapai, there is no fuel until Mapinhane.

PARQUE NACIONAL DE BANHINE (BANHINE NATIONAL PARK)

Banhine is currently completely undeveloped as a protected area and has no large wildlife of note. Camping is possible but there are no facilities and you'll need to be completely self-sufficient.

PARQUE NACIONAL DE ZINAVE (ZINAVE NATIONAL PARK)

Actually in Inhambane province, except for a tiny corner extending into Gaza, Zinave is also completely undeveloped, although rehabilitation of park infrastructure is underway. It's wild, beautiful and somewhat wetter than Banhine, thanks to the Rio Save along its northern border, and an intriguing birding destination, though also with no large wildlife of note. It's sometimes used as an overnight stop by those transiting the rugged bush route to the coast but for any camping you'll need to be self-sufficient.

QUISSICO

Quissico, capital of Zavala district, is noteworthy for being one of the main meal and bathroom stops on long-haul bus routes along the EN1. If the bus stops for long enough, look down the escarpment eastward to a chain of shimmering, pale blue lagoons in the distance. Quissico's other claim to fame is that it's the centre of the famed Chopi *timbila* (marimba) orchestras, and site of the annual *timbila* festival.

About 11km from Quissico, **Praia Mar e Sol** (www.reviteresort.com; camping per adult/child US$12/6, chalet per person US$34) is sandwiched between the beach and the lagoon, on the inland side of the dunes. It has 10 campsites set amidst the vegetation, each with its own braai area, plus a six-person self-catering chalet. There's no restaurant; bring all supplies.

On the EN1, **Pousada de Zavala 'Quissico'** (☎ 293-65007; r US$10-14) is the main place to stay in the town centre, with undistinguished rooms sharing bathrooms, and a restaurant. Just behind is a good viewpoint over the lagoons.

Quissico is 130km northeast of Xai-Xai on the EN1. To reach the lagoon and Praia Mar e Sol, take the signposted turn-off just north of town, from where it's 11km down to the water (4WD).

PRAIA DE ZÁVORA

About 55km north of Quissico and about 80km south of Inhambane is Praia de Závora (Závora Beach), yet another beautiful stretch of southern Mozambican coastline. There's a reef here for snorkelling and the fishing is rumoured to be good. Otherwise, the main activities are relaxing and taking walks to the nearby lighthouse.

Závora Lodge (www.zavoralodge.com; camping per person US$8.50-12.50, 4-/6-person bungalows US$94/140, 8-person house US$212) has camping, including a few sites on the seaside of the dunes, some with *barracas* (food stalls) and all with basic ablutions; self-catering reed bungalows with hot and cold water; a couple of self-catering houses on the beach; and meals (with advance notice). The bungalows and houses come with bedding and mosquito nets but otherwise bring everything with you. The turn-off is signposted 11km north of Inharrime town (no public transport), from where it's 17km further down a sandy track that's usually negotiable with 2WD.

Just north of the Závora Lodge turnoff, and about 12km from Inharrime town, is the turnoff for the more upscale and not-yet-operational **Dolphin Lodge** (www.zavora.co.za).

INHAMBANE

With its serene waterside setting, tree-lined avenues, faded colonial-style architecture and exotic mixture of Arabic, Indian and African influences, Inhambane is one of Mozambique's most charming towns and well worth a visit. It has a history that reaches back at least 10 centuries, making it one of the oldest settlements along the coast. Today Inhambane is the capital of Inhambane province, although

it's completely lacking in any sort of bustle or pretence. It is also the gateway to a superb collection of beaches, including Tofo and Barra.

History

As early as the 11th century, Inhambane served as a port of call for Arabic traders sailing along the East African coast. Textiles were an important commodity, and by the time the Portuguese arrived in the early 16th century, the area boasted a well-established cotton-spinning industry. In 1560 Inhambane was chosen as the site of the first Jesuit mission to the region. Development was also helped along by Inhambane's favourable location on a sheltered bay, and before long, it had moved into the limelight as a bustling ivory trading port. By the early 18th century, the Portuguese had established themselves here, together with traders from India. This mixture of Indian, Christian and Muslim influences continued to characterise Inhambane's development in later years, and is still notable today.

In the coming decades, the focus of trade shifted from cloth and ivory to slaves. By the mid-18th century, an estimated 1500 slaves were passing through Inhambane's port each year, and this human trafficking had become the town's economic mainstay.

In 1834 Inhambane was ravaged by the army of the Gaza chief, Soshangane. However, it soon recovered to again become one of the largest towns in the country. The abolition of the slave trade in the late 19th century dealt Inhambane's economy a sharp blow. The situation worsened in the early 20th century as economic focus in the region shifted southwards to Lourenço Marques (now Maputo). Many businesses moved south or closed, and Inhambane began a gradual decline from which it still has not recovered.

Information

There's a good map of Inhambane, complete with historical background information, published by GTZ. Ask around town, or at Bar Babalaza at the Tofo–Barra junction.

Banco Austral (Av da Independência) Two branches just up from the ferry, with an ATM on the north side of the road.

BIM (Av Acordos de Lusaka) Opposite Á Maçaroca restaurant; ATM.

Centro Provincial de Recursos Digitais de Inhambane (Av da Moçambique; per min US$0.02; ☯ 8am-4pm Mon-Fri, 9am-4pm Sat; ☒) Internet access.

TANGERINAS DE INHAMBANE

Mention Inhambane province to a Mozambican, and chances are they will say something about *tangerinas de Inhambane*. In season, you'll see bushel baskets lining the roadsides piled to overflowing. The fruit has even made it into local pop culture through the poem, *As saborosas tanjarinas d'Inhambane*, written by renowned Mozambican poet José Craveirinha.

INHAMBANE

INFORMATION
Banco Austral..................................1 A4
BIM...2 A5
Centro Provincial de Recursos Digitais de
Inhambane..................................3 B5
Telecomunicações de Moçambique...........4 A5

SIGHTS & ACTIVITIES
Cathedral of Nossa Senhora de Conceição....5 A4
Market...6 B5
Museum..7 B4
New Mosque....................................8 B4
Old Mosque....................................9 A4

SLEEPING
Escola Ferroviária de Moçambique..........10 B4
Pensão Pachiça...............................11 A4

EATING
Á Maçaroca....................................12 A5
Bakery..13 B5
Fatima's Paradise.............................14 A5
Fatucha Café..................................15 A4
Restaurant Tic-Tic............................16 B5
Supermarket...................................17 A5

ENTERTAINMENT
Zoom Disco....................................18 A5

SHOPPING
Associação Gunduru Gombeni...................19 B5
Casa de Cultura...............................20 A5

TRANSPORT
Bus & Chapa Stand.............................21 B5
Ferry & Dhows to Maxixe.......................22 A4

Baía de Inhambane

Baía de Inhambane

To Lindela (35km);
ENI (35km)

To Airstrip
(5km); Tofo
(22km); Barra
(22km)

Train Station
(disused)

Telecomunicações de Moçambique (Av Eduardo Mondlane; 7am-10pm) Domestic and international telephone calls; head right coming off the ferry jetty.

Sights & Activities

Strolling around Inhambane's quiet traffic-free streets comes as a treat if you've been frequenting some of Mozambique's other urban areas.

The stately **Cathedral of Nossa Senhora de Conceição**, dating from the late 18th century, is one of the main landmarks. It rises up behind the newer cathedral, just north of the jetty. North of here, reached by following the waterfront road, is the small **old mosque** (1840). The **new mosque** is several blocks further east. Don't miss strolling along the **waterfront** at sunset, and watching the sun sink into the flamingo-frequented Baía de Inhambane (Inhambane Bay).

Inhambane's colourful **market** is at its best in the early morning. Also recommended is the tiny **museum** (Av da Vigilância; admission free, donations welcome; 8am-3pm Mon-Sat) near the new mosque. Its displays include collections of traditional musical instruments, clothing and household items from the surrounding area, with some captions in English.

About 10km northeast of Inhambane in the bay are two islands, **Ilha dos Ratos** (Isle of Rats) and **Ilha dos Porcos** (Isle of Pigs). Boats can be arranged through Pensão Pachiça; allow at least five hours for the trip.

Sleeping

Pensão Pachiça (293-20565, 293-20046; farolturismo@teledata.mz; Rua 3 de Fevereiro; dm/d US$11/40) This fine backpackers on the waterfront near the cathedral has been given a complete refurbishing and is the best place to stay. It has dorm beds, a few private rooms, an outdoor restaurant-bar-pizza area, a rooftop with sunset views, and a resident masseur and beauty centre. Rooms have nets and clean shared bathrooms, and the owner can assist with arranging excursions. The same management also runs the campsite at Barra lighthouse (p92). Take a left coming off the ferry jetty; Pensão Pachiça is about 300m down.

Escola Ferroviária de Moçambique (293-20781; Av de Moçambique; r without/with fan US$15/19) By the train station at the eastern edge of town, this is the only other choice. It has functional but soulless attached doubles (no nets), with each two-room unit sharing a bathroom. Unless they are full, you'll usually only be charged per occupied bed, rather than for the entire room. From the ferry jetty, continue straight through town to the end of the main road and look for the grey monstrosity.

Eating

For inexpensive local meals try **Fatucha Café** (Av da Independência; meals from US$2; 8am-8pm Mon-Sat), with outdoor seating, or **Restaurant Tic-Tic** (Av da

SOUTHERN MOZAMBIQUE

SOUTHERN MOZAMBIQUE

LAND OF THE GOOD PEOPLE

On arrival in Inhambane, 15th-century Portuguese explorer Vasco da Gama was reportedly so charmed by the locals that he gave the area the name *terra da boa gente* or 'land of the good people'.

Revolução 227a; meals US$2-3), diagonally opposite the market. Next to the market is a **bakery** (Av da Revolução), with piping hot, fresh rolls.

Fatima's Paradise (Av da Independência) has a shaded outdoor seating area, with snacks and drinks from the adjoining Takeaway Sazaria. Upstairs is a rooftop bar without much of a drink selection but with views over town and the bay.

One block south of Av da Independência, **Á Maçaroca** (☎ 293-20489; Av Acordos de Lusaka; meals US$6-10; ☼ 9am-11pm Mon-Sat) is Inhambane's only midrange restaurant, with a selection of grilled fish, meat, curries and other dishes.

There's a reasonably well-stocked **supermarket** (Av da Independência) just up from the jetty.

Shopping & Entertainment

For woodcarvings and other crafts, try the **Associação Gunduru Gombeni** (☼ 8am-5pm Mon-Fri, 8am-noon Sat), next to the market. They are also a good contact for local cultural events and theatre productions.

The provincial Casa de Cultura (House of Culture), across from the cinema, is a good place to meet local musicians or arrange lessons.

Zoom Disco, just off Av Acordos de Lusaka and behind the Pep Store, is the main nightspot, but it's much nicer to go have a drink at the popular bar at Pensão Pachiça.

Getting There & Away

AIR

There are three flights weekly to/from Maputo (US$164 one-way) on LAM that connect reasonably well with onward flights to Johannesburg. There are also frequent charter flights to/from Johannesburg. Check with places listed in the Tofo and Around Inhambane Sleeping sections for an update on charter operators. If you are unable to find a Johannesburg–Inhambane flight, another option is flying from Johannesburg to Vilankulo (p95) and then taking a bus to Inhambane.

BOAT

Between about 6am and sunset, an old and precipitously overloaded ferry runs sporadically throughout the day between Inhambane and Maxixe (US$0.50, 20 to 25 minutes), alternating with smaller motor boats. Minor mishaps, such as getting stuck on sandbanks during low tide, are routine. Dhows do the trip more slowly for US$0.15 and one of Inhambane's great morning sights is sitting on the jetty and watching them load up. To charter a motorboat for yourself costs US$5 for the boat; the journey takes about 10 minutes.

BUS

The bus station is behind the market. Chapas to Tofo depart throughout the day (US$0.60, one hour). Oliveiras buses to Maputo depart at 6am and 11am (US$9, seven hours, 450km). It's faster to catch one of the 30-seaters – at the moment the main lines are Inhambane Ceu and Inhambane Expresso – which depart at 5am (US$8). For other southbound buses, and for all northbound transport, you'll need to head to Maxixe.

Coming from Maputo, Inhambane Ceu and other smaller buses depart Junta between 5am and 7am. Alternatively, take any northbound bus to Maxixe.

For shuttles between Swaziland and Tofo, see p188.

AROUND INHAMBANE

The coast southeast of Inhambane is lined by a succession of attractive beaches, and is a good destination for families. Facilities are geared toward drive-in visitors looking for a self-catering holiday though most can also organise transfers to/from Inhambane. Most places have only limited facilities during the off-season (any time other than South African holidays), and during the holidays they're often fully booked. All are accessed by well-signposted, sandy (4WD) access roads, branching off the main road between about 10km and 35km south of Inhambane. Listings here are roughly north to south.

Sleeping

Coconut Bay (Baía dos Cocos; ☎ 293-20882, 82-311 7250; www.coconutbay.co.za; camping per person US$12 plus per site from US$8, s/d casitas US$42/75, 4-person rondavels US$128, 6-person chalets from US$188) This pleasant, low-key place has camping barracas amidst the palms, plus a range of self-catering rondavels and

AROUND INHAMBANE

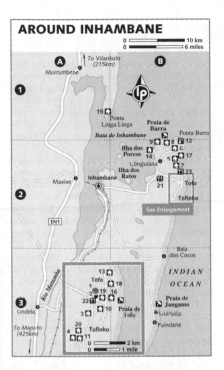

chalets, most set back from the beach, and some on the edge of the dune overlooking the water. There are also a few no-frills *casitas* with bathroom, but without self-catering facilities, a restaurant/bar and a dive centre (certified divers only). The turn-off is signposted about 10km south of town, from where it's 17km further.

Jeff's Palm Resort (☎ 293-56063, in South Africa 013-750 2439; www.jeffsmoz.com; 8-person camping barracas US$34, plus per person US$10, 4-/8-person houses US$129/300) Another good spot, the small Jeff's Resort is nestled in the palm groves behind the dunes, with a collection of self-catering houses, plus barracas for camping, each with its own ablutions block and cooking area. There's a restaurant and bar, and diving and fishing can be arranged. Bring your own towels and mosquito nets (and, for the barracas, all camping gear).

Jangamo Beach Resort (☎ in South Africa 013-750 2439; www.jangamo.co.za; d US$55, 6-person chalets US$155, 6-person houses US$219) About 22km off the main road and immediately south of Jeff's Resort, Jangamo is set on the dunes overlooking and somewhat back from the sea. Rooms include doubles in the main lodge, reed and thatch chalets and some six- to eight-person houses.

All have hot water and the chalets and houses have their own bathrooms. There's a bar and a good restaurant and fishing charters can be organised.

Guinjata Bay Resort (☎ in South Africa 013-741 2795; www.guinjata.com; camping per person US$17, 2-/3-/4-bedroom chalets US$146/211/273) A large, sprawling place set among the dunes, with a range of camp sites and self-catering chalets, plus a restaurant. Fishing charters can be arranged with advance notice and there's diving (including instruction).

Sea Blue Scuba Safaris (☎ 84-644 8370, in South Africa 013-744 0357; www.seablue.co.za; 2-/3-/4-room chalets from US$159/239/212) Sea Blue is mainly a dive centre that's recently expanded and now offers its own accommodation, with stone-and-thatch chalets on the dunes, including some with private bathrooms, some with self-catering facilities and some with views of the water. There's also a restaurant, and half-board rates are available.

Paindane Beach Resort (☎ 082-569 3436; www .paindane.com; camping per adult/child US$10/5, 4-/6-person chalets from US$91/118, 8-person villas from US$250)

About 35km southeast of Inhambane by road, the good Paindane has camping barracas, as well as reed-and-thatch chalets on the dunes overlooking the sea and larger, less-appealing 'villas'. All are self-catering (bring your own sleeping bag or sheets), though there's a good restaurant and bar as well. Diving and instruction are available, and there's snorkelling equipment for rent and wonderful snorkelling at low tide just offshore.

TOFO & TOFINHO

Thanks to its sheltered azure waters, long stretches of white sand, easy access and fine diving, the beach at Tofo has long been legendary on the Southern Africa holiday circuit. The beach runs in a long arc, at the centre of which is a small town with a perpetual party-time atmosphere. Just to the south and easily accessed from Tofo is Tofinho, set on a green hillside looking out over turquoise waters, and known for its strong currents, its good wave and its surfing vibe. Many people come to Tofo expecting to spend a few days, and instead stay several weeks or more. If the partying crowd isn't your scene, head around the point to quieter Barra, or further north or south.

Tofo On-Line (per hr US$5; ☺ 10am-6pm Thu-Tue), in the town centre, has internet access and milkshakes. The closest banks and ATMs are in Inhambane.

Diving

Tofo is Mozambique's unofficial diving capital. For diving information, see p43. Dive operators (both PADI Gold Palm) include:
Diversity Scuba (☎ 293-29002; www.diversityscuba .com) In the town centre.
Tofo Scuba (☎ 82-826 0140; www.tofoscuba.com) Based at Casa Barry.

Surfing

Surfers should head straight to Tofinho's Turtle Cove – check out their website (www.feralsurf .com) for a description of conditions. The Waterworks Surf & Coffee Shop, near Diversity Scuba, rents and sells gear (for diving, too).

Sleeping

TOFO

Budget

Bamboozi (☎ 293-29040; camping US$9, dm US$14, 2-/4-person bungalows US$23/46, 4-person chalets/honeymoon ste US$94; 🖳) Justifiably popular, with a large,

thatched and circular dorm plus camping, hot-water ablutions, a kitchen area, bungalows and chalets nestled amongst the palms behind a high dune, a dune-top bar-restaurant with fantastic views and a dive operator. It's 3km north of town along a sandy road. Management was changing when we passed through, and we've received some complaints, but hopefully things should be sorted out by now. Wednesday and Friday are party nights.

Fatima's Nest (☎ 82-414 5730; www.mozambiqueback packers.com; camping per person US$5, dm US$7-9, 2-/3-person bungalow US$24/36) A low-key, rather makeshift place about 1.5km south of Bamboozi's in a (sometimes very) breezy setting on low dunes directly overlooking the beach. On offer: camping, tents for rent, no-frills reed bungalows, a kitchen, bar, pool table and – if the partying doesn't wear you out – a trampoline, plus good dinners and evening beach bonfires. Staff can help sort you out with pick-ups from Inhambane and excursions.

Pensão Tofo (☎ 82-827 4590, in South Africa 083-308 0733; dm/d US$8/23 🕮) Small, clean and without the beach vibes, but nevertheless a good budget bet – especially if you're visiting during the rainy season, when the beachside backpackers tend to get flooded out. It has several rooms – including a six-bed dorm with fan and nets, plus an air-con double, all with shared bathroom and a kitchen. A restaurant, bar and pizzeria are coming soon. It's opposite Tofo On-Line in the town centre.

Nordin's Lodge (☎ 293-29009; 2-/4-person chalets with bathroom US$50/100) The quiet Nordin's is at the far northern end of town, just south of Fatima's Nest. It has rustic but spacious thatched chalets with hot water, fridge and self-catering facilities.

Midrange

Casa Barry (☎ 293-29007, in South Africa 082-808 5523; www.casabarry.com; camping per site US$8, d reed/brick casita US$70/86, 4-/6-person chalets US$172/206) Well-located on the beach at the southern end of town, this is one of the better midrange choices. To the back of the compound is a camping area, and to the front a collection of closely spaced, rustic reed-and-thatch self-catering chalets and a beachfront restaurant. Fishing charters can be arranged, and there's an onsite dive operator.

Albatroz (☎ 293-29005, 293-29034; restalbatroz@ teledata.mz; s/d US$32/48, 4-/6-/8-person chalets

US$74/112/132) Mainly known as one of Tofo's better restaurants, with some reasonable if rather cluttered self-catering chalets (including well-outfitted kitchens with microwaves) and a handful of rooms. Most rooms have an exterior window and a semi-interior one covered with thatching that blocks ventilation.

Aquático Lodge (☎ 82-857 2850; aquatico .lodge@teledata.mz; 5-person chalet US$141) This self-catering place is at the far northern end of the beach, about 3.5km from town. There are a handful of five-person A-frame houses set behind the dunes, all with loft and raised veranda, plus a restaurant and quad bikes for hire.

Mango Beach (☎ 82-943 4660; luckylil@webmail .co.za; r US$20, 4-person house US$55, 6-person chalet US$102) Tofo's northernmost lodge at the moment, about 500m up from Aquático Lodge and about 4km from town via road. There's a dune-top bar-eating area with impressive views over the long beach, plus a large cluster of cabanas and chalets behind the dunes. Rooms are basic – with shared bathrooms and you'll need your own linens. Much nicer are the houses (also with shared bathroom), and the chalets, which come with their own kitchenette, bathroom and all bells and whistles. For swimming, best to head a bit south, to avoid the rocks just in front.

Hotel Tofo Mar (☎ 82-294 5150; hoteltofomar@yahoo .com.br; s/d US$38/70, with sea view from US$42/75; ☒) In a prime location directly on the beach in the town centre, this is the only hotel (ie, nonbungalow style place). Although rather faded these days, management is planning an upgrade. Once completed, it will be worth checking out. There's a restaurant and a bar, and the sea-view rooms have small, breezy balconies overlooking the beach.

To rent no-frills **private beach houses** (4-person house from US$100) in Tofo town, ask around at Pensão Tofo or Dino's bar.

TOFINHO

With its superb turquoise vistas and top-notch surfing, Tofinho – just over the escarpment from Tofo – draws its own crowd.

Budget

Turtle Cove (☎ in South Africa 011-803 4185; www.feral surf.com; camping per person US$8, dm US$12, r per person with bathroom in reed/stone bungalows US$16/22) Turtle Cove has been completely rebuilt after being damaged several years ago in a fire, and is *the*

place to go if you're interested in surfing or chilling. There are pleasant stone-and-thatch casitas, plus simpler reed and thatch bungalows (gradually being upgraded to stone) set amidst the palm trees. All have private bathroom and there's a common area with Moorish overtones. Other attractions: evening bonfires, yoga instruction, surf board rental (guests only), video equipment for filming your surfing and good meals. Bring your own bedding for the dorms.

Midrange

Annastasea (☎ in South Africa 011-803 4185; bookings@ mozcon.com, or through Turtle Cove; 12-person house US$390) This classy and spacious house with ochre, tile and wood overtones and a vaguely Moorish ambience is an optimal choice if you're in a group. It's set on expansive lawns, with full facilities – beautiful kitchen, washing machine, etc – in the main house and four adjoining three-person cottages, all with mosquito netting. In high season it's only rented in it's entirety but off-season is generally available for about US$23 per person.

Casa de John (Casa Amarela; ☎ 82-451 7498, in South Africa 011-827 5745; www.casajohn.co.za; 6-person house US$189; ☒) Very nice, fully equipped two- and three-bedroom self-catering houses in a breezy setting on the cliff overlooking the sea.

Eating
TOFO

Casa de Comer (☎ 82-764 8160; meals US$7; ☒ 10am-9pm Wed-Mon) This is Tofo's classiest cuisine, with a Mozambique-French fusion menu that changes daily (delicacies include seafood lasagne and fish creole with saffron) plus wines, all reasonably priced and served against a backdrop of candlelight and classical music.

Waterworks Surf & Coffee Shop (breakfasts US$2-3.50, light meals US$4; ☒ 7am-5pm Tue-Sun) Another great addition to the Tofo dining scene, with excellent breakfasts plus a small menu of light meals and (coming soon) evening hours and dinners. It's next to Diversity Scuba in the town centre.

Dino's Beach Bar (meals from US$2; ☒ 10am-late Thu-Tue) Good vibes, good music and good food on the beach just past Fatima's Nest, this is Tofo's main hangout. On offer: pizzas, seafood, toasted sandwiches, salads, full breakfast, desserts and more.

Albatroz (☎ 293-29005; restalbatroz@teledata.mz; meals from US$5, breakfast buffet US$14; ☒ lunch & dinner)

At the top of the hill in the town centre, and worth the walk or drive up, this restaurant offers delicious seafood dishes, generally prompt service and a good Sunday breakfast buffet.

TOFINHO

Turtle Cove is the place to go, with its eclectic mix of dishes, sometimes featuring sushi, and a laid-back ambience. Bar closing time is at 11.30pm. Everywhere else in Tofinho is self-catering.

Getting There & Away

There are chapas throughout the day along the 22km asphalt road between Tofo and Inhambane, with the first reliable departure from Tofo about 6am (US$0.60, one hour). There's no direct transport to Maputo or points north; you'll need to go via Inhambane or Maxixe, which means that to catch an early northbound or southbound express bus, you'll need to stay in Inhambane the night before. If you leave early from Maputo, it's possible to get to Inhambane in time to continue straight on to Tofo that day, with time to spare.

Tofinho is a 15- to 30-minute walk from Tofo, depending on which route you take.

BARRA

Barra's beach is just as beautiful as that at Tofo, featuring surf, sand dunes and palm groves. It's set at the tip of the Barra peninsula, at the point where the waters of Baía de Inhambane mix with those of the Indian Ocean. On the bay side are stands of mangrove and wetland areas that are good for birding. There's been a building spree in recent years – mostly South African–run self-catering places – but unlike Tofo, there's no town here, and everything's quite spread out. This is no problem if you have your own transport – many self-drivers prefer Barra's generally quieter scene and its greater range of midrange lodging options – but Tofo is a better bet if you're backpacking.

Diving

For general diving information see p43. Dive operators (all offer instruction, and can organise snorkelling and other water sports) include:

Barra Lodge Scuba Diving (www.barradiveresorts .com; Barra Lodge) Also arranges diving around Pomene.
Barra Reef Divers (www.barrareef.co.za; Barra Reef)

Fishing

Barra has long been a popular angler's destination. Good contacts include **Hains Fishing Charters** (www.hainsfishingcharters.co.za) and Barra Lodge.

Sleeping & Eating

Farol de Barra (☎ 82-960 3550, 82-355 9590; www .barralighthouse.com; camping per adult/child US$12/6, electricity per day per site US$5) Under the same management as Pensão Pachiça in Inhambane, has rustic camping on the beach at Barra point (nothing but your tent, sand, sea grasses and sea), and a simple bar-restaurant with tasty seafood. There are about 30 campsites, plus hot and cold ablutions, plug points, good security and views. Tents can sometimes be hired, boats can be launched and quad bikes aren't permitted. Take the signposted sandy (4WD only) right off the Barra road, when coming from Bar Babalaza.

Barra Lodge (☎ 293-20561, in South Africa 011-314 3355; www.barralodge.co.za; dm US$13, casita s/d with half board US$132/221, 6-person self-catering cottages US$181) This midrange establishment is one of Barra's largest, longest-running and most outfitted places, with a range of accommodation – from small twin-bedded reed casitas with bathroom to larger self-catering cottages – plus a beachside bar-restaurant. It offers a full range of activities, including diving, horseback riding and quad bikes, plus fly-in packages from Johannesburg and excursions (including diving) to Pomene. Backpacker facilities include a divers' bunkhouse with hot showers and a cooking area.

Barra Reef (☎ 293-56035, 82-712 6640; www.barra reef.co.za; s/d bunkhouse US$26/31, 4-person casitas US$109, 5- to 6-person self-catering villas US$125) About 1km further on is the relaxing Barra Reef, with a good setting – directly on the beach, with open views of the coast. There's a choice of simple self-catering chalets, including some double-storey A-frames with upstairs veranda, plus casitas sharing a communal kitchen, a bunkhouse and a beachside restaurant-bar. In addition to diving, there's kayaking and other activities.

Bali Hai Lodge (☎ 293-56017, 293-56082; www .balihailodge.com; s/d chalet US$59/88, 8-person main house US$391) Rather more reminiscent of South Africa than the South Pacific but nonetheless quite pleasant, with a main house consisting of four doubles with private bathrooms around a large common area plus some separate two-room chalets. It's all self-catering (no restaurant) and fishing charters can be arranged.

Flamingo Bay Water Lodge (☎ 293-56001, in South Africa 011-314 3355; www.flamingobay.co.za; s/d with half board US$250/391; ✗ 🖳 ☎) Barra's most up-scale choice, with 20 luxurious wood-and-thatch stilt houses lined up in a neighbourly row over the bay plus an overflow pool, a restaurant and little golf carts to take you from the main lodge down the long wooden walkways to your room. It's just past Barra Lodge and signposted. No children under 12 years of age.

Apart from the lodge restaurants, the main option is **Bar Babalaza** (meals from US$2), about 6km from Barra at the junction where the roads to Tofo and Barra diverge. It's a local institution, with meals and drinks, air for your tyres and local information. In Barra itself, there are no shops or nonhotel restaurants but fish is available from local fishers.

Getting There & Away
AIR
For air connections to/from Inhambane (from where all the Barra lodges do transfers), see p88. Barra Lodge and several other places offer fly-in packages from Johannesburg.

BUS
There are lots of daily chapas between Inhambane and Conguiana village along the Barra road, from where you'll need to sort out a pick-up or walk (about 4km to Barra Lodge).

CAR & MOTORCYCLE
The turn-off for Barra is about 15km from Inhambane en route to Tofo – bear left at the Bar Babalaza junction. You can easily make it in 2WD most of the way, but you'll need 4WD to reach Barra lighthouse and the self-catering anglers' places at the point. Hitching is easy in season from Bar Babalaza.

MAXIXE
Maxixe (pronounced 'ma-sheesh') is about 450km northeast of Maputo on the EN1, and has nothing to recommend it except its convenient location as a stopping point for traffic up and down the coast. It's also the place to get off the bus and onto the boat if you're heading to Inhambane, across the bay.

There are ATMs at BIM, just in from the main road near Pousada de Maxixe, and

at Banco Austral – about 600m north, and just in from the EN1. Telecomunicações de Moçambique (TDM), near Banco Austral, has internet access.

Sleeping & Eating
Maxixe Camping (☎ 293-30351; EN1; camping per person US$5, 2-person beach bungalows from US$32) Next to the jetty, with reasonable ablutions and self-catering facilities. In addition to camping, there are also a few faded bungalows with bathrooms. You can arrange to leave your vehicle here while visiting Inhambane.

Pousada de Maxixe (☎ 293-30199; EN1; d without/with bathroom US$16/24), Across the road from Maxixe Camping, this relic of the past has grubby rooms and sporadic water supplies, but surprisingly good local food in the evenings.

Stop (☎ 293-30025; EN1; meals from US$2; ☉ 6am-10pm; r US$26; ✗) Overlooking the water on the northern edge of the jetty and a good place to dine while waiting for the ferry. The same management also rents clean rooms with bathroom and TV next to Banco Austral (no meals).

For self-catering, try Taurus, just in from the EN1, with South African imports, meats and cheeses.

Getting There & Away
Thirty-seater buses to Maputo (US$8, 6½ hours, 450km) depart from the bus stand by the Tribunal beginning at 6am. For chapas to Morrumbene, Vilankulo (US$6, 3½ hours) and other points north, go to Praça 25 de Setembro (just ask for the 'praça'), a couple of blocks north of the Tribunal bus stand in front of the Conselho Municipal. For information on the Inhambane ferry, see p88.

PONTA LINGA LINGA
This old whaling station is about 15km from Inhambane at the tip of a small peninsula on the northern side of Baía de Inhambane. The offshore waters are home to a population of dugong. Onshore is a small village, nestled among the coconut palms.

The only accommodation is **Funky Monkeys** (camping per person US$4, dm US$4), a bare-bones backpackers. It's is run by Lúcio and his wife, who is an excellent cook, and if you wind up staying longer he's usually willing to negotiate with prices. He can also help you arrange canoeing in the nearby mangroves.

SOUTHERN MOZAMBIQUE

> **TROPIC OF CAPRICORN**
>
> There are no signs marking the spot, but you cross the tropic of Capricorn – the southernmost latitude (22.5°) at which the sun is directly overhead – about 15km south of Massinga town on the border between Massinga and Morrumbene districts.

Linga Linga can be reached from Morrumbene or by dhow from Inhambane (about US$5, bring extra water and shade). There's nothing regular, so you'll need to charter one – ask staff at Pensão Pachiça (p87) to point you in the right direction.

MORRUMBENE

This town on the EN1 30km north of Maxixe is notable as the place to get a dhow to Ponta Linga Linga. If you get stuck for the night, **Pousada do Litoral** (EN1; r US$10) has undistinguished rooms.

Chapas run throughout the day to/from Maxixe (US$0.80, 30 minutes) and in the mornings to/from Vilankulo (US$3, 3½ hours). From the chapa stand, you'll need to walk about 20 minutes to the water (ask for the *ponta*), where you can catch a boat to Linga Linga (US$0.20). Sailings depend on the winds, but there's usually a 'public' boat departing daily (except Sunday) about 11am. Otherwise, you can hire your own for about US$6, though after about 3pm it's difficult to find willing captains. When approaching Linga Linga, ask the captain to take you all the way to the point. Otherwise they'll drop you along the side of the peninsula, from where you'll need to walk another couple of kilometres to Funky Monkeys.

MASSINGA

Massinga is a bustling district capital on the EN1. It's decidedly free of tourist attractions, though there is an interesting mural on the main street. Like many parts of coastal Inhambane province, the town is surrounded by landscapes lush with coconut palms. In contrast, much of northern Massinga district (which stretches north and west from Massinga town) and other inland areas are arid and browner, and dotted with enormous baobab trees. There are some particularly impressive baobab stands about 50km north of Massinga, just west of the EN1 at the turn-off for Chicomo locality. Local residents use hollows in the trunks of the trees for storing water during the dry season. These same communities rely on hunting as an important food source. It's normally done with bow and arrow, mostly at night when the landscape is illuminated by a full moon.

There's a TDM office diagonally opposite the bank for domestic and international telephone calls, and several ATMs in the town centre.

The friendly **Dalilo's Hotel** (☎ 293-71043; EN1; r with/without bathroom from US$20/30; 🔀) at the northern end of town is the best place to stay and **Dalilo's Restaurant** (meals from US$3) is the place to go for information on what's happening.

Getting There & Away

Most north–south buses stop at Massinga. The first departure to Maputo is about 6am. Going north, buses from Maputo begin to arrive in Massinga by about 2.30pm, en route to Vilankulo (US$5 between Massinga and Vilankulo).

MORRUNGULO

Several kilometres north of Massinga is the signposted turn-off for Praia de Morrungulo, a particularly beautiful and seemingly endless stretch of coast lined by palm trees and striking low cliffs.

Amongst the bougainvilleas and palm trees bordering the beach sits the attractive, self-catering **Morrungulo Beach Resort** (www.morrungulo.co.za; camping per adult/child US$11/5.50, bungalow d US$78, 4-person chalets US$144, bunkhouse per person about US$31). It has reed-and-thatch chalets with kitchenette and bathroom, thatched shelters (*barracas*) with plug points and an eight-bed bunkhouse; bring your own bed sheets and linen. There's also a dive centre (book instruction in advance) and fishing charters can be arranged. Advance bookings are essential during South African and Zimbabwean school holidays. Excellent value and a great place for families. No restaurant.

Also recommended is the laid-back **Baobab Lodge** (☎ 82-865 6980, 21-455010; baobab_lodge@yahoo.co.uk; camping/barraca per person US$5/8, dm US$8, cliff/beach d US$30/35, 6-person cottage US$75-100), located between Morrungulo Beach Resort and Sylvia Shoal. It has rooms and a self-catering cottage at the top of the small escarpment (about five minutes on foot down to the sea), camping with hot water showers, and more self-catering cottages and camping down near the water. There's a good restaurant with seafood grills and local meals, plus homemade pizzas, and a cultural centre that sometimes has traditional dance performances. Staff can help you arrange visits to nearby villages.

On the beach about 3km north of Morrungulo Beach Resort, **Sylvia Shoal Lodge** (La Rosa; ☎ in South Africa 011-884 6055, 082-900 4886; camping per person US$15, 2-person bungalow US$95) is a small, agreeable place with camping with hot-water showers and barracas, a few self-catering bungalows and (in season) a beachside bar and restaurant. There's a resident dive instructor (the beautiful Sylvia Shoal reef is offshore) and dive gear for rent.

Just before reaching Morrungulo is a tiny bakery selling fresh bread daily.

Getting There & Away
Morrungulo is 13km from the main road down a good sand track that is negotiable with 2WD. Sporadic chapas run to locations within walking distance of the lodges. The turnoffs for Sylvia Shoal and Baobab Lodge are signposted. For Morrungulo Beach Resort, continue straight.

POMENE
Pomene, the site of a colonial-era beach resort, is known for its fishing, birding and its striking estuarine setting. The surrounding area is part of the Pomene Reserve, which was gazetted in 1972 with 20,000 hectares to protect the mangrove ecosystems, dune forests and marine life of the area, including dugongs and turtles. The reserve is now neglected but the beach here is lovely. It's on the coast about halfway between Inhambane and Vilankulo off the EN1. Massinga is the best place to stock up. There's an airstrip for charter flights.

Pomene Lodge (☎ in South Africa 011-314 3227; www.pomene.co.za; camping per person US$16, d dive hut US$55, s/d chalet US$66/102, tr cabin US$125, 6-/8-person chalets US$250/334) is a relaxing, remote place set on a spit of land between the estuary and the sea. It has a collection of no-frills self-catering chalets, all with bedding and mosquito nets, plus basic reed beach huts sharing ablutions (bring your own bed sheets). There's also camping (hot and cold water), a restaurant-bar and diving, and estuary boat trips can be arranged, as can transfers to/from Barra Lodge (p92). Check locally

about swimming, due to strong currents. The turn-off is 12km north of Massinga, from where it's another 55km down a sandy track (4WD) to the lodge; there's no regular public transport.

Pomene View (☎ in South Africa 083-962 9818; www.pomeneview.com; 5-person chalets US$156; ☎) lacks Pomene Lodge's beachside setting (it's set on a rise amidst the mangroves and coastal vegetation on the mainland side of the estuary), but it's friendly, small and tranquil, with its own special appeal and wide views. Accommodation is in self-catering brick-and-thatch chalets, each with bedding, mosquito nets and braai area, and there's a bar. Take the same turnoff north of Massinga as for Pomene Lodge, and then follow the Pomene View signs. Transfers across the estuary are easily arranged, as are mangrove excursions and fishing charters.

VILANKULO
Vilankulo is the finishing (or starting) point of Mozambique's southern tourist circuit, and an institution on the Southern Africa backpackers' loop, as well as on the South African overlander scene. It's also the gateway for visiting the nearby Archipélago de Bazaruto, separated from the mainland by an expanse of turquoise sea. During South African holidays, Vilankulo is overrun with pick-ups and 4WDs, but otherwise it's a quiet, slow-paced town.

Orientation
Vilankulo is spread over about 5km and chapas are few and far between, so you may spend a fair amount of time walking. The bus stand, market area and main centre of activity are at the southwestern end of town, while most accommodation starts about 20 minutes on foot northeast of here along the seafront. Bairro

---

VILANKULO

Like many towns in Mozambique, Vilankulo takes its name from an early local chief (régulo), Gamala Vilankulo Mukoke. The name was rendered as 'Vilanculos' during colonial times, but was then changed back to Vilankulo after independence. Bairro Mukoke (Mucoque), west of BIM Expresso, is named after Gamala Vilankulo's son, who lived there.

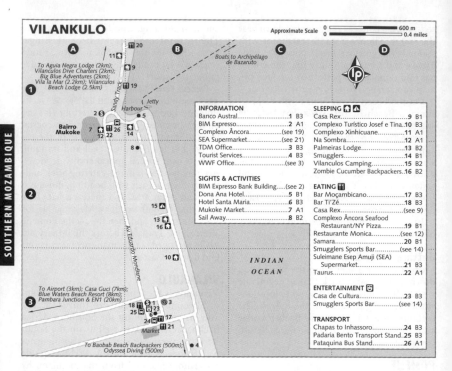

VILANKULO

Approximate Scale

INFORMATION		
Banco Austral	.1	B3
BIM Expresso	.2	A1
Complexo Âncora	(see 19)	
SEA Supermarket	(see 21)	
TDM Office	.3	B3
Tourist Services	.4	B3
WWF Office	(see 3)	

SIGHTS & ACTIVITIES		
BIM Expresso Bank Building	(see 2)	
Dona Ana Hotel	.5	B1
Hotel Santa Maria	.6	B3
Mukoke Market	.7	A1
Sail Away	.8	B2

SLEEPING		
Casa Rex	.9	B1
Complexo Turístico Josef e Tina	.10	A1
Complexo Xinhicuane	.11	A1
Na Sombra	.12	A1
Palmeiras Lodge	.13	B2
Smugglers	.14	B1
Vilanculos Camping	.15	B2
Zombie Cucumber Backpackers	.16	B2

EATING		
Bar Moçambicano	.17	B3
Bar Ti'Zé	.18	B3
Casa Rex	(see 9)	
Complexo Âncora Seafood Restaurant/NY Pizza	.19	B1
Restaurante Monica	(see 12)	
Samara	.20	B1
Smugglers Sports Bar	(see 14)	
Suleimane Esep Amuji (SEA) Supermarket	.21	B3
Taurus	.22	A1

ENTERTAINMENT		
Casa de Cultura	.23	B3
Smugglers Sports Bar	(see 14)	

TRANSPORT		
Chapas to Inhassoro	.24	B3
Padaria Bento Transport Stand	.25	B3
Pataquina Bus Stand	.26	A1

INDIAN OCEAN

Mukoke, reached by following the tarmac road (Av Eduardo Mondlane) north for about 2km from the bus stand, is a second centre of sorts, with an ATM, a market and several sleeping options within easy reach.

Information

INTERNET ACCESS

Complexo Âncora (per ½hr US$1.60; 8am-8pm Wed-Mon;) Lots of terminals and sea views, located along the waterfront.

TDM (per min US$0.04; 8am-3pm Mon-Fri;) Internet access and international telephone calls; one block behind Banco Austral.

MONEY

Banco Austral (Av Eduardo Mondlane) ATM, and changes cash dollars; at the junction where the road from Pambara comes into town.

BIM Expresso (Av Eduardo Mondlane, Bairro Mukoke) ATM.

SEA Supermarket (near the market) Has an ATM.

TOURIST INFORMATION

Tourist Services (293-82228; margie@teledata.mz; 2-5pm Mon-Sat) Very helpful, sells town maps and can assist with flight bookings, info and excursions. It's about

500m north of Baobab Beach Backpackers and one road in from the beach.

WWF Office (293-82383; 7.30am-noon, 2pm-4pm Mon-Fri) Near TDM and the place to pay entry fees for Archipelago de Bazaruto.

Dangers & Annoyances

Vilanculo's beaches are generally fine during the daytime, as long as you're within sight of the hotels or the crowds. However, especially after sundown, avoid the stretch by the old Dona Ana Hotel near the washed away road. Also avoid the route through the villages leading from the market area down to Baobab Beach Backpackers – ask staff from the backpackers to accompany you if you need to leave before dawn to catch the bus.

Sights

It's worth taking a stroll through the bustling **market** area near the bus stand. Nearby is the now derelict **Hotel Santa Maria**, built by tycoon-entrepreneur Joaquim Alves. At the northern end of town on the beach is the rambling, currently derelict and soon to be rehabilitated **Dona Ana Hotel**, also built by Alves. Just inland are the

BIM Expresso bank building, which used to be Alves' residence, and the colourful **Mukoke market**.

Activities

DIVING & SNORKELLING

For general information see p43. Dive operators (all also arrange day snorkelling trips and island transfers) include:

Odyssea Diving (☎ 293-82492, 82-781 7130; www .odysseadive.com; Baobab Beach Backpackers) PADI instruction.

Vilanculos Dive Charters (☎ 82-856 2700; bigblue@teledata.mz; Aguia Negra Lodge) A long-standing outfit offering PADI instruction and dive-accommodation deals.

DHOW SAFARIS

The recommended **Sail Away** (☎ 293-82385, 82-387 6350; www.sailaway.co.za) is the best contact for island dhow safaris, with various day and overnight sails in the archipelago (check out their website for a sampling). Prices are very reasonable: a day trip including snorkelling around the islands of Magaruque or Benguera, a good lunch, refreshments, park entry fees and snorkelling equipment costs US$47, with discounts sometimes available for walk-ins. Overnight safaris range from two to four days and cost from US$70 per person per day, with everything that the day trip includes, plus full board and accommodation. All boats have extra motors, safety and first-aid equipment and communication on board. Sail Away's Vilankulo base is on the road paralleling the beach road and about 400m south of the Dona Ana Hotel.

FISHING & OTHER WATER SPORTS

For fishing charters, boat hire, snorkelling and other water sports, contact **Big Blue Adventures** (☎ 293-82425; bigblue@teledata.mz), based at Aguia Negra Lodge.

Sleeping

Vilankulo has one of the best accommodation selections along the southern coast, especially for midrange travel. Advance bookings are essential if you'll be travelling around the Christmas-New Year's or Easter holidays.

BUDGET

Zombie Cucumber Backpackers (www.zombiecucumber.com; dm US$10, d chalet US$28; 🖳) An excellent backpackers, and prime for relaxing, with lots of green space, hammocks, a bar and a circular 10-bed dorm, plus small, spotless cha-

lets, most with double bed, net and fan, and hot water when the weather's cool. It's just back from the beach road, south of Palmeiras Lodge. The owner cooks up great meals each evening (order by 5pm) and breakfast is available (US$2 to US$5).

Baobab Beach Backpackers (☎ 293-82202, 82-731 5420; baobabmoz@yahoo.com; camping US$6, dm US$8, chalet d US$20, beachfront chalet d with bathroom US$40) Has a beachside setting (though camping and most accommodation is inland) and a definite party vibe (full moon parties are a regular feature) plus camping space, a kitchen, a bar-restaurant and several chalets. It's at the southern end of town, reached from the bus station–market area via a sandy path winding through the village. Get someone to accompany you (a modest fee is expected), especially at night or in the predawn hours.

Vilanculos Camping (☎ 293-82043, in South Africa 015-516 1427; www.vilanculoscamping.co.za; camping per person US$11, chalets per person US$16, with bathroom US$23) This large, shaded camping area is in a good setting on the inland side of the beach road and rather lacking in atmosphere, but otherwise is wellkept and a good bet. There's plenty of room for tents or caravans, plus ablution blocks, and some straightforward rooms and bungalows with bedding.

Complexo Turístico Josef e Tina (☎ 293-82140; camping per tent US$10, d/q rondavel US$24/32, d in main house from US$30) A local-style place on the beach road just up from Zombie Cucumber with camping, a self-catering area, no-frills rooms in reed bungalows and several rooms in the main house with bathroom and communal kitchen facilities.

Na Sombra (☎ 293-82429; s/tw/d/q US$11/14/16/21) Just southwest of BIM in the Mukoke section of town, with small, no-frills rooms – all with fan and shared bathroom – and the good Restaurante Monica. The owner has a minivan available for rental and can help organise excursions.

MIDRANGE

Smugglers (☎ 293-82253; www.smugglers.co.za; s/d US$38/55, s/d with bathroom US$44/66; 🅿 🖳) Just southwest of the Dona Ana Hotel on the inland side of the road, this well-run place has pleasant rooms – most twin-bedded with shared hot-water bathrooms, fans and nets – set around lush, green gardens with two small pools, and rooftop sprinkler systems to keep things cool during the afternoon heat. There are also a few

SOUTHERN MOZAMBIQUE

family-style rooms with bathrooms, and a good restaurant. Children's discounts are available.

Aguia Negra Lodge (☎ 293-82387; www.aguianegra .co.za; 6-person chalets about US$147, s/d chalet US$55/86, luxury s/d US$86/140; ⓟ ⓡ ⓧ) About 2km north of the Dona Ana Hotel, the popular Aguia Negra has breezy, rustic six-person A-frame chalets set around a large, grassy compound overlooking the sea, each with an open loft area, plus a bathroom with hot water. There's a restaurant and a resident dive and water sports operator. The newer 'luxury rooms' to the side of the property have air-con, TV and minifridge, and canoe and windsurfing equipment is available for guests; rates include a good full breakfast.

Palmeiras Lodge (☎ 293-82257, or through Vilanculos Beach Lodge; s/d cottages US$66/109, 6-person self-catering bungalow US$211; ⓡ) Spread out on tranquil green grounds bordering the beach at the eastern edge of town, the good Palmeiras has accommodation in very nice whitewashed stone-and-thatch cottages, or in a more rustic eight-person self-catering block. There's no restaurant but the chalets include continental breakfast.

Vilanculos Beach Lodge (☎ 293-82388; www .vilanculos.co.za; s/d from US$117/203; ⓟ ⓡ) A large, busy resort-style place about 1km north of Aguia Negra Lodge, with accommodation in chalets – each with verandas – set back from the water on a hillside, plus a restaurant and a range of water sports.

Blue Waters Beach Resort (www.vilanculosresorts .com/bluewaters; camping per person US$9, d bungalow US$47, 4-person chalet US$133) About 8km south of town past the airport and signposted from the main road into town, with large grounds and good camping, simple double bungalows, self-catering chalets and a beachfront bar and restaurant. You'll need your own transport.

TOP END

Casa Rex (☎ 293-82048; www.casa-rex.com; s/d from US$95/150; ⓡ) This is the place to go if you're after a small, upmarket getaway. It sits in peaceful, manicured grounds about 500m north of the old Dona Ana Hotel, with comfortable rooms – ranging from garden to premium to luxury suites – in terracotta cottages with mosquito netting, plus delicious home-cooked cuisine.

Vila la Mar (☎ 293-82302; vilalamar@teledata.mz; 6-/10-person houses US$250/280) This good-value self-catering place has spacious, fully furnished chalets – most with sea views, and all with

spotless, modern kitchens, fans, netting and attractive décor. It's between Aguia Negra and Vilanculos Beach Lodge.

Complexo Xinhicuane (☎ 293-82450; r per person US$130-150; ⓧ) A new place up the road from Casa Rex on the inland side and just about to open when we passed through. It has a large garden, plush and tastefully appointed rooms and attractive common areas with carved wood décor. A pool and a restaurant are planned.

Casa Guci (☎ 82-868 6540; www.casaguci.com; s/d US$116/172; ⓡ) Another new and very nice place about 7km south of town overlooking the water, and signposted from the main road into town. It has modern, well-equipped two- and four-person self-catering chalets set around large, green grounds. Self-catering rates are also available.

Eating

Complexo Âncora Seafood Restaurant/NY Pizza (☎ 293-82444; pizzas & meals US$4-10; ⓨ 7am-10pm Wed-Mon) This place on the waterfront by the port is a piece of Americana in the middle of Mozambique, with large meals, apple pie for dessert plus a breezy waterside eating area. Everything's halal (no alcohol) and they have a free takeaway/delivery service.

Samara (☎ 293-82068; meals US$9-14; ⓨ lunch & dinner Tue-Sun) A cosy waterfront eatery tucked away about 200m off the main road on the beach, north of Casa Rex. Specialities include seafood platters, prawns and crayfish.

Most listings under Sleeping also have good restaurants, especially the restaurant at **Casa Rex** (☎ 293-82048; meals from US$12), with seafood and gourmet fare (advance bookings only); **Smugglers Sports Bar** (☎ 293-82253; www.smugglers.co.za; meals from US$3), with good breakfasts and hearty pub fare, and volleyball out front; **Restaurante Monica** (☎ 293-82429; meals US$2.50-US$6), at Na Sombra, featuring tasty local cuisine and **Aguia Negra** (☎ 293-82387; meals US$5-US$7).

For self-catering, there are fruits and vegetables at the market and, in the afternoons, fresh seafood which you can usually arrange to get grilled up at your hotel. Also try **SEA Supermarket** (ⓨ 9am-1pm & 3pm-7pm Mon-Fri, 9am-2pm Sat) near the market and **Taurus** (☎ 293-82326), diagonally opposite BIM, with South African imports, meats and cheeses, plus soft serve ice cream.

Other recommendations:

Bar Ti'Zé (meals from US$1) A small local eatery on the main road near the bus stand, with fresh, inexpensive meals.

Bar Moçambicano (snacks US$1; ⏱ 8am-5pm Mon-Fri) Just down from the market, with cheap snacks and burgers, and a bakery (also open Saturday) next door.

Entertainment

There's sports TV at **Smugglers Sports Bar** (☎ 293-82253; www.smugglers.co.za). Casa de Cultura, just down from the market, is the best contact for special events and traditional music.

Getting There & Away

AIR

If your budget permits, it's worth flying at least one-way into Vilankulo to see the incredible panorama of the Archipélago de Bazaruto from the air (assuming your pilot does a fly-over route, and the weather is clear) – seas in brilliant hues of turquoise and jade laced with shimmering white sand banks.

LAM, with a representative at the airport, flies four times weekly to/from Maputo (US$216 one way), with links three times weekly to/from Chimoio and weekly to/from Beira. **Pelican Air** (☎ 293-82348, 293-82149, in South Africa 011-973 3649; www.pelicanair.co.za; Airport), trading in Mozambique as TTA, has daily flights between Johannesburg and Vilankulo (US$266 one-way), with onward connections to Bazaruto and Benguera islands (about US$312 one-way from Johannesburg to the islands). There are also twice-weekly links from Kruger Mpumalanga International Airport (near Nelspruit) to Vilankulo (though no connections on this stretch in the opposite direction). **Swazi Express** (☎ in Swaziland 518-6840; www.flyswazi .com; Airport) has three flights weekly connecting Vilankulo with Durban (from US$148 one-way) and Swaziland's Matsapha Airport (from US$89 one-way).

The airport is about 3km from town. There are no taxis, so you'll need to arrange a lift with a hotel, or hitch (usually easy).

BUS

Vilankulo is 20km east of the EN1 down a tarmac access road, with the turnoff at Pambara junction. Chapas run regularly between the two throughout the day (US$0.80). Except as noted, all transport departs from the main road just down from Padaria Bento.

To Maputo (US$16, nine to 10 hours), there are two to three buses daily, departing town by about 4.30am – get to the stand by 4.15am, and you should find something. If you're staying in the Mukoke section of town, it's more convenient to board the bus at Pataquina (down the small street opposite BIM Expresso); the first bus of the day (an express) usually departs from here between 3am and 3.30am, before stopping at the main stand near Padaria Bento. Pass by Pataquina in the late afternoon the day before to get an update from the driver. Wherever you board, arrive early if you're choosy about your seat, as there's no advance booking.

Coming from Maputo, aim to be in Junta by about 4.30am. One of the better lines is Xiluva, departing Junta about 5am. The fastest option (unless they break down – not infrequent) is the Panthera Azul bus to Beira, which will drop you at Pambara junction at about 2pm, from where it's easy to catch a chapa into town.

To Beira (US$12, nine hours), 30-seater buses depart Vilankulo at 4.30am. Unlike the Maputo buses, you should book the afternoon before (which also means you can choose a seat).

To Chimoio, there's a daily 30-seater bus departing Vilankulo at 4am (US$14, 8½ to nine hours). Otherwise, you'll need to go via Inchope or Beira.

To Maxixe (for Inhambane), minibuses run throughout the day (US$6, four hours).

To Inhassoro (US$2, 45 minutes), chapas depart throughout the morning from opposite SEA supermarket.

Getting Around

Vilankulo is very spread out and there are no taxis, but lifts are easy to find. Occasional chapas run along the main road, but not out to the beach places on the northeastern edge of town.

ARCHIPÉLAGO DE BAZARUTO

Rising out of the sea 10km to 25km offshore between Vilankulo and Inhassoro is the spectacular Archipélago de Bazaruto. It's about as close to a tropical paradise as you'll find (except for the Quirimbas islands further north, see p158), and is one of Mozambique's highlights, especially for honeymooners or anyone wanting a relaxing getaway. Among its attractions: clear, turquoise waters; tranquil, white-sand beaches; a plethora of colourful birds; and rewarding diving and snorkelling.

The archipelago consists of five main islands: Bazaruto, Benguera (also spelled

ARCHIPÉLAGO DE BAZARUTO

0 ————— 14 km
0 ————— 8 miles

Inhassoro

Ilha de Bazaruto
Park Headquarters

Sitone

Ilha de Santa Carolina

Baía de Bazaruto

Ilha de Benguerra

Mozambique Channel

To EN1 (5km);
Inhassoro (75km);
Maxixe (230km);
Maputo (690km)

PARQUE NACIONAL DE BAZARUTO

Ilha de Magaruque

Vilankulo

Ilha de Bangué

Ponta São Sebastião

SLEEPING 🏠 ⛺
Bazaruto Lodge...................1 B1
Benguerra Lodge................2 B3
Dugong Beach Lodge.........3 B4
Indigo Bay.........................4 B2
Linene Island Resort...........5 B4
Marlin Lodge......................6 B3
Ponta Dundo Camp............7 B2

Benguerra, and formerly known as Santo António), Magaruque (Santa Isabel), Santa Carolina (Ilha do Paraíso) and tiny Bangué. Until about 10,000 years ago – relatively recent in geological terms – the larger islands were connected to the mainland at Ponta São Sebastião (see p102). The small population of Nile crocodiles that laze in the sun in remote corners of both Bazaruto and Benguera islands is evidence of this earlier link.

Since 1971 much of the archipelago has been protected as a **national park** (per adult/child US$8/2) under the auspices of the WWF (Worldwide Fund for Nature). In late 2002 the park boundaries were extended southwards to encompass all of the islands, bringing the area under protection to about 1400 sq km.

Thanks to this protected status, and to the archipelago's relative isolation from the ravages of war on the mainland, nature bursts forth here in full force. You'll see dozens of bird species, including soaring fish eagles and graceful pink flamingos. There are also red duikers, bushbucks, and, especially on Benguera, the Nile crocodiles. Dolphins swim through the clear waters, along with 2000 other types of fish, plus loggerhead, leatherback and green turtles. Most impressive, perhaps, are the elusive dugongs (see p38), who spend their days foraging among sea-grass meadows around the archipelago. As a backdrop to all this are excellently preserved coral formations, with up to 100 species of hard coral and over two dozen soft coral species identified thus far.

Living amidst all the natural beauty are about 3500 Mozambicans who call the archipelago home.

History

Although many of the island residents are relatively recent arrivals who sought haven during the war years, the archipelago's history reaches well back. The islands – which previously were known as the Hucicas or Vacicas – were long famed for their pearls and ambergris. By at least the 15th century, they were the site of a thriving maritime community sustained by the coastal dhow trade. The earliest Portuguese trading settlements dated from the mid-16th century, while the first permanent Portuguese settlement was established on Santa Carolina in the mid-19th century. Today, all of the islands are inhabited except Bangué.

At various times leading up to the colonial period, several of the islands – most notably Santa Carolina – served as penal colonies not only for Vilankulo, but for the entire region, including places as distant as present-day Beira. According to local lore, the variety of ethnic groups necessitated development of a common language, which led to growth of a unique dialect now considered indigenous to the southern part of the archipelago. Although this dialect has largely been replaced by Xitswa (one of the major languages of Inhambane province) and Portuguese, it's still spoken by some older inhabitants.

Information

Entry fees should be paid in advance at the WWF office in Vilankulo, unless your hotel has taken care of doing this for you (all the island-based hotels do so, as does Sail Away in Vilankulo, for those on its dhow safaris). Park headquarters are located at Sitone, on the western side of Ilha de Bazaruto. While fees for diving, walking and other activities within the archipelago have been approved in principle, they aren't currently being enforced.

If you're with your own boat, you'll also need to arrange the necessary licences and boat permits at the WWF office.

Activities
DIVING
Diving is wonderful here – see p43 for general information. Dives, equipment rental and certification courses can be organised by any of the top-end lodges, or by the Vilankulo-based dive operators listed on p97.

FISHING
Game fishing – including for sailfish, tuna, barracuda and black, blue and striped marlin – is also excellent (and is all tag-and-release), and can be arranged by all of the lodges.

SAILING & DHOW SAFARIS
Away from the lodges, the best contact for arranging sailing trips around the archipelago is Sail Away (p97). The closest islands for day trips from Vilankulo are Magaruque (12km offshore) and Benguera (15km).

Sleeping & Eating
All tourist facilities are on the western side of the islands where waters are calmer, currents less strong and sunset views superb.

All hotels and lodges are top end, and all require advance bookings through their head office or through a tour operator, although if you turn up at Vilankulo or Inhassoro and talk to a boat owner with a radio link to the islands you can often arrange something on the spot. For years, the only concession on the archipelago to budget travellers was Gabriel's Camp on Ilha de Benguera, which is currently closed for upgrading to a luxury hotel. Fortunately, a new community-run camp, Ponto Dundo, is being built to fill the gap and should be open by the time this book is published. Otherwise, the best options if you have limited purse strings are arranging an island dhow cruise, or visiting in the off-season, when some of the lodges offer special deals.

ILHA DE BAZARUTO
Ponta Dundo Camp (camping per person US$15) This soon-to-open place – the only budget accommodation in the archipelago – is on the southern point of Bazaruto island. It's run by the local community in partnership with the national park, and plans to offer accommodation in permanent two-person tents. Bring your own food and drink (there will be a kitchen area), and get an update in Vilankulo before heading over.

Bazaruto Lodge (☎ 21-305000; reservas@pestana .co.mz; s/d with full board from US$225/365; ⊠) This unpretentious four-star getaway sits at the northwestern end of the island in a prime location overlooking a small and placid bay, and Ilha de Santa Carolina in the distance. Accommodation is in 24 A-frame chalets nestled amidst lush gardens beneath the sand dunes. All have been recently renovated, some have sea views and the lodge offers good overall value. There's also a honeymoon suite and two family-style chalets, plus a restaurant and water sports. The lodge is under the same management as Hotel Pestana Rovuma in Maputo and Pestana Inhaca Lodge on Ilha de Inhaca, and combination itineraries can be arranged. A new five-star property under the same management is planned for the northern end of the island; check with Pestana's Maputo offices for an update.

Indigo Bay (☎ 293-82340, in South Africa 011-465 6904; www.indigobayonline.com; s/d US$365/540) Under the same ownership as Pemba Beach Resort Hotel, Indigo Bay is the largest and most outfitted lodge in the archipelago. You have your choice of private beachfront chalets or rooms that are set back on the lawn overlooking the water – all well appointed with telephones, televisions and other amenities to remind you that there's life beyond the palm trees waving just outside. There's also a full range of activities including horseback riding in the surf, guided birding walks and water sports. While it lacks the laid-back island touch of most of the other places (expansions and more activities are planned), for some visitors this will be compensated for by the high level of comfort, service and amenities.

ILHA DE BENGUERA
Benguerra Lodge (☎ in South Africa 011-452 0641; www .benguerra.co.za; s/d with full board from US$534/790; ⊠) Generally considered to be one of the best and most intimate of the island lodges, with

accommodation in 11 well-spaced and spacious luxury chalets set near a good beach amidst patches of forest. It's in the centre of the island's western coastline, and offers dhow cruises, diving, snorkelling, fishing and guided birding walks. There are also two beachside honeymoon suites, each with their own plunge pool, and a private honeymoon villa set off on its own.

Marlin Lodge (☎ in South Africa 012-543 2134; www .marlinlodge.co.za; s/d with full board from US$320/430) Several kilometres south of Benguerra Lodge, and with a somewhat more bustling ambience, Marlin Lodge has accommodation in 19 pleasant reed and thatch chalets along the beach, all with hammocks, verandas and pleasing wood tones, plus a handful of spacious luxury suites. Also on offer is a range of activities, including fishing (marlin is probably the best choice on the islands for anglers), diving, water sports and dhow cruises.

ILHA DE MAGARUQUE
The hotel on Magaruque – founded by tycoon-entrepreneur Joaquim Alves in colonial days, and long a favoured haunt of the rich and famous – is undergoing renovation and not yet open. For now, the small island is ideal if you fancy walking around a small patch of tropical sand; it can be circled in a few hours, but bring plenty of shade or sunscreen. There's also good snorkelling in the crystal clear shallows just off the idyllic beach on the island's southwestern corner.

ILHA DE SANTA CAROLINA
The prettiest of the islands, with stands of palm and other vegetation, Santa Carolina was formerly the site of another Joaquim Alves property. Today, the old hotel is closed and crumbling, although renovation is planned. Meanwhile, several **rooms** (☎ 82-320 9970; per person US$35) in an annex have been maintained for visitors, and offer surprisingly pleasant accommodation, with nets, clean linens and fresh towels, plus wonderful views over the water. There are no facilities otherwise and you'll need to bring your own food. For diversion, snorkelling is the highlight – Santa Carolina's waters offer among the best snorkelling in the archipelago, and it is possible just offshore. Sail Away in Vilankulo (see p97) has two-night, three-day dhow safaris to Santa Carolina for US$234 per person all-inclusive.

THIEVES' ISLAND

Between Vilankulo and Ilha de Benguera is a large sandbar, visible only at low tide. According to local lore, it used to be known as 'Ilha dos Ladrões' ('Thieves' Island'), and lawbreakers were brought here and left to drown when the tides came in. Now, it's called 'Meu Sócio' ('My Partner' or 'My Helper') by sailors, who know it as a place of refuge if their dhow starts to sink.

Getting There & Away
AIR
There are airstrips on Bazaruto, Benguera, Magaruque and Santa Carolina, though only the ones on Bazaruto and Benguera are regularly used. All of the top-end lodges offer fly-in packages from Johannesburg. Pelican Air has scheduled flights between Johannesburg or Nelspruit and Vilankulo, with connections on to the islands; see p99.

BOAT
All the top-end lodges can arrange speedboat transfers for their guests if you prefer not to go by plane. For day-trippers, speedboat charter from Vilankulo costs between US$100 and US$200 return, depending on the island. Good contacts include Vilankulo dive operators and Big Blue Adventures (p97). For a speedboat transfer between Inhassoro and Ilha de Santa Carolina (about 30 minutes), expect to pay from US$100 return.

Alternatively, you can reach the islands by dhow from Vilankulo, best arranged through Sail Away (p97). There are also numerous freelancers who will offer to take you over. While some are reliable, others may quote tempting prices, and then ask you to 'renegotiate' things once you're well away from shore. Check with tourist information or with your hotel for recommendations; expect to pay from about US$60 per boat for a day sail and don't pay until you're safely back on land.

For nonmotorised dhows, allow plenty of extra time to account for wind and water conditions; from Vilankulo to Benguera or Magaruque takes two to six hours.

PENINSULA DE SÃO SEBASTIÃO
This isolated promontory just south of the Archipélago de Bazaruto is now part of the Vilanculos Coastal Wildlife Sanctuary – a private

and somewhat controversial conservation and tourism initiative that's meant to combine the allure of wildlife safaris (once the now-stalled wildlife restocking plans are completed) and the languor of a tropical beachside getaway into one grand package (see www.thesanctuary .co.za). It's dotted with small lakes, lagoons and stands of mangrove and surrounded by the same turquoise waters that lap the islands of the archipelago, and is worth considering if you're interested in birding or just breaking away from it all. While there are small populations of bushbuck, duiker and other small animals, the main attractions are the flamingos and other water birds, and the tranquillity.

Set on the western side of São Sebastião peninsula is the exclusive **Dugong Lodge** (☎ in South Africa 011-463 3551; www.dugonglodge.co.za; chalet s/d with full board from US$350/500; ⊠) There are 10 luxurious tented chalets, some right on the beach, and all with shaded verandas and large baths. There's no diving, but snorkelling and deep sea fishing can be organised, as can sea kayaks and excursions to nearby Bangué island, with nothing on it but white sands lapped by turquoise waters, and a few trees.

Linene Island Resort (www.linene-island.com; per person full board from US$133) is a rustic angler's hideaway on the eastern side of the peninsula, with small twin-bedded wooden chalets linked by a raised walkway and a full range of fishing.

Getting There & Away

The sanctuary is reached via air charter (US$60 per person one-way) or speedboat (US$25 per person one-way, 30 minutes) from Vilankulo, arranged with the lodges.

INHASSORO

Inhassoro's proximity to some prime fishing areas in the channel between the mainland and the Archipélago de Bazaruto has made the town a popular destination for anglers.

It's also the last of the southern beaches before the EN1 turns inland and begins the wild journey north. With its unhurried pace and wide stretches of sand, Inhassoro is also a welcome change from the more touristy towns further south.

The best place to stay is **Hotel Seta** (☎ 293-91000/1, 82-302 0990; camping per adult/child US$8/4, chalets US$32-45). A long-standing, straightforward establishment with good camping, it has faded but agreeable white stone-and-thatch cottages and a restaurant. Inhassoro is a convenient jumping-off point for Bazaruto and Santa Carolina islands, and the hotel can help arrange boat transfers.

Getting There & Away

Inhassoro is about 15km east of the main road. Several chapas run daily to/from Vilankulo (US$2, 45 minutes). There are also direct buses to/from Maputo (US$15, 10 hours). To Beira, the best bet is to head out to Macovane (the junction with the EN1) and wait for passing northbound buses from there. Driving northwards, there's a **bridge** (toll US$0.80; ☽ 5am-8pm) over the Rio Save.

BARTOLOMEU DIAS (PONTA MACOVANE)

From Inhassoro, it's possible to continue northwards along a rough and sandy spur road (4WD only) for about 40km (allow two to three hours for the distance) to Bartolomeu Dias, where there's not much but sand, fresh air and sea views. If you can manage to overlook environmental concerns and the official ban against beach driving, the journey takes about 30 minutes following the coast (low tide only).

Once opened, the still-in-progress **BD Lodge** (☎ 84-390 5700, in South Africa 042-243 3552; www.moz adventures.com; 2-/4-person chalets US$94/140) will offer stilted, rustic self-catering chalets, with both sunrise and sunset views over the water, plus a bar-restaurant and fishing charters.

Central Mozambique

In the annals of ancient Africa, central Mozambique – Sofala, Manica, Tete and Zambézia provinces – should get top billing. It was here, at the old port of Sofala, that 15th-century traders from as far away as India and Indonesia gathered in search of vast caches of gold. And it was here that some of the region's most powerful kingdoms arose, including the Karanga (Shona) confederations along the Zimbabwe border and the legendary kingdom of Monomotapa southwest of Tete. It was also in central Mozambique – along the course of the Rio Zambezi – that early explorers and traders first penetrated the vast Mozambican hinterlands. During the 17th and 18th centuries, they set up a series of *feiras* (gold-trading fairs) that reached as far inland as Zumbo on the Zambian border.

Today, the tides have turned: visitors are but a small trickle, and central Mozambique is seldom given more than passing mention in the tourist brochures. Yet, while it lacks the accessible beaches of the south, the region has a few gems that are well worth seeking out. In addition to wildlife watching at Parque Nacional de Gorongosa, these include vibrant traditional cultures, Mozambique's highest peaks and alluring mountain landscapes. The highland terrain is at its most beautiful in western Manica and northwestern Zambézia provinces, where rolling, mist-covered hills stretch into the horizon. Central Mozambique is also a major transit zone, flanked by the Beira corridor, connecting landlocked Zimbabwe with Beira and the sea, and the Tete corridor, linking Zimbabwe and Malawi.

Places in this chapter are described roughly south to north and clockwise, going from Sofala province to Manica, to Tete, and then to Zambézia.

HIGHLIGHTS

- Wander into the wilds at wonderful **Parque Nacional de Gorongosa** (p111)
- Dine on port city Beira's famous **seafood** (p109)
- Marvel at the massive **Barragem de Cahora Bassa** (p121) and go fishing on the lake
- Hike in the hills around **Gurúè** (p128), or scale misty **Monte Namúli** (p128)
- Go birding in the twittering, chirping bird-filled forests south of **Caia** (p123)

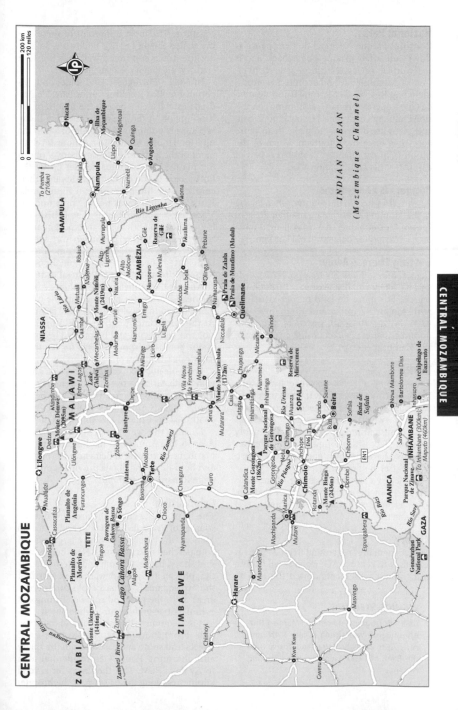

CENTRAL MOZAMBIQUE

National Parks

Beautiful Parque Nacional de Gorongosa is slowly but surely making a comeback, and is well worth a visit if you are in the area; see p111. Central Mozambique's other protected areas – including Reserva de Marromeu and Reserva de Gilé – operate primarily as hunting concessions, although occasional birding groups visit, and plans are underway to make them more accessible for general tourism. Much of the Montes Chimanimani are protected as part of a transfrontier conservation area.

Dangers & Annoyances

As with elsewhere in the country, when hiking in the Montes Chimanimani or other areas of central Mozambique, stick to well-used footpaths to avoid the dangers of old land mines.

Getting There & Away

Central Mozambique is a transport crossroads and it's likely you'll at least pass through the region. For more on land border crossings with Malawi, Zambia and Zimbabwe, see p186. For north–south travellers, the main point of interest is likely to be crossing the Rio Zambezi – see p123.

BEIRA

Beira, capital of Sofala province, is Mozambique's second-largest city. It's also the country's busiest port, and as famed for its seafood as for its tawdry nightlife. Yet, despite a somewhat tarnished image, Beira is a reasonably pleasant place with a compact central area, an addictive harbour-town energy and a short, breezy stretch of coastline.

Beira has a reputation as one of the easiest places in the country to catch malaria, so cover up well in the evenings, and travel with a net.

History

Settlement of the area around Beira dates to at least the 9th century AD, when small fishing and trading settlements dotted the nearby

---

POUNDS STERLING

Unlike Portuguese-dominated Maputo, British influence was strong in late 19th- and early 20th-century Beira, and for a time the Bank of Beira even circulated sterling currency.

---

coastline. The most important of these was the fabled Sofala (p112). Following Sofala's decline, trade continued well into the 19th century, although on a smaller scale.

In 1884 a Portuguese landholder and imperialist named Joaquim Carlos Paiva de Andrada established a base at the mouth of the Rio Púngoè, at the site of present-day Beira, as a supply point for his expeditions into the interior. He also wanted to promote development of the Mozambique Company – one of the many charter companies set up by the Portuguese in their attempts to solidify their control over the Mozambican hinterlands. Paiva de Andrada was not the only one enamoured of Beira's charms. The British also found the area enticing as an export channel from their landlocked inland territories to the sea. Over the next decade, it became a focus of dispute between the two colonial powers before ultimately going to Portugal in 1891.

Andrada, who meanwhile had made Beira the headquarters for his Mozambique Company, began to develop its harbour facilities. At the same time, a railway line to the interior was completed and Beira soon became a major port and export channel for Southern Rhodesia (Zimbabwe).

From the mid-20th century, Rhodesia's links with South Africa increased, cutting into Beira's transport monopoly. Yet, by this time Beira's significance as a port was established and it continued to be one of Mozambique's hubs.

During the war years, Renamo leader Afonso Dhlakama had his headquarters at Marínguè, northwest of Beira near Gorongosa, and both Beira and Sofala province continue to be Renamo strongholds.

Orientation

The heart of the city is the area around the squares of Praça do Município and Praça do Metical (the latter marked by a large metical coin perched on a pedestal). Near here, you'll find shops, banks, telecom and internet facilities, plus an array of sidewalk cafés. North of the two squares is the baixa (old commercial area), with the port and some charming old colonial-style architecture, while about 1km east is Maquinino, the main bus and transport hub. From Praça do Município, tree-lined streets lead south and east through the shady and charming Ponta Gêa residential area to Av das FPLM. This then runs for several kilometres along the ocean past the hospital

BEIRA

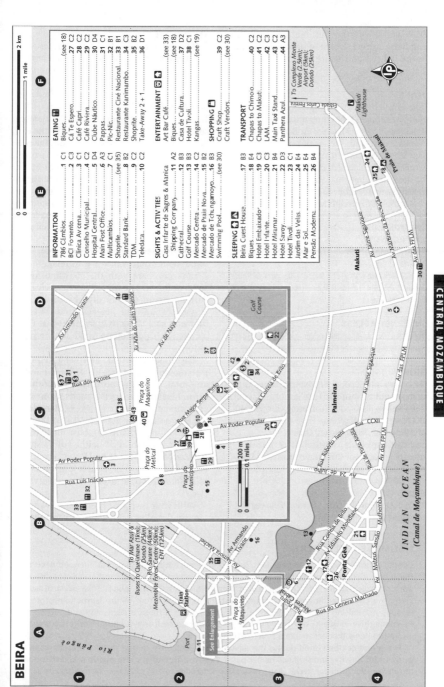

INFORMATION
786 Câmbios..................................1	C1
BCI Fomento.................................2	C3
Clínica Av cena............................3	C1
Conselho Municipal.......................4	C2
Hospital Central............................5	D4
Main Fost Office...........................6	A3
Multicâmbios................................7	C1
Shoprite................................(see 35)	
Standard Bank..............................8	B2
TDM..9	C2
Teleda......................................10	C2

SIGHTS & ACTIV TIES
Casa Irfarte de Sagres & Manica	
Shipping Company.......................11	A2
Cathecral..................................12	B3
Golf Course.................................13	B3
Mercado Centra...........................14	C2
Mercado de Praia Nova..................15	B2
Mercado de Tchungamoyo............16	B3
Swimming Pool......................(see 30)	

SLEEPING
Beira Guest House.......................17	B3
Biques.......................................18	E4
Hotel Embaixador.......................19	C3
Hotel Ifante..............................20	C3
Hotel Miramar............................21	B4
Hotel Savoy...............................22	D3
Hotel Tivoli................................23	C1
Jardim das Velas.........................24	E4
Mar e Sol..................................25	E4
Pensão Moderna........................26	B4

EATING
Biques................................(see 18)	
Cá Te Espero...............................27	C2
Café Capri.................................28	C2
Café Riviera...............................29	C2
Clube Náutico............................30	D4
Pappas......................................31	C1
Pic-Nic.....................................32	B1
Restaurante Ciné Nacional............33	B1
Restaurante Kanimambo...............34	C3
Shoprite...................................35	B2
Take-Away 2 + 1........................36	D1

ENTERTAINMENT
Art Bar Café.........................(see 33)	
Biques................................(see 18)	
Casa de Cultura..........................37	D2
Hotel Tivoli..........................38	C1
Kangas.............................(see 19)	

SHOPPING
Craft Shop.................................39	C2
Craft Verdors.......................(see 30)	

TRANSPORT
Chapas to Chimoio.....................40	C2
Chapas to Makuti........................41	C2
LAM..42	C3
Main Taxi Stand..........................43	C2
Panthera Azul............................44	A3

CENTRAL MOZAMBIQUE

INDIAN OCEAN
(Canal de Moçambique)

Rio Púngoè

to Makuti – another residential area fringing Beira's small stretch of beach. At the end is the old red-and-white Makuti lighthouse, dating to 1904.

MAPS

The excellent *Planta de Endereçamento da Cidade da Beira* and the companion map booklet, *Endereçamento da Cidade da Beira – Guia das Vias* are part of the series of maps put out by Coopération Française in cooperation with the Conselho Municipal. Copies are hard to come by these days, but you can try at the **Gabinete de Endereçamento da Cidade da Beira** (☎ 23-329165; 5 Praça do Município) at Conselho Municipal.

Information

EMERGENCY

Central Hospital (☎ 23-312073/4; Av das FPLM) Malaria testing.
Clínica Avicena (☎ 23-327990, 84-302 1520; Av Poder Popular; ☒ 24hr) For medical emergencies. Just north of Praça do Metical.

INTERNET ACCESS

Teledata (Rua de Moçambique; per hr US$2; ☒ 7.30am-7pm) Diagonally opposite the telecom office.

MONEY

There are numerous ATMs, including at the airport and at Shoprite (Av Samora Machel).
786 Câmbios (Rua Machado dos Santos) Changes cash.
BCI Fomento (Rua Major Serpa Pinto) ATM; opposite LAM.
Multicambios (Rua dos Açores) Changes cash.
Standard Bank (Praça do Metical) ATM; also rather reluctantly changes travellers cheques (minimum US$35 per transaction, original purchase receipts required).

POST

Main post office (Rua Correia de Brito) Northwest of the cathedral.

TELEPHONE

TDM (Telecomunicações de Moçambique; Rua Companhia de Moçambique; ☒ 7am-10pm) Domestic and international telephone calls. North of Praça do Município; look for the green and white building.

Sights & Activities

Beira's spired **cathedral** (Av Eduardo Mondlane), southeast of the centre, was built in the early 20th century with stones taken from the ruins of San Caetano fort in Sofala. Also worth a look are the surrounding **Ponta Gêa** area, with some charming old houses; **Praça do Metical**; and the area around the port, where the streets are lined with faded colonial-era buildings. One to watch for is the restored **Casa Infante de Sagres**, now the offices of Manica Shipping Company.

Praia de Makuti (Makuti Beach; Av das FPLM) is one of the better places in town to relax, though it can't compare with the coastline further south or north. The water is moderately clean, currents strong (ask locally where swimming is possible) and the breezes good. There's a **swimming pool** (Av das FPLM; per day US$4) at Clube Náutico and a **golf course** in the southern part of town.

The chaotic **Mercado de Tchungamoyo** (Tchungamoyo Market; Av Armando Tivane), known locally as 'Goto', is in the northeastern corner of town. It's full of imported goods, contraband and some unsavoury characters. **Mercado Central** (Central Market; Rua Correia de Brito) in the town centre is quieter, and the best place to buy fruit and vegetables. If neither of these suit, try **Mercado de Praia Nova** (Praia Nova Market), west of Praça do Município, with piles of fresh seafood, and just about everything else.

With your own transport, Rio Savane (see opposite) makes a fine day or overnight trip.

MEZIMBITE FOREST CENTRE

Central Mozambique's forests have long been plundered, but there's finally some good news on the scene. If you have extra time and are interested in learning about local sustainable development projects, take a few hours to visit Mezimbite Forest Centre, about 50km west of Beira along the EN6. In addition to promoting sustainable conservation of the surrounding forests through maximising the forests' benefits to local residents, it trains artisans and craftpersons to be competitive in quality at the highest levels, producing exclusive furniture designs, jewellery and other items that are marketed internationally.

The centre can be visited during the daytime (and preferably during the dry season, when it buzzes with activity) and staff will be happy to show you around. It's also possible to order some of their products online (www.allanschwarz.com/bracelet.php).

Sleeping

While Beira doesn't distinguish itself with accommodation options, it has enough of a choice to satisfy most tastes and there are a few nice, new places.

BUDGET

Biques (☎ 23-313051; Praia de Makuti; camping per person US$3.50; P) Set on a breezy rise overlooking Praia de Makuti, this camping ground has seen better days, and doesn't receive too many travellers these days. Security isn't what it once was, nor are the ablutions. However, the bar (with satellite TV) and restaurant are popular and it's a good spot for watching the sunset. Take any chapa towards Makuti and ask them to drop you at the turnoff, from where it's about 400m further on foot. Taxis from town cost about US$3.

Hotel Savoy (☎ 23-329302; cnr Ruas Major Serpa Pinto & Pedro Amilcar Cabral; s/tw US$8/16, d with bathroom US$22) In an ageing grey high rise near Hotel Embaixador and worth a look if you're on a shoestring but don't want to camp at Biques. The rooms are mediocre but the central location is convenient.

Hotel Miramar (☎ 23-322283; Rua Vilas Boas Truão; s/tw/d US$14/16/20; ✷) The Miramar is another faded classic, with no-frills rooms – some with private bathroom – near the water (no beach), but inconvenient to the rest of town and not optimal for solo women travellers. There's no food.

Pensão Moderna (☎ 23-329901; Rua Alferes da Silva; d/tr US$24/31, d with bathroom & air-con US$34; ✷) This is one of the better budget choices. Rooms – most with fan and shared bathroom – are faded but adequate, there's a patio out front and meals can be arranged. It's two blocks south of the cathedral and opposite the park with an old aeroplane in the centre; all the taxis know it.

Hotel Infante (☎ 23-326603; Rua Jaime Ferreira; s/d with fan US$24/28, with air-con US$26/30; ✷) In a high-rise building near Hotel Embaixador, Hotel Infante has small, clean rooms with bathroom, and a restaurant.

Rio Savane (☎ 23-323555, 82-385 7660; camping per person US$3, 5-person barracas US$6 plus per person US$6, d/q self-catering bungalow US$50/100) If you have your own vehicle and want to escape for a day or two, it's well worth driving out to this rustic place, which is in a serene setting on the Rio Savane, separated from the sea by a narrow peninsula. In addition to camping, there are several rustic *barracas* (food stalls), self-catering chalets and

meals. The nearby wetlands are ideal for birding. Follow the Dondo road past the airport to the right-hand turn-off for Savane. Continue 35km to the estuary, where there's secure parking and a small boat (until 5pm) to take you to the camp site. Transfers from Beira can sometimes be arranged with the camp.

MIDRANGE & TOP END

Beira Guest House (☎ 23-324030; 1311 Av Eduardo Mondlane; r/ste US$75/100; ✷ ▣) This residential style B&B in the Ponta Gêa area has pleasant rooms with minifridge, TV and laundry service. Breakfast is included and there's a cook available for other meals if you bring food. It's near Farmácia Beira.

Jardim das Velas (☎ 23-312209; jardimdasvelas@yahoo.com; 282 Av das FPLM; d/f US$75/85; ✷) We've heard good reports about this new place at the end of Praia de Makuti near the lighthouse. The doubles come with minifridge, mosquito nets and TV and the apartment-style family room has a kitchenette. There are no meals. Look for the peach-coloured place with the red roof.

Hotel Embaixador (☎ 23-323785, 23-329057; cnr Ruas Major Serpa Pinto & Belegard da Silva; s/d US$38/50; ✷ P) A few blocks southeast of Praça do Município, this was once Beira's top hotel. These days, it's rather down at the heel and often empty. But the location is convenient, the rooms spacious (albeit a bit musty) and it's worth a look if your budget doesn't stretch to the Hotel Tivoli.

Hotel Tivoli (☎ 23-320300; h.tivoli-beira@teledata.mz; cnr Av de Bagamoyo & Rua da Madeira; s/d US$83/99; ✷ ▣ P) In a busy area of the baixa, the Tivoli has captured Beira's business market, with small but tidy rooms with TV and amenities, and a sleek restaurant-bar. Buffet breakfast is included in the price.

The old **Mar e Sol** (Av das FPLM, Makuti) was being renovated as a guesthouse and restaurant when we passed through – worth asking around to see if it's been completed.

Eating

Beira's restaurants and cafés are full of faded charm, and the dining scene is where you can experience this old-fashioned port city at its best.

CAFÉS

Café Riviera (Praça do Município; snacks & light meals from US$1.50; ⏰ 7.30am-9pm) This classic, pink Old

World sidewalk café is a wonderful spot to sit with a cup of coffee and *bolo de mandioca* (almond cake) and watch the passing scene, with soft, plump sofas inside and outdoor tables overlooking the beach.

Café Capri (Praça do Município; snacks & light meals from US$1.50; 🕑 6.45am-9pm Mon-Fri, Sat 7am-8.30pm, Sun 8am-8pm) Another Beira classic, just down from Café Riviera, and with good *café espresso*.

RESTAURANTS

Pic-Nic (🕾 23-326518; Rua Costa Serrão; meals from about US$4.50; 🕑 breakfast, lunch & dinner) For years, this place was reputed to be one of the city's best restaurants and while its reputation is somewhat outsized for what you get, portions are large and service reasonable. Dining is in a windowless red-draped interior, with black-suited waiters at your beck and call.

Restaurante Kanimambo (🕾 23-323132; meals US$4-7; 🕑 lunch & dinner Sun-Fri) Behind Hotel Embaixador, with Beira's best Chinese food and a friendly proprietor.

Restaurante Ciné Nacional (Rua Costa Serrão; meals from US$6; 🕑 lunch & dinner Mon-Sat) A dark, windowless place just opposite Pic-Nic in the cinema building and known for its curries (which should be ordered in advance). Portions are small but it's a reliable bet for vegetarians.

Pappas (Rua dos Açores; meals from US$2.50) There are no tables here – you get your meals at the L-shaped bar – but the steak and seafood grills on hot sizzle platters are delicious, and the ambience convivial. It's close to Hotel Tivoli.

Popular waterside hangouts include the restaurant at **Biques** (🕾 23-313051; Praia de Makuti) and **Clube Náutico** (🕾 23-311720; Av das FPLM; meals US$6-11, plus per person entry US$0.40; 🕑 lunch & dinner), a colonial-era swimming and social club, with average food made enjoyable by the beachside setting. On Saturday afternoons, there are all-comers-welcome rugby matches on the sand in front.

Other recommendations:

Cá Te Espero (🕾 82-447 8860, 82-562 6950; Rua Companhia de Moçambique; meals from US$5-12; 🕑 8am-10pm) Portuguese-style seafood and grills in a dark and smoky pub atmosphere.

Take-Away 2 + 1 (Av Artur do Canto Resende; meals from US$2; 🕮) A usually empty takeaway counter, and a tiny restaurant serving a modest selection of inexpensive local fare on plastic checked table cloths. It's just northeast of Praça do Município.

Self-caterers should head to **Shoprite** (cnr Avs Armando Tivane & Samora Machel).

Entertainment

Art Bar Café (Ciné Nacional, Rua Costa Serrão; 🕑 4pm to late Wed-Sat) This promising place in the cinema building was about to open when this text was written. It's run by the same people who used to run one of Beira's best bars (now closed) and will have snacks, drinks and a DJ after 11pm.

Complexo Monte Verde (🕾 23-302341; Estrada Carlos Pereira; entry US$2) Beira's main nightclub is midway between Praia de Makuti and the airport.

Casa de Cultura (🕾 23-327858; Rua Major Serpa Pinto) Opposite Hotel Embaixador, with theatre and dance performances. Information on upcoming programmes is posted by the entrance.

Other bars include Biques (Praia de Makuti), with satellite TV; the smarter Kangas (Hotel Embaixador) and the classy albeit stuffy bar at the Hotel Tivoli.

Shopping

The vendors near Clube Náutico hawk a modest array of woodcarvings and other crafts. Pricier but worth a look is the small **craft shop** (Rua Companhia de Moçambique; 🕑 4pm-6pm Mon-Fri, 8am-6pm Sat) opposite TDM and next to Cá Te Espero.

Getting There & Away

AIR

There are flights on **LAM** (🕾 23-324141/2; 85 Rua Major Serpa Pinto) weekly to/from Johannesburg, daily to/from Maputo, and three to six times weekly to/from Tete, Nampula, Quelimane, Pemba, Vilankulo and Lichinga. The LAM office is opposite Hotel Embaixador. **Air Corridor** (🕾 23-302222/3; Airport) stops at Beira on its daily run up and down the coast. **SAAirlink** (🕾 23-301569/70; www.saairlink.co.za; Airport) flies three times weekly between Beira and Johannesburg.

BUS & CHAPA

Beira's main transport stand is at Praça do Maquinino. There's no real order to things – you'll need to ask locals where to go for buses to your destination.

To Maputo, **Panthera Azul** (🕾 23-325042, 82-394 4551; www.pantherazul.com; 43 Av Mouzinho de Albuquerque, Complexo SNJ) goes weekly (US$44, 17 to 18 hours), departing at 5am on Thursday from the Panthera Azul office at Prédio Grelha, at the southwestern end of Av Samora Machel. Otherwise, there's usually an 'express' bus (US$30, 18 hours) and/or one regular bus daily (US$24), both departing by about 4.30am from Maquinino; buy tickets the day before. Coming from Maputo, the express bus departs Junta by about 5am, and the normal buses – which overnight at the Rio Save bridge – between about 6am and 7.30am. If you get stuck at the bridge, it's best to sleep in the bus.

To Vilankulo (US$12, nine hours, 470km), there's a direct bus daily departing Maquinino by about 5am. Otherwise, get any southbound bus to drop you at Pambara, the junction town on the EN1, from where chapas regularly ply the final 20km to Vilankulo.

To Chimoio (US$5, three hours, 200km) and Machipanda (US$6, four hours), there are minibuses throughout the day from Praça do Maquinino.

To Tete (US$16, 10 hours, 600km), there are direct buses at least several times weekly, but it's best to go first to Chimoio and get transport there. This will mean overnighting in Chimoio since transport from there to Tete leaves in the morning.

To Quelimane (US$16.50, nine hours), buses depart from Mar Azul in Pioneiros bairro, about 1km north of the centre, and go via the new tarmac road running west of Gorongosa park to Caia.

Another option, for any northbound or southbound transport, is to head out to Inchope, 130km west of Beira, where the EN6 joins the EN1, and try your luck with passing buses there, though they are often full and waits are long. Inchope is the epitome of a scruffy junction town, with no accommodation except a few unappealing *pensões*. Chapas run between Beira and Inchope throughout the day (US$2, two hours).

TRAIN
Passenger services to Zimbabwe have been indefinitely suspended. You'll need to take road transport over the border into Zimbabwe, where you can continue by rail to Harare.

Getting Around
TO/FROM THE AIRPORT
The airport is about 7km northwest of town (US$8 in a taxi).

BUS & CHAPA
Chapas to Makuti (US$0.30) depart from Maquinino, with some also leaving from Rua Major Serpa Pinto near Hotel Embaixador.

CAR
Rental agencies include **Imperial** (☎ 23-302650/1; www.imperial.co.za) and **Avis** (☎ 23-301263, 82-502 5360; avis.beira@teledata.mz), both at the airport.

TAXI
The main taxi stand is at the western edge of Praça do Maquinino. Taxis don't cruise for business, and companies come and go, so ask your hotel for the updated numbers.

AROUND BEIRA
Parque Nacional de Gorongosa
About 170km northwest of Beira is **Parque Nacional de Gorongosa** (Gorongosa National Park; www .gorongosa.net; adult/child/vehicle US$8/2/8; ⌫ closed 1 Dec-1 Apr), which was gazetted in 1960 and soon made headlines as one of Southern Africa's premier wildlife parks. It was renowned for its large prides of lions, as well as for its elephants, hippos, buffaloes and rhinos. During the 1980s and early 1990s, hungry soldiers and poachers brought an end to this abundance. Because Renamo headquarters were nearby, the surrounding area was heavily mined and the park's infrastructure was destroyed. Rehabilitation work began in 1995, and in 1998 Gorongosa reopened to visitors. In recent years, the park has received a major boost thanks to assistance from the US-based Carr Foundation, which has joined hands with the Government of Mozambique to fund Gorongosa's longterm restoration and ecotourism development.

While animal numbers still pale in comparison with those of the park's heyday, wildlife is making a definite comeback and the park is well worth a visit if you are in the area. It's likely that you will see impalas, waterbucks, oribis, kudus, warthogs, hippos, elephants and – with luck – even a lion or two. A wildlife sanctuary has been created in the park, where restocking of zebras, buffaloes, wildebeests and other animals has begun. Meanwhile, a major attraction is the birdlife, with over 300 species, including many endemics and near-endemics, and an abundance of water birds in the wetland areas to the east around the Rio Urema.

Also alluring is the park's unique mixture of ecological zones. Within its 5370 sq km it encompasses the southernmost part of the Great Rift system, the hulking Gorongosa massif, expanses of coastal plain and the Zambezi valley, and is considered to be the most biologically diverse of all Mozambique's conservation areas.

Since Gorongosa's reopening, infrastructure has been being gradually upgraded, with many more improvements planned for the near future. Check the enticing website (www .gorongosa.net) for updates.

Park headquarters (☎ 23-535012, 23-535003; travel@ gorongosa.net) are in Chitengo, about 15km east of the entry gate, from where rough tracks branch out to other park areas. Vehicle rental and guides for wildlife drives (including night drives) can be arranged at park headquarters, and walking safaris will be starting soon. Many areas of the park are inaccessible during the rainy season. Note that park entry fees are payable in meticais only.

SLEEPING

There is a **camp site** (camping per person US$4) with ablution blocks and hot water at park headquarters, and six plain but pleasant **rondavels** (s/d US$26/38) with bathrooms and nets, and more rondavels coming soon. Bookings should be made through park headquarters. There's also a reasonably priced restaurant serving good local-style meals, and braai facilities for self-caterers. Luxury bungalows are planned for Chitengo in the near future, as is a new restaurant. Also coming imminently is a new camping ground, plus a travellers dorm.

GETTING THERE & AWAY

Gorongosa has an airstrip for charter flights.

By road, the turn-off for Gorongosa from the main Beira–Chimoio road is at Inchope, about 130km west of Beira. From Inchope, it's another 43km along excellent tarmac to Nota village and the park access road, and from there, 17km east along an all-weather gravel road to the park gate. Once at the gate, it's about 15km further to the Chitengo headquarters, where you pay your fees. You can easily reach the park entrance with 2WD, but for exploring, you'll need 4WD. Pick-ups from Chimoio and Beira can be arranged with the park. Via public transport, take any transport heading north from Inchope to Gorongosa town ('Vila Gorongosa'). The park plans to open an information office here in the near future, from where reasonably priced pick-ups can be arranged to the park or to Monte Gorongosa (see following). Pink Papaya Backpackers in Chimoio (see p116) organises all inclusive overnight trips to Gorongosa Park for between US$50 and US$100 per person, depending on group size.

Monte Gorongosa

Outside the park boundaries to the northwest is **Monte Gorongosa** (Mt Gorongosa, 1863m), Mozambique's fourth-highest mountain. Steeped in local lore, it's known for its rich plant and birdlife and its abundance of lovely waterfalls. The mountain's slopes are the only place in Southern Africa to see the green-headed oriole, and one of just a handful of places where you can see the dappled mountain robin and Swynnerton's forest robin.

SOFALA

About 40km south of Beira and just south of the Rio Búzi is the site of the ancient gold-trading port of **Sofala**, dating from at least the 9th century AD. Sofala's importance lay in its role as the major link between the gold trade of the interior and the powerful sultanate at Kilwa in present-day Tanzania. By the 15th century, it had become one of East Africa's most influential centres, with ties as far away as Madagascar, India and even Indonesia. San Caetano, the first Portuguese fort in Mozambique, was built at Sofala in 1505 with stones shipped from Portugal. However, soon after the Portuguese arrived, trade routes shifted northwards, Ilha de Moçambique eclipsed Sofala as the main coastal base and Sofala and its fort rapidly sunk into oblivion. Today nothing remains of Sofala's former glory. The ruins of the fort (which lay a few kilometres outside present-day Sofala) have been completely overtaken by the sea.

There is no tourist infrastructure at Sofala and unless you're an avid history buff, it's difficult to think of a persuasive reason to visit. To get here from Beira by public transport, take any bus heading along the EN6 towards Chimoio and get off at Tica, from where there is sporadic public transport south to Búzi along a rough road that's slated for rehabilitation. If you are approaching by road from the EN1, the turn-off is at Chiboma; ask locally about conditions from Chiboma to the coast. Alternatively, there's a daily ferry for US$4 from Beira, which stops at various points along the coast, including the small modern-day port of Sofala.

Monte Gorongosa is considered sacred, but it's possible to climb to its upper slopes with a local guide. The Carr Foundation, which is financing the rehabilitation of Gorongosa park, is also supporting a community-based ecotourism and reforestation project on the mountain, centred around hiking trails and birding, with a focus on conserving the mountain ecosystems that are essential for maintaining wildlife populations in the park. The project, which aims to give local communities alternative sources of livelihood other than slash-and-burn agriculture, is still in the early stages, but once going, it will encompass all tourism and hiking on the mountain. A base camp for hikers and birders is being set up near the beautiful Morumbodzi Falls, which are on the mountain's western side at about 950m. From the camp, there are paths to the falls (about one hour's easy walk away), birding walks and overnight climbs to the summit (about six hours one-way). A booking office and information centre for the mountain and park is planned for Gorongosa town, where guides and porters can also be arranged. Meanwhile, to organise hikes contact park headquarters at travel@gorongosa.net. All fees (to be determined soon – watch the park website for details) will go to the local communities.

According to tradition, no red can be worn when climbing the mountain and the climb must be undertaken barefoot, though this latter requirement seems to be conveniently waived these days. This is just as well: the mountain receives about 2000mm of rain a year, and its wet, humid conditions, combined with the steepness of the path on the upper reaches, make the going slippery approaching the summit. Good shoes and a reasonable degree of fitness are essential.

To get to the Morumbodzi base camp area, follow the EN6 from Beira to the turn-off at Inchope. Continue north along the tarmac road, passing the turnoff for Gorongosa park and continuing another 25km or so further to Gorongosa town. About 10km beyond Gorongosa town, turn off the main highway to the right, and continue 10km along an unpaved track to the base camp. Once the booking and information office in Gorongosa town is open (reachable via public transport from Inchope), transfers will be available from there to the base camp.

CHIMOIO

Chimoio is the capital of Manica province, and Mozambique's fifth-largest town. While its tourist attractions are decidedly modest, it's a pleasant place with an agreeable climate and worth a stop if you're in the area. It's also the jumping-off point for exploring the Montes Chimanimani (Chimanimani Mountains) to the southwest.

About 5km northeast of town is **Cabeça do Velho**, a large rock that resembles the face of an old man at rest. To get here, take Rua do Bárue past Magarafa market and continue along the dirt road; you'll see the rock ahead of you in the distance. Once at the base, you can climb up in about 10 minutes to enjoy some views. As with all mountains and high places in Mozambique, there are legends and traditions associated with this one and locals may still offer a prayer to the spirits once at the top.

Information

The moneychangers loitering around the bus stand should be avoided.

BIM (Av 25 de Setembro) ATM.

Shoprite (EN6) ATM.

Standard Bank (cnr Av 25 de Setembro & Rua Patrice Lumumba) ATM.

TDM (cnr Ruas do Bárue & Patrice Lumumba) International calls.

TDM (Shoprite; per 30 min US$1.20; ⊗ 9am-8pm Mon-Sat, 9am-3pm Sun) Internet access.

Teledata (cnr Av 25 de Setembro & Rua Mossurize; per min US$0.04; ⊗ 8.30am-6pm Mon-Fri, 9am-2pm Sat) Internet access.

Sleeping

BUDGET

Pink Papaya (☎ 82-555 7310, 82-237 2980; http://pink papaya.atspace.com; cnr Ruas Pigivide & 3 de Fevereiro; camping per person US$4, dm/d US$8/24) A welcoming and popular backpackers and the best budget option, with camping, dorm beds and doubles, and a kitchen and braai area. The owner can sort you out with horse riding and excursions in the area (including to Parque Nacional de Gorongosa), plus visits up to Pink Papaya Forest Retreat (p116).

Residencial Flôr de Vouga (☎ 251-22469; cnr Av 25 de Setembro & Rua Dr Araújo de la Cerda; s/d US$8/19) Above the old Banco Austral building, this homy place has a handful of no-frills, breezy rooms on the second floor, all with fan and clean shared bathroom, and some with balcony. Breakfast can be arranged for a modest extra cost.

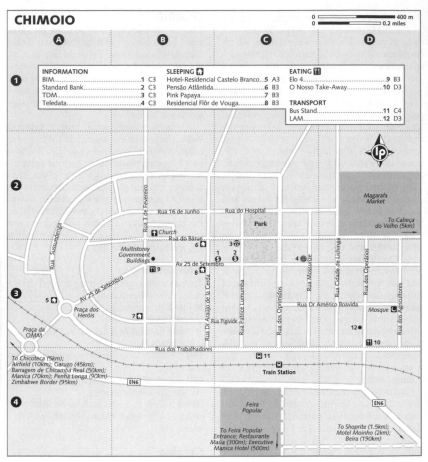

CHIMOIO

INFORMATION		SLEEPING		EATING	
BIM	1 C3	Hotel-Residencial Castelo Branco	5 A3	Elo 4	9 B3
Standard Bank	2 C3	Pensão Atlântida	6 B3	O Nosso Take-Away	10 D3
TDM	3 C3	Pink Papaya	7 B3		
Teledata	4 C3	Residencial Flôr de Vouga	8 B3	**TRANSPORT**	
				Bus Stand	11 C4
				LAM	12 D3

Pensão Atlântida (☎ 251-22169; Rua do Bárue; s/d US$12/20, r with bathroom US$24, r with bathroom & air-con US$32; ✷) Inferior to the other options, but worth a look if elsewhere is full, with spacious, slightly musty rooms in a cavernous, noisy building near the post office. Formerly known as Pensão Flôr de Vouga.

MIDRANGE
Motel Moinho (☎ 251-24762; r US$20, r in windmill US$24-28) This atmospheric place has musty but pleasant rooms in an old windmill – all with views over the surrounding flower gardens and countryside – and simple, nicer and non-musty rooms in a separate building nearby. All have their own bathroom, fan, TV and hot water. It's about 2km east of town, and about

1km off the EN6 from Beira – inconvenient unless you have your own transport. Breakfast costs extra. If you're arriving from Beira via bus, ask to get dropped on the main road near the windmill *(moinho)* turnoff, to avoid the hike back from the bus station.

Hotel-Residencial Castelo Branco (☎ 251-23934; Rua Sussundenga; r without/with breakfast US$50/62; ℗ ✷) The nicest rooms in town, in a large white house overlooking small gardens just off Praça dos Heróis, and frequented by business travellers and aid workers. Everything is modern and spiffy; the twin-bedded rooms come with bathroom, minifridge and a small balcony.

Executive Manica Hotel (☎ 251-23135; r/ste US$65/100; ℗ ✷) This longstanding place is

Manica's only other upscale hotel, with efficient service, somewhat overfurnished but nevertheless comfortable rooms with TV in the main building and similarly appointed but better, brighter rooms around a small garden in an adjoining annexe. There's also a restaurant. It's near the Feira Popular and signposted off the eastern bypass road at the edge of town.

Eating

Elo 4 (Av 25 de Setembro; meals US$3-8) Opposite the government building in the town centre, this is the most popular eatery in town, with good pizzas and Italian dishes.

O Nosso Take-Away (cnr Ruas dos Trabalhadores & dos Operários; meals from US$1; 6am-10pm Wed-Mon) At the eastern edge of town near the railway tracks, and a reasonable choice for shoestring dining.

Chicoteca (meals from US$4; lunch & dinner Wed-Mon) Serves grills and standard fare. It's about 5km out of town: follow the main road west to the signposted turnoff. Go south from here for about 500m, then left for 250m, then left again to the restaurant.

The Feira Popular at the southern edge of town has several good restaurants (most closed on Monday), including the longstanding **Maúa** (meals from US$2; lunch & dinner Tue-Sun), with local fare.

Self-caterers can try **Shoprite** (EN6), 2km east of the town centre.

Getting There & Around

AIR

There are several flights weekly on **LAM** (251-22531; Rua dos Operários, at Mafúia Comercial) to Vilankulo, Tete and Maputo. The airfield is 10km from town, and signposted about 5km west of Chimoio along the Manica road.

BUS & CHAPA

All transport leaves from near the train station. To Tete, there's a daily bus departing Chimoio at 4am (US$9, six hours), and sometimes continuing on to Zóbuè on the Malawi border. Chapas and minibuses to Beira (US$5, three hours) run throughout the day, as do chapas to Manica (US$1.80, one hour) and on to the border.

For Quelimane, you'll need to make your way in stages via Inchope and Caia. Watch for touts trying to sell you 'direct' tickets – you'll still need to get out at Inchope and wait for northbound transport.

To Vilankulo, there's a direct bus leaving daily at 4am (US$14, 10 hours). Otherwise, you'll need to go via Beira (and overnight there), or get out at Inchope and wait there for southbound transport.

TAXI

Chimoio has a couple of taxis – look for them in front of the park on Av 25 de Setembro or by the market, or ask your hotel to ring one.

AROUND CHIMOIO

About halfway between Chimoio and Manica is the placid **Barragem de Chicamba Real** (Chicamba Real Dam), set among low hills and popular with bass anglers. The sporadically functioning **Casa Msika** (251-66009; fax 251-22675; camping per person US$5, d US$30, 3-bed rondavels US$50) has camping, plus faded rooms and rondavels overlooking the lake. There's a restaurant, though it's sometimes closed. Call or ask around in Chimoio for an update before heading out, as the complex was only erratically open when this book was researched and its future was uncertain. The signposted turnoff is about 45km west of Chimoio, from where

AROUND CHIMOIO

0 ———— 40 km
0 ———— 20 miles

To Pink Papaya Forest
Retreat (55km);
Tete (320km)

To Harare
(260km)

Penha Longa

Mutombomwe

Machipanda   Manica

Garuzo

Mutare

Vumba

Chinamapere
Rock Paintings

Casa Msika

EN6

To Beira
(192km)

Chicamba   Chimoio

Vumba
Mountains

Barragem de
Chicamba Real

A9

Monte Tsetserra   **Manica**

Tsetserra
Camp

Mutambara

Rotanda

Mavita

Rio Revúe

Z I M B A B W E

Montes Chimanimani

Chimanimani

Chikukwa Camp

Monte Binga
(2436m)   Zomba Camp

Dombe

it's 4km further south to Casa Msika. There's no public transport from the turnoff.

Opposite the turnoff for Barragem de Chicamba Real and about 10km north of the main road is sleepy **Garuzo**, once a busy stop on the train line and now a very quiet town. Nearby is a small waterfall. The road running through Garuzo used to be the main Chimoio–Manica route before the highway was built.

About 100km northwest of Chimoio and about 6km off the road to Tete is **Pink Papaya Forest Retreat** (☎ 82-555 7310, in Zimbabwe 091-207064; helenmlarge@hotmail.com; camping per person US$5, dm US$10, rondavels per person US$15, day excursions including lunch about US$20), a camping and self-catering place under the same management as Pink Papaya backpackers in Chimoio and not yet open when this book was researched. It's set on a large farm southeast of Catandica. In addition to camping and a dorm, rondavels are planned, as is a bar. The owner plans to offer canoe trips along the river, hikes or biking in the forest and other excursions. Check with Pink Papaya for an update. Watch for the signposted turnoff 6km north of the Rio Púngoè bridge.

MANICA

Tiny, picturesque Manica, 70km west of Chimoio, is situated in what was once the heart of the kingdom of Manica and an important gold trading area. About 5km from town are the **Chinamapere rock paintings**. To get here, go west from Manica about 3km, and then south along a dirt road, following signs for 'pinturas rupestres'. The site of the paintings is considered sacred by local residents, and before your visit, an elderly lady will conduct a brief prayer ceremony. According to tradition, no pregnant or menstruating women can visit the site.

Several kilometres south of Manica is **Vumba** (which means 'mist' in the local Manika language) and the bottling plant for Mozambique's Água Vumba mineral water.

There's an ATM at **BIM Expresso** (EN6).

Sleeping & Eating

Pensão Flamingo (☎ 251-62385; r US$18) On the main road, a few blocks west of BIM Expresso, this spiffy place has simple rooms – all with bathroom and fan – plus a garden and a restaurant.

Motel Guida (☎ 251-62437; r US$14-26) In the unlikely event that Pensão Flamingo is full,

---

THE MUTASA

Since long before colonial boundaries were drawn, the people of Penha Longa have been loyal to the *mutasa*, the dynastic title of the ruler of the kingdom of Manica, who controls the area from present-day Mutare (Zimbabwe). Despite a divisive 1891 Anglo–Portuguese treaty that put western Penha Longa under British control, and the eastern part under Portuguese control, cross-border ties remain strong and Mozambican residents of Penha Longa still profess loyalty to Nyakwanikwa (the present-day *mutasa*) in Mutare.

---

this hotel is a decent budget alternative, with spacious, no-frills rooms with fan and shared bathroom. It's at the western edge of town just before the turnoff for Manica Lodge. Meals can be arranged.

Manica Lodge (☎ 251-62452; manica.lodge@teledata .mz; small/large rondavels US$20/30, 6-person house US$40) At the western end of town, and about 400m off the main road (watch for the signposted turnoff just after the immigration office), this amenable place has stone rondavels scattered around tranquil, manicured gardens. The larger ones are nice – all reasonably spacious, with TV and private bathrooms. In back are several less appealing rondavels that are tiny, and without TV. There's also a restaurant and a three-room self-catering house.

Also recommended:

Estalagem Selva (☎ 82-5702480; EN6; r with fan & bathroom US$20, swimming pool per person US$1; 🖭) About 42km east of Manica, with sterile rooms in large grounds with a restaurant and a tiny tourist information centre. Mostly used as a day getaway from Chimoio.

O Outro Lado (EN6; meals US$3-4) A small restaurant along the main road at the edge of the pine forest, about 25km east of Manica.

Getting There & Away

All transport departs from the market, diagonally opposite BIM Expresso. Chapas run frequently to/from Chimoio (US$1.80, one hour) and to the Zimbabwe border (US$0.60, 30 minutes). Four times weekly (currently Monday, Tuesday, Thursday and Saturday), there are direct chapas from Manica to Rotanda village in the Montes Chimanimani. Ask the driver to drop you at 'Paragem do João' (two to three hours from Manica), which is within a 1km walk of the campsite at the base of Monte Tsetserra (see p118).

PENHA LONGA

The mountainous Penha Longa area straddles the border with Zimbabwe, beginning about 20km north of Manica. It's cool and scenic and offers many walks, all of which can be easily undertaken from the local accommodation spots. Although there is plenty of local cross-border activity, the only official border crossing is between Machipanda and Mutare (Zimbabwe) on the main road.

Penha Longa is home to the Shona people, and you'll see their traditional painted dwelling compounds dotting the hillsides. These typically consist of a cluster of buildings, including a large round kitchen which often doubles as a children's sleeping area. Nearby is a smaller square building, usually raised off the ground by a few stones at the corners and used by adults for sleeping. There are often small storage areas on the compound as well. The dwellings are made of brick and then layered with ochre-, grey- and olive-coloured clays. The distinctive decorations on the outside walls are achieved by mixing various types of clay which are then embellished with paints made from natural pigments, most often in designs of black and white.

It's sometimes possible to arrange to sleep at **Casa Gaswa** (rondavel US$6), a simple three person rondavel in the Mutombomwe area of Penha Longa. Bring food and drink from Manica; hiking guides can be arranged. If Casa Gaswa is occupied, you can also pitch a tent on the grounds for a negotiable fee or arrange something with local villagers. Better – ask the caretaker to show you the way to **Quinta da Fronteira**, an old mansion about 3km from Casa Gaswa with a refreshing stream nearby. It's slowly being rehabilitated, but meanwhile they have a few basic rooms and you can camp. You'll need to bring your own food and drink here, too. For information in Manica, contact Dinis Zandamela (☎ 251-62217, 251-62222) at Kwaedza Simukai Manica, opposite the market.

Getting There & Away

Chapas run several times daily between Manica and Penha Longa (US$1, one hour). From the chapa terminus in Penha Longa, it's a 20-minute walk to Mutombomwe and Casa Gaswa, and from there, 3km further to Quinta da Fronteira. Ask locals to point the way.

Driving, turn north at the intersection in the centre of Manica town towards the market. Continue past the market, staying left at the first fork, then right at the second. Mutombomwe bairro is reached after about 20km. Casa Gaswa will be on the hillside to your left. The road is unpaved, but in reasonable condition during the dry season.

MONTES CHIMANIMANI

Silhouetted against the horizon on the Zimbabwe border southwest of Chimoio are the Montes Chimanimani, with Monte Binga (2436m), Mozambique's highest peak, rising up on their eastern edge. The mountains are beautiful – with stands of pine and mahogany – and exceptionally biodiverse, and together with Chimanimani National Park in Zimbabwe have been designated part of a transfrontier conservation area. Chimanimani is particularly notable for its abundance of

---

A LEGEND OF PENHA LONGA

During the late 19th century, Penha Longa lay in the centre of a disputed area. To the west were the lands of the kingdom of Manica. To the southeast was the territory of the powerful Gaza chief Ngungunhane.

These two kingdoms had long been enemies, and Ngungunhane's troops staged frequent raids into Manica. To protect themselves from the invaders, the people of Penha Longa would send heralds up the mountain to Mudododo village (on what is now the Zimbabwe border), from where they had wide views down over the valleys. When these heralds saw the forces of Ngungunhane coming, they would notify the villagers, who would set out roots from a certain plant for the invaders and then flee the village. Although this type of root closely resembled yam, a local staple, it was actually poisonous. The invaders were not able to tell the difference and would eat it and then fall ill. In this way, the residents of Penha Longa were able to protect themselves and resist the Gaza invaders.

plants. At least 50 unique species have been identified here, many of which are prized for their medicinal value by traditional healers. There is also a multitude of birds, including the rare southern banded snake eagle and the barred cuckoo. Rounding out the picture are bushbuck, eland, sable, duiker, klipspringer and countless smaller animals.

Like the Penha Longa area to the north, the Montes Chimanimani have a long history and rich traditional life. Rock paintings similar to those at Chinamapere (see p116) have been found at several locations. Many of the rivers and pools in this area are considered sacred by local communities, as are some of the forest areas in the foothills of the mountains, and some of the peaks themselves. Traditional beekeeping is widely practised and you're likely to see odd-looking hives (made from the bark of *brachystegia* trees) hanging from tree branches.

Hiking in the Montes Chimanimani

There's a fledgling network of very rustic campsites and hikes (ranging from several days up to a week) for anyone wanting to explore the mountains and surrounding plains on foot. Everything's very basic and access is limited during the rainy season, but if you're self-sufficient, have access to a good 4WD and don't mind doing without the amenities, it's a good way to get acquainted with the local culture. For help arranging guides (which can also be arranged at the campsites), stop by the **Direcção Provincial de Agricultura** (DPA; ☎ 251-22075, 251-22706; Rua Pigivide; ◷ 7.30am-3.30pm Mon-Fri) in Chimoio and ask for the Chimanimani section.

The easiest camp to reach is Tsetserra Camp, at the base of Monte Tsetserra, and reachable on public transport from both Chimoio and Manica. From here, you can climb through some beautiful forest to the top of Monte Tsetserra (five hours return), or do various day or overnight walks. At the summit are the ruins of an old mansion, and another area where you can camp.

Another option (reachable only by 4WD) is the camp at Chikukwa village, which is scenically located in a valley surrounded by forest, and which is the base for climbing Monte Binga, as well as for other hikes. There are also camps at the low-lying Zomba, (reachable by public transport) and several other villages.

For all hikes, you'll need to have a guide, and be fully self-sufficient. Waterproofing your gear is also a good idea, as is bringing along a bag to pack out your trash. Chimoio is the best place for stocking up for hikes. Before heading off, it's worth having a chat with your guide to sort out who is expected to bring what food and supplies. Fees are about US$5 per day for a guide, US$3 per meal, and US$8 per two-person hut. Stick to beaten paths to avoid the dangers of old landmines.

Climbing Monte Binga

The main way to climb Monte Binga is to approach from Zimbabwe. If you have your own transport, it's also possible to climb from Mozambique, beginning at Chikukwa Camp on the Zimbabwe border (see preceding section). Allow a total of four days for the climb from Mozambique, including travel time between Chimoio and Chikukwa. You'll need to be self-sufficient with food and water and a guide is essential (best arranged at Chikukwa Camp).

Getting There & Away

The best access to the Chimanimani area on the Mozambique side is from Chimoio via Mavita and Rotanda. For Monte Tsetserra and Tsetserra Camp, take the signposted turnoff for Barragem de Chicamba Real for about 15km southwards to the dam administration buildings. From here, continue southeast (4WD) as the road winds scenically for about 60km to the top of Tsetserra peak.

To reach Chikukwa Camp on your own steam, take a chapa from Chimoio to Sussendenga, from where you'll need to wait for another vehicle going towards Mavita and Rotanda. After passing Mavita, watch for the signposted Chimanimani/Chimbuwane turnoff, from where it's about 30km further on foot to Chikukwa (a guide is necessary). For self-drivers, 4WD is essential.

TETE

Dry, dusty Tete doesn't have much in the way of tourist attractions and its reputation as one of the hottest places in Mozambique often discourages visitors. Yet, the arid, brown landscape, dotted with baobab trees and cut by the wide swathe of the Rio Zambezi, gives it a unique charm and an atmosphere quite unlike that of Mozambique's other provincial capitals.

History

Tete was an important Swahili Arab trading outpost well before the arrival of the Portuguese and today remains a major transport junction. It grew to significance during the 16th and 17th centuries when it served as a departure point for trade caravans to the gold fields further inland. At the end of the 17th century, it was all but abandoned when the Portuguese lost their foothold in the hinterlands. In the 18th century, it again began to prosper with the opening of the gold fair at Zumbo to the west and the expansion of goldmining north of the Zambezi. It became a regional administrative centre in 1767, and a hospital and a house for the governor were built. More recently, Tete received a boost with the building of the dam at Cahora Bassa, which opened in 1974. Today, with a population of roughly 50,000, it is one of the major towns in the Mozambican interior.

The main languages are Nyungwe, around Tete city; Chewa near the Malawi border; and Ngoni.

Information

BIM Expresso (Av Julius Nyerere) ATM.
Immigration office (Rua Macombre) A few blocks up from Hotel Zambeze.
MBC Internet Café (Av Julius Nyerere; per min US$0.04; 7.30am-noon & 2pm-5.30pm Mon-Fri, 8am-1pm Sat) Diagonally opposite and up from Prédios Univendas.
Standard Bank (cnr Av Julius Nyerere & Av da Independência) ATM and can change cash dollars; next to Hotel Zambeze.
TDM (Av 25 de Junho; 7am-10pm) Domestic and international telephone calls.

Sights & Activities

Tete's main sights are the impressive 538m-long **suspension bridge** that spans the Rio Zambezi and the remains of an old Portuguese **fort** on the river near the bridge.

TETE PROVINCE

Tete province is an anomaly within Mozambique, lying inland and almost divided from the rest of the country by Malawi. While the south is hot and arid, northern Tete, much of which lies at altitude, enjoys a delightfully cool climate, with beautiful hill panoramas. Tete is also interesting as one of the few areas of Mozambique (in addition to Cabo Delgado) where you'll see masked dancing.

About 25km northwest of Tete overlooking the river is the **Missão de Boroma** (Boroma Mission). Founded in 1885 by Jesuit missionaries, it was known for its school (colégio), its carpentry-training centre and its attractive church. After being abandoned for many years, activities have recommenced on a small scale.

Northeast of Tete near the Malawi border is the district of **Angónia**, which is set on a plateau between 1000m and 1500m in altitude, and has a wonderfully cool and refreshing climate, especially if you've just come from Tete. It's also a scenic area and good for walks, although there are no tourist facilities. Ulóngwe, its pleasant capital, is just 20km west of the border and is closely tied into the Malawian economy; kwacha are accepted here as well as meticais.

Sleeping

Hotel Zambeze (252-23100/3; Av Eduardo Mondlane; s/d US$10/14, with air-con from US$16/22;) Cheap and centrally located, but otherwise highly unappealing, this cavernous, grey high-rise is the main budget option. Rooms are moderately clean, the shared bathrooms less so (and they don't have hot water, despite what staff may tell you). There's also a restaurant. It's in the lower part of town next to Standard Bank.

Complexo Piscina (252-23079; s/d/tr US$12/20/24;) Piscina, on the riverbank under the bridge, is a step or two up, with small but tolerable rooms – all with their own bathroom – and a restaurant. Breakfast costs extra.

Prédios Univendas (252-23198/9, 252-22670; Av Julius Nyerere; s/d US$22/31, with bathroom from US$42/52;) The entrance to the rooms (most with fan, air-con, TV and shared bathroom) is just around the corner from the Univendas shop on Av da Independência.

Motel Tete (252-22345; EN103; r US$42;) On the river about 1km past Piscina, and about 25 minutes on foot from the town centre along the main road to Changara, this unassuming place is Tete's most upmarket option. The low-ceilinged but spacious rooms have private bathroom, TV and placid river views with breezes. There's a good restaurant (no alcohol) and helpful management.

Eating

Pastelaria Confiança (Av 25 de Junho; snacks & light meals from US$0.80; 7.30am-8pm Mon-Sat;) Clean and cool (good air-con), with a good selection of snacks, hamburgers, omelettes and other light meals, plus pastries and beverages.

Pino's Pizza (Av Eduardo Mondlane; pizzas from US$2.50; ☻ dinner) This Italian-run place on the ground floor of Hotel Zambeze (go right from reception) has the best pizza in town, with fresh cheese and lots of trimmings.

Freitas (meals US$6-8; ☻ lunch & dinner Wed-Mon) Next door to Piscina and known for its chicken *zambeziana*.

Of the hotels, **Motel Tete** (☎ 252-22345; EN103; meals from US$3) has the best dining, with riverside views, a good menu selection and relatively fast service. **Supermercado Tete** (Av 25 de Junho) is the best bet for self-caterers.

Drinking & Entertainment

Good spots to enjoy a cool drink while watching the sun set over the Zambezi include the outdoor patio at Motel Tete, or (only go in a group) any of the small bars lining the river under the bridge.

Casa de Cultura (Av Eduardo Mondlane), near the Municipal Garden III Congresso at the lower end of town, provides information on upcoming cultural events.

Getting There & Away

AIR

There are flights on **LAM** (☎ 252-22056; Av 24 de Julho) connecting Tete three to four times weekly with Maputo, Beira, Lichinga, Nampula, Quelimane and Chimoio.

The airport is 6km out of town on the Moatize road; take any chapa heading to Moatize. There are no taxis.

BUS & CHAPA

For Malawi, chapas run to Zóbuè (US$2, two hours) and Dedza from Mercado da OUA on the western side of town. At the border you'll need to change to Malawian transport. The daily bus from Chimoio also continues on to Zóbuè, departing Tete about 10am from Av 25 de Junho, down from Pastelaria Confiança. Alternatively, catch the bus that stops in Tete on its route between Harare and Blantyre.

For Harare (Zimbabwe), take a chapa from Mercado 1 de Maio (along Av 25 de Junho) to Changara (US$2.80, 1½ hours) and get transport from there. Another (pricier) option is to wait at the intersection of the bridge road and the road to Harare and try to catch one of the daily Harare–Blantyre buses.

For Zambia, take a Moatize chapa over the bridge past the SOS compound to the petrol station, where you'll find chapas to Matema, and from there, infrequent transport to Cassacatiza (on the border).

For Chimoio (US$9, six hours), all transport leaves from opposite Prédio Emose near Prédios Univendas, with the first departures between 4.30am and 5am.

Chapas to Moatize (US$0.35) depart throughout the day from the Moatize bus stand on Rua do Qua.

To Songo (for Barragem de Cahora Bassa), several pick-ups depart daily from the old Correios (post office) building in the lower part of town near the cathedral.

The Tete to Lichinga journey via Blantyre and Mandimba is best done in stages.

To Boroma, there are occasional direct chapas leaving from Mercado da OUA. It's possible to hitch, although the going is slow. The best place to wait is at the Boroma road junction, about 1.5km west of Mercado da OUA.

To Ulóngwe, there is at least one direct chapa departing daily from Mercado da OUA. Otherwise, take any car heading to Zóbuè, get out at the Angónia junction about 15km

---

RIO ZAMBEZI

The mighty Zambezi tumbles into Mozambique at Zumbo in western Tete province and flows about 1000km through the country before spilling into the sea near Chinde, south of Quelimane.

Up to 8km wide at points, it has long served as a highway between the coast and the interior. Among the notables it has carried was Livingstone, who took a paddle steamer upriver from the Zambezi delta to Tete before his progress was thwarted by the Cahora Bassa rapids. Earlier, Arab traders had made their way upriver at least as far as Sena and Tete, and the Portuguese had built settlements near the river delta in the hope of gaining access to western gold fields.

Apart from the Caia ferry (soon to be replaced by a bridge), the only links over the Mozambican portion of the river are the suspension bridge at Tete and the Dona Ana bridge between Mutarara and Sena.

before Zóbuè and get onward transport from there.

The management at Motel Tete can help arrange car rental; expect to pay about US$100 per day plus fuel.

BARRAGEM DE CAHORA BASSA & SONGO

About 150km northwest of Tete near the town of Songo is massive Cahora Bassa, the fifth-largest dam in the world. The dam, which was completed in 1974, is set at the head of a magnificent gorge in the mountains and makes a good day or overnight trip from Tete. It's also a wonderful destination for anglers, and is renowned for its tiger fish.

History

Barragem de Cahora Bassa had its beginnings during the colonial era, when it was proposed as a means of flood control and for water storage to irrigate plantations downstream. The scheme was later enlarged to include a hydroelectric power station, with South Africa agreeing to buy most of the energy. Construction of the dam was highly politicised, with the Portuguese government intending it as a statement of its permanent presence in the region. Plans were made to place up to one million settlers, white and African, on the new farmland that the dam waters would irrigate. This was vigorously opposed by Frelimo. Party leadership viewed Cahora Bassa as a perpetuation of white minority rule in Southern Africa and made blocking the dam's construction a major objective in the late 1960s. Opposition was organised on an international scale, as sympathetic groups in Western countries worked to discourage private investment.

Ultimately the contracts were signed and, despite repeated Frelimo attacks during construction, the massive undertaking was completed in 1974. To move all the equipment needed for the dam, existing roads and railways had to be modified, and a suspension bridge was built across the Zambezi at Tete. While resettlement of people living in the area was not as great a problem as it was with the construction of the nearby Kariba Dam on the Zambia–Zimbabwe border, more than 24,000 new homes had to be built.

Yet, three decades after its construction, Cahora Bassa has not come close to fulfilling early expectations. One major reason was

---

LAGO CAHORA BASSA

Lago Cahora Bassa, the lake created by the dam, stretches for 270km westwards to the confluence of the Zambezi and Luangwa rivers on the Zambian border, and has the potential to generate more than 3500 megawatts of energy – enough to illuminate the entire region. En route, it partially covers the thundering Cahora Bassa rapids, which blocked David Livingstone's attempt to find a direct route through Rio Zambezi in the late 1850s.

---

destruction of power lines by Renamo rebels in the 1980s. Even after repairs were completed, power supplies remained grounded by contractual and pricing disputes between Mozambique, South Africa and Portugal. Silt has been another impediment. Most of it is brought in via the Luangwa River, where overgrazing and poor farming practices lead to soil erosion and turn the waters muddy brown. Now, with the late 2005 agreement for a turnover of majority control from Portugal to Mozambique, perhaps the dam finally has a chance of reaching its potential.

Information

The dam can be visited, including the impressive underground turbine rooms. To arrange a tour, contact the offices of **Hidroeléctrica de Cahora Bassa** (HCB; ☎ 252-82157, 252-82221/4; rp.sng@hcb .co.mz) in Songo town and ask for Relações Públicas (Public Relations), which will help you organise things. There's no charge for a visit, and permits are no longer necessary to enter Songo. If you're already in Songo, ask locals to point you towards the HCB office in the *'substação'* (substation).

Sleeping & Eating

Centro Social do HCB (☎ 252-82215, 252-82454, 252-82508; r/ste US$30/36; 🏊) This pleasant place in the town centre has clean and comfortable twinbedded rooms – all with fridge, window screens and private bathrooms with hot water – set in large manicured green grounds. Breakfast costs extra. Also here is Restaurante O Teles (meals US$5 to US$10).

Ugezi Tiger Lodge (☎ 82-599 8410, fax 252-82049; c61@mweb.co.za; camping per person US$11, chalets per person US$19-25, with air-con US$23-30; 🏊) Anglers – or anyone wanting an escape to nature – will love this rustic fishing camp perched on a hill overlooking Lago Cahora Bassa. There's a choice of camping (tent rental possible), or accommodation in chalets on the densely vegetated hillside, some with air-con and private bathroom. It's all very no-frills but the morning scenery on the lake at the base of the property (there's no beachfront) is beautiful. Boats are available for fishing charters and for lake tours up towards the dam. It's about 14km from Songo town and 6km beyond the dam. The restaurant (meals from about US$11) serves superb grilled fish.

Getting There & Away

There are frequent charter flights between Tete and Songo; check with listed accommodation for details or ask at the airfield about seat availability.

Chapas run several times daily between Tete and Songo (US$4, three to four hours), departing Tete from the old *correios* (post office) building. Once in Songo, it's another 7km down to the dam, which you'll have to either walk or hitch. Ugezi Tiger Lodge does pick-ups from Tete.

ZÓBUÈ

Zóbuè, 115km northeast of Tete, is the main border town between Tete province and Malawi. There are a few basic *pensões*, and numerous moneychangers. Several vehicles go between here and Tete (US$2, two hours) daily. For more on getting to/from Malawi, see p186.

ZUMBO

Remote Zumbo's history dates back to at least 1715, when the Portuguese established a gold trading fair at the eastern edge of the Luangwa River at its confluence with the Zambezi. The settlement grew rapidly and by the mid-18th century was one of the most prosperous European cities in Southern Africa, with numerous Portuguese trading houses. This boom was shortlived, and by 1765, Zumbo's wealth began to decline. The difficult overland journey along the Zambezi from Tete, shifting trade patterns, the town's fragile economic foundation and drought were all factors. By the mid-19th century, Zumbo had been all but abandoned and today it is little more than an oversized village.

Near Zumbo is **Tchuma Tchato** (camping per person US$3, bungalows per person US$10), a community-based natural resources project in which the local community has organised itself to bring a halt to poaching of local wildlife – elephants and other large animals abound – and earn some revenue. They run a small campsite here on the bank of the Rio Zambezi opposite Zumbo and about 5km from the Zimbabwe border. There are also some basic bungalows with shared facilities and meals can be arranged, though it's best to bring food supplies with you. Soda and beer are sometimes available at the camp, but bring drinking water or a filter. For more details, or to arrange a booking, contact the **Direcção Provincial do Turismo** (☎ 252-24225; dpturismo@teledata .mz; Rua 3 de Fevereiro) in Tete.

Well southeast of Zumbo, on the southern side of Lago Cahora Bassa, are several hunting concessions that also cater to anglers. Access is via Mukumbura on the Zimbabwe border, or from Tete via Chinhanda (there's a fishing camp just west of Chinhanda). If you're interested in these, contact www.tgsafari.co.za for more information.

The easiest access to Zumbo from Tete is via Zimbabwe. On the Mozambican side, you can reliably get as far as Fingoé (north of the lake, and at the midway point between Songo and Zumbo) via public transport. From Fingoé to Zumbo, there's no public transport, but the road is passable with a good 4WD.

SENA & MUTARARA

About 250km downstream from Tete along the Zambezi are the twin villages of Sena and Mutarara, known for the 3.6km Dona Ana railway bridge (built in 1934) which spans the river here. The bridge has been converted to take vehicles; it's open from sunrise to sunset, and – because of its narrow width – alternates directions roughly every hour. There are a few basic *pensões* in both towns, including Pensão São Francisco in Mutarara, and Mira Zambezi in Sena. The river here is known for its hippos, which you can sometimes see if you happen to be flying over in a charter flight, or by asking the *pensão* to help you organise a local boat.

From Mutarara, you can continue north on an unpaved but reasonable road and a generally hassle-free border crossing into Malawi, or eastwards over the Shire River (bridged by a small ferry, US$2) and then on to Morrumbala (where there's a good *pensão*) and the main road to Quelimane.

CAIA

About 60km further downstream is Caia, the main north–south crossing point. There's no accommodation worthy of the name in Caia itself, but in Catapu, 32km south of Caia along the main road, is the very good **M'phingwe Camp** (www.dalmann.com; s/d cabins US$18/24, with bathroom US$22/30), with six rustic but spotless double cabins sharing facilities, plus one with its own bathroom. Breakfast can be arranged with advance notice (US$6.50) and there's a restaurant with steaks and other meals (US$6.50 to US$9) and cold drinks. Although most people just stop for an overnight en route north, the surrounding forest is a rewarding birding area and worth longer exploration. M'phingwe can also be used as a base for climbing Monte Gorongosa (p112) and a guide can be arranged at the camp. The turnoff is signposted on the main road, from where M'phingwe is about 2km further.

The road from Inchope to Caia via Gorongosa village is good tarmac the entire way. From Caia northwards, it's being rehabilitated, though it's in reasonable shape as far as Alto Molócuè.

Work has started on a bridge over the Zambezi, which should be completed around 2010. For now, the river at Caia is crossed by two ferries (per vehicle with driver US$4, per person US$0.05) that run roughly every half hour or so from 7am to 5pm, except at midday when the captains take off to have lunch.

MARROMEU

Marromeu is an old sugar-growing centre beside the Rio Zambezi, dating back to the late 19th century when the Portuguese Sugar Society of East Africa built a plantation and sugar factory here. After many years of neglect, the factory has been rehabilitated under Mauritian ownership, and is now Mozambique's largest sugar processing mill. There is no infrastructure to speak of other than that connected with the sugar company.

About 45km upriver from Marromeu is the town of **Chupanga**, where Mary Moffat, wife of the missionary and explorer David Livingstone, is buried. She died here on 17 April 1862.

South of Marromeu begin the extensive wetlands of the Rio Zambezi delta, which are home to a wealth of water birds, including wattled crane, flamingo and pelican. On the coast is the **Reserva de Marromeu** (Marromeu Reserve) which formerly was known for its vast herds of buffalo – put by some estimates at about 55,000 in the 1970s. Today, only a fraction of that number remain, although plans are underway for restocking. For now, the area is of interest primarily to hunters (there are several hunting concessions here) and birders – in 2003, it was proclaimed as a 'wetland of international importance' under the Ramsar convention.

In Marromeu, there's accommodation at the basic **Pensão Domino** (☎ 23-640420; r about US$16). It's better, however, to base yourself at Catapu and explore the area from there.

Getting There & Away

There is an airstrip at Marromeu for charter planes. Chapas go daily to Marromeu from both Inhamitanga and Caia.

QUELIMANE

Bustling Quelimane is the capital of Mozambique's densely populated Zambézia province and heartland of the Chuabo people. While lacking the architectural charm of some other Mozambican towns – with the exception of the abandoned Portuguese **cathedral** near the waterfront, and the nearby **mosque** – its compact size and energetic atmosphere make it an agreeable place to break your travels.

Well outside town are several **beaches** that can't rival the coastal stretches further north or south, but make good getaways if you're based in Quelimane longer term. The **riverfront** is at its best at sunset.

History

Quelimane stands on the site of an old Arab trading settlement dating to at least the 15th century and built on the banks of the Rio dos Bons Sinais in the days when this was still linked to the Rio Zambezi. Until the 19th century, when the river channel became clogged with silt, Quelimane served as the main entry port to the interior. It was also an important export point for agricultural products, and a major slave-trading centre. Today few traces of this long history are evident and, apart from the cathedral, almost no old buildings remain.

Information

The excellent series of maps done by Coopération Française in collaboration with the local Conselho Municipal covers Quelimane – *Planta de Endereçamento da Cidade de Quelimane*. It's hard to find – try **Gabinete de Endereçamento da**

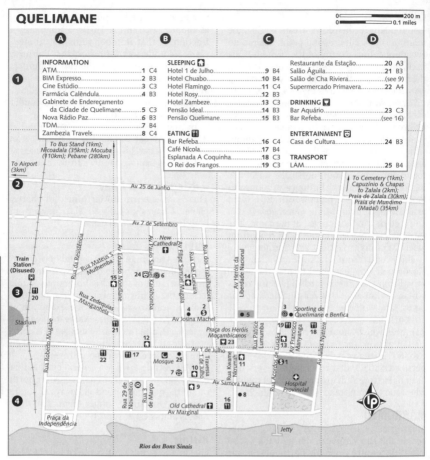

QUELIMANE

INFORMATION	
ATM	1 C4
BIM Expresso	2 B3
Cine Estúdio	3 C3
Farmácia Calêndula	4 B3
Gabinete de Endereçamento da Cidade de Quelimane	5 C3
Nova Rádio Paz	6 B3
TDM	7 B4
Zambezia Travels	8 C4

SLEEPING	
Hotel 1 de Julho	9 B4
Hotel Chuabo	10 B4
Hotel Flamingo	11 C4
Hotel Rosy	12 B3
Hotel Zambeze	13 C3
Pensão Ideal	14 B3
Pensão Quelimane	15 B3

EATING	
Bar Refeba	16 C4
Café Nícola	17 B4
Esplanada A Coquinha	18 C3
O Rei dos Frangos	19 C3

Restaurante da Estação	20 A3
Salão Aguila	21 B3
Salão de Cha Riviera	(see 9)
Supermercado Primavera	22 A4

DRINKING	
Bar Aquário	23 C3
Bar Refeba	(see 16)

ENTERTAINMENT	
Casa de Cultura	24 B3

TRANSPORT	
LAM	25 B4

Cidade de Quelimane (☎ 24-214912; 558 Av Josina Machel) in the Conselho Municipal building.

INTERNET ACCESS
Cine Estúdio (cnr Av Josina Machel & Rua Acordos de Lusaka, 1st fl; per min US$0.04; ✆ 7am-8pm Mon-Fri, 8am-7pm Sat) A few computers and a sporadically functioning internet connection; while waiting, head to the tiny café next door, with views down onto lively basketball games at the adjoining sports club.
Nova Rádio Paz (Av Paulo Samuel Kankhomba; ✆ in theory 8.30am-8pm) Quelimane's only other internet connection; opposite the Casa da Cultura.

MEDICAL SERVICES
Farmácia Calêndula (☎ 24-213393; Av Josina Machel; ✆ 8am-8pm Mon-Sat, 9am-1pm Sun)

MONEY
ATM (Hospital Provincial, cnr Rua Acordos de Lusaka & Av Samora Machel)
BIM Expresso (Av Josina Machel)

TELEPHONE
TDM (cnr Avs Samora Machel & Filipe Samuel Magaia) Near Hotel Chuabo.

TRAVEL AGENCIES
Zambezia Travels (☎ 24-216174; www.zambezia.ch; Rua Kwame Nkrumah) A recommended Swiss-Mozambican run travel agency specialising in Mozambique north of the Rio Save, and the best contact for arranging visits to Gurúè, climbing Monte Namúli, and anything else in central Mozambique. It's on a small side street diagonally opposite Hotel Chuabo and just off Av Samora Machel.

Sleeping

BUDGET

Hotel 1 de Julho (cnr Av Samora Machel & Rua Felipe Samuel Magaia; tw US$16, with bathroom & air-con US$28) Near the old cathedral, this reasonable budget choice has no-frills rooms, all with fan and sink, and meals available (breakfast costs extra).

Pensão Quelimane (☎ 24-212359; Av Eduardo Mondlane; s/d/tw US$12/14/16, with bathroom & air-con from US$18/22/24; 🗶) More no-frills rooms (not quite as good as those at Hotel 1 de Julho), and no breakfast.

Hotel Rosy (☎ 24-214969, 24-213825; cnr Avs 1 de Julho & Paulo Samuel Kankhomba; s/d US$24/28; 🗶) Centrally located near the central mosque, this place has quite decent rooms – those on the ground floor have air-con, while those upstairs are marginally nicer, but with fan only. Breakfast is included in the price, and meals can be arranged.

Other recommendations:

Pensão Ideal (☎ 24-212731; Av Filipe Samuel Magaia; s/tw US$13/18, d with bathroom US$20) Ideal only for its price, with musty, stuffy rooms with sagging beds and continental breakfast.

Hotel Zambezi (Rua Acordos de Lusaka; s/d US$10/14) Reasonably clean rooms, a shiny floor leading out to a small courtyard and bucket baths. Breakfast costs extra.

MIDRANGE

Hotel Flamingo (☎ 24-215602; sogetra@teledata.mz; cnr Rua Kwame Nkrumah & Av 1 de Julho; s/d US$50/60; 🗶 🖵) This nice and newish place, under the same management as Restaurante da Estação, has quite decent rooms, all with bathroom and air-con, plus a small pool (entry per adult/child US$2/US$3) and a tiny gym. Full breakfast is included in the price.

Hotel Chuabo (☎ 24-213181/2; fax 24-213812; Av Samora Machel; s/d US$56/60; 🗶) The Chuabo is a Quelimane institution – one of the few hotels anywhere in the country that managed to stay running throughout the war years. The large rooms come with TV, fridge and air-con, and many with views over the river. The rooftop restaurant (meals from US$6) has reasonable meals, waiters in starched shirts and views over town. It's rumoured that the hotel will soon undergo renovations and an upgrade, so get an update before booking.

Eating

Quelimane has plenty of cafés that offer light meals starting at about US$3, including **Café Nícola** (Av 1 de Julho); **Salão Águila** (cnr Avs Josina Machel & Eduardo Mondlane) next to Cinema Águila; and the less atmospheric but spiffier **Salão de Cha Riviera** (cnr Avs Samora Machel & Felipe Samuel Magaia), underneath Hotel 1 de Julho. **O Rei dos Frangos** (Av Josina Machel), opposite Sporting de Quelimane e Benfica has takeaway grilled chickens with fries for US$4.

Esplanada A Coquinha (cnr Avs Josina Machel & Julius Nyerere; meals from US$4; 🕑 lunch & dinner) Opposite and about 100m past Cinema Benfica, this is one of the best places to try local Zambézian cuisine. There's a large menu selection, outdoor seating under a few large, thatched shelters, and a Sunday lunch buffet (US$6) featuring local dishes.

Bar Refeba (Av Marginal; meals from $2.50) Overlooking the waterfront near the old cathedral, this is a popular spot for a meal and an evening drink. The menu features good grilled prawns, plus grilled chicken and a few other choices.

Restaurante da Estação (☎ 24-213/30; Rua da Resistência; meals from US$5) This spiffy restaurant near the train station is a popular hangout for expats and aid workers, with a pizza oven, good-value Italian meals and porch seating.

None of Quelimane's restaurants are renowned for speedy service, so order before you're hungry or, better, stop by in advance to place an order.

For self-catering, try **Supermercado Primavera** (Av 1 de Julho), a block down from and opposite Hotel Rosy.

Drinking

Popular bars include **Bar Refeba** (Av Marginal) and **Bar Aquário** (Av 1 de Julho) in the gardens near City Hall.

Entertainment

The best place to find out about upcoming events is the **Casa de Cultura** (Av Paulo Samuel Kankhomba), near the new cathedral. Montes Namúli, Zambézia province's excellent traditional song and dance group, is based here, and it's often possible to watch their rehearsals.

Well-known local theatre groups include Falados da Zambézia, and Xenhê (pronounced wen-yay, the Chuabo word for 'scorpion'). As elsewhere in the country, theatre pieces here are frequently used to draw attention to social themes, or to carry out civic education on issues such as AIDS. For information on performances (all in Portuguese or Chuabo) ask at the Casa de Cultura.

ZAMBEZI DONAS

Just as much a part of Quelimane history as the Rio dos Bons Sinais is the old Portuguese *prazo* system. As the Portuguese saw things, *prazos* were land-holdings granted to private individuals by the Portuguese government in an attempt to solidify control over the Mozambican hinterlands. The *prazo* holder *(prazeiro)* had to be a female Portuguese citizen who would then pass the *prazo* on to her female offspring married to white Portuguese. All sorts of rules and duties applied: the *prazeiro* was allowed to employ Africans, to raise a private army (generally made up of slaves) and to trade, and was responsible for maintaining law and order within the *prazo* area.

While some *prazos* were small, others were hundreds of square kilometres in extent. At the height of the system, the area encompassed by *prazos* was said to have been greater than the entire area of Portugal. By the 18th century, some *prazos* were effectively functioning as independent states, and the 'Zambezi donas', as the *prazeiros* were known, enjoyed positions of prominence and power. Over time, the system became the basis for the rise of an Afro-Portuguese ruling elite, and formed a type of feudal aristocracy that dominated the affairs of the region.

However, the *prazo* system was inherently unstable and ultimately failed due in part to rivalries among the prazeiros, a scarcity of Portuguese women, African resistance, and poor economic performance. By the late 19th century, many of the *prazeiro* families had emigrated and the system lay in shambles. *Prazos* were finally abolished in the early 20th century when António Salazar came to power in Portugal.

Getting There & Away

AIR

There are flights four to five times weekly to/from Maputo, Beira, Nampula and Tete on **LAM** (☎ 24-212801; Av 1 de Julho). **Air Corridor** (☎ 24-216333/93; Av 25 de Junho) stops in Quelimane on its run up and down the coast.

The airport is about 3km northwest of town at the end of Av 25 de Junho – start walking and you'll find a lift or ask your hotel to call one of Quelimane's handful of private taxis.

BUS & CHAPA

The bus stand is at the northern end of Av Eduardo Mondlane. Chapas run frequently to/from Nicoadala at the junction with the main road (US$1.50, 45 minutes).

To Nampula, a Grupo Mecula bus departs daily at 4.30am (US$14, 10 hours). Several vehicles also run daily to Mocuba (US$4, two to three hours), from where you can get onward transport to Nampula via Alto Molócuè, or to the Malawi border at Milange.

To Gurúè (US$9.60, six to seven hours), there's a small (30-seater) bus departing daily at about 4.30am, for which you should buy a ticket the afternoon before to be certain of a seat. (Even with a ticket, it's a good idea to show up early at the bus stand.)

Heading south, buses to Beira depart daily at 5am (US$16.50, nine hours). If you're driving, it's also possible to cross further upriver via the bridge between Sena and Mutarara.

AROUND QUELIMANE

The closest beach to Quelimane is **Praia de Zalala**, about 30km northeast of town. It's long and wide, with sunrise views, a row of fringing palms, and water of questionable cleanliness (as it's used as a toilet by local villages). However the drive out from Quelimane is scenic, through extensive coconut plantations formerly owned by Companhia da Zambézia.

Complexo Kass-Kass (☎ 24-212302; bungalows US$32) is the only accommodation, with basic four-person bungalows that haven't seen a dust rag in years and a mediocre restaurant. Due to incidents of petty theft, camping isn't recommended. If you have your own transport, head for the day to the quieter **Praia de Mundimo** (usually called Praia de Madal); there are no facilities.

Chapas to Zalala (US$1.60, 45 minutes) depart Quelimane from the Capuchin mission (*Capuzínio*), about 1km from the cemetery on the Zalala road. To Praia de Mundimo, you'll need a 4WD and someone to point the way. There's an unmarked righthand turnoff from the Zalala road about 15km from Quelimane. From there it's another 20km or so on unmarked tracks through the coconut plantations.

Much of the area south of Quelimane surrounding the Rio Zambezi delta consists of various hunting concessions, and is known for its birdlife. **Mahimba Hunting Camp** (bookings through www.tgsafari.co.za) caters to birders out of season.

PEBANE

About 280km northeast of Quelimane is Pebane – a fishing port and popular holiday destination during colonial times, and today a charming (albeit faded) and quiet town not far from a long beach. There's a basic **campsite** (camping per tent US$2) on the sand near Ponta Matirre, about 4km from town, and inexpensive rooms with bucket baths and meals at **Pensão Jamaima** (r US$12).

About 5km north of town on the beach is **Macucuane Lodge** (☎ in Zimbabwe 011-611298; www .macucuane.com; per person self-catering US$35), a rustic and still-in-process Zimbabwean-run anglers camp with a few double chalets and fishing boat charters, and several more self-catering houses planned. Advance bookings recommended.

Pebane is reached in slow stages by public transport or with a 4WD, via Namacurra, Olinga (Maganja) and Mucubela. From Pebane northwards, the road paralleling the coast continues as far as the Rio Ligonha, which is bridged only by dugout canoe, and from there on to Moma. There's no regular public transport along this route until you get to Moma, from where there are chapas to Angoche and on to Nampula. It's much better to go via Olinga to Mocuba and the main road northwards. Another option from Pebane heads north along a bush track (4WD) via the **Reserva de Gilé** (Gilé Reserve) to Gilé village and on to Alto Ligonha, from where it's straightforward to continue on to Nampula.

Prior to the war, the 2100 sq km Reserva de Gilé was home to elephants, buffaloes and other wildlife. It's relatively inaccessible now (the best road access is via Pebane or Alto Molócuè), and no recent surveys have been conducted, though it's rumoured to still have decent populations of large animals. There are ruins of an old camp on the reserve's western edge, but no other facilities.

MOCUBA

Mocuba is the junction town for travel from Quelimane to Nampula or Malawi. About 40km north, near Munhamade in Lugela district, are some **hot springs**. Also in Lugela district are the large **cavernas do Monte Mulide**, caves used during the war as a place of refuge by local populations. Both spots are considered sacred, and there are no facilities at either.

Pensão Cruzeiro (☎ 24-810184; Av Eduardo Mondlane; r US$14; meals from US$2), on Mocuba's main street, has basic rooms and meals.

Transport to Quelimane (US$4, two to three hours) leaves from the market. Transport to Nampula (US$11, eight hours) leaves from the northern end of the main street. The road is tarmac but potholed from Mocuba to Nampevo junction, from there under construction to Alto Ligonha, and then tarmac to Nampula. There are several vehicles daily to Milange (US$6.50, four hours) departing from Mocuba's market, though you'll maximise

---

CULTURE ZAMBÉZIA STYLE

Zambézia province's rich culture is best discovered by getting out of Quelimane and into the surrounding districts. Namarrói, in the north of the province, is known for its snake dancers (cobras de Namarrói). After first performing a ritual to ensure success and safety, they go into the bush to capture snakes, dance with them and then return them alive to the bush.

In Morrumbala in southwestern Zambézia, and in bordering areas of Tete province's Mutarara district, you'll find marimba (known locally as varimba or valimba) players. Unlike the Chopi timbila (marimba) orchestras found in southern Mozambique, where each instrument is usually played by one person at a time, the large Morrumbala/Mutarara marimbas may be played by two or three people at once, often switching parts several times within the same song. The Morrumbala marimbas are also made using different materials and techniques, giving them a distinctive tone, although purists consider the tone quality of the timbila to be superior.

Gilé, northeast of Quelimane, is known for its dancers.

The best time to see local groups performing is on the dia da cidade (city/town day). Check with the Casa de Cultura or the local district administrator for information about upcoming events. None of these places have tourist facilities; you'll need your own vehicle or plenty of time to take public transport.

your chances of a lift by walking west past the airstrip to the Milange road junction.

MILANGE

Milange is a peppy town about 3km east of the Malawi border. BIM Expresso has an ATM; moneychangers can help with Malawian kwacha.

Pensão Lili (r US$12) has meals and no-frills rooms.

Finding a lift between Milange and Mocuba usually isn't a problem. To Gurúè, there's sporadic public transport northeast along a rehabilitated road to Molumbo, and from there on to Lioma, from where you can get a chapa the rest of the way.

Also see p186.

GURÚÈ

The charming and picturesque town of Gurúè is set amidst lush vegetation and tea plantations in one of the coolest, highest and rainiest parts of the country. Tea has long been one of the most important crops, and there are extensive holdings dating from colonial days. Only a small proportion have been rehabilitated. The surrounding area offers good walking and if you don't mind foregoing the comforts, it would be easy to spend up to a week here hiking in the hills.

BIM (Av da República) has an ATM. There's internet access (plus domestic and international telephone calls) at **TDM** (per min US$0.04).

Sights & Activities

A good place to start is with a walk through the jacarandas on the northern edge of town. To get here, find the small church in the centre of Gurúè and head north along the road running in front of it. Continue for five to 10 minutes, following the edge of the hill and staying on the uphill side at the forks.

A popular destination for longer hikes is the **cascata** (waterfall) in the hills north of town. To get here, head first to the UP4 tea factory (also known as Cha Sambique), which you can see in the distance to the north; ask locals to point out the way and allow about 45 minutes on foot. From UP4, it's another 1½ hours on foot through overgrown tea plantations and forest to the falls, which will be to your right. En route are several detours offering beautiful views back towards Gurúè. Swimming is possible in the pools above the falls. There are said to be some wild

horses from colonial days in the surrounding hills, as well as herds of cattle. As the falls are situated in the middle of tea plantations, you will need permission to visit. This is free and can be obtained from the Gulamo company at their UP6 warehouse, a complex of white buildings several kilometres out of town off the Quelimane road; ask for Senhor Rafiq. If you don't have your own vehicle, you may be able to arrange a lift out to UP6 with the Gulamo office in the centre of town diagonally opposite the bank.

At UP6 you can also arrange to tour one of the tea factories, which still have much of their original equipment, including an old steam engine.

In the hills about 12km northeast of town is **Casa dos Noivos** – originally a honeymoon spot (hence its name, 'House of the Newlyweds'). It's well past its prime, but makes a good spot for watching the sunset. The house itself consists of a single room, with several other smaller houses on the property, presumably used to accommodate the accompanying entourage.

Climbing Monte Namúli

Rising up from the hills about 15km northeast of Gurúè are the mist-shrouded slopes of Monte Namúli (Mt Namúli, 2419m), from which flow the Licungo (Lugela) and Malema rivers. If you find yourself in the area with time to spare, it makes a good, and very scenic climb, manageable by anyone who is reasonably fit. The mountain is considered sacred by the local Makua people, so while climbing is permitted, you'll need to observe the local traditions. It's also highly advisable to go with a guide, as the route isn't straightforward and it's easy to get lost.

Before setting out, buy some *farinha de mapira* (sorghum flour), rice and sugar at the market in Gurúè (it shouldn't cost more than US$1.50 for everything), to be used to appease both the spirits and the local *régulo* (chief).

The climb begins about 6km outside Gurúè near UP5, an old tea factory. To reach here, head south out of Gurúè along the Quelimane road. Go left after about 2km and continue several kilometres further to UP5. With a vehicle, you can drive to the factory and park there. With a 4WD it's also possible to drive further up the mountain's slopes to Mugunha Sede, about 40km from Gurúè by road and the last village below the summit. There's no public transport.

Shortly before reaching UP5 you'll see a narrow but obvious track branching left. Follow this as it winds through unrehabilitated tea plantations and stands of bamboo and forest, until it ends in a high, almost alpine, valley about 800m below the summit of Monte Namúli. The views en route are superb. On the edge of this valley is Mugunha Sede, where you should seek out the chief and request permission to climb the mountain. If you don't speak Portuguese, bring someone along with you who knows either Portuguese or the local language, Makua. If you've come this far with a 4WD, you'll need to arrange to leave it here. The sorghum flour that you bought in Gurúè should be presented to the chief as a gift, who may save some to make traditional beer and scatter the remainder on the ground to appease the ancestors who inhabit the area. The chief will then assign someone to accompany you to the top of the mountain, where another short ceremony may be performed for the ancestors.

About two-thirds of the way from the village is a spring where you can refill your water bottle, although it's considered a sacred spot and it may take some convincing to persuade your guide to show you where it is. Just after the spring, the climb becomes steeper, with some crumbling rock and places where you'll need to use your hands to clamber out. Once near the summit, the path evens out and then gradually ascends for another 1.5km to the mountain's highest point. The top of Namúli is often shrouded in clouds, so you'll likely have better views during the climb than from the summit itself. After descending the moun-

---

THE MAKUA

Although widely scattered today throughout large areas of central and northern Mozambique, most Makua consider Monte Namúli as a common home. According to tradition, the Makua ancestors – all once living in the area around the mountain – split into several groups. Some followed the Rio Malema from its source on the mountain northwards into Nampula province, while others made their way southwards along the Rio Licungo (which also has its source on Namúli) into present-day Zambézia, thus resulting in the distinct Makua groupings of modern times.

MAKUA MARRIAGE CUSTOMS

Women contemplating marriage could take a tip from the matrilineal Lomwe-Makua people who live around Gurúè. Instead of the traditional exchange of gifts (*lobola* – bride price or dowry) to seal an engagement, an exchange of services is often required – anything from repairing a fence to building a house – so that the man is able to prove he can work. Another tradition stemming from the matrilineal culture is that after marriage, the groom sets up his house near that of his mother-in-law.

---

tain, present the rice that you bought at the Gurúè market to the chief as thanks.

OVERNIGHT OPTIONS
It's possible to do the climb in a long day from Gurúè if you get an early start and drive as far as Mugunha Sede, from where it's about three hours on foot to the summit. The road to Mugunha Sede has been rehabilitated and is in rough but decent condition.

To do the entire climb on foot from Gurúè, allow three days, walking the first day as far as Mugunha Sede (about seven to eight hours from Gurúè), where the *régulo* will show you a spot to camp or arrange basic accommodation in a local house. The second day, head up to the summit and back, spending the night again in Mugunha Sede and returning the next day to Gurúè. With an early start and good fitness levels, it's possible to combine the second and third stages into one long day. If you have an extra day available, there's a longer detour route possible via the UP4 warehouse and a beautiful waterfall. Camping on the summit isn't permitted (and isn't a good idea anyway because of rapidly and often dramatically changing weather conditions). Be prepared for frequent rain and cold. Also, if it's raining, the guide will definitely want an extra incentive to continue up to the summit. Guides can be arranged in Quelimane through Zambézia Travels (p124), or in Gurúè through Pensão Monte Verde and Residencial Likungo.

Sleeping & Eating
Pensão Gurúè (☎ 24-910050; Av da República; r US$14) On the main street near Pensão Monte Verde, this was once Gurúè's best option, though it's now

run down. There are basic rooms (most sharing facilities) and a struggling restaurant.

Residencial Likungo (☎ 82-442 0290; Av 25 de Setembro; d & tw from US$16) A decent place, with five clean rooms in a large house, all with shared bathroom. Breakfast is included in the price and meals can be arranged. It's in the town centre near Escola Primária dos Monte Namúli. You can also make bookings and get information through Salão de Cha Riveiera in Quelimane (p125).

Pensão Monte Verde (☎ 24-910245; Av da República; s/d US$20/30) Rooms here are quite reasonable, with their own bathroom and hot water, and there's a restaurant (breakfast included). It's on the main street near BIM.

For food, other than what you can arrange at the hotels, there are inexpensive plates of rice and beans at the market and a bakery just down from Pensão Gurúe. For self-catering, try **Aquíl Comercial** (Av da República) near BIM.

Getting There & Away

There's a daily chapa to Quelimane (US$9.60, six to seven hours) departing about 4.30am from near the market. Otherwise there are several vehicles daily to Mocuba (US$5, 3½

to four hours), where you can get onward transport to Quelimane. The road from Gurúe south to the Nampevo junction with the EN104 is good tarmac.

For Nampula, there's at least one vehicle daily in the dry season to Alto Molócuè, from where there is frequent onward transport. Alternatively, catch a chapa to Mutuali – they run whenever there's a train connection – and wait for the train to Nampula (or Cuamba). Cuamba can also be reached via a decent road, though there's little traffic, as almost everyone takes the train (see p145). If you leave Gurúe early enough (no later than 5am), you can take any Mocuba or Quelimane transport to Nampevo junction, get out there and wait for a passing bus or truck on to Nampula.

The fastest way to get to Milange with public transport is via Mocuba.

ALTO MOLÓCUÈ

This agreeable town is a refuelling point between Mocuba and Nampula.

Pensão Santo António (d US$16; meals from US$3) on the main square has clean doubles. Vehicles go daily to/from Nampula (US$4, 3½ hours) and Mocuba (US$4, four hours).

Northern Mozambique

If southern Mozambique's lures are the accessible beaches and relaxing resorts, in the north it's the paradisal coastal landscapes, the sense of space and the sheer adventure of travel. This is one of Africa's last frontiers – wild, beautiful and untamed. Inland are vast expanses of bush where enough lions and elephants still roam to be the stuff of local lore and wreak havoc on villages. Along the coast is an almost endless succession of unspoiled beaches and islands, plus Ilha de Moçambique – one of Southern Africa's top attractions.

In many respects, the north – the provinces of Nampula, Niassa and Cabo Delgado – might as well be a separate country. It's divided from the rest of Mozambique by several major rivers and hundreds of kilometres of road. And, although home to one-third of Mozambique's population, it accounts for only one-fifth of the gross national product, has the lowest adult literacy rates and often seems to drop out of sight for the southern-oriented government.

Culturally, northern Mozambique is intriguing as the home of many matrilineal tribes, in contrast with the strictly patrilineal south. Islamic influences are also stronger here, with centuries-old ties to the old Swahili trading networks. The north is also the birthplace of Mozambique's independence struggle. It was here, in the bush, that the Frelimo cadres did their training, and it was here – in the unlikely village of Chai – that the first shots of war were fired.

In the main destinations – Nampula, Ilha de Moçambique, Pemba, the Archipélago das Quirimbas and Lichinga – there is enough infrastructure to travel as comfortably as you like. Elsewhere, journeys are rough and rugged.

Places in this chapter are described clockwise from south to north.

HIGHLIGHTS

- Wander at dawn through the streets of **Ilha de Moçambique** (p137), taking in its surreal, time-warp atmosphere
- Go island hopping by dhow or chill out on your private slice of paradise in the **Archipélago das Quirimbas** (p158)
- Revel in the rugged remoteness of the **Lago Niassa** (p148) shoreline and spend a night at the wonderful **Nkwichi Lodge** (p150).
- Chill out on Pemba's **Praia de Wimbi** (p154)
- Set off on one of the wildest safaris of your life in the **Reserva do Niassa** (p150)

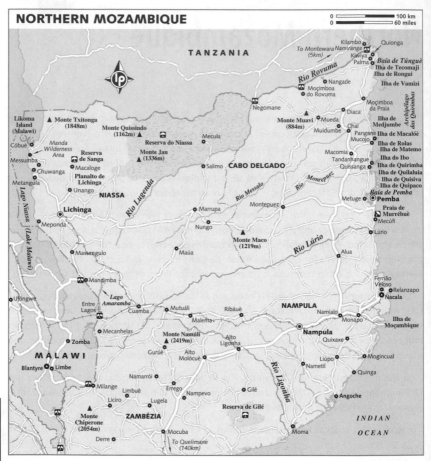

NORTHERN MOZAMBIQUE

Climate
In theory, the rainy season starts somewhat earlier in Mozambique's far north – from late December until March – although in recent years the rains have held off until later, around February, and have continued through to April. There's less rainfall along the coastal areas and more in inland areas at altitude.

National Parks
The big drawcards here are the Reserva do Niassa (p150) and the Archipélago das Quirimbas (p158), much of which is protected as a national park; see also p40. In the far northwest is the Manda Wilderness Area (p149).

Getting There & Away
There are straightforward air and road connections linking northern Mozambique with Tanzania and Malawi, and if your focus is on this part of the country, it's often less expensive and more time-efficient to enter this way, than via Maputo; see p186. Within Mozambique, there are good north–south air links. While the north–south road situation is improving (it's mostly tarmac the whole way, following main routes), it's still a long, rugged journey, so allow ample time for overland travel.

NAMPULA
Bustling Nampula is Mozambique's third-largest city, a convenient transport hub and – as the jumping-off point for visiting Ilha de Moçam-

bique – an inevitable stop for many travellers. While there are few, if any, tourist attractions, the city's good facilities, broad avenues and its main plaza, graced by an imposing white cathedral and rimmed by flowering trees, make it an amenable enough spot to spend a night or two.

The surrounding countryside is dotted with enormous inselbergs – large masses of smooth volcanic granite which intruded into the earth's crust aeons ago and were then exposed over the millennia by erosion of the softer surrounding rock. Some soar close to 1000m into the air. Climbing them is tempting, but before doing so check with locals about the presence of land mines. For any technical climbing, you'll need to get permission from the local district administrator.

History

It's only recently that Nampula has come into its own, having spent much of the 19th century languishing in the shadow of nearby Ilha de Moçambique. The construction of a rail link from the coast in the 1930s and the expansion of the city's port in the late 1940s boosted Nampula's growth as a rail junction and administrative centre. Today, it's the capital of Nampula province (Mozambique's second most populous province after Zambézia) and the commercial centre of the north.

Orientation

The train station and main transport stand are at the northern edge of town. About 10 minutes on foot southwest of here is the cathedral, a major landmark. Once at the cathedral, internet cafés, ATMs and several hotels are within easy reach, scattered around within about a 1km radius.

The best map, if you can manage to find one – check in local stationery shops or at **Gabinete de Endereçamento da Cidade de Nampula** (☎ /fax 26-213848; 256 Rua Daniel Napatima) – is the excellent *Planta de Endereçamento da Cidade de Nampula*. There are **BIM Expresso** branches with ATMs on Av Eduardo Mondlane, and on the corner of Avs da Independência & Francisco Manyanga.

Information

INTERNET ACCESS

IT Services (Av Eduardo Mondlane; per hr US$2; ☽ 7am-9pm) Next to Frango King.

Teledata (Av Eduardo Mondlane, Centro Comercial de Nampula; per hr US$1.60; ☽ 7.30am-8pm Mon-Fri, 7.30am-1pm & 3pm-8pm Sat) Next to Hotel Girassol.

MEDICAL SERVICES

Farmácia Calêndula (Av Eduardo Mondlane; ☽ 8am-8pm Mon-Sat, 9am-1pm Sun) One block up from the museum.

Hospital Provincial (Praça da Liberdade) Malaria testing.

MONEY

Centro Comercial de Nampula (Av Eduardo Mondlane) ATM; next to Hotel Girassol.

Shoprite (Rua dos Continuadores) ATM.

Standard Bank (Av Eduardo Mondlane) ATM, and changes travellers cheques for a minimum US$35 commission per transaction; just up from the museum.

TELEPHONE

TDM (Telecomunicações de Moçambique; Rua Monomotapa) International and domestic calls; near the cathedral.

Sights & Activities

The **Museu Nacional de Etnografia** (National Ethnography Museum; Av Eduardo Mondlane; admission free, donations welcome; ☽ 2-4.30pm Tue-Thu & Sat, 2-6pm Fri, 10am-noon & 2-4pm Sun) is well worth a visit, with a well arranged collection documenting various aspects of local life and culture and explanations in English and Portuguese.

Nampula doesn't have as much to offer architecturally as Maputo and Beira, but there are a few intriguing buildings. The main one is the imposing **Catedral de Nossa Senhora de Fátima**, in a large plaza flanked at one end by the governor's house.

The public **swimming pool** (Clube CFM; Rua 3 de Fevereiro; entry US$2) is a decent spot to cool off. The **pool** (Ribáué Rd; adult/child US$3/2) at Complexo Bamboo is smaller, but the surrounding greenery is pleasant.

About 5km north of town is a **monastery** run by a contemplative women's order, with an interesting church that is periodically open to the public. Follow the airport road out of town past the roundabout to the first major fork; take the first left and watch for the small signpost.

Sleeping

What Nampula lacks in sights, it makes up for in its array of sleeping options, which is reasonably wide at the upper end of the spectrum, although mediocre at the budget level.

NORTHERN MOZAMBIQUE

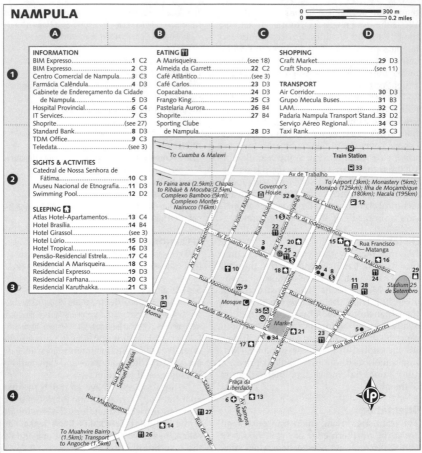

NAMPULA

0   300 m
0   0.2 miles

INFORMATION
BIM Expresso.....................1 C2
BIM Expresso.....................2 C3
Centro Comercial de Nampula......3 C3
Farmácia Calêndula....................4 D3
Gabinete de Endereçamento da Cidade
  de Nampula...........................5 D3
Hospital Provincial...................6 C4
IT Services...........................7 C3
Shoprite...........................(see 27)
Standard Bank......................8 D3
TDM Office..........................9 C3
Teledata...........................(see 3)

SIGHTS & ACTIVITIES
Catedral de Nossa Senhora de
  Fátima............................10 C3
Museu Nacional de Etnografia....11 C3
Swimming Pool.......................12 D2

SLEEPING
Atlas Hotel-Apartamentos........13 C4
Hotel Brasília......................14 B4
Hotel Girassol....................(see 3)
Hotel Lúrio.........................15 D3
Hotel Tropical......................16 D3
Pensão-Residencial Estrela.......17 C4
Residencial A Marisqueira..........18 C3
Residencial Expresso................19 D3
Residencial Farhana.................20 C3
Residencial Karuthakka.............21 C3

EATING
A Marisqueira.......................(see 18)
Almeida da Garrett................22 C2
Café Atlântico.....................(see 3)
Café Carlos........................23 D3
Copacabana.........................24 D3
Frango King........................25 C3
Pastelaria Aurora..................26 B4
Shoprite...........................27 B4
Sporting Clube
  de Nampula........................28 D3

SHOPPING
Craft Market.......................29 D3
Craft Shop.........................(see 11)

TRANSPORT
Air Corridor.......................30 D3
Grupo Mecula Buses.................31 B3
Padaria Nampula Transport Stand..33 D2
Serviço Aéreo Regional............34 C3
Taxi Rank..........................35 C3

BUDGET

Hotel Lúrio (☎ 26-218631; Av da Independência; s/d US$20/32, ste s/d US$48/60) A large, cavernous high-rise a few blocks south of the train station, with faded rooms, all with fans and without hot water, that are among the cheapest in town. Continental breakfast is included.

Hotel Brasília (☎ 26-217531; 26 Rua dos Continuadores; tw/d US$26/30; ⊠) Hotel Brasília has clean, decent-value rooms with bathroom and a small restaurant (snacks from US$1, meals and pizzas US$2.50 to US$7) featuring Mozambican and standard cuisine. It's close to Shoprite, but otherwise a bit of a walk to internet cafés and the transport depots.

Pensão-Residencial Estrela (☎ 26-214902; Av Paulo Samuel Kankhomba; tw without/with bathroom US$32/56)

Proudly displaying its single star (only about half of which is actually merited), this shoestring establishment has overpriced twin-bedded rooms with fan – some with TV and minifridge – a tolerable shared bathroom, and a central but noisy and rather seedy location one block downhill from the post office. There's no food.

Residencial A Marisqueira (☎ 26-213611; cnr Avs Paolo Samuel Kankhomba & Eduardo Mondlane; s/d/tw US$36/41/53; ⊠) Several big steps up is the well-located and central A Marisqueira, with no-frills rooms (ask for one of the newer ones), all with TV, and a restaurant downstairs. There's no hot water.

Residencial Farhana (☎ 26-212527; Av Paulo Samuel Kankhomba; s/d/tw US$35/48/62; ⊠) Formerly Pensão Marques, this large, rather dingy edifice has a row of straightforward rooms – the doubles come with a rattling air-conditioner and musty private bathroom – plus hot water and TV. There's no food. Rooms to the front have small balconies, but they get the street noise; those to the back are quieter, but ventilation isn't as good.

MIDRANGE & TOP END

The selection improves if you're willing to pay a bit more, with several more upper-end places under construction.

Residencial Expresso (☎ 26-218808/9; fax 26-218806; Av da Independência; s/d from US$53/67; ✸) Six large, spotless, modern rooms with fridge and TV. Breakfast is included and meals can be arranged.

Residencial Karuthakka (☎ 26-216730, 82-670 7320; residencialkaruthakka@hotmail.com; Rua 3 de Fevereiro; r without/with breakfast US$45/50, ste US$60; ✸) A new place behind the market with a large front veranda, plus spacious, spotless rooms, some with balcony, and all with minifridge, TV, fan, air-con and hot water.

Atlas Hotel-Apartamentos (☎ 26-218222; fax 26-218233; Av Samora Machel; s/d US$70/80; ✸) Spacious (though the bedroom itself is smallish) and rather heavily furnished self-catering apartments with sitting room, kitchenette and fridge. It's at the southern edge of town near the hospital.

Hotel Tropical (☎ 26-213220, 82-499 7670; Rua Macombre; s/d/tw US$53/62/77; ✸) Behind the museum, this hotel was once Nampula's only midrange choice and still does a steady business, though it's seen better days and isn't as good value as the other options in this category. Rooms come with TV, bathroom and breakfast buffet and there's a popular restaurant downstairs.

Complexo Bamboo (☎ 26-217838; www.teledata.mz/bamboo; Ribáuè Rd; s/tw/d US$60/80/80; ✸ 🛒) Pleasant, well-maintained rooms (the twins are nicer than the doubles) in expansive grounds with a tiny playground make this a good choice for families. All rooms have TV and minifridge and there's a restaurant. It's about 5km out of town – follow Av do Trabalho west from the train station, then right onto the Ribáuè Rd; Bamboo is 1.5km down on the left.

Hotel Girassol (☎ 26-216000; www.girassolhoteis.co.mz; Av Eduardo Mondlane; s/d US$90/105, ste US$130-150; ✸) Upstairs in the Centro Comercial de Nampula high-rise, this good four-star place catering to business travellers has efficient service and Nampula's best rooms. All have small, modern bathrooms, plus TV, telephone and minifridge and some have excellent views over the cathedral and town.

Complexo Montes Nairucco (☎ 26-240081; idalecio@teledata.mz; Ribáuè Rd; camping per person US$4, s/tw/d US$50/65/65, day visitors per person US$2) This Portuguese-run getaway is nestled under the towering Monte Nairucco on a large farm planted with mango and orange groves about 16km west of town. It makes a peaceful weekend retreat or day trip (6am-10pm), with a reservoir where you can swim, a restaurant (meals US$4 to US$8; breakfast, lunch and dinner), a bar and a braai area, plus walks in the vicinity. The camping ground overlooks the reservoir and has hot-water ablutions. Taxis from town charge from about US$10. Driving, follow the Ribáuè Rd for about 15km to the signpost, from where it's 1km further down a small lane.

Eating
RESTAURANTS

Copacabana (☎ 26-218121; Rua Macombre; pizzas & meals US$4-8; ⊗ closed Sun) Opposite Hotel Tropical, with covered outdoor seating, fresh pasta, pizzas and a large menu featuring grilled seafood and meat dishes.

Sporting Clube de Nampula (Av Eduardo Mondlane; meals US$4-8; ⊗ 8am-10pm) Next to the Museu Nacional de Etnografia, this popular watering hole features the usual chicken and fish grills, plus *fejoada* (a bean-and-sausage dish) and more. Sit inside or outdoors – there's a playground at the adjoining school for children.

Café Carlos (☎ 26-217960; Rua José Macamo; meals from US$4; ⊗ closed Sun) Just off Rua dos Continuadores, this pleasant place has seafood grills, a pizza oven and seating in a small, outdoor courtyard.

Almeida da Garrett (Av Francisco Manyanga; meals US$6; ⊗ 9am-11pm Wed-Mon & Tue 5pm-11pm) A darkish, rather seedy establishment with pool tables inside and nicer dining on a small balcony. The large menu features good Goan cuisine, including some vegetarian dishes, plus a range of burgers, grills and other standards. Stop by in the morning to place your order.

Complexo Bamboo (☎ 26-217838; www.teledata.mz/bamboo; Ribáuè Rd; meals from US$4; 🛒) The restaurant at this hotel serves all the usual dishes in pleasant, leafy surroundings.

CAFÉS & FAST FOOD

Café Atlântico (Av Eduardo Mondlane, Centro Comercial de Nampula; snacks & meals from US$1; ☺ 6am-9pm; ☒) Burgers, pizzas and other light meals.

A Marisqueira (☎ 26-213611; cnr Avs Paulo Kankhomba & Eduardo Mondlane; meals US$4) Reasonably priced plates of the day, plus snacks and sweets, in a bright dining room with views of the passing scene.

Pastelaria Aurora (Rua dos Continuadores; dishes from US$2) This place, near Hotel Brasília has light meals and snacks, and is known for its curries. Also on offer are a few Chinese dishes.

Frango King (Av Eduardo Mondlane; half/whole chicken US$3/5; ☺ 7.30am-4am) Grilled chicken to go.

Self-caterers can try **Shoprite** (Rua dos Continuadores; ☺ 9am-8pm Mon-Sat, 9am-3pm Sun).

Shopping

The best place for crafts is the Sunday morning **craft market** (☺ dawn to dusk) in the large stadium field downhill from Hotel Tropical. The best time to go is from about 7am, before things get hot and crowded. Leave your bags at home, and watch out for pickpockets.

The craft shop behind the museum has ceramic Makonde pots, basketry and woodcarvings.

Getting There & Away

AIR

There are flights on **LAM** (☎ 26-213322, 26-212801; Av Francisco Manyanga; ☺ 7.30am-12.30pm, 2.30-5.30pm Mon-Fri) to Maputo (daily), Beira, Lichinga, Quelimane, Tete and Pemba (all several times weekly).

Air Corridor (☎ 26-214444, 26-213333; aircorridor@ teledata.mz; cnr Av Eduardo Mondlane & Rua 3 de Fevereiro) stops in Nampula on its daily run up and down the coast.

Serviço Aéreo Regional (SAR; ☎ 26-212401, sargaw@ teledata.mz; Rua Cidade de Moçambique), opposite the market, flies twice weekly between Nampula and Cuamba (US$72 one-way).

The airport is about 4km northeast of town (US$4 in a taxi).

BUS & CHAPA

Grupo Mecula has daily buses to Nacala (US$4, two to three hours); Pemba (US$7, seven hours); Quelimane (US$14, 11 hours); Montepuez (US$7, eight hours); and Mueda (US$12, 13 hours). All depart at 5am except the bus to Nacala, which departs at 1pm. Departures are from the Grupo Mecula garage

(in the area known as 'Roman') on Rua da Moma, just off Av 25 de Setembro and one block south of Rua Cidade de Moçambique.

To Ilha de Moçambique (US$3.60, three to four hours), there are chapas departing between about 5am and 11am from Padaria Nampula transport stand along Av do Trabalho, east of the train station. Look for one that's going direct – many that say they're going to the island go only as far as Monapo, where you'll need to wait for another vehicle. Currently, the best connection is on the *tanzaniano* chapa departing Nampula about 10am (get there about 9am to be sure of a seat) and continuing more or less nonstop to Ilha. Alternatively, ask for one of the other *tanzaniano* chapas, which depart Nampula anywhere between around 7am and 10am, depending on how early they arrive from Ilha. The Padaria Nampula transport stand is also the place to find chapas to Mossuril, Namapa, and other points north and east.

Transport to Angoche (US$4.80, three hours) departs from Muahvire bairro, along the extension of Av das FPLM, beginning about 5am.

Chapas to Ribáuè and Mocuba (US$11, eight hours) leave from the western end of Av do Trabalho, about 2.5km west of the train station near the Ribáuè road junction in the Faina area. There are also buses several times weekly from here to Cuamba, and the road is in decent shape most of the way, although most people go by train. If you drive, there's accommodation en route at **Complexo Turístico Malaya** (☎ 26-340004; d US$22; ☒) in Malema, with small and surprisingly decent rondavels, and a restaurant.

TRAIN

A six-times weekly passenger train connects Nampula and Cuamba; see p145.

Getting Around

The main **taxi rank** (Moti Taxi; ☎ 82-352 0970; Av Paulo Samuel Kankhomba) is near the market. Moti Taxi is planning to open another stand soon next to the main bus station opposite Padaria Nampula.

Car rental agencies include the very efficient and helpful branch of **Imperial** (☎ 26-216312, 82-300 5170; imperial.npl@teledata.mz; Airport); and **Moti Rent-A-Car** (☎ 82-352 2770; Airport). Moti Rent-A-Car takes Visa cards only and doesn't offer any insurance.

MOGINCUAL

Mogincual, an old trading settlement 175km southeast of Nampula, sits near an estuary divided by a narrow finger of land from the sea, surrounded by wetland areas that are good for birding.

Bay Diving (p144) runs a basic bush camp (advance reservations essential) on the estuary about 3km from town. However, it's soon to be relocated closer to Nacala; check with them for an update.

Getting There & Away

Take any chapa running along the Nampula–Nacala road and disembark at the Monapo junction. From here, you'll have to walk a few minutes to the market in Monapo town, from where chapas run once or twice daily to Mogincual.

ANGOCHE

This quiet, somewhat dilapidated district capital has a long and intriguing history. While few reminders of its past remain, it has stayed relatively isolated and is worth a visit if you're in the area. About 7km north of town is the attractive **Praia Nova**, and about 45km further on is the village of **Quinga**, near another beautiful stretch of sand.

Stretching well south of Angoche towards Moma and on to Pebane are the **Archipélagos das Ilhas Primeiras e Segundas** (soon to be Mozambique's newest protected area – see p40), several of which are favoured as nesting areas by local green turtles and many of which are encircled by coral reefs. Dugongs are also frequent visitors. There are no tourist facilities.

History

Angoche (formerly António Ennes) is an old Muslim trading centre dating from at least the 15th century. It was one of Mozambique's earliest settlements and an important gold and ivory trading post. By the late 16th century, Angoche had been eclipsed by Quelimane as an entry port to the interior. However, it continued to play a role in coastal trade and was an important economic and political centre, with close ties to Ilha de Moçambique. In the 19th century, Angoche became the focus of the clandestine slave trade, which continued until the 1860s when the town was attacked by the Portuguese. While effective Portuguese administration was not established until several decades later, the attack marked the be-

ginning of Angoche's downfall and the town never regained its former status.

Sleeping & Eating

Inas Casa de Hospedes (☎ 26-720232; r US$52; 🞕) Angoche's most comfortable accommodation has straightforward rooms and meals. It's behind the Catholic church; ask for Mooxelele (mo-oh-sheh-*lay*-lay).

Otherwise, there are several basic *pensões* (inexpensive hotels) with no-frills rooms for about US$4, including Pensão Mafamede and Pensão Parapato. For meals, try **Restaurante O Pescador** (Av Liberdade; meals from US$2), on the main street near BIM bank.

Getting There & Away

Daily chapas connect Nampula and Angoche during the dry season, departing Nampula about 5am (US$4.80, three hours). It's also possible to reach Angoche from Monapo. Most public transport on this route only goes as far as the village of Liúpo, where you'll need to change vehicles.

Quinga can be reached with your own vehicle from Angoche (going inland via Namaponda), or via Liúpo, from where there's a daily chapa on to Quinga. There is no direct public transport from Angoche.

Dhows to the offshore islands can be arranged at Angoche's bustling fish market.

ILHA DE MOÇAMBIQUE

Tiny, crescent-shaped Ilha de Moçambique (Mozambique Island) measures only 3km in length and barely 500m in width at its widest section. Yet it has played a larger-than-life role in East African coastal life over the centuries, and today is one of the region's most fascinating destinations. Close your eyes for a minute and imagine the now-quiet streets echoing with the footsteps of Arab traders, ushered in on the monsoon winds. Or hear the crisp voice of the Portuguese governor-general barking orders from his plush quarters in the Palácio de São Paulo. Or try to imagine the sweat, anger and despair of the Africans herded into the closed cells of the Fortaleza de São Sebastião before being sold into slavery.

Today, Ilha de Moçambique is an intriguing anomaly – part ghost town and part lively fishing community. It's also a picturesque and exceptionally pleasant place to wander around, with graceful praças rimmed by once-grand churches, colonnaded archways

NORTHERN MOZAMBIQUE

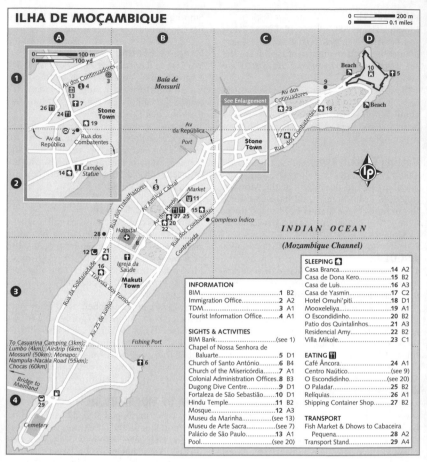

ILHA DE MOÇAMBIQUE

INFORMATION	
BIM...**1** B2	
Immigration Office....................**2** A2	
TDM...**3** A1	
Tourist Information Office.........**4** A1	

SIGHTS & ACTIVITIES	
BIM Bank.................................(see 1)	
Chapel of Nossa Senhora de Baluarte................................**5** D1	
Church of Santo António..........**6** B4	
Church of the Misericórdia.......**7** A1	
Colonial Administration Offices.**8** B3	
Dugong Dive Centre..................**9** D1	
Fortaleza de São Sebastião.....**10** D1	
Hindu Temple...........................**11** B2	
Mosque.....................................**12** A3	
Museu da Marinha.................(see 13)	
Museu de Arte Sacra................(see 7)	
Palácio de São Paulo...............**13** A1	
Pool...(see 20)	

SLEEPING	
Casa Branca..............................**14** A2	
Casa de Dona Kero...................**15** B2	
Casa de Luís..............................**16** A3	
Casa de Yasmin.........................**17** C2	
Hotel Omuhi'piti.......................**18** D1	
Mooxeleliya..............................**19** A1	
O Escondidinho........................**20** B2	
Patio dos Quintalinhos.............**21** A3	
Residencial Amy........................**22** B2	
Villa Mikole...............................**23** C1	

EATING	
Café Âncora..............................**24** A1	
Centro Náutico........................(see 9)	
O Escondidinho......................(see 20)	
O Paladar.................................**25** B2	
Reliquias...................................**26** A1	
Shipping Container Shop...........**27** B2	

TRANSPORT	
Fish Market & Dhows to Cabaceira Pequena.............................**28** A2	
Transport Stand........................**29** A4	

and stately colonial-era buildings lining the quiet, cobbled streets of the Stone Town. In Makuti Town, with its thatched-roof huts and crush of people, narrow alleyways echo with the sounds of playing children and squawking chickens, while fishermen sit on the sand repairing their long, brightly coloured nets.

Since 1991, this cultural melting pot has been a Unesco World Heritage site and – while there are still many crumbling ruins – there's fresh paint and restoration work aplenty.

Interestingly, there are no wells on Ilha de Moçambique; it was settled despite the lack of water sources because of its favourable location and natural harbour. To compensate, most houses in the early days had cisterns, as

did the Fort of São Sebastião, which had three. Now, water is piped in from the mainland.

History

For most of its history, Ilha de Moçambique has served as a meeting point of cultures and a hub of Indian Ocean trade. As early as the 15th century it was an important boat-building centre, and its history as a trading settlement – with ties to Madagascar, Persia, Arabia and elsewhere – dates back well before that. Vasco da Gama landed here in 1498 and in 1507 a permanent Portuguese settlement was established on the island. Unlike Sofala to the south, where the Portuguese also established a foothold at about the same time, Ilha de Moçambique prospered as both a trading

NORTHERN MOZAMBIQUE

station and naval base, with connections to places as far away as Macau and Goa. In the late 16th century, the sprawling Fort of São Sebastião was constructed. The island soon became capital of Portuguese East Africa – a status that it held until the end of the 19th century when the government was transferred to Lourenço Marques (Maputo). As focus shifted southwards, Ilha de Moçambique's star began to fade. The construction of a rail terminus at Nacala in 1947 and the development of the Nacala port during the 1950s sealed the island's fate and sent it into an economic decline from which it never recovered.

Apart from its early strategic and economic importance, Ilha de Moçambique also developed as a missionary centre. Beginning in the 17th century, numerous orders established churches here and Christians intermixed with the island's traditional Muslim population and Hindu community. Various small waves of immigration over the years – from places as diverse as East Africa, Goa, Macau and elsewhere – contributed to the ethnic and cultural mix and the resulting melange is one of the island's most intriguing aspects. Over the last century, as the Portuguese presence on the island has faded into obscurity, Muslim influence has reasserted itself and, together with local Makua culture, is now dominant.

Orientation

Ilha de Moçambique's fusion of cultures is best seen in Stone Town, as the cobwebbed, quiet northern half of the island is known. Here, you'll find the majority of historic buildings – most constructed between the early 16th and late 19th centuries when the Portuguese occupied the island and most original residents were banished to the mainland. Makuti Town – the island's younger, more colourful southern half – reflects Ilha de Moçambique's other face. It dates from the late 19th century, and is where most islanders now live, with daily Makua life going on much as it has for centuries. The waterfront in between, along the island's eastern edge, is known as the *contracosta*.

Maps are available from the tourist information office.

Information

BIM (Av Amilcar Cabral; ⏲ 8am-3pm Mon-Fri) On the western side of the island; has an ATM, and changes cash dollars, euro and rand.

Immigration Office Diagonally opposite Mooxeleliya, down from the Church of the Misericórdia.

TDM (per min US$0.04; ⏲ 7.30am-8pm) Just up from the tourist information office; internet access and international calls.

Tourist information office (☎ 26-610081; Av de Continudores; ⏲ 9am-noon & 2-5pm, in theory) Information on things to see and do, island guides and accommodation listings.

Sights
PALÁCIO DE SÃO PAULO

The imposing **Palácio de São Paulo** (☎ 26-610081; fax 26-610047; adult/child US$4/1; ⏲ 9am-4pm) – the former governor's residence and now a museum – dates from 1610 and is the island's historical showpiece. The interior has been renovated to give a remarkable glimpse into what upper-class life must have been like during the city's 18th-century heyday. In addition to an impressive collection of knick-knacks from Portugal, Arabia, India and China, there are many pieces of original furniture, including an important collection of heavily ornamented Indo-Portuguese pieces. In the chapel, don't miss the altar and the pulpit, the latter of which was made in the 17th century by Chinese artists in Goa. On the ground floor is the small **Museu da Marinha** (Maritime Museum), with relics hauled up from the surrounding depths. Behind the palace are the **Church of the Misericórdia** (still in active use) and the **Museu de Arte Sacra** (Museum of Sacred Art, closed at time of writing), containing religious ornaments, paintings and carvings. The museum is housed in the former hospital of the Holy House of Mercy, a religious guild that assisted the poor and sick in several Portuguese colonies from the early 1500s onwards. The ticket price includes entry to all three museums.

FORTALEZA DE SÃO SEBASTIÃO

The island's northern end is dominated by the massive **Fortaleza de São Sebastião** (admission free, guide US$2; ⏲ 8am-5pm), which is the oldest complete fort still standing in sub-Saharan Africa. Construction began in 1558, and about 50 years later the final stones were laid. Guides can be arranged with the tourist information centre. Just beyond the fort, at the island's tip, is the whitewashed **Chapel of Nossa Senhora de Baluarte**. Built in 1522, it's considered to be the oldest European building in the southern hemisphere and one of the best examples of

---

MUSIRO

All along the northern coast, and especially on Ilha de Moçambique, you'll frequently see women with their faces painted white. The paste is known as *musiro* (also *n'siro* or *msiro*), and is used as a facial mask to beautify the skin, and sometimes as a sunscreen by women working in the fields, or as a medicinal treatment (though the medicinal paste usually has a yellowish tinge). *Musiro* was also traditionally applied in ways that conveyed messages – for example whether the wearer was married, or whether her husband was away – although most of the meanings have since been lost.

Musiro is made by grinding a branch of the *Olax dissitiflora* tree (known locally as *ximbuti* or *msiro*) against a stone with a bit of water. Local women usually leave the mask on for the day, and sometimes overnight. If you go walking in villages early in the morning and see women with white paste on their hands, chances are that they are in the midst of preparing *musiro*.

Manueline vaulted architecture in Mozambique (add that one to your store of cocktail party trivia). At the southern tip of the island, keeping watch over the fishing port, is the impressive, white and no-longer-used **Church of Santo António**.

OTHER SIGHTS

Other places to watch for while wandering through Stone Town include the restored ochre-toned **BIM bank** (Av Amilcar Cabral) and the ornate **colonial administration offices** overlooking the gardens east of the hospital. A few blocks north of the market is a **Hindu temple** and on the island's western edge a fairly modern **mosque** painted an unmissable shade of green.

Activities

Ilha has several small beaches, the cleanest of which is Praia Nancaramo, next to the fort. Strong tidal flows make it dangerous to swim around the northern and southern ends of the island. Better quality beaches are located in Chocas (p142) or points further north. For cooling off, try the small **pool** (Av dos Heróis; adult/child US$2/1) at O Escondidinho.

Dugong Dive Centre (☎ 26-610027, 82-454 7810; caku@teledata.mz; Centro Náutico; ◷ 8am-5pm Tue-Sun) can sort you out with diving around Goa and Sena, two tiny islands off Ilha de Moçambique, plus overnight dhow safaris (September to November only), sea kayaking and boat transfers to Chocas. Their base is opposite Hotel Omuhi'piti.

Sleeping

There's a reasonably good range of accommodation on the island, but at the budget level, many of the rooms are small and poorly ventilated. If your funds permit, it's often worth paying a modest amount more for one of the midrange places.

BUDGET

Casuarina Camping (lenavie@hotmail.com; Lumbo; camping per person US$3, r per person US$20, vehicle US$4, day visitor US$0.40) Casuarina is on the mainland opposite Ilha de Moçambique, just a two minute walk from the bridge. On offer: camping on a small beach (where you can also swim), plus no-frills bungalow-style rooms, ablution blocks with bucket-style showers and meals.

Otherwise, the cheapest options are in homes with local families, generally offering small, no-frills rooms in the family quarters. They include:

Casa de Luís (O Macutini; Travessa dos Fornos, Makuti Town; camping per person US$4, s/d US$8/14) Quite basic, and not the best option in heavy rains, as the yard gets flooded, but the owner is friendly and has been welcoming shoestring travellers for years. Take the first left after passing the green mosque (to your right), then the first left again; ask one of the small boys who will inevitably attach themselves to you to show you the way.

Casa de Dona Kero (☎ 26-610034; Rua dos Combatentes, Contracosta; r US$10, d/tr US$14) A small house with small rooms, all with fans but no nets, and on the stuffy side, but the proprietors are friendly. Prices include continental breakfast. It's opposite Complexo Índico.

Residencial Amy (Av dos Heróis; d/tr US$16/18) Near the park, with several basic, dark rooms – most lacking exterior windows – in the main house and a common area with TV. Breakfast costs US$2.

Casa de Yasmin (☎ 26-610073; Rua dos Combatentes; r US$20) At the northern end of the island, with a handful of small, clean rooms – some with private bathroom – in an annex next to the family house. A few air-con rooms with bathroom are planned. No breakfast.

MIDRANGE

Casa Branca (☎ 26-610076; flora204@hotmail.com; Rua dos Combatentes; r US$24) On the island's eastern side near the Camões statue, Casa Branca has three simple but spotless rooms with views of the turquoise sea just a few metres away and a shared kitchen. One room has its own bathroom, and the other two share. Rates include breakfast. Adjoining is a seaside garden/sitting area.

Mooxeleliya (☎ 26-610076; iannika@teledata.mz; d/f US$22/48) Under the same management as Casa Branca and equally good value – the Makua name translates roughly as, 'Did you rest well?' – with five large, high-ceilinged rooms upstairs and two darker 3- to 4-person family-style rooms downstairs. All have their own bathroom, breakfast is included and a backyard garden is planned. It's just down from the Church of the Misericórdia.

Patio dos Quintalinhos (Casa de Gabriele; ☎ 26-610090; www.patiodosquintalinhos.com; Rua da Solidariedade; s/d without bathroom US$20/25, d US$30, q & ste US$35) Opposite the green mosque, with a handful of comfortable, creatively designed rooms around a small courtyard, including one with a loft, and a suite with its own star view skylight and private rooftop balcony with views to the water. All have bathroom, except for two tiny rooms to the back. There's also a rooftop terrace and secure parking (per night US$6); breakfast is included and meals can sometimes be arranged, as can bicycle and vehicle rental and excursions to the outlying islands.

Villa Mikole (Casa Dugong; ☎ 26-610156, 82-454 7810; s/d US$50/70) On a small side street just down from Centro Náutico, this private, well-furnished house run by Dugong Dive Centre has several comfortable rooms to rent, a shaded, airy common area and self-catering and braai facilities. Advance bookings are essential.

O Escondidinho (☎ 26-610078; ilhatur@itservices.co.mz; Av dos Heróis; r US$36/52; ☒) An atmospheric place with spacious, high-ceilinged rooms, all with nets, ceiling fans and mosquito netting in the windows, plus a garden courtyard, and a good restaurant. A few rooms have private bathroom. Advance bookings advisable. It's near the public gardens.

Hotel Omuhi'piti (☎ 26-610101; h.omuhipiti@teledata.mz; s/d from US$60/72; ☒) In a good setting at the island's northern tip, this three-star establishment is Ilha de Moçambique's concession to luxury, with modern, quiet rooms, some with views over the water. Breakfast is included and there's a restaurant.

Eating

O Paladar (meals from US$3; ☽ lunch & dinner) At the eastern corner of the old market and unmarked, O Paladar is the place to go for local cuisine. Stop by in the morning and place your order with Dona Maria for lunchtime or evening meals.

O Escondidinho (☎ 26-610078; meals US$6-8) The restaurant at this hotel has some of Ilha's best dining, with a changing daily menu featuring shrimps, crayfish and other seafood dishes with French overtones and tables near the small garden.

Relíquias (☎ 26-610092; Av da República; meals US$4-10; ☽ 10am-10pm) Another good spot, with a range of seafood and meat dishes, including prawn curry, matapa and coconut rice. It's close to the museum.

Café Âncora (☎ 26-610006; brunch US$9; ☽ 8am-11pm) Newly reopened, Café Âncora, directly opposite the Church of Misericórdia, has delicious brunches (10am to 2pm Sunday), with fresh yogurt and juice, muesli, waffles and more, plus a menu featuring sandwiches, seafood and homemade ice cream.

Centro Náutico (snacks & beers US$1) Drinks and snacks on a breezy waterside terrace opposite Hotel Omuhi'piti.

For self-caterers, there's a well-stocked shipping container shop next to the market.

Entertainment

Ilha de Moçambique is a good place to see *tufo* dancing. Ask at the tourist information office about upcoming events.

The best time to experience Ilha de Moçambique's time-warp atmosphere is just before dawn, or on an evening when the power goes off (a fairly frequent occurrence), especially if there's a full moon.

Getting There & Away

AIR

There's an airstrip at Lumbo on the mainland for charter flights. For regularly scheduled flights to/from Nampula, see p136.

BUS & CHAPA

Ilha de Moçambique is joined by a 3.5km bridge (built in 1967) to the mainland. Most chapas stop about 1km before the bridge in Lumbo, where you'll need to get into a smaller pick-up to cross over Baía de Mossuril (Mossuril Bay), due to vehicle weight restrictions on the bridge.

NORTHERN MOZAMBIQUE

All transport departs from the bridge. The only direct cars to Nampula (US$3.60, three hours) are the *tanzaniano* minibuses, with one or two departing daily between 3am and 5am. The best thing is to ask your hotel to help you get a message to the chapa driver to come collect you. Currently only one (departing about 5am) goes non-stop to Nampula. After about 6am, the only option is open pick-up trucks to Monapo (US$1.20, one hour), where you can get transport on to Nampula (US$2.20, two to three hours) or Nacala (US$2, one hour). Once in Nampula, there are daily buses north to Pemba and south to Quelimane, though both leave early so you'll need to overnight in Nampula. To head direct to Pemba, take the 4am *tanzaniano* chapa as far as Namialo, where – with luck – you should be able to connect with the Mecula bus from Nampula, which usually passes Namialo about 6am.

Chapas to Lumbo cost US$0.20. If you're driving: wide vehicles won't pass over the bridge, and maximum weight is 1.5 tonnes. There's a US$0.40 per vehicle toll payable on arrival on the island.

AROUND ILHA DE MOÇAMBIQUE
Ilha de Goa
This tiny island shimmers offshore, about 5km east of Ilha de Moçambique. It has a lighthouse built during the 1870, run by the lighthouse keeper and his family, who have lived on Goa for more than 20 years. Its name comes from the island's position on the sea route from Goa – the base for local government between 1509 and 1662. The lighthouse is now solar powered, and according to the keeper, the batteries give out about 1am. You can climb to the top for some views.

Before visiting, get permission from the port captain (*capitania*) on Ilha de Moçambique; it's free and can often be arranged on the spot. You'll also need to hire a motorised dhow (about US$60 for a 10 to 15 person boat). Be prepared for choppy seas, and tidal limits on the length of time you can spend on the island. Allow about 40 minutes one-way with favourable winds and currents, otherwise at least double this. Ask at your hotel for a reliable captain.

Ilha de Sena
About 2km south of Ilha de Goa, and prettier, is the Ilha de Sena (also known as the Ilha das Cobras). It takes its name from its

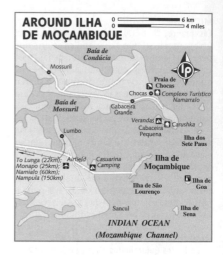

location along the old sea route aiming towards the trading centre of Sena, on the Rio Zambezi. The beach here is attractive and there's snorkelling offshore. In the interior are some rock pools lined with mangrove forests. Permission from the port captain on Ilha de Moçambique is necessary to visit and details for getting here are the same as for Ilha de Goa. Centro Náutico (p141) rents snorkelling equipment.

Ilha de São Lourenço
Just off the southern tip of Ilha de Moçambique is this tiny island, which is completely covered by a small eponymous fort dating from 1695. You can walk across the channel at low tide (watch that you don't get stuck out there), but will need to clamber up over the walls, as the ladder into the fort is missing.

Lumbo
Sleepy Lumbo, on the mainland opposite Ilha de Moçambique, was formerly the terminus of a railway line from the interior. Today it's of interest for its Commonwealth war cemetery, a once grand but now abandoned hotel, a few old Portuguese houses and salt flats.

South of Lumbo on Baía de Mocambo (Mocambo Bay) is Lunga, future site of a new, upscale hotel.

CHOCAS
Just to the north of Ilha de Moçambique and across Baía de Mossuril is the old Portuguese holiday town of Chocas. It makes an agreeable

day or overnight excursion, except during holiday weekends when it's completely overrun.

Nearby are two villages formerly used as getaways by wealthy residents of Ilha de Moçambique. **Cabaceira Grande** is the more interesting of the two, with a well-preserved church dating from the late 16th century, the ruins of the old governor-general's palace dating to the mid-19th century and a tourism training school. **Cabaceira Pequena**, a few kilometres southeast, has some old houses, an old Swahili-style mosque and the ruins of a cistern used as a watering spot by Portuguese sailors. It's near the tip of the Mossuril isthmus, connected by a narrow strip of land.

Nearby is the tiny and underwhelming **Ilha dos Sete Paus**, with snorkelling offshore.

Sleeping & Eating

Complexo Turístico Namarralo (☎ 26-660049; 2-/4-person bungalows with bath US$40/80; 🗷) The busy Namarralo has straightforward stone bungalows in a large, fenced compound on the beach. All have bathroom and breakfast included and there's a restaurant serving Portuguese cuisine. It's signposted from the entrance to Chocas.

Carushka (☎ 82-516 0173; ophavela@teledata.mz; 4-/8-person bungalows US$32/64) Ideal for a quiet getaway (except on holiday weekends), Carushka has rustic, spotless bungalows set back from the water between the mangroves and one of the best stretches of beach. Wooden walkways take you through the mangroves to the water. A restaurant is planned, but for now you'll need to bring all food and drink with you and staff will prepare it (the bungalows aren't self-catering). It's about 2km south of Chocas town, en route to Cabaceira Pequena. Get here by 4WD or on foot from Chocas town, or hire a boat from Ilha de Moçambique to drop you at the beach.

Verandas (camping per person US$2) Camping (bring your own tent) under simple thatched shelters on the beach at Cabaceira Pequena, several kilometres past Carushka. Bring everything with you, although more facilities (and even horse riding) are planned.

Getting There & Away

There are one or two direct chapas daily between Chocas and Nampula; the *tanzaniano* chapa departs Nampula anywhere between 10am and noon and departs Chocas about 4am (US$4). Otherwise, take any transport between Monapo and Ilha de Moçambique, disembarking at the signposted Mossuril

junction 25km southeast of Monapo. Sporadic chapas go from here to Mossuril (20km), and then on to Chocas (12km further), along an unpaved but good road.

From Chocas, it's about a 30-minute walk at low tide to Cabaceira Pequena, and from one hour to 1½ hours to Cabaceira Grande. Alternatively, dhows depart daily in the morning for Cabaceira Pequena from the fish market near the green mosque on Ilha de Moçambique (US$0.20). Departures from Cabaceira Pequena back to Ilha de Moçambique are also in the morning, so if you want to return the same day, you'll need to charter a boat (about US$20 for a motorised dhow). If there's no wind, the trip across the bay can take up to six hours or more. Dugong Dive Centre (p140) organises boat trips to Chocas, as do all of Ilha de Moçambique's midrange hotels and the tourist office.

NACALA

Nacala is set on an impressive natural harbour and is northern Mozambique's busiest port, developed in the mid 20th century. The town itself has nothing of interest for travellers, but there's good diving, and attractive beaches nearby. The most popular are **Fernão Veloso** to the north, with a resident dive operator, and **Relanzapo** to the east.

Orientation

The first part of Nacala you'll enter is Nacala-Alta (the high town) which merits no more time than it takes to drive through. After several kilometres, you'll see the bay ahead of you, and the main street (Rua Principal) begins to head downhill to the train station and harbour in the baixa or Nacala-Porto (port) area. The market, transport stand, banks and most shops are along or just off Rua Principal during its route downhill. The best place to get off the bus is at the top, near Hotel Maiaia. The beaches are about 10km to 15km north and west of town, reached via a turnoff in Nacala-Alta.

Information

Banco Austral (cnr Rua Principal & Rua 8) ATM.
BIM (Baixa) ATM; in an isolated highrise.
BP Petrol Station (Nacala-Alta) ATM.
Farmácia Calêndula (Rua 8; 🕐 8am-6pm Mon-Fri, 8am-noon Sat)
TDM (per min US$0.04; 🕐 7.30am-10pm) Internet access; diagonally opposite Hotel Maiaia.

Sleeping & Eating

Residencial Bela Vista (☎ 26-520404; Nacala-Alta; s/d from US$10/18, d with bathroom US$31; ✂) This shoestring place in Nacala-Alta is only worth considering if you don't want to be by the beach, don't have the budget for Hotel Maiaia and don't have onward transport to anywhere better. Rooms are very basic – most share bathrooms – and there's a restaurant. Turn left off the main road at the town entrance in front of Mini-Bar Owannhoka. Chapas to the baixa (US$0.20) pass nearby.

Bay Diving (☎ 26-520017; www.fimdomundosafaris .com; Fernão Veloso; camping per person US$6, dm US$8, d US$21.50, 2- to 4-person chalets with bathroom US$31-41, breakfast per person US$6; ✂) Almost everyone heads to this popular divers' base on an escarpment overlooking the beach at Fernão Veloso. It has rustic reed and thatch A-frame chalets with fans and nets, plus dorm beds, camping with hot water, a good restaurant (ask about the chocolate cake) and a steam room. They offer PADI and NAUI instruction and equipment rental, plus sea kayaking and road excursions to Ilha de Moçambique. There's also a customised dhow for overnight or day dhow safaris, including to Ilha de Moçambique, and day trips or overnight camping on a deserted stretch of beach across the bay. Follow directions to Fernão Veloso (see right) and then follow the Bay Diving signs. Pick-ups can be arranged from Nacala town. Alternatively, pay any chapa heading to Fernão Veloso a bit extra to take you all the way to Bay Diving.

Complexo Turístico Napala (☎ 26-520608; Fernão Veloso; d/q chalets US$40/70; ✂) A new establishment directly on the beach northeast of Bay Diving, with small stone rondavels – all with TV, minifridge, bathroom and hot water – and a waterside restaurant. Chapas to/from town run nearby.

Hotel Maiaia (☎ 26-526842; inturhoteis@teledata .mz; Rua Principal; s/d from US$60/70; ✂) The centrally located three-star Maiaia is where most business travellers stay. It has a restaurant and spiffy, modern rooms with TV (some also have a small balcony). It's on the main street diagonally opposite the central market, where the road starts its final descent into the baixa. Visa cards are accepted.

All the hotels have restaurants. Otherwise, try the slightly seedy **Baía Azul** (Rua 8; meals US$2) or **Restaurante Sandokan** (Rua 8; meals from US$2), on the opposite side of the main road, and temporarily closed when we passed through.

Pastelaria Carioca (cnr Ruas Principal & 8), near Banco Austral, has light meals and pastries.

Getting There & Around

Grupo Mecula buses to Nampula (US$4, 2½ hours) and Pemba (US$7, seven hours) depart daily at 5am from the Mecula garage. Head down Rua Principal to the large roundabout, then follow the street going left and uphill next to Mozstar. Mecula is about 400m up on the left, behind an unmarked wall.

There are also chapas each morning to Nampula and Monapo (US$1.20, one hour), departing from the blue shipping container diagonally opposite Hotel Maiaia, and also from next to the BP petrol station in Nacala-Alta. Once in Monapo (ask your hotel for help in timing the connection), you can find transport to Ilha de Moçambique and Namialo, the junction town for Pemba.

To Fernão Veloso: take the turn-off for the airport and military base at the Nacala town entrance. After about 9km watch for the signposted turn-off opposite the base, from where it's about another 1.5km. Chapas to Fernão Veloso (US$0.20) depart from the Nacala-Alta market near the Catholic church, or you can catch them at the airport turn-off.

Relanzapo is reached by taking the same turn-off for the airport and military base. Turn right on the dirt road immediately before the base and continue 15km east. There's no public transport.

Nacala has a few metered taxis; dial **Moti-Taxi** (☎ 26-526111).

CUAMBA

This lively rail and road junction (formerly known as Novo Freixo), with its dusty streets, flowering trees and large university student population, is the economic centre of Niassa province and a convenient stop-off if you're travelling to/from Malawi. The surrounding area is known for its garnet gemstones.

Information

BIM Expresso (Av Eduardo Mondlane) ATM; near the post office.

TDM (Av Eduardo Mondlane; per min US$0.04) Internet access and telephone calls.

Sleeping & Eating

Namacha (s/d US$12/18) Just off the main road (Av Eduardo Mondlane) in the town centre and one of the better bets for budget accom-

---

FIM DE MONDO

'Fim do mundo' ('the end of the world') is how many Mozambicans describe Niassa – the least populated of Mozambique's provinces – and as far as the rest of the country is concerned, it might as well be. This wild, remote and beautiful area is generally overlooked by the government and other locals and ignored by tourists. Yet, if you're after adventure and time in the bush, it's an ideal destination. Apart from Niassa's scenic rugged terrain, the main attraction is the alluring Lago Niassa (Lake Niassa) coastline. Much of the northern part of the province enjoys protected status – from the Manda Wilderness Area between the coast and the Rio Messinge (see p150), to the Reserva de Sanga (p147), which goes from the Rio Messinge east to the edge of the buffer zone around Reserva do Niassa, and then the vast Reserva do Niassa (p150), which reaches east to the Rio Lugenda and the border of Cabo Delgado province.

---

modation, with surprisingly decent rooms and a pleasant courtyard.

Pensão-Restaurante São Miguel (r without/with bathroom US$15/18) Between Namacha and Hotel Vision 2000 and of similar standard to Namacha. Rates include breakfast.

Hotel Vision 2000 (☎ 271-62632; h-vision2000@ teledata.mz; cnr Avs Eduardo Mondlane & 25 de Junho; r US$50-70; 🖳) On the main intersection, this is Cuamba's only midrange option. Rooms in the main building are faded but spacious and quite decent, with TV and mini-fridge, and there's a restaurant. Staff here can help you arrange a visit to one of the gemstone mines near Cuamba.

Getting There & Away

AIR
There are twice-weekly flights to/from Nampula on **Serviço Aéreo Regional** (sargaw@teledata.mz) for US$72 one-way. Hotel Vision 2000 is the booking agent.

BUS, CAR & CHAPA
The main transport stand is at Maçaniqueira market, at the southern edge of town and just south of the railway tracks. Most chapas also pick up passengers at the train station closer to the town centre. The best times to find transport are between 5am and 6am, and again in the afternoon at the station, on days when the train from Nampula arrives.

To Nampula, there's at least one vehicle daily along a long, red ribbon of road winding past beautiful inselberg landscapes. However, it's cheaper and generally at least as 'fast' to travel by train.

To Gurúè, the best way is via train or chapa to Mutuáli, from where you can find vehicles for the remainder of the journey. Via train, this works best going from Cuamba to Gurúè.

In the other direction, vehicles usually leave Gurúè for Mutuáli in the morning, which means you may have to wait for up to six hours for the train on to Cuamba.

To Lichinga, there are several cars daily, departing by 6am from Maçaniqueira market (US$12, six to eight hours).

To Malawi, vehicles go daily from Cuamba to both Entre Lagos (US$3.50, four hours) and to Mandimba (US$6, 3½ hours). Once at Entre Lagos, there's a weekly train on the Malawi side to Liwonde. For more on these routes, see p186.

TRAIN
A train connects Cuamba with Nampula (US$20/10/4 for 1st/2nd/economy class, 10 to 11 hours, sometimes much longer), departing in each direction at 5am on alternate days. (Currently departures from Cuamba are on Wednesday, Friday and Sunday; there are no trains in either direction on Monday.) First class has been temporarily discontinued and second class sometimes doesn't run. If you're travelling on a day when there's third class only, try heading to the more comfortable dining car and ingratiating yourself with staff – though we have heard from some travellers that they had to buy something every hour or so for the privilege of sitting there. Women travelling alone in 1st- or 2nd-class will be given seats in a females-only cabin. The ride is enjoyable, stopping at many villages along the way and offering a good slice of Mozambican life.

To transport your vehicle on the train (about US$90), you'll need to load it the night before and arrange a guard. During the journey you can ride with the car.

Train service between Cuamba and Entre Lagos is suspended.

MANDIMBA

Mandimba is a small, bustling border town and transport junction.

Pensão Massinga (r US$8-32) is the best place to stay, with clean rooms with fan and meals.

En route between Mandimba and Lichinga is the town of **Massangulo**, the site of the first Catholic mission in Niassa. Its church, about 2km off the main road, is worth a detour if you have your own vehicle.

Vehicles go daily to Lichinga and Cuamba. For border information, see p186.

LICHINGA

Niassa's capital is pretty, low-key Lichinga (formerly Vila Cabral), which sits at about 1300m altitude, with an invigorating cool climate and quiet jacaranda-lined streets. It's worth a day or two in its own right and is also the best jumping-off point for exploring the lake. The surrounding area – home mainly to Yao, as well as smaller numbers of Nyanja and Makua people – is dotted with pine groves and ringed by distant hills.

Orientation

Lichinga is set out in a series of concentric circles, with a large plaza at the centre and the main transport stand at its southeastern edge near the market. It's easy to cover on foot – nothing is more than about a 10-minute walk.

The section of road running past the governor's mansion on the northwestern edge of town is closed to vehicle traffic and the area immediately in front of the mansion is also closed to pedestrians.

Information

Acord (Av Filipe Magaia; 9am-4pm Mon-Fri) Internet access.

Banco Austral (Av Samora Machel) ATM.

BIM (cnr Av Samora Machel & Rua Filipe Samuel Magaia) Also has ATM.

Hotel Girassol Lichinga (Rua Filipe Samuel Magaia) Internet access.

Immigration Just off the airport road, diagonally opposite Escola Industrial e Comercial Ngungunhane.

Sleeping

BUDGET

Hotel Chiwindi (271-20345; Av Julius Nyerere; r without/with bathroom US$25/30) No-frills rooms in a convenient location near the bus stand and market.

Ponto Final (271-20912; Rua Filipe Samuel Magaia; r with bathroom US$22, with bathroom, fridge & TV US$27)

This long-standing place at the northeastern edge of town has reasonable rooms with bathrooms and low ceilings, and a bar.

MIDRANGE

Pousada de Lichinga (271-20176, 271-20177; Rua Filipe Samuel Magaia; s/d without bathroom US$30/34, s/d US$36/40) The Pousada has a convenient central location, straightforward rooms and a restaurant. Prices include continental breakfast.

Casa Nurbay (271-20819; Rua de Nachingwea; r per person US$20) This private house rents out good rooms, one with bathroom, the others with shared facilities. From Av Samora Machel, take the second right down from the post office.

Hotel Girassol Lichinga (271-21280, 271-21279; www.girassolhoteis.co.mz; Rua Filipe Samuel Magaia; s/d US$85/92, with advance booking US$70/80;) Hovering between three and four stars, this is Lichinga's most upmarket option and one of the few places in the province catering to business travellers. There's a restaurant, tennis courts and rooms with satellite TV and all the trimmings. Book in advance for a discount.

Eating

O Chambo (271-21354; meals from US$2.50) The unassuming and long-standing O Chambo, in the FEN (Feira Exposição Niassa) compound next to the market, is Lichinga's best-known restaurant. Great soups cost US$1 and there are delicious local dishes and other meals.

Pousada de Lichinga (271-20176, 271-20227; Rua Filipe Samuel Magaia; meals from US$3) This hotel restaurant has reasonably prompt service and tasty grills and other meals.

Other recommendations:

O Gordo (Av Julius Nyerere; meals from US$3.50) On the airport road near Escola Industrial e Comercial Ngungunhane, with hearty Portuguese fare.

Lanchonete Modelo (Av Samora Machel; snacks & meals from US$2) Burgers, chips and light meals; it's several blocks down from BIM on the main street.

Planalto (271-20385; Rua Filipe Samuel Magaia; meals US$3) On the western side of town near the provincial government buildings, with a modest selection of standards.

Supermarkets include **Translândia** (Av Julius Nyerere), opposite O Gordo, and Nurbay's **Comércio Geral** (Av Samora Machel).

Entertainment

Lichinga has an active cultural scene. One of the highlights is Niassa province's renowned

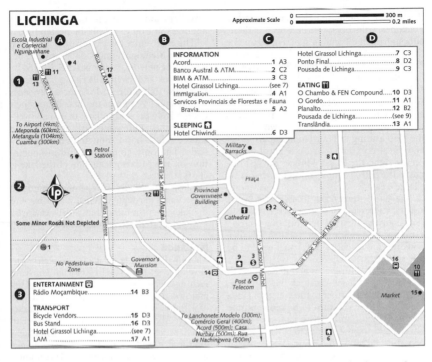

LICHINGA

Approximate Scale

INFORMATION	
Acord	1 A3
Banco Austral & ATM	2 C2
BIM & ATM	3 C3
Hotel Girassol Lichinga	(see 7)
Immigration	4 A1
Servicos Provinciais de Florestas e Fauna	
Bravia	5 A2

SLEEPING	
Hotel Chiwindi	6 D3

Hotel Girassol Lichinga	7 C3
Ponto Final	8 D2
Pousada de Lichinga	9 C3

EATING	
O Chambo & FEN Compound	10 D3
O Gordo	11 A1
Planalto	12 B2
Pousada de Lichinga	(see 9)
Translândia	13 A1

ENTERTAINMENT	
Rádio Moçambique	14 B3

TRANSPORT	
Bicycle Vendors	15 D3
Bus Stand	16 D3
Hotel Girassol Lichinga	(see 7)
LAM	17 A1

song and dance group, Massukos, which is based here and gives occasional performances, usually on holidays and other special occasions. For information on their schedule, and on other cultural events, ask at **Rádio Moçambique** (Rua Filipe Samuel Magaia), near Pousada de Lichinga and just off Av Samora Machel.

Getting There & Away
AIR
There are four flights to/from Maputo, going via Tete, Nampula and/or Beira on **LAM** (☎ 271-20434, 271-20847; Rua da LAM). Their office is just off the airport road.

BUS & TRUCK
All transport departs from next to the market, with vehicles to most destinations leaving by around 6am. There are several chapas daily to Cuamba (US$12, 6½ hours) via Mandimba along a road that's reasonably good to Mandimba and then good from there to Cuamba, with a couple of vehicles daily to Metangula (US$5, 2½ hours) and to Meponda (US$2.50 1½ hours). If you're trying to hitch from Lichinga to Cuamba, the best place to wait

for a lift is at the police checkpoint about 5km south of town at the beginning of the Mandimba/Cuamba road.

Lichinga is easily accessed from Malawi, via Likoma Island and Cóbuè. See p189, and p150.

GETTING AROUND
There are no taxis, but Lichinga is easily covered on foot. Alternatively, you can arrange bicycle rental at the market.

Hotel Girassol Lichinga is the best contact for arranging car hire.

AROUND LICHINGA
Reserva de Sanga
About 150km north of Lichinga, towards the Tanzanian border and edging the buffer zone of Reserva do Niassa, is **Reserva de Sanga** (Sanga Reserve, or Chipange Chetu; entry per person per visit US$10), the site of a community-oriented wildlife conservation project. It's temporarily closed to visitors, but hopefully to reopen soon. When functioning, it offers the chance to experience one of the wildest and most isolated parts of Southern Africa. Birding is good and

the wildlife – including elephants, buffalos, antelopes, wildebeests and zebras – is there, although often difficult to spot. For an update on the reserve's status, stop by the **Serviços Provinciais de Florestas e Fauna Bravia** (Provincial Forestry Department; ☎ 271-20986, 271-20977, 271-20917; Av Julius Nyerere) in Lichinga. You'll also need to stop by here anyway to get a permit (free) to enter the reserve area. The forestry office is on the northwestern edge of town. Follow the road leading to Translândia supermarket and the airport, and look for a petrol station on the right; the forestry offices are just opposite the petrol station and signposted, near a large tree.

The basic **Uzuzu Camp** (zambezihunters@yahoo .com; tented accommodation per person including guide about US$5) is primarily used by a hunting concession, but also takes other visitors; advance bookings are essential, and you'll need to be self-sufficient.

The reserve entrance is about 20km north of Macaloge village. Once at the entrance, it's about 30km further to the village of Nova Madeira, where you turn right and continue 6km to Uzuzu Camp. There's a truck several times weekly from Lichinga to Nova Madeira, departing Lichinga at 5.30am (US$5, five to six hours). For a negotiable extra fee, the driver is usually willing to take you the 6km in to the camp. Several times weekly, the same truck that goes to Nova Madeira continues north along a bush track to the Rio Rovuma, from where you can enter Tanzania (arrange a visa in advance).

LAGO NIASSA (LAKE MALAWI)

The Mozambican side of Lago Niassa is beautiful and – in contrast to the Malawian side – almost completely undeveloped. It sees a small but steady stream of adventure travellers and is an excellent destination for anyone wanting to get off the beaten track.

The main area for exploring is the coast between Metangula and Cóbuè, with a succession of narrow, sandy beaches backed by mountains and steep hills rising up directly from the lakeshore. Most local residents are Nyanja ('People of the Lake'), and their distinctively painted square, thatched dwellings dot the countryside. Fishing is the main source of livelihood, though it's mostly small scale. The only commercial fishing operation on the Mozambican side of the lake is at Metangula.

Allow plenty of time for getting around and be prepared to rough it. When venturing onto the lake, keep in mind that squalls can arise suddenly, often with strong winds.

Meponda

This small, lakeside village is completely undeveloped and a possibility for a day trip from Lichinga. The tiny harbour to the south of the main road as you enter Meponda is the hub of activity, with the town centre and market nearby. About 1km north of here is a small beach, which is ideal for picnicking and watching the fish eagles. Local fishermen will take you out on the lake for about US$2 per hour.

The only accommodation is at the very basic and not very appealing **O Pomar das Laranjeiras** (rondavel per person US$6), on the beach about 500m north of the harbour, which can also arrange food with lots of advance notice.

GETTING THERE & AWAY

Meponda is 60km southwest of Lichinga. A few chapas run between the two towns daily (US$2.50, 1½ hours). Schedules don't usually cooperate to make a day trip possible. However, on weekends, if you take a chapa out in

---

SWIMMERS, TAKE CARE

In addition to being home to countless colourful fish, Lago Niassa also hosts healthy populations of the tiny snail that causes bilharzia. While there is less risk of bilharzia infestation on the Mozambique side of the lake, you should still use caution when swimming: don't swim anywhere with reeds and other shoreline growth, or in shallow, still water. If you swim anyway (and many people do, with no ill effects), get a bilharzia test once you return home. Keep in mind, though, that if you are infected, it won't show up for at least six weeks or longer, and several tests may be necessary. One place where you can enjoy Lake Malawi without worrying about bilharzia is in the crystal clear waters around Nkwichi Lodge (p150).

Another water-related danger to watch out for is the crocodile. Locals say that they lurk in the river that joins Lago Niassa near Meponda and in other river mouths along the lakeshore.

the morning, it's usually easy to find a lift back to Lichinga in the afternoons.

Meponda was formerly linked with Malawi's Senga Bay via the weekly MV *Mtendere*. It's currently not running, but worth asking around to see if ferry services have resumed.

Metangula

Bustling Metangula is the capital of Distrito do Lago, the largest Mozambican town along the lakeshore, and the site of a small naval base. The town is divided into two areas – the staid administrative quarters perched on a small escarpment with wide views over the lake and the lower lying residential areas along the lake shore. Metangula itself has little for visitors. However about 8km north of town is the tiny village of **Chuwanga**, which is on an attractive beach, and is a popular weekend getaway from Lichinga. About 5km northeast of Chuwanga is **Messumba**, site of a well-known Anglican mission that traces its history back to the arrival of the first missionaries in the area in 1882. Until being forced to close during the war, Messumba served as headquarters for Anglican missionary activity in northern Mozambique. It was renowned for its hospital and for the Colégio de São Felipe, where numerous notables studied, including several members of Frelimo's elite. Most of the mission buildings are now in disrepair, although you can still visit the impressive church and walk around the grounds. Today, the only secondary school in Distrito do Lago is in Metangula.

Chuwanga Beach Hotel (Complexo Cetuka or Catawala's; camping per person US$5, s/d bungalows US$15/20) On

the beach at Chuwanga, this is where everyone stays. It has camping and simple bungalows on the sand. Meals are available and there's a grill for cooking your own.

Otherwise, there are a few basic guesthouses in town; if you get stuck, ask at Bar Triângulo at the main junction. It's also occasionally possible to get a **room** (niassa@skyfile.com; US$20) at the Mtendere Estates guesthouse on the escarpment.

GETTING THERE & AWAY

Several chapas daily connect Metangula and Lichinga (US$5, 2½ hours). Most depart early, though there is usually at least one vehicle in each direction at about 1pm. Departures in Metangula are from the fork in the road just up from the market. The all-weather road from Lichinga is tarmac for the first 75km and then good dirt for the final 29km to Metangula. The final 20km or so winding down to the lakeshore is very scenic.

There are occasional chapas between Metangula and Chuwanga, and hitching is easy on weekends. To get to Messumba, you'll need your own 4WD.

For information on the *Ilala* ferry between Metangula and Cóbuè, see p189. Local boats leave Metangula from the small port down from the market and below the Catholic church.

Cóbuè

Tiny Cóbuè is the gateway into Mozambique if you're travelling from Malawi via Likoma Island, about 10km offshore. The island is surrounded by Mozambican waters, but belongs to Malawi.

In addition to its immigration post, Cóbuè's attractions include a lakeside setting and the ruins of an old Catholic church and school. The school was used as a wartime base by Frelimo, which means that there still may be some land mines, so use caution when walking around the grounds.

The community-owned **Manda Wilderness wildlife reserve** (entry per person about US$5) is being established south of town by local residents with support from Nkwichi Lodge and the Swedish government. Fees and guides can be arranged at any of the places listed under Sleeping.

SLEEPING

Hotel Inyati Yoyela (White Buffalo; r US$12) Somewhat of a Cóbuè institution, and long the

NORTHERN MOZAMBIQUE

main backpackers' stop, with basic rooms and meals, and now under new management.

Mira Lago (r about US$10) In Cóbuè town just behind Hotel Inyati Yoyela, this new-ish place is no-frills, clean and pleasant, with solar-powered lighting and sometimes TV.

Mchenga Wede (per person US$5, meals about US$7-10) About 5km south of Nkwichi Lodge near Mbueca village, Mchenga Wede is a good choice if you are backpacking around the lake, with bush walks, snorkelling and local canoe trips. It's run by some enterprising staff from Nkwichi Lodge, and in addition to camping, they have no-frills bungalows and a small restaurant and bar. Bookings can be made through Nkwichi (Mchenga Wede should also feature soon on the Nkwichi website) or you can just show up.

Nkwichi Lodge (info@mandawilderness.org; www.mandawilderness.org; s/d with full board US$240/380) Apart from its convenient location as part of a larger Southern Africa circuit linking Mozambique and Malawi, the main reason to come to Cóbuè is to get to this wonderful and highly recommended lodge. It offers the chance to explore an area of Southern Africa that is about as remote as it gets, while enjoying all the comforts and contributing to the local community and environment as well. The lodge is part of the Manda Wilderness Area – a privately initiated conservation area along the lakeshore that also promotes community development and responsible tourism. The surrounding bush is full of birds, with ospreys, palm nut vultures, Pell's fishing owls and fish eagles all regularly seen. There's also a reasonable amount of wildlife roaming around and with luck, you may see the occasional elephant or antelope.

Accommodation is in seven lovely hand-crafted bungalows, with private outdoor baths and showers built into the trees, each looking out onto its own little white-sand cove. The lake here is crystal clear and safe for swimming and there's a dhow for sails and sunset cruises. You can also arrange canoeing and multinight wilderness walking safaris. Staff will come meet you in Cóbuè and boat transfers can be arranged from Cóbuè (per person US$50), Likoma Island, Mbueca village or Metangula. Advance bookings are essential.

GETTING THERE & AWAY

There's an airstrip in Cóbuè for charter flights. More common is to charter flight from Lilongwe (Malawi) to Likoma Island (US$535 for a three-passenger plane, arranged through Nkwichi Lodge) and then arrange a boat transfer from there with the lodge.

The weekly *Ilala* ferry runs between Cóbuè and Metangula, and between Cóbuè and Likoma Island; see p189. A local dhow sometimes meets the *Ilala* in Cóbuè, and goes down the coast with many stops, including at Nkwichi Lodge and Mchenga Wede.

Otherwise, there are a couple of slow boats sailing weekly between Cóbuè and Metangula. These boats take at least two days to Cóbuè and sometimes longer, stopping frequently en route, which means passengers have to sleep on the beach. Many of the boats continue on to Likoma Island. It's also possible to hire or hitch a ride with one of the occasional speedboats doing business along the lakeshore. These take between six and eight hours to/from Metangula, and are more easily arranged in Metangula than in Cóbuè. Guests of Nkwichi Lodge can arrange boat transfers (dhow or speedboat) with the lodge from Cóbuè, and from Likoma Island. The lodge's dhow, the *Miss Nkwichi*, can also be chartered for pickups from Metangula (six hours).

The 75km road between Cóbuè and Metangula is rough (4WD) but improving, though there's no regular public transport. If you have your own vehicle and are heading to Nkwichi Lodge, there's secure parking at Mira Lago in Cóbuè and at Mchenga Wede in Mbueca.

Walking takes about two days, going along the river via the villages of Ngoo and Chia and past remote wilderness and beautiful, untouched beaches. Guides and porters can be arranged at Nkwichi Lodge or Mchenga Wede. Allow four to five hours on foot between Cóbuè and Mchenga Wede.

Reserva do Niassa

About 160km northeast of Lichinga on the Tanzanian border is the **Reserva do Niassa** (Niassa Reserve; entry per person/vehicle for three days US$5/10, may increase), a vast tract of wilderness with the largest wildlife populations in Mozambique. It's particularly notable for its elephants (estimated to number about 12,000), sable antelopes (over 9000), buffaloes and zebras. They are kept company by duikers, elands, leopards, wildebeests, hippos and even a population of the endangered African wild dog, as well as over 400 different types of birds.

The reserve – which is Mozambique's largest protected area and twice the size of South Africa's Kruger National Park – was established in the early 1960s to protect local elephant and black rhino populations. However, because of inaccessibility, scarce finances and the onset of war it was never developed. Although wildlife populations here suffered during the 1980s from poaching and the effects of armed conflict, losses were far less than those in other protected areas further south. In more recent times, significant progress has been made in curbing poaching, and there has been a trend of increasing animal numbers.

In the late 1990s Reserva do Niassa was given new life when a group of private investors, working in partnership with the Mozambican government, was granted a 10-year renewable lease on the area. The reserve's size was increased to about 42,000 sq km, and the boundaries now stretch from the Rio Rovuma in the north to the Rio Lugenda in the south and east. Much of the area in between is covered by woodland and dotted with massive granite inselbergs.

An estimated 20,000 people live within the reserve's boundaries, which also encompass a 20,000 sq km buffer zone and there are plans for community-based tourism, although these are in the future. A recent proposal introduced by the Peace Parks Foundation in South Africa aims to tie the Reserva do Niassa into an enormous protected swathe stretching from Lago Niassa in the west to the Indian Ocean in the east and northwards to Tanzania's Selous Game Reserve.

One of the main reasons the Reserva do Niassa has been able to maintain its magnificent wildness and impressive wildlife populations up to this point has been its relative isolation from almost everywhere. However, with the building of a bridge over the Rovuma at Negomane, this isolation is likely to come increasingly under threat in the coming years.

INFORMATION

Headquarters are about 40km southwest of Mecula at Mbatamila, and the main gate is near Salimo in the reserve's southeastern corner.

Wildlife in Reserva do Niassa is spread relatively thinly over a vast area, with dense foliage and only a skeleton network of bush tracks. As a result, most tourism to date has

been exclusively for the well-heeled, with the most feasible way to visit by charter plane from Pemba. With the imminent opening of the reserve's first safari camp and the gradual upgrading of road connections linking Cabo Delgado and Niassa provinces, this is beginning to change, although the reserve's main markets are likely to remain top end for the foreseeable future. For more information, contact **reserve headquarters** (rdn01@bushmail.net) or the **Sociedade de Gestão e Desenvolvimento da Reserva do Niassa** (www.niassa.com), the private concern overseeing development of the reserve. Vehicle safaris are possible using the limited network of bush tracks and walking safaris can be arranged at reserve headquarters.

SLEEPING & EATING

Until now, most visitor activity has centred around hunting safaris. The first luxury safari camp for photographic tourism – **Lugenda Bush Camp** (www.raniresorts.com), on the Lugenda River near the eastern edge of the park – is set to open soon, primarily offering fly-in safaris based out of Pemba Beach Resort Hotel (p156), with both walking and vehicle safaris. The same management also operates the **Luwire Hunting Camp** (www.luwire.com) on the reserve's southeastern edge.

At reserve headquarters, there are three twin-bedded **chalets** (per chalet US$30) with bathrooms, and three large two-person **tents** (per tent US$20) sharing hot- and cold-water ablutions, plus a communal kitchen/dining area. Bush **camping** (per person US$5) is also permitted, though you'll need to be completely self-contained.

GETTING THERE & AROUND
Air
There are about 11 airstrips that can accommodate charter flights, including one at Mecula. The reserve sits roughly midway between Lago Niassa to the west and the Indian Ocean to the east, both about an hour's flight away via small plane. The easiest charter access is from Pemba (arrange through Pemba Beach Resort Hotel, p156, or Kaskazini, p152), or from Nkwichi Lodge (opposite). Charter rates from Pemba start from around US$360 per hour for a five-seater plane.

Car
The reserve is accessible during the dry season with a 4WD from Lichinga via Muembe and Mataca (allow at least one full day); from

NORTHERN MOZAMBIQUE

Cuamba via Maúa, Marrupa and Salimo; and, from Pemba via Montepuez, Marrupa and Salimo (usually at least a two-day drive, the stretch between Balama and Marrupa is in bad condition). Before setting out, inquire locally about road conditions, as there are several bridges en route that occasionally wash away and make road access impossible. To undertake any of these journeys, you'll need to be self-sufficient and equipped with spares for everything, as there's nothing available en route. For any driving within the reserve, take a guide from reserve headquarters to maximise your chances of seeing wildlife. There's a nine-seater safari vehicle that can be rented at headquarters for US$150 per day with driver.

MONTEPUEZ

Montepuez, a busy district capital, previously rivalled Pemba as the largest town in Cabo Delgado. Today, it's known for its marble quarries, and as the start of the wild road west across Niassa province to Lichinga. About 2km southeast of town, and signposted off the main road, is **Aurora** (☎ 84-781-3820, 82-633 4150; www.auroramozambique.com; dm with full board & cultural activities US$50, s/d/tr with full board & cultural activities US$75/120/165), which offers visitors the chance to immerse themselves in local Mozambican life at a level that normally isn't possible unless you're based in the country long-term. Among other things, you can spend a day in the bush with a traditional medicinal practitioner, learn local cooking or pottery techniques, take guided botanical walks, watch *mapiko* dancing or visit Makonde carvers at work. Accommodation is in spacious, rustic rooms – all with mosquito nets – in a refurbished colonial-era house near the old São José mission church, with hot water, solar power and good cuisine (vegetarian and other special meals are available on request).

If this doesn't suit, there are several basic *pensões* in the town centre.

Several chapas go between Pemba and Montepuez (US$4, three hours, daily), along a good road; the first departure from Pemba is at 5am. If you're headed for Aurora, ask to get dropped at the turnoff, from where it's about 600m further on foot. The road from Montepuez west to Lichinga is passable in a well-equipped 4WD. Allow at least three days for the journey and inquire locally about conditions before setting out.

PEMBA

Pemba sprawls across a peninsula jutting into the enormous and magnificent Baía de Pemba, one of the world's largest natural harbours. It was established in 1904 as administrative headquarters for the Niassa Company and for much of its early life was known as Porto Amelia. Today, it's capital of Cabo Delgado province, the main town in Mozambique's far north, and gateway to the Archipélago das Quirimbas and an endless string of white-sand beaches. The town is also a relaxing and enjoyable stop in its own right, with almost perpetual sunshine and blue skies, a long, palm-fringed beach just down the road and a lazy, languid ambience.

Orientation

Pemba's baixa area is home to the low-lying port and old town, with a row of small shops and traders lining Rua do Comércio, the main street. Steeply uphill from here, the busier and less atmospheric town centre is the place to get things done, with banks and offices, a few restaurants and unappealing hotels, and the main bus stand. About 5km east of the town centre is Praia de Wimbi (also spelled Wimbe), the main hub of tourist activity and the favoured destination of most visitors.

MAPS

The best map is *Planta de Endereçamento da Cidade de Pemba*, part of the series done by Coopération Française in cooperation with the local Conselho Municipal, usually on sale at Artes Maconde's main branch, at Pemba Beach Hotel. Kaskazini also has a free Pemba tourist map.

Information
IMMIGRATION
Immigration office (Rua 16 de Junho; ☼ 7.30-11am & 2-4pm Mon-Fri) Just off Rua Base de Moçambique.

INTERNET ACCESS & TELEPHONE
PrestaServe/Skylink (Av 25 de Setembro; per hr US$3; ▧) Internet.
Super Wimbi (Av Marginal, Praia de Wimbi; per hr US$5) Internet.
TDM (cnr Avs Eduardo Mondlane & 25 de Setembro; per hr US$4, ☼ 7am-10pm) Internet, plus domestic and international telephone calls.

MEDICAL SERVICES
Hospital Provincial (cnr Ruas Base Beira & 1 de Maio) Malaria tests.

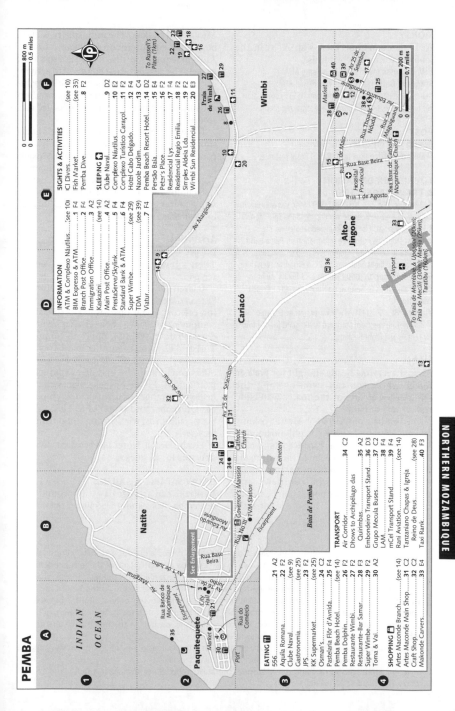

PEMBA

INDIAN OCEAN

To Russell's Place (1km)

INFORMATION
ATM & Complexo Náutilus..........(see 10)
BIM Expresso & ATM...................1 F4
Branch Post Office........................2 F4
Immigration Office.........................3 A2
Kaskazini..................................(see 14)
Main Post Office...........................4 A2
PrestaServe/Skylink.......................5 F4
Standard Bank & ATM....................6 F4
Super Wimbe..............................(see 29)
TDM...7 F4
Viatur..

SIGHTS & ACTIVITIES
CI Divers..................................(see 10)
Fish Market..............................(see 35)
Pemba Dive.................................8 F2

SLEEPING
Clube Naval.................................9 D2
Complexo Náutilus.....................10 E2
Complexo Turístico Caraçol..........11 F2
Hotel Cabo Delgado.....................12 F4
Nacole Jardim.............................13 C4
Pemba Beach Resort Hotel............14 D2
Pensão Baía................................15 E4
Peter's Place...............................16 F2
Residencial Lys...........................17 F4
Residencial Regio Emilia...............18 F2
Simples Aldeia Lda......................19 E3
Wimbi Sun Residencial.................20 E3

EATING
556..21 A2
Aquila Romana............................22 F2
Clube Naval...............................(see 9)
Gastronomia...............................23 F2
JPS...24 C2
KK Supermarket.......................(see 25)
Osman's...................................25 C2
Pastelária Flôr d'Avnida................26 F2
Pemba Beach Hotel...................(see 14)
Pemba Dolphin............................27 F2
Restaurante Wimbi.....................28 F3
Restaurante-Bar Samar...............29 F2
Super Wimbe..............................30 A2
Toma & Vai................................

SHOPPING
Artes Maconde Branch...............(see 14)
Artes Maconde Main Shop............31 C2
Craft Shop..................................32 F2
Makonde Carvers.........................33 E4

TRANSPORT
Air Corridor................................34 C2
Dhows to Archipélago das
    Quirimbas...............................35 A2
Embondeiro Transport Stand..........36 D3
Grupo Mecula Buses....................37 C2
LAM..38 F4
mCel Transport Stand...................39 F4
Rani Aviation............................(see 14)
Tanzaniano Chapas & Igreja.........(see 28)
Reino de Deus.............................40 F3
Taxi Rank..................................

NORTHERN MOZAMBIQUE

Paquitequete

Natite

Wimbi

Cariacó

Alto-Jingone

Airport

To Praia de Murrébué & Upésoul (20km);
Praia de Mecúfi (30km); Marúfo (75km);
Taratíbu (160km)

Wimbi

Catholic Mozambique Church

Hospital Provincial

Market

Baía de Pemba

Praia de Wimbi

MONEY

At Praia de Wimbi, there's an ATM in the lobby of Complexo Náutilus.

BIM Expresso (Av Eduardo Mondlane) ATM.

Standard Bank (Av Eduardo Mondlane) ATM; also changes travellers cheques (minimum US$35 commission per transaction, original purchase receipts required).

POST

Branch post office (Av 25 de Setembro)

Main post office (Rua No 1, Baixa) Poste restante.

TOURIST INFORMATION & TRAVEL AGENCIES

Kaskazini (☎ 272-20371, 82-309 6990; www.kaskazini .com; Av Marginal, Praia de Wimbi; ⏰ 8am-3pm Mon-Fri, 8.30am-noon Sat) Efficient, knowledgeable and the best first stop. They give free information on Pemba and elsewhere in northern Mozambique, help with accommodation and flight bookings and can organise everything from dhow safaris to sunset cruises on a luxury yacht to car hire and visits to Reserva do Niassa. Based at Pemba Beach Hotel.

Viatur (☎ 272-21431; www.viatur.net; Av Eduardo Mondlane) Just up from Standard Bank; good for city tours, car rentals and flight bookings.

Sights

Almost everyone heads straight for **Praia de Wimbi**, where you can swim or enjoy the sea breezes at one of the many waterside restaurants or bars.

On Pemba's outskirts are several colourful and vibrant *bairros* (neighbourhoods). The most intriguing is **Paquitequete**, which is on the southwestern edge of the peninsula and is Pemba's oldest settlement. In contrast with the other bairros, which are newer and more heterogeneous, the population here is almost exclusively Muslim, and predominantly Mwani and Makua. The atmosphere is at its best in the late afternoon just before sunset. At Paquitequete's northern edge is a small **fish market**. The nearby beach buzzes with activity in the early morning as *makuti* (dried palm fronds used for constructing roofs), bamboo and other building materials are unloaded and readied for market.

Up on the hill behind the governor's mansion is a large **cemetery**, with fragrant frangipani trees shading the Christian and Muslim graves. Close to the sea is a section containing Commonwealth war graves.

Beginning about 10km south of town is a string of tranquil, attractive beaches, including **Murrébuè** and **Mecúfi**.

Activities

DIVING

There's rewarding diving around Pemba; see p46.

CI Divers (☎ 272-20102; www.cidivers.com; Complexo Náutilus, Av Marginal, Praia de Wimbi) is the main operator, offering PADI open-water certification, equipment rental and boat charters. Further down Praia de Wimbi, opposite Complexo Turístico Caraçol, is another good operator, **Pemba Dive** (☎ 82-661 1530, ☎ /fax 272-20820), which offers equipment hire and dives (though no instruction). Either of these places can also help you arrange excursions to Archipélago das Quirimbas and rental of jet skis, fishing boats, sailboards, windsurfing equipment and bicycles.

Pemba Beach Hotel has resident dive instructors for its guests.

DHOW SAFARIS & SAILING

Kaskazini can arrange day trips around Baía de Pemba (from about US$40 per person per

---

CABO DELGADO

Although remote from Maputo, Cabo Delgado province has played a disproportionately important role in recent Mozambican history. It's known in particular as the birthplace of the independence struggle, which began here supported from bases in nearby Tanzania. Cabo Delgado is also where some of the most protracted wartime fighting took place during the 1980s. At the height of the war, it could take up to a month to travel – convoy-style, and moving only at night – between Pemba and Moçimboa da Praia, which makes the seven-hour bus ride today seem like a stroll in the park. Another legacy of the war years is that most district capitals in the north have airstrips, including some large enough to accommodate jets.

As in neighbouring Niassa province, large tracts of Cabo Delgado are wild and trackless and local lore is full of tales about the dangers of lions and the like.

Major ethnic groups include the Makonde, the Makua and, along the coast, the Mwani.

half day, minimum four people) or overnight dhow safaris to Archipélago das Quirimbas (from about US$150 per boat, up to six people). Together with Pemba Beach Hotel, they also offer an upscale sunset cruise for US$50 per person, including drinks. Pemba Beach Hotel's private luxury yacht, the *MY Fantastique*, can be chartered for sails.

Sleeping

TOWN CENTRE

Central Pemba has slim accommodation offerings – all budget, at least in standard, if not in price – and is only worth considering if you can't find anything at Praia de Wimbi or if you have an early morning bus.

Pensão Baía (cnr Ruas 1 de Maio & Base Beira; d with fan US$16, with bathroom & air-con US$20; 🔀) Basic and spartan, with no-frills rooms and meals with advance notice. No clothes washing allowed.

Hotel Cabo Delgado (☎ 272-21552; cnr Avs 25 de Setembro & Eduardo Mondlane; s/d/tw US$19/24/29) This ageing hotel on the main street is well past its prime, although the central location, diagonally opposite the mCel transport stop, is convenient. The faded rooms come with bathroom, fan and continental breakfast.

Residencial Lys (☎ 272-20951; sulemane@teledata .mz; Rua 1 de Maio; r US$18, with fan and bathroom US$24, with air-con US$36; 🔀) Acceptable but somewhat seedy and noisy, and not recommended for women alone. The no-frills rooms have fans and some have bathrooms. It's one block in from Av Eduardo Mondlane.

PRAIA DE WIMBI

Almost everyone stays at the beach. Book in advance if travelling during the December/January and Easter South African school holidays.

Budget

Russell's Place (Cashew Camp; ☎ 82-686 2730; www .pembamagic.com; camping per person US$6, dm US$4, 2-/3-person chalet with bathroom US$35) About 3.5km beyond Complexo Náutilus along the beach road extension, Russell's place has camping, dorm beds and a few A-frame chalets. The ablution blocks have bucket-style showers with hot water, and there's a bar, well water for drinking, a self-catering area and a restaurant with evening buffets and pizzas. The beach is just a few minutes' walk away across the road (high tide swimming only).

Nacole Jardim (☎ 82-661 1530; info@kaskazini.com; camping/chalet per person US$5/15) A tranquil spot well-suited for families or anyone interested in birdlife, coastal ecosystems and traditional medicine. One of the owners is a traditional healer and can give a fascinating two-hour botanical walking tour focusing on local medicinal plants. Three mangrove gardens and 40 baobab trees are scattered throughout the property, including one enormous tree used during the war as local refuge. In addition to camping, there's a self-catering chalet (with more planned), and a beachside bar and braai area. It's about 10 minutes from town (US$6 in a taxi), behind the airport on the bay (so the only place in these listings not on Praia de Wimbi) and about 5km off the main road along an unpaved track. It's under the same management as Pemba Dive.

Midrange

Peter's Place (☎ 272-20102; cidivers@teledata.mz; Av Marginal; d US$45) Along the extension of the Wimbi beach road directly opposite SAL, this good-value place consists of one small but wonderfully airy room on the shady, green grounds of a private residence, with a few more rooms planned. Just outside is a huge, beautiful baobab tree, with a sitting area built into its upper branches. There's no food.

Residencial Regio Emilia (☎ 272-21297; c.forna@ teledata.mz; Av Marginal; r from US$50; 🔀) Next door to Peter's Place (look for the Italian flag), this is another good-value choice, with a handful of comfortable chalets (15 rooms total, in a mix of smaller and family-style chalets) set in large, green and quiet grounds. One chalet has a veranda (more are planned) and all come with kitchenette. The owner, Carlos, is extremely knowledgeable about Cabo Delgado and can give cultural tours in various languages. Continental/full breakfast costs US$5/10 extra.

Wimbi Sun Residencial (☎ 82-318 1300; Av Marginal; r US$45-60; 🔀) A new place with modern, clean rooms – the best are the spacious 'suites'. None have nets and all have bathrooms. It's at the start of the Wimbi Beach strip, diagonally opposite Complexo Náutilus on the inland side of the road. Breakfast costs US$6.

Complexo Turístico Caraçol (☎ 272-20147; sule mane@teledata.mz; Av Marginal; s/d US$40/50, 1-/2-room apt US$75/85; 🔀) This place is well-located – on the inland side of the beach road just beyond Complexo Náutilus – and nothing fancy but good value for money. The rooms are straight-forward – all set in a row of apartment blocks and all with either fan or air-con. The apartments have hot plate and minifridge and some have views to the water.

Simples Aldeia Lda (SAL; ☎ 272-20134; Av Marginal; s/d from US$42/55; 2-room cottage s/d US$88/115; ⊠) This self-catering place, about 1.5km beyond Caraçol, and on the opposite side of the road, has simple rooms in three small cottages, all with twin beds, TV, screens, fridge and hot-plate.

Complexo Náutilus (☎ 272-21520; nautiluscas@ teledata.mz; Av Marginal; 2-/4-person bungalows from US$120/140; ⊠ ⊠) A good setting directly on the beach, marred only by indifferent service and management. Accommodation is in closely spaced beachside bungalows of varying sizes, all with TV and minifridge, and there's a restaurant. Ask for one of the 'newer' front bungalows. Rates include breakfast.

Top End

Pemba Beach Resort Hotel (☎ 272-21770, in South Africa 011-465 6904; www.pembabeachresort.com; Av Marginal; s/d US$160/220; ⊠ ⊠ ⊡) This five-star establishment is a beautiful spot to relax for a few days. It's built on large grounds overlooking the water, with a good restaurant, a seaside pool and a luxury yacht for charters around the Archipélago das Quirimbas and deep-sea fishing. Package deals from Johannesburg are available.

Clube Naval (☎ 272-21770; www.pembabeachresort .com; Av Marginal; 4- to 6-person self-catering apt US$312) Next door to Pemba Beach Resort Hotel and under the same management, Club Naval has well-equipped, upscale self-catering apartments. All have two bedrooms, kitchens, washing machines and cable TV, and accommodate up to four adults and two children.

Eating

TOWN CENTRE

Restaurante-Bar Samar (☎ 272-20415; Av 25 de Setembro; meals US$3-8; 9am-10pm Sun-Fri) Tucked away in the parking lot of the Igreja Reino de Deus, this good-value place features a wide array of delicious Portuguese cuisine and covered outdoor seating with lots of plants and greenery.

Pastelaria Flôr d'Avineda (☎ 272-20514; Av Eduardo Mondlane; meals from US$3) A long-standing and informal eatery, with outdoor tables on a small, street-side plaza, and a good selec-tion of standards and pastries. Indian food, including vegetarian dishes, is available with 24-hour notice.

Gastronomia (☎ 272-21038; Av Eduardo Mondlane; sandwiches US$5; closed Sun) A small shop next to Flôr d'Avineda, selling imported meats and cheeses, plus tasty sandwiches to takeaway.

556 (☎ 272-21487; Rua No 1; meals US$6-14; 10am-11pm Mon-Sat; ⊠) On the hill overlooking the port and bay, this is the best place for carnivores, with a good selection of South African meats, plus chicken grills, pizza and pub food.

Toma & Vai (Rua do Comércio; meals from US$2) In the baixa area near the port, with a few tables and a small selection of Italian and local dishes.

For self-catering try **Osman's** (Av 25 de Setembro), about 1.5km east of the main junction, or **KK Supermarket** (Av Eduardo Mondlane) next to Pastelaria Flôr d'Avineda.

PRAIA DE WIMBI

Budget

Super Wimbe (Av Marginal; meals US$2-3; from 7am) This inexpensive local hangout with burgers and omelettes is just past Complexo Caraçol.

JPS (Av Marginal extension; half chicken & chips US$4) A local haunt on the inland side of the road just beyond SAL, with grilled chicken, matapa and other local dishes, and screened-in eating areas. Service isn't speedy, but the price is right and the food is good.

Restaurante Wimbi (Av Marginal; meals US$3-4) A local place featuring seating on the beach, seafood grills and good service.

Pemba Dolphin (Av Marginal; seafood grills from US$5) Directly on the beach, with music and a beach-bar ambience, plus seafood grills. Grilled *lagosta* (crayfish) starts at US$14.

Midrange

Aquila Romana (☎ 272-21972; Av Marginal, Praia de Wimbi; pizzas & meals US$4-10; 6.30pm-10pm Tue-Fri, 9am-10pm Sat & Sun) In a tranquil beachside setting about 200m after the tarmac ends, this good place has pizza, homemade pasta and delicious Italian food.

Clube Naval (☎ 272-21770; Av Marginal, Praia de Wimbi; meals US$5-11; 10am-midnight) A waterside restaurant-bar next to Pemba Beach Hotel, with a breezy setting directly on the beach and a large menu featuring salads, seafood, chicken, ribs, pizzas and desserts (apple pie, ice cream and more). There's a volleyball area in the sand, plus a tiny playground for children.

Pemba Beach Hotel (☎ 272-21770; Av Marginal, Praia de Wimbi; breakfast/dinner buffet US$14/18) The restaurant here features breakfast and dinner buffets plus dining *á la carte*, with seating indoors or outside on the covered veranda.

About 20km south of Pemba at Murrébuè is **Upeponi** (meals from US$3) with good seafood on a beautiful, quiet beach and basic accommodation. Follow the tarmac road out of town for about 10km, then go left on an unpaved road towards Mecúfi, branching left again near a small power station.

Shopping

Pemba has some wonderful crafts, and is an especially good place to buy Makonde carvings.

Artes Maconde (☎ /fax 272-21099, 272-21100; ceebee@teledata.mz; Town Centre Av 25 de Setembro; Praia de Wimbi Pemba Beach Hotel) has an excellent selection of carvings and other crafts from around the country. They do international air and sea shipping and also take orders for local crafts and carvings. For anyone interested in high-quality Mozambican crafts, it's an essential stop.

There's a group of **Makonde carvers** (EN106) in Alto-Gingone near the large mango tree opposite the airport, where you can get some good pieces at very reasonable prices. Also try the small **craft shop** (Av do Chai) on the road between town and Wimbi beach. It's about 700m down from Av 25 de Setembro on the left side and unmarked.

Getting There & Away

AIR

There are daily flights on **LAM** (☎ 272-21251; Av Eduardo Mondlane; ✆ 7am-5pm Mon-Fri, 8am-noon Sat) to/from Maputo (often via-Nampula and/or Beira), and three times weekly to/from Dar es Salaam, Tanzania.

Air Corridor (☎ 272-20799, 272-28012; Av 25 de Setembro), diagonally opposite Osman supermarket, has daily flights down the coast, stopping at Nampula, Beira, Quelimane and Maputo.

Charters to the Archipélago das Quirimbas or west to Reserva do Niassa or Lago Niassa can be booked through Rani Aviation (contact through Pemba Beach Hotel), **Quirimbas Aviation** (☎ 272-21808; aircharters-quirimbas@plexusmoz.com) and Kaskazini.

BOAT

For local dhows to the Archipélago das Quirimbas, ask around at the beach behind the mosque at Paquitequete; also see p154 and p161.

BUS & CHAPA

Grupo Mecula (☎ 272-20821) has daily buses to Nampula (US$7, seven hours), Nacala (US$7, seven hours), Moçimboa da Praia (US$6.50, 7½ hours) and Mueda (US$6.50, eight hours). For Ilha de Moçambique, take the Nacala bus as far as Monapo, where you'll need to get out and catch a chapa for the remaining 55km. All departures are at 4.45am from the Grupo Mecula office (where you buy your ticket), on a small side street behind Osman's supermarket, just off the main road and about 1.5km from the centre. All buses also pass by the mCel office at the corner of Avs 25 de Setembro and Eduardo Mondlane to pick up more passengers, before departing town by around 5am.

If you miss the bus, try your luck with other transport at mCel or head to Embondeiro transport stand, about 3km from the centre, to the left of the main road (US$2 in a taxi). Alternatively, *tanzaniano* chapas depart in all directions from Igreja Reino de Deus from 4am, with high speeds and prices marginally cheaper than the Mecula buses.

Getting Around

Pemba's **taxi rank** (☎ 272-20187; Av Eduardo Mondlane) is just past the mCel office (from US$2 from town to Wimbi beach).

For car rental, try **Moti Rent-A-Car** (☎ 272-21687; motimoz@teledata.mz), based at the airport, or arrange through Kaskazini or your hotel.

Chapas only run sporadically between Praia de Wimbi and town (US$0.20), but it's easy enough to find lifts. Most of the beach hotels can arrange lifts from US$5 per person.

CI Divers (p154) rents bicycles for US$5 per hour.

AROUND PEMBA

Within about a 2½ to three hour drive from Pemba are several new camps and lodges, all of which offer visitors a chance to experience a part of Cabo Delgado's wild, untamed bush and possibly see an elephant or two.

Mareja (www.mareja.com; camping per person US$10, r without/with bathroom US$20/30) is an impressive community-focused project where you can experience local life in the bush, including traditional dancing, wildlife watching and walks. Luxury fly-camps are planned, but for now, there's camping, dorm beds and a couple of rustic but pleasant guesthouse rooms. It's about 40km northwest of Pemba as a bird flies; allow about 2½ hours by road. Mareja may be able to help with transfers.

Beautifully set on the northern side of Pemba Bay, **Londo Lodge** (www.londolodge.com; per person full board US$350; 🐾) has six luxury beach-facing villas, a restaurant, a range of water sports, and safaris and bushwalking planned, though they weren't yet open when this book was researched.

Taratibu (Veka) is located about 160km northwest of Pemba in Ancuabe district in a wild area known for its elephants. Four chalets are planned, but for now it's just camping and self-catering. Kaskazini (see Information) is the Pemba booking agent.

ARCHIPÉLAGO DAS QUIRIMBAS

The Archipélago das Quirimbas consists of about two dozen islands and islets strewn among the turquoise waters along the 400km stretch of coastline between Pemba and the Rio Rovuma. Some are waterless and uninhabited, while others have histories as long as the archipelago itself.

Throughout, the archipelago's natural beauty is astounding, with searing white patches of soft sand surrounded by brilliant turquoise and azure waters alternating with greener and vegetated islands, fringed in part by mangroves. Dense mangrove forests also link many of the islands with each other and with the coast, with only skilled dhow captains able to navigate among the intricate channels that were cut during Portuguese times.

Today, many of the southern islands, including Ibo, Quirimba, Matemo and Rolas, are part of the **Parque Nacional das Quirimbas** (Quirimbas National Park; entry per adult/child US$8/2), which also includes large inland areas on the fringing coastline. Fees are currently collected by hotels within the park area, although this is likely to change. There are also various other park fees, including US$4 per person per day for camping, but their enforcement status is still in flux.

In addition to its pristine natural beauty, the archipelago is known for its diving, which is considered to be especially good around Quilaluia, Vamizi and Rongui; see p46.

History

Ibo and Quirimba, the two main islands in the archipelago, were already important Muslim trading posts when the Portuguese arrived in the 15th century. The islands were renowned in particular for their production of silks, cottons and maluane cloth – on some old maps, they are shown as the Maluane Islands. Ivory, ambergris and turtle shell were also important items in local commerce, and trade extended south as far as Sofala, Zambézia and north to Malindi, off the Kenyan coast.

By the early 17th century the Portuguese had established a mission on Quirimba and a fortified settlement on Ibo. They also built cisterns to store rainwater, which encouraged the development of agriculture, and the islands began to supply food to Ilha de Moçambique. Beginning in the mid 18th century, the archipelago – particularly Ilha do Ibo – served as a base for the clandestine slave trade, attracting boats from as far away as Zanzibar and Kilwa in present-day Tanzania. In the late 19th century, as the slave trade came to an end and colonial attention shifted to the mainland, trade in the archipelago began to decline. Today Quirimba, with its coconut and sisal plantations, is probably the most economically active of the islands, though all are quiet – largely ignored until recently and caught in a fascinating time warp.

Ilha do Ibo

Ibo, the best-known of the Quirimbas islands, is an enchanting place, its quiet streets lined with dilapidated villas and crumbling, moss-covered buildings and echoing with the silent, hollow footsteps of bygone centuries. Architecturally it is more open than Ilha de Moçambique, although its ambience is more insulated and its pace more subdued. The

---

TO TIDE YOU OVER

Unless you're travelling by chartered plane (which is easily arranged and often reasonably priced), access to most of the islands of the Archipélago das Quirimbas is dependent on winds and tides. To avoid getting stranded, always check tide tables before setting out. Dhows only come and go at high tide, setting sail just before the high tide point.

Tide tables are available at the port in Pemba. Otherwise, ask at shops in town or inquire of resident expatriates. Tide tables for the entire country are available at Inahina in Maputo (see p175).

best time to visit is during a clear, moonlit night, when the old colonial houses take on a haunting, almost surreal aspect.

Ibo was fortified as early as 1609 and by the late 18th century had become the most important town in Mozambique after Ilha de Moçambique. During this era, the island was a major export point in the slave trade, with demand spurred by French sugar plantation owners on Mauritius and elsewhere. In the late 19th century, it served briefly as headquarters for the Niassa Company. However, in 1904, the headquarters were relocated to Pemba (then Porto Amelia) to take advantage of Pemba's better sea access routes and harbour, and Ibo faded into oblivion.

At the island's northern end is the star-shaped **Fort of São João**, which was built in 1791 and designed to accommodate up to 300 people. In the days when Ibo was linked into the slave trade, the fort's dark, cramped lower chambers were used as slave holding points. Today it's known for the **silver artisans** who have set up shop near the entrance. Much of the silver used is made from melted-down coins and is often of inferior quality, but the distinctive and refined Swahili artisanship is among the best in the region.

There are two other forts on the island, neither well preserved. The **Fort of São José** to the southwest dates from 1760, but ceased to have any military use once the larger fort of São João was built. The **Fort of Santo António** near the market was built around 1830. Other places of interest include a large church near the fort of São José, and the island's three cemeteries, including an old Hindu crematorium along the road running northwest from the port.

Traditional religious practices are alive and well on Ibo and if you spend some time on the island, you'll undoubtedly come into contact with them. One of the best times to see dancing is in late June, when the feast of São João is celebrated with numerous festivities.

Ibo doesn't have many beaches, but as compensation there are magical sunset views over the mud flats just north of the tiny port.

SLEEPING & EATING

The accommodation situation on Ibo was in a state of flux as this book was researched, with almost all everywhere moving rapidly upscale. Especially if you're on a budget, stop at Kaskazini in Pemba (p154) for an update before heading out this way, as much of the following information is likely to be outdated.

Karibuni (Casa de Janine; ibo_pemba@yahoo.fr; camping per US$3, r US$24) The long-standing Karibuni is located in Vila Ruben, an old house along the waterfront just northwest of the tiny port. It's cheap and friendly, with a few clean, no-frills rooms with shared bathroom and bucket bath and delicious meals on order. Plans are underway for this entire strip of waterfront, including Vila Ruben, to be converted to a luxury property, so get an update before setting your plans.

Telecomunicações de Moçambique Guesthouse (☎ 272-43001, 272-43000; r US$26) About 500m east of the port near the telecom building, this guesthouse has spacious, clean rooms, occasional electricity and a TV in the common area, plus clean bucket showers. It's a good deal – the only problem is that there's not always someone around to open it up for you, and when there is, it's often filled with official guests. The tiny **Bar São João**, diagonally opposite, has cheap meals and drinks and sometimes sells bottled water.

Ibo Island Lodge (☎ in South Africa 021-702 0643; www.iboisland.com; s/d with half board US$360/560) This atmospheric and very promising 12-room luxury boutique hotel (it was about to open as this book was researched) is housed in three charming, restored mansions overlooking the water just northwest of the dhow port, with spacious, high-ceilinged rooms and wonderful sunset views. It's operated by Ocean Island Safaris (p190); check with them for the latest information.

Ilha de Quirimba

Quirimba, just south of Ibo, is the most economically active island of the archipelago, with large coconut plantations, a sizeable sisal factory and an airstrip. While it is more bustling than Ibo, it is far less interesting from an architectural and historical perspective and not nearly as scenic as the little patches of paradise further north. It is possible to walk between Quirimba and Ibo at low tide, but the route is through dense mangrove swamps, and you'll need a guide.

Historically, Quirimba was an important Muslim trading centre well before the arrival of the Portuguese. In 1522 it was raided by the Portuguese and the town was destroyed, although it was later rebuilt. In the 16th century

Quirimba served as a centre for missionary work.

There is currently no accommodation on the island, though this is likely to soon change.

Quilaluia

Until recently, tiny Quilaluia was inhabited only by seasonal fishing communities. Now, it's a protected marine sanctuary and home to **Quilálea** (☎ 272-21808; www.quilalea.com; per person all-inclusive full-board from US$375), a luxurious private resort, and the place to come if you're looking for a secluded tropical island retreat. Accommodation is in nine well-spaced private chalets of rock, teakwood and other natural materials, each with sea-facing verandas, king-sized beds and billowing mosquito nets – though the nets are hung more for the ambience than anything else, as the island is considered to be mosquito-free. There's excellent cuisine, and the sea stretches out before you to the horizon. The surrounding waters offer prime diving and snorkelling immediately offshore.

Medjumbe & Matemo

Idyllic Medjumbe is a narrow sliver of island draped with white coral sand and home to **Medjumbe Island Resort** (☎ in South Africa 011-465 6904; www.medjumberesort.com; s/d with half-board US$389/576; ✗ ☒). Accommodation is in 13 thatched wooden chalets set directly on the sand. Diving and fishing are available just offshore.

Unlike Medjumbe, which is unpopulated except for the resort, the much larger island of Matemo, north of Ibo, has been inhabited for generations, and was an important centre for cloth manufacture into the 17th century. Today villages dot much of the north and interior of the island. At its tip is **Matemo Island Resort** (☎ in South Africa 011-465 6904; www.matemoresort.com; s/d with half-board US$389/576; ✗ ☒), the largest of the island developments, with 24 chalets – all with sliding glass doors opening onto the beach, indoor and outdoor showers and Moorish overtones in the common areas.

Both lodges are run by Rani Africa, which also runs the Pemba Beach Hotel in Pemba (p156), and island-mainland packages are available.

Vamizi, Rongui & Macalóè

These three islands are part of the **Maluane Project** (www.maluane.com) – a privately-funded and highly impressive community-based conservation project. Ultimately it will encompass not only the islands, but also an adjoining coastal strip and a 33,000 hectare inland area, where wildlife safari-tropical island combinations will be possible. For now only Vamizi has accommodation, with lodges on Rongui and Macaloé and an inland luxury bush lodge to follow soon.

MAPIKO DANCING

If you hear drumming in the late afternoons while travelling around Cabo Delgado, it likely means *mapiko* – the famed masked dancing of the Makonde.

The dancer – always a man – wears a special wooden mask or *lipiko* (plural: *mapiko*), decorated with exaggerated features, hair (often real) and facial etchings. After being carved, the masks are kept in the bush in a special place known as the *mpolo*, where only men are permitted to enter. Traditionally, they cannot be viewed by women or by uncircumcised boys unless they are being worn by a dancer.

Before *mapiko* begins, the dancer's body is completely covered with large pieces of cloth wrapped around the legs, arms and body so that nothing can be seen other than the fingers and toes. All evidence that there is a person inside is supposed to remain hidden. The idea is that the dancer represents the spirit of a dead person who has come to do harm to the women and children, from which only the men of the village can protect them. While boys learn the secret of the dance during their initiation rites, women are never supposed to discover it and remain in fear of the *mapiko*. (*Mapiko* supposedly grew out of male attempts to limit the power of women in matrilineal Makonde society.)

Once the dancer is ready, distinctive rhythms are beaten on special *mapiko* drums. The dance is usually performed on weekend afternoons, and must be finished by sunset. The best places to see *mapiko* dancing are in and around Mueda and in Macomia. To take a mask home, look in craft shops in Pemba and Nampula.

Historically, the most important of the three islands was Vamizi – a narrow, paradisal crescent about midway between Moçimboa da Praia and Palma at the northernmost end of the archipelago. It was long a Portuguese and Arabic trading post and there are ruins of an old Portuguese fort at its western end, plus a large village and several stunning beaches to the north and east. All three islands are important seasonal fishing bases.

Vamizi Island Lodge (www.vamizi.com; r per person with full board & activities from US$485) This 24-bed luxury getaway sits on a long arc of spectacular white sand draped along Vamizi's northern edge and is without doubt one of the most beautiful places to relax along the northern Mozambican coast. The 10 spacious beach chalets have large, open sitting areas and private verandas, plus all the comforts you could want, presented in a tasteful and low-key way. Offshore is first-class diving and snorkelling; deep-sea fishing can be arranged, plus walks – including to some hawksbill and green turtle nesting areas – and birding.

Other Islands

Tiny **Quipaco**, about midway between Pemba and Quissanga and the first island in the Quirimbas string, is notable for its birdlife and mangrove ecosystems. The surrounding waters, especially at the nearby Ponto do Diablo, are considered prime fishing areas and the island itself makes a tranquil stop, although it lacks the tropical backdrop of some of the other islands further north. There are a few A-frame houses that can be booked through jam@teledata.mz or Kaskazini in Pemba; bring all food and drink.

Further north is small **Quisiva**, which has no infrastructure, although you can still see some old Portuguese plantation houses. The tiny and densely vegetated **Rolas** is uninhabited except for some seasonal fishing settlements and a fascinating population of coconut crabs. The island is part of the Quirimbas national park area and a WWF campsite is planned.

Getting There & Away

AIR
Several of the islands, including Ibo, Quirimba and Matemo, have airstrips for charter flights. Island lodges all organise plane and/or motorboat transfers for their guests. Individual seats are often available; Pemba to Ibo costs US$65 per person one way.

COCONUT CRABS

Ilha das Rolas is known for its giant coconut-eating land crabs. These nocturnal creatures, considered to be the largest arthropods in the world, sometimes grow up to 1m long. They get their name from their proclivity for climbing coconut palms, shaking down the nuts, and then prying the cracked shells open to scoop out the flesh.

BOAT
To reach Ibo or Quirimba on your own steam, you'll need to go first to Quissanga, on the coast north of Pemba, and from there to the village of Tandanhangue, where you can get dhows to the islands. From Pemba, there's a direct chapa to Quissanga (US$4, five hours) from the fish market behind the mosque in Paquitequete , departing about 4am daily. In a private car, the trip takes about 3½ hours.

Once in Quissanga, most vehicles continue on to the village of Tandanhangue (US$4 from Pemba), which is the departure point for dhows to Ibo (locals pay US$0.80 – foreigners are often quoted rates up to ten times higher) and Quirimba islands.

If you're driving, take the dirt track to the left about 2km before Quissanga town to reach Tandanhangue (4WD). There's secure parking at Casa de Isufo (signposted 2km before the Tandanhangue port – you'll need to walk back to the port) for US$1.50 per day.

Dhows leave Tandanhangue only at high tide, and take from one to six hours. There's no accommodation in Tandanhangue or Quissanga, but if you get stuck, Isufo (at Casa de Isufo) can help you find a meal and has an enclosed area where you can sleep on the ground.

An alternative to a dhow is to try and charter a local motor boat, for which you should expect to pay about US$40. For those with larger budgets, it's easy to arrange speedboat charters from Pemba direct to the islands. The best contact for this is Kaskazini.

For island-hopping along the coast, contact Kaskazini. Guludo (p162) arranges dhow safaris for its guests. When planning a route, check that the winds are in your favour (see p191).

MACOMIA

The small district capital of Macomia is the turn-off point for the beach at Pangane. If you find yourself stuck here on a weekend, chances are good that you'll be able to see some *mapiko* dancing. Soccer is also popular and there are frequent matches pitting local teams against those from Pemba and elsewhere in the area.

The only place to stay is the very basic **Pensão Kwetu-Kumo** (r US$9), about 1.5km west of the main road, with tiny, grubby rooms.

Several vehicles daily go to Mucojo, sometimes continuing on to Pangane. Hitching is possible but very slow. If you're stranded, a good place to ask for a lift is at Chung's Bar, at Macomia's main intersection.

To continue southwards to Pemba, the Mecula buses from Moçimboa da Praia and Mueda pass Macomia from about 8.30am or 9am. Going northwards, you'll often need to wait until around 9am or 10am for a vehicle to pass through.

CHAI

It was in the large village of Chai that Frelimo's military campaign against colonial rule began in 1964. There's a small monument near the main road and every year on 25 September (Revolution Day), national attention turns here as the independence struggle is remembered with visits by high-ranking officials and reenactments of historical events.

Chai is about 40km north of Macomia along the main road between Pemba and Moçimboa da Praia. Take any vehicle heading to/from Pemba and ask to be dropped off, but do it early enough in the day that you have a chance of onward transport, as there's no accommodation.

PANGANE

Pangane is a large village on a long, palm-fringed beach about 10km north of Mucojo, and 50km off the main north–south road. Many seasonal fishermen come up from Nacala and other places in the south, so the sand isn't always the cleanest, but the setting is beautiful. Just offshore is Macaloé island, part of the Maluane project, and beyond that the St Lazarus Banks, renowned for their diving and fishing.

Sleeping & Eating

Hashim's Camp (camping per person US$6, bungalow US$10) Run by the helpful Hashim, this place is set at Pangane's breezy point on the nicest stretch of sand and is ideal for sitting back for a few days. Staff will prepare grilled fish and other-

wise take care of you and while everything's very basic, it's clean and relaxed. Sleeping is in three reed bungalows with sand floors, mattresses, and decent ablutions.

Guludo (☎ in UK 01323-766 655; www.guludo.com) This upscale fair-traded camp – set against a backdrop of palm groves, white sands and turquoise seas – makes a fine base if you want to get a taste of northern Mozambique's coastal paradise while learning about and supporting local community development initiatives. On offer are nine spacious, sea-facing safari-style tents, island excursions, diving and even elephant tracking. (The surrounding area is one of the best places in these parts for spotting the giant pachyderms.) A bush lodge is planned and staff can also arrange walks to see the village school and other community initiatives. It's about 15km south of Mucojo junction; transfers can be arranged from Pemba and Macomia, as well as from Montepuez; Aurora (p152) makes a good combination itinerary with Guludo if you want to continue the theme of learning about local life.

Alternatively there are several guesthouses, the best of which is the long-running **Pensão Suki** (r US$12). It's owned by the same people who run Chung's Bar in Macomia, so you can inquire there as you're passing through.

Getting There & Away

There's at least one vehicle daily between Pangane and Macomia (where fuel is sometimes available). Otherwise, there are several chapas daily between Macomia and the Mucojo junction (US$2), from where you can find a pick-up on to Pangane (US$0.80), 10km further north. Driving, the road from Macomia is sandy (4WD). From both Pangane and Guludo, it's easy to arrange a dhow to various islands of the Archipélago das Quirimbas, including Ibo (12 to 20 hours, depending on the winds); check with Hashim's Camp or Guludo. For the well-heeled, there's an airstrip at Mucojo for charter planes.

MUEDA

Mueda – the main town on the Makonde Plateau and the centre of Mozambique's Makonde people – is rather lacking in charm. However, this is compensated for by a wonderfully cool climate, a rustic, highland feel and an attractive setting, with views down from the escarpment along the southern and

---

THE MAKONDE

The Mueda Plateau around Mueda is home to the Makonde, who are renowned throughout Africa for their amazing woodcarvings. Like many tribes in the north, the Makonde are matrilineal. Children and inheritances normally belong to the woman and it's common for husbands to move to the village of their wives after marriage, setting up house near their mothers-in-law. Settlements are widely scattered – possibly a remnant of the days when the Makonde sought to evade slave raids – and there is no tradition of a unified political system. Each village is governed by a hereditary chief and a council of elders.

Due to their isolated location, the Makonde remained largely insulated from colonial and postcolonial influences. Even today, many Makonde still adhere to traditional religions, with the complex spirit world given its fullest expression in their carvings.

Traditionally, the Makonde practised body scarring and while it's seldom done today, you may see older people with markings on their faces and bodies. It's also fairly common to see elderly Makonde women wearing a wooden plug in their upper lip, or to see this depicted in Makonde artwork.

---

western edges of town. The surrounding area holds the potential for some good hiking, but it was heavily mined during the war, so stick to well-trodden paths. The plateau itself lies at about 800m altitude, with water available only on its slopes and at its base.

Sights & Activities

Mueda was originally built as an army barracks during the colonial era. In 1960 it was the site of the infamous massacre of Mueda. There's a statue commemorating Mueda's role in Mozambican independence and a mass grave for the 'martyrs of Mueda' at the western end of town. Maria José Chipande – wife of Alberto Chipande, who was a well-known Makonde guerrilla commander during the independence struggle, one of the founding members of Frelimo and a former Minister of Defence – is also buried here. Just behind this monument is a ravine (known locally as *xiudi*) over which countless more Mozambicans were hurled to their deaths.

The outlying villages are good places to see Makonde woodcarvings.

About 50km northwest of Mueda on the edge of the Makonde Plateau is the outpost town of **Moçimboa do Rovuma**, which offers views down to the Rio Rovuma, although it's inaccessible unless you have your own vehicle.

Sleeping & Eating

Pensão Takatuka (Rua 1 de Maio; r US$10, in annexe US$12) Takatuka has reasonably clean but very basic rooms in the main building or in an annexe out back, all with shared bucket bath. Food can be arranged, but order well in advance. It's on the tarmac road in the town centre.

Motel Sanzala (Rua 1 de Maio; r US$10) The only other choice, with similarly basic rooms, but the advantage of running water. It's just down the road from Pensão Takatuka.

Getting There & Away

Grupo Mecula has daily buses to Pemba (US$7, eight hours) and Nampula (US$12, 13 hours), both departing at 5am from the main road. There are also several vehicles each morning to Moçimboa da Praia (US$3.50, seven hours).

There's usually one chapa daily to Moçimboa do Rovuma (US$4, two hours), from where you can cross the border into Tanzania; see p188. All transport leaves from the main road opposite the market and it all leaves early. After about 10am, it's difficult to find vehicles to any destination.

If you're driving, there are two roads connecting Mueda with the main north–south road. Most traffic uses the good road via Diaca (50km). The alternate route via Muidumbe (about 30km south of Diaca), is scenic, winding through hills and forests, but rougher. Near Muidumbe is **Nangololo**, a mission station and an important base during the independence struggle, with an old airstrip large enough to take jets.

MOÇIMBOA DA PRAIA

This bustling outpost is the last major town before the Rio Rovuma and the Tanzanian border. Most local residents are Mwani

---

THE STORY OF THE NÁVILO

Once upon a time, the Yao and the Makonde, two of the largest tribes in northern Mozambique, were great enemies. This enmity arose in bygone days when Mataka was the most powerful Yao chief and M'Bavale an important leader among the Makonde. In those days the Yao (most of whom live in present-day Niassa province) earned their livelihood from hunting, fishing and trading. However the Makonde, who are at home in northern Cabo Delgado province, were farmers. As links between the coast and the interior grew, the Yao began to cross through the territory of the Makonde in order to trade with Arab coastal merchants. This intrusion on their territory angered the Makonde, and led to many battles. Before long, the Yao and the Makonde were sworn enemies, enmeshed in what seemed to be an intractable conflict.

Weeks, months and years passed. Finally, Mataka and M'Bavale reached an agreement that their people would stop fighting against each other. Not only that, but they would also embody this truce in a special relationship, known as the *návilo*. Under the *návilo*, the Yao and the Makonde would meet each other in peace. They would also each be bound to go to any length necessary to meet the needs of the other, and in turn would have full liberties with the property of the other. A Yao would thus always be welcome into the home of a Makonde and treated as a royal visitor, and a Makonde would receive the same treatment from a Yao. The demands made by each side would be tempered by the knowledge that the other party could request the same of them. According to many Yao and Makonde, this special relationship between the two groups endures to this day.

('People of the Sea') – a Swahili and hence Muslim people known for their textiles and silver craftsmanship, as well as for their rich song and dance traditions. Moçimboa da Praia does brisk a trade with Tanzania, both legal and illegal, and from here northwards, a few words of Swahili will often get you further than Portuguese.

The town itself is long – stretched over several kilometres between the main road and the sea. In the somewhat scruffy, upper-lying section is a small market, several *pensões* and the transport stand. About 2km east near the water are a few more places to stay, police and immigration, a lively fish market and the colourful dhow port.

Information

If you're travelling by dhow and enter or leave Mozambique here, have your passport stamped at the immigration office near Complexo Miramar. An immigration officer meets arriving charter flights.

Banco Austral (Av Eduardo Mondlane) Changes US dollars cash; out of hours, try changing with some of the Indian shop owners.

TDM (Av 7 de Março; per min US$0.60) Internet access.

Sleeping & Eating

Pensão Leeta (☎ 272-81147; Av Samora Machel; camping US$5, r US$10) At the entrance to town near the transport stand, with no-frills and slightly scruffy twin-bedded rooms sharing bucket-style baths. They'll also let you pitch a tent on their grounds.

Pensão-Residencial Magid (☎ 272-81099; Av Eduardo Mondlane; r US$12) Convenient to the Grupo Mecula bus garage, with basic rooms sharing facilities.

Complexo Miramar (Complexo Natasha or Chez Bebé; ☎ 272-81135/6; s/d US$18/24) Several steps up from the previous two listings, with a breezy, waterside location, three no-frills rondavels with just a trickle of running water, and a popular restaurant-bar (meals from US$3). Follow the main road downhill to the water, near the police station.

Hotel Chez Natalie (☎ 82-527 9094; natalie@teledata .mz; camping per tent US$8, 4-person chalet US$68) This tranquil place – designed by the same architect responsible for Carushka in Chocas (p142) – is the best bet in town, especially if you have your own transport. On offer are camping (though with only minimal ablutions), and three rustic and very pleasant chalets, each with a double bed and two twins in a family-style setup, plus a refrigerator, running water, electricity, internet access if you happen to have your own laptop, a bar and meals with advance arrangement (or pans and a small grill, if you want to cook your own). Breakfast is included in the room price, and staff can help you arrange bicycles for around town or dhow excursions. It's about 2km from the town centre (no public transport), overlooking some mangroves and the estuary that rims Moçimboa to the north. Watch for the signposted turnoff near Clubé de Moçimboa.

Getting There & Away

AIR

There's an airstrip outside town for charter flights (currently used mainly for charters to Vamizi island in the Archipélago das Quirimbas).

BOAT

It's easy to arrange dhows from Moçimboa da Praia. Expect to pay from US$10 to US$15 per day, and read the boxed text on p191 first.

BUS & PICK-UP

The transport stand is near the market at the entrance to town. Two pick-ups go to/from the Rovuma via Palma (US$10, four hours) daily, leaving Moçimboa da Praia by around 3.30am or 4am latest; arrange with the drivers the afternoon before to be collected from wherever you're staying. The village on the Mozambican side of the border is known locally as Namoto. Allow two to three hours between Moçimboa da Praia and Palma, and another 1½ to two hours to the border. If all goes smoothly, you can do the entire journey to Mtwara (Tanzania) in half a day in the dry season; see p188. During the rainy season, it takes much longer and sometimes isn't possible at all.

To Pemba, the Mecula bus departs daily at 4.30am sharp (US$7, seven hours). The best place to get it is at the garage where it's kept during the night, about midway between Complexo Miramar and the bus stand. Other-wise, there are usually one or two chapas or pickups that do the journey as well, departing by 7am from the main road in front of the market.

PALMA

The large fishing village of Palma is nestled among the coconut groves about 45km south of the Tanzania border. It's a centre for basketry and mat weaving – though most of this is done in the outlying villages – and for boat making, and it is fascinating to watch craftspeople using centuries-old techniques. The area is also a melting pot of languages, with Makwe, Makonde, Mwani, Swahili and Portuguese all spoken.

About 15km offshore across Baía de Túnguè is idyllic **Ilha de Tecomaji**, which is usually deserted except for some local fishermen who use it for drying octopus. Dhows can be arranged from the small harbour near Hotel Palma; allow about three hours with good winds, and bring water and everything else with you. Just south of Tecomaji is **Ilha de Rongui**, followed by **Ilma de Vamizi**, both of which are privately owned as part of the Maluane Project (p160). Beaches in town are not clean enough for swimming.

About 20km north of Palma is tiny Kiwiya junction, where a sandy track branches about 17km seawards to **Cabo Delgado** – the point of land from which Cabo Delgado province takes its name – and a lighthouse.

COASTAL LIFE

Life along much of the northern Mozambican coast centres around fishing and dhow building, often using centuries-old methods and equipment. Dhows are often constructed without nails, using only wooden pegs and tightly fitted wooden slats, which are sealed and waterproofed with a mixture of natural gum and resin.

One of the main catches in Palma and other areas of the far north is octopus. Fishermen head out to sea armed only with a snorkel mask and a spear or handmade spear gun. Once well offshore, they leave their boats and swim to locate the octopus, which they then target between the eyes.

At night, look out to sea and you'll see little lanterns bobbing up and down on the waves – rigged on dhows to lure fish into large nets spread out in the surrounding waters. Sometimes, groups of fishermen will pull trawl nets – some up to 100m long – through shoreline waters in search of fish that feed on sea grass meadows in the shallows. In delta areas and around mangrove creeks, you may see traps – some up to 50m long – made from mangrove poles. Smaller reed traps and baskets are often used in the southern part of the country and in inland lakes. A common sight at low tide is women in their brightly coloured capulanas and head scarves wading into the sand flats to harvest clams, oysters and other shellfish.

Orientation

Palma has an upper, administrative section of town with immigration, the post office and a small market, and a lower section, about 2km downhill along the water, with the main market, the hotel and many local houses. There's nowhere to change money, although changing meticais and Tanzanian shillings at the markets is no problem.

Sleeping & Eating

Hotel Palma (r US$8) The friendly, family-run and very basic Hotel Palma, about 2km downhill from the immigration office, is the only place to stay. Meals can be arranged or you can get plates of rice and sauce at the market.

Getting There & Away

For travel between Palma and Tanzania, see p188. Chapas from Moçimboa da Praia en route to the Rio Rovuma pass Palma between about 6am and 8am and charge US$5 from Palma. Transport from the Rovuma south to Moçimboa da Praia passes through Palma between 11am and 2pm, and there's usually a car from Palma to Moçimboa da Praia each morning (US$5, 2½ hours).

All transport leaves from the Boa Viagem roundabout at the entrance to town, about 3km from Hotel Palma. Some drivers continue down to the market near Hotel Palma, or will at least be willing to drop you at the top of the hill.

Directory

ACCOMMODATION

Accommodation in Mozambique ranges from the most basic rooms to five-star luxury and stunning island lodges. There's a wide choice in most major cities and tourist destinations. Elsewhere, selection is limited. Throughout the country, accommodation tends to be more expensive than elsewhere in the Southern Africa region, though a few good deals are available, especially in the top-end category, which includes some idyllically situated island lodges.

Accommodation along the coast, and especially in the south, fills up around Christmas and during the South African school holidays (see p175); book in advance if you'll be travelling then. Discounts are often available during the low season, and sometimes also midweek, so always ask. Almost all places offer children's discounts as well, and extra beds can usually be arranged for US$10 to US$20. When quoting prices, many establishments distinguish between a *duplo* (a room with two twin beds) and a *casal* (double bed).

Sleeping listings in this book are divided into budget, midrange and top-end categories. See the inside front cover for approximate price ranges.

Backpackers Lodges

There are a few backpacker lodges (usually called 'backpackers') in Mozambique, similar to those found in South Africa, and the network is slowly expanding, especially in the south. Most offer a choice of dorm beds or private rooms, plus cooking facilities and sometimes camping. They're always worth hunting down and are usually the best-value budget accommodation. The price of a dorm bed averages US$10.

Camping

There are plenty of camping grounds along the southern coast, plus enough others scattered around the country that it's well worth carrying a tent if you're trying to save money (and essential if you're cycling or spending significant time in rural areas). Camping avoids grubby *pensões* (cheap local hotels), and some of the beachside camping grounds are wonderful, with the surf in front or just over the dunes. Officially, camping is permitted only in designated areas. The realities of land mines, wildlife and general security risks mean that it's not wise to free camp anyway, particularly if you're on your own. In rural parts of the country, or wherever there is no established camp site, ask the local chief (*régulo*) for permission; you'll invariably be welcomed and well taken care of, and should reciprocate with a modest token of thanks. (Generally what you would pay at an official camping ground or a bit less should be fine.)

DIRECTORY

Hotels & Pensões

The cheapest hotels *(pensão*, singular, or *pensões*, plural) average from about US$8 per room. For this price you can expect a tiny, nonventilated box of a room with a communal toilet and bucket bath. There may or may not be electricity.

For midrange standards, including a private bathroom, hot running water, electricity, air-conditioning (sometimes) and a restaurant on the premises, expect to pay from about US$40 per room.

Top-end hotels offer all the amenities you would expect, and cost from around US$150 per room.

In out of the way areas, if you happen to be in a district capital and stuck for accommodation, check with the district administrator, who will generally have some sort of guesthouse for official visitors that you may be permitted to use if it's empty (from about US$15 per person). There are usually no amenities and you'll need to look elsewhere for drinks and meals.

Self-Catering & Rentals

South African–style self-catering accommodation – with sleeping facilities plus a kitchenette or braai area – is very common,

especially along the southern coast. Many of the beach places offer self-catering options and there are many places geared exclusively to self-caterers (ie they don't offer meals or other hotel services, so you'll need to bring all your food with you, though most places at least have a bar). Most self-catering places have kitchen utensils and plug points. Some supply bed linens, mosquito nets and, occasionally, towels, while for others you'll need to bring these yourself.

It's also possible in some coastal areas to rent private beach houses. Several have been listed in the individual town sections of this guide. Otherwise, look in the Mozambique pages at the back of *Getaway* magazine (see p190) or ask at travel agents.

ACTIVITIES

Mozambique is a prime destination for diving and snorkelling, as well as birding, fishing and surfing. Dhow safaris are also increasingly popular and there are several established rugged hikes, plus wildlife-watching both underwater and on land.

Birding

Mozambique offers excellent birding, and because much of the country is still uncharted territory, you may even have the chance to record some first-sightings. Among the best birding areas are the Archipélago de Bazaruto (p99), Parque Nacional de Gorongosa (p111) and nearby Monte Gorongosa (p112), the Montes Chimanimani (p117), the area around Monte Namúli (p128), the southern coastal wetlands (around Xai-Xai, p81), Reserva Especial de Maputo (p79), and the area around Catapu (near Caia; p123) in central Mozambique.

In 1996 the Mozambique Bird Atlas Project was initiated – a massive undertaking aimed at charting the distribution and abundance of all bird species in the country, beginning in the south and moving northwards. The project can be contacted through the South Africa–based **Avian Demography Unit** (http://web.uct. ac.za/depts/stats/adu/p_mozat.htm) at the University of Cape Town or through the **Endangered Wildlife Trust** (www.ewt.org.za), also in South Africa. It welcomes correspondence from travellers in Mozambique with records of sightings. In addition to these two entities – both of which can provide bird lists for the country – good initial contacts for Mozambique birding in-

clude the Pretoria-based **Indicator Birding** (www
.birding.co.za), which organises occasional birding
trips to Mozambique; **Southern African Birding**
(www.sabirding.co.za); and the **African Bird Club** (www
.africanbirdclub.org).

Dhow Safaris, Boating & Kayaking

Good places for arranging dhow safaris include Vilankulo and the Archipélago de Bazaruto (contact Sail Away, p97); and northern
Mozambique around Pemba, Pangane and the
Archipélago das Quirimbas (contacts include
Kaskazini, p154, and Guludo, p162). In these
places, in Moçimboa da Praia and elsewhere
along the coast, it's also easy enough to organise things on your own (from around US$15
per local boat per day), though always ask at
your hotel for recommendations of reliable
captains, travel with the prevailing winds and
read the boxed text on p191.

For upmarket yacht and boat charters
around Pemba and the Archipélago das
Quirimbas, see p154. Most lodges on the Archipélago de Bazaruto also arrange charters.
In Maputo, the best contacts are top-end hotels, **Clube Naval** (☎ 21-492690, 21-494881, Avenida
Marginal), and the speedboat-charter operators
listed on (p73).

Sea kayaking is in its infancy, which means
that for any major jaunts you'll need to bring
boats and all other equipment with you. A few
resort areas, including Ilha de Inhaca and the
dive shops at Praia de Wimbi in Pemba, rent
small sea kayaks suitable for short paddles
close to shore. Another option, if you're self-
equipped, is kayaking along the Lago Niassa
coastline (see p148).

Diving & Snorkelling

Diving and snorkelling are Mozambique's
main 'activity' draws and there are excellent
opportunities for both. See the Diving chapter
(p43).

Fishing

Among anglers, the waters off the Mozambican coast have long been legendary, particularly in the south between Ponta d'Ouro and
Inhassoro, and in the far north around Pemba,
which is within easy reach of the famed St
Lazarus Bank, east of Quilaluia in the Archipélago das Quirimbas. Saltwater fly-fishing
is also increasingly popular. Inland, the most
popular fishing areas are Barragem de Cahora
Bassa near Tete, and Barragem de Chicamba

Real near Chimoio. A recommended initial
contact for fishing in northern Mozambique
is **Visagie World Charters** (www.world-charters.com).
For Barragem de Cahora Bassa, contact Ugezi
Tiger Lodge (p121).

Many people bring their own boat and
equipment from South Africa. Fishing charters can also be arranged through most of the
coastal resorts and upscale hotels. If you're
signed up with a charter, all the necessary
paperwork should be taken care of. If you
are bringing your own boat to Mozambique,
you will need a sportfishing license (about
US$16 per month), as well as a Form ORI/IIP
(Registration Form for Captured Sports Fish).
Launching is allowed from designated beach-
access roads with a permit (from about US$15),
available from the local *capitania* (maritime office) found in major coastal towns. Both fishing
licenses and launch permits can usually also be
sorted out with most coastal resorts.

Species you are likely to encounter include
marlin, kingfish, tuna and sailfish. Marlin season is from October/November to February/
March. For sailfish, it is generally year-round.
Tag and release is encouraged at many resorts.
Officially, no more than 6kg of any one type
of catch from sport- and deep-sea fishing can
be taken out of the country.

Hiking & Rock Climbing

For almost all hiking in Mozambique you'll be
on your own, as there's very little organised.
One of the better mountain climbs is up Monte
Namúli, which needs no special equipment.
Monte Gorongosa is also good, and equally
straightforward. Monte Binga is normally accessed from Zimbabwe, though it's possible
to climb from the Mozambique side. The surrounding Montes Chimanimani are beautiful
for hiking, but without any infrastructure other
than a handful of basic camp sites. Other areas
for hikes include Penha Longa, west of Chimoio,
and the hills around Gurúè. For information on
all of these places, see the Central Mozambique chapter (p104). For all except Monte
Gorongosa, you'll need a tent, and wherever
you hike, don't stray off established footpaths.

For rock climbing, the most appealing area
is west of Nampula towards Cuamba, with its
towering granite domes and sheer faces. However, there's nothing organised and it's not
particularly feasible unless you have a 4WD
and are self-sufficient. All the usual warnings
about landmines apply here too.

BEACH BITS

Mozambique's beaches are idyllic, but there are some things to watch out for.

Crime Don't tempt someone by leaving your belongings unguarded on the beach, and avoid isolated areas.

Currents The strong pulls that often accompany tidal ebbs and flows make swimming risky in some areas, so check with locals first before plunging in.

Jellyfish Bluebottles and other creatures with stinging tentacles are common in some seasons and areas. Most are painful rather than seriously harmful, but ask around locally if you see them on the beach.

Seashells, sea urchins & worms Sharp shells, sea urchins and the like inflict painful cuts that are slow healing in the tropics, so sandals or other footwear are a good idea if you'll be wading. They're also a good idea for beach walking, as more than one visitor has become infected with creeping eruption (also called cutaneous larva migrans or migrating larvae). This ailment, which probably sounds worse than it is, is spread through the droppings of humans, dogs and other animals.

Tides Keep an eye on water levels if you're travelling by dhow. For swimming, the water goes far out at low tide and many beaches are only good for swimming at high tide.

Surfing

The best waves are at Ponta d'Ouro (see p77) in the far south of the country and (for skilled surfers) at Tofinho (see p90) – Mozambique's unofficial surfing capital. Boards can be rented at both places.

Wildlife Watching

Some of the best wildlife watching is underwater; see the Diving chapter (p43). A particular highlight here is whale-watching (see boxed text, p47).

On the terrestrial side, wildlife-watching in Mozambique is very much for those with an adventurous bent who are seeking an alternative to southern and East Africa's established safari circuits. Unlike in some neighbouring countries, where the herds practically come to you, in Mozambique you'll need to spend considerable time, effort and, in some cases, money to seek them out – though the adventure and rugged bush backdrops compensate for often-challenging sightings. For more, see the Wildlife and National Parks & Reserves sections in the Environment chapter (p37 and p40), and the individual park and reserve listings.

BUSINESS HOURS

For business hours, see the inside of the front cover; exceptions are noted in individual listings. Most *casas de câmbio* (foreign-exchange bureaus) are open from about 8.30am to 5pm Monday to Friday, and on Saturday until about noon. Many shops and offices close for an hour or two between noon and 2pm. In northern Cabo Delgado, where dawn comes early, many places open by 7am or

7.30am, and close by about 5pm or 5.30pm, particularly in towns without good electricity supplies.

CHILDREN

Mozambicans are generally very friendly, helpful and protective towards children. The main considerations for travel here will likely be the scarcity of decent medical facilities; the length and discomfort involved in many road journeys; the problem of maintaining a balanced diet outside the major towns; and the difficulty of finding clean bathrooms outside of midrange and top-end hotels.

Many of the southern resorts, which are among the most family-friendly, offer special children's rates. These often include free accommodation for those under five years old and significant discounts (usually 50%) for those between five and 12 years of age. Similar discounts are increasingly available in other parts of the country as well, and many midrange and top-end hotels in tourist areas have swimming pools.

It's a good idea to travel with a blanket to spread out and use as a makeshift diaper-changing area. Powdered full-cream milk (but not skimmed milk) is available in almost all midsized and larger towns, as is bottled water. Nappies (diapers) are available in Maputo, Beira, Chimoio and Nampula, as is prepared baby food. (Shoprite branches and well-stocked pharmacies are the best places to find baby supplies in all these towns.) Cots and spare beds are easily arranged at most midrange and top-end places. Useful items to bring from home include a good supply of wet wipes (though these are often available in major cities), eye baths and antibiotic eardrops.

If you will be travelling with an infant, pushchairs (strollers) are not practical. Much better is some sort of harness or cloth that allows you to carry the baby on your back, Mozambican style, or in front of you. For long journeys, always take extra food and drink along (for the baby and for yourself).

In beach areas, be aware of the risk of hookworm infestation in populated areas, as well as the risk of bilharzia in lakes. Other things to watch out for are sea urchins at the beach, and thorns and the like in the brush.

For malaria protection, it's essential to bring nets from home for your children and ensure that they sleep under them. Also bring mosquito repellents from home, and check with your doctor regarding the use of prophylactics. Long-sleeved shirts and trousers are the best protection at dawn and dusk.

Maputo-based car-hire agencies can arrange child seats with advance notice, and upscale hotel restaurants sometimes have child seats. Breast-feeding in public is a non-issue in Mozambique, as women do it everywhere. Child care can generally be arranged informally through your hotel.

Lonely Planet's *Travel with Children* by Cathy Lanigan is full of tips for keeping children and parents happy while on the road.

CLIMATE

Southern Mozambique becomes unpleasantly hot for only a short period between late December and February, when temperatures can climb at midday to over 30°C, and unpleasantly wet between January/February and late March/April. For the rest of the year, it has an abundance of clear, blue skies and sunny days, with temperatures averaging around 24°C. From June through August the weather can get chilly at night, so bring a light jacket.

Heading north along the coast, temperatures and humidity levels rise, though conditions are moderated by sea breezes. At the height of the rainy season between February and early April, secondary roads often get too wet to negotiate.

The hottest areas of the country are in the dry west around Tete city and along the humid Zambezi River Valley, where the mercury frequently exceeds 30°C. The coolest areas – where a light jacket is essential in the winter months from June through August – are elevated parts

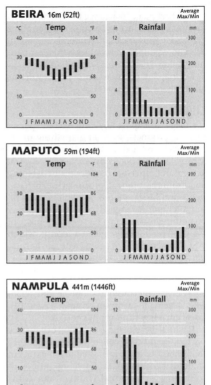

of Nampula and Niassa provinces, and northern Tete province.

Rainfall averages 750mm annually in Maputo, and between 800mm and 900mm along the northern coast. In the rainiest parts of the country – such as around Gurúè, southeast of Milange, and along the Zimbabwe border near Mt Binga – annual rainfall can be as high as 1800mm to 2200mm. Mozambique's zones of lowest precipitation are in the southwest, including parts of northwestern Gaza and western Inhambane provinces.

COURSES

There are several Portuguese language schools in Maputo (see p63). Elsewhere, private tutors can be easily arranged for Portuguese and for local languages, although don't expect books or formalised instruction. Rates start at about US$10 per hour.

The best place to arrange music, especially drumming, or dance instruction is at one of the provincial *casas de cultura* (cultural centres). In Maputo, a good initial contact is the Companhia Nacional de Canto e Dança (p68).

Diving-certification courses are available all along the coast; see p43.

CUSTOMS

It's illegal to export any endangered species or their products, including anything made from ivory or tortoiseshell. If you bring in a bicycle, laptop computer, video camera, generator, deep freeze or other major camping and fishing equipment, or similarly expensive items into Mozambique, you will need to fill out a temporary import permit (which may be nothing more than a handwritten piece of paper). You'll then be given a receipt, which you'll need to present again (with the item(s) declared) when leaving the country.

You're also supposed to declare any cash that you bring in excess of US$5000 or the equivalent. You'll need to show the form again when leaving to justify any amounts over this. Local currency cannot be exported.

If you'll be stocking up in South Africa on food and other consumables, remember that import of these is limited to a maximum value of US$200. 'Reasonable' quantities of souvenirs for personal (rather than commercial) purposes can be exported without declaration.

Firearms of any type, including sporting firearms, aren't permitted to be brought into Mozambique unless you have a permit. (These are arranged by hunting companies for their clients.)

DANGERS & ANNOYANCES

Mozambique has calmed down considerably from the war days, when going anywhere by road meant a convoy and a high risk of attack. Today, it's a relatively safe place and most travellers shouldn't have any difficulties. That said, there are a few areas where a bit of caution is warranted.

Crime

If you are a Western-looking traveller, you will stand out as someone who is wealthy, which increases your vulnerability and means extra precaution is necessary.

Petty theft is the main risk: watch your pockets or bag in markets; don't leave personal belongings unguarded on the beach or elsewhere; and minimise (or eliminate) trappings such as jewellery, watches, headsets and external money pouches. If you leave your vehicle unguarded, expect windscreen wipers and other accessories to be gone when you return. Don't leave anything inside a parked vehicle.

In Maputo and southern Mozambique, due to the proximity of South African organised-crime rings, carjackings, muggings and more violent robberies occur with some frequency. Most incidents can be avoided by taking the usual precautions: avoid driving at night; keep the passenger windows up and the doors locked if you are in a vehicle (including taxis) at any time during the day or night; don't wander around isolated or dark streets; and avoid walking – alone or in a group – at dusk or at night, particularly in isolated areas or on isolated stretches of beach. At all times of day, try to stick to busier areas of town, especially if you are alone, and don't walk alone along the beach away from hotel areas. If you're driving and your car is hijacked, hand over the keys straightaway. The flashier the car, the higher the risk, with new 4WDs the main targets.

When riding on chapas or buses, keep your valuables well inside your clothes to avoid falling victim to unscrupulous entrepreneurs who take advantage of overcrowded conditions to pick their fellow passengers' pockets.

Hassles & Bribes

More likely than violent crime are simple hassles with underpaid authorities in search of a bribe. If you do get stopped you should not have any problem as long as your papers are in order. Being friendly, respectful and patient helps (and you won't get anywhere otherwise), as does trying to give the impression that you know what you're doing and aren't new in the country. Sometimes the opposite tack is also helpful – feigning complete ignorance if you're told that you've violated some regulation, and apologising profusely. If you are asked to pay a fine (*multa*) for a trumped-up charge, playing the game a bit (asking to speak to the supervisor or *chefe*, and requesting a receipt) helps to counteract some of the more blatant attempts, as does insisting on going to the nearest police station or *esquadrão*, (which you should always do anyway).

Land Mines

Thanks to a massive de-mining effort, many of the unexploded land mines in Mozambique – a legacy of the country's long war – have been eliminated. However, mines are still a risk, which means that it's unsafe to free camp or to go wandering off into the bush anywhere without first seeking local advice. Even then, stick to well-used paths where other people have obviously gone before. Areas that should always be avoided include the bases of bridges, old schools or abandoned buildings, and water tanks or other structures. Also take special care on roadsides in rural areas – if you need to relieve yourself, stay on the road or seek out a trodden path. Mine-removal work is ongoing; you may see trucks or red and white markings in areas where mines have been identified for removal.

EMBASSIES & CONSULATES
Mozambican Embassies & Consulates

Mozambican diplomatic representations in the region and around the world include the following:

France (☎ 01 47 64 91 32; 82 Rue Laugier, Paris 75017)
Germany (☎ 030-3987 6500; Stromstrasse 47, 10551 Berlin; emoza@aol.com)
Italy (☎ 06-3751 4852; Via Filippo Corridoni 14, 00195 Rome; segreteria@ambasciatamozambico.it)
Malawi Lilongwe (☎ 01-774100; off Convention Drive); Limbe (☎ 01-643189; 1st Fl, Celtel Bldg, Rayner Ave, Limbe, near Blantyre)
Portugal (☎ 021-797 1747, 797 1994; Av de Berna 7, 1050-036 Lisbon)
South Africa Pretoria (☎ 012-401 0300, 012-321 2288; 529 Edmund St, Arcadia); Johannesburg (☎ 011-484 6427; 11 Boundary Rd, cnr with Carse O'Gowrie Rd, Houghton); Cape Town (☎ 021-426 2944; 45 Castle St, Castle Bldg, 7th fl); Durban (☎ 031-304 0200; 320 West St, Room 520); Nelspruit (☎ 013-752 7396; 32 Bell St)

TRAVEL ADVISORIES

Government travel advisories are good sources of updated security information:
Australia www.dfat.gov.au
Canada www.voyage.gc.ca/dest/ctry/reportpage -en.asp
UK www.fco.gov.uk
US http://travel.state.gov

Swaziland (☎ 404 3700; Mountain Inn Rd, Mbabane)
Tanzania (☎ 022-211 6502; 25 Garden Ave, Dar es Salaam)
UK (☎ 020-7383 3800; 21 Fitzroy Square, London W1T 6EL; www.mozambiquehc.org.uk)
USA (☎ 202-293 7146; 1990 M St, NW, Suite 570, Washington, DC 20036; www.embamoc-usa.org)
Zambia (☎ 01-239135; 9592 Kacha Rd, off Paseri Rd, Northmead, Lusaka)
Zimbabwe (☎ 04-253871; 152 Herbert Chitepo Ave, Harare)

Embassies & Consulates in Mozambique

Countries with diplomatic representations in Maputo include the following. For a more complete listing check the telephone directory. Most are open from about 8.30am to 3pm, often with a midday break.

Australia (☎ 21-322780; cnr Av Zedequias Manganhela & Vladimir Lenine, 33 Storey Bldg, 1st fl; www.embassy .gov.au/mz.html)
Canada (☎ 21-492623; 1128 Av Julius Nyerere; www .dfait-maeci.gc.ca/mozambique/menu-en.asp)
France (☎ 21-490444, 21-492896; 2361 Av Julius Nyerere; www.ambafrance-mz.org)
Germany (☎ 21-492714; 506 Rua Damião de Gois; www.maputo.diplo.de)
Ireland (☎ 21-483524/5, 21-491440; 3332 Av Julius Nyerere; ireland@virconn.com)

AVISO! (NOTICE)

All foreigners are required to carry a copy of their passport when out and about. Rather than carrying the original, it's much better to carry a notarised copy of the name and visa pages, as well as notarised copies of your drivers license and other essential documents. If you're stopped on the street or at a checkpoint and asked for any of these, always hand over the notarised copy, rather than parting with the original. Notary facilities are available in Maputo and other major cities; ask at your hotel for a recommendation. Some Mozambique embassies will also provide this service before you travel. The notarised copies will also be helpful in getting replacements, should your originals get stolen: bring the copies with you to the police station, where you will then be given a temporary travel document that should get you through the remainder of your travels.

Italy (☎ 21-491605; 378 Av Kenneth Kaunda; ambasciata@italia.gov.mz)
Malawi (☎ 21-492676; 75 Av Kenneth Kaunda)
Netherlands (☎ 21-490031; 285 Rua de Mukumbura; www.nlembassy.org.mz)
Portugal (☎ 21-490316; 720 Av Julius Nyerere; embaixada@embpormaputo.org.mz)
South Africa (☎ 21-490059, 21-491614; 41 Av Eduardo Mondlane; consular@tropical.co.mz)
Swaziland (☎ 21-492117, 21-492451; Rua Luís Pasteur; swazimoz@teledata.mz)
Tanzania (☎ 21-490110; 852 Av Mártires de Machava)
UK (☎ 21-320111, 21-310111; 310 Av Vladimir Lenine; bhc.maputo@teledata.mz)
USA (☎ 21-492797; 193 Av Kenneth Kaunda; www .usembassy-maputo.gov.mz)
Zambia (☎ 21-492452; 1286 Av Kenneth Kaunda)
Zimbabwe (☎ 21-490404, 21-486499; 1657 Av Mártires de Machava)

EMERGENCIES

Meagre salary levels, poor organisational infrastructure and low morale mean that Mozambique's police are often not particularly useful in an emergency. To facilitate things, always carry a copy of your insurance information (including contact telephone numbers) with you. Before beginning your travels, also make copies of all other important documents, including passport, travellers cheque purchase receipts, credit cards, air tickets, drivers licence and international health card. Leave one copy with someone at home and keep another with you, separate from the originals.

If you'll be travelling upcountry for an extended period, try to register with your embassy in Maputo, and carry a copy of their telephone number with you as well (although remember that there are limits on what the embassy can do). It's a good idea to have emergency dollars hidden somewhere in case you should need them. If you have had items stolen and need a police statement for insurance purposes, you'll need to go to the police station responsible for the section of town where the robbery occurred. The procedure is generally straightforward enough, although time consuming. See the boxed text on p173.

FESTIVALS & EVENTS

Apart from national holidays – most of which are celebrated with parades, and song and dance performances – Mozambique has few countrywide festivals. Smaller events abound though, most with no advertising. For concerts and larger happenings, watch for posters around town, and announcements in *Notícias*, and check with the Centro Cultural Franco-Moçambicano (p56).

Music Crossroads Southern Africa (January; www .jmi.net/activities/crossroads/) A showcase for young musical talent from throughout Southern and East Africa, including Mozambique; times and locations vary.

Gwaza Muthini (February) Marracuene's commemoration of the Battle of Marracuene and the start of the *ukanhi* season; date varies, usually early February; see boxed text, p73.

Baluarte Festival (June; www.ccfmoz.com) Held on Ilha de Moçambique to celebrate local Makua culture, and to promote cultural links between Mozambique and its French-speaking Indian Ocean neighbours; dates vary.

Timbilas Festival (July/August) The famed timbila festival of the Chopi around Quissico; see boxed text, p83.

Avante Mozambique! (August/September; avantemozambique@yahoo.com) A celebration of Mozambique's art and cultures, including song, music and dance; just getting started, but planned to be an annual event; held in Maputo over two weeks in late August-early September.

FOOD

Eating listings are ordered by budget and divided into three price ranges: Budget, Midrange and Top End; see inside the front cover for price ranges. For more on dining in Mozambique, see the Food & Drink chapter (p48).

GAY & LESBIAN TRAVELLERS

Mozambique tends to be more tolerant than some of its neighbours, although gay sexual relationships are for the most part culturally taboo. The country's small gay scene, centred in Maputo, has traditionally been quite discrete, but things are starting to open up. From an official viewpoint male homosexuality is illegal in Mozambique, although this statute is rarely enforced and gay travellers should anticipate no particular difficulties.

There is very little tourism information available that is Mozambique-specific. Probably the easiest way to break into things is to contact gay establishments in neighbouring South Africa. A good place to start is the **International Gay & Lesbian Travel Association** (www.iglta .org), which can link you up with gay-friendly travel agents in the Southern Africa region. Also check out www.mask.org.za, following links to articles (including those in the archive) on Mozambique.

HOLIDAYS

Most Mozambican public holidays are celebrated with parades, and song and dance performances.

New Year's Day 1 January

Mozambican Heroes' Day 3 February – commemorating the country's revolutionary heroes

Women's Day 7 April

International Workers' Day 1 May

Independence Day 25 June – Mozambique's Independence from the Portuguese colonial government in 1975

Lusaka Agreement/Victory Day 7 September – the signing of the independence treaty

Revolution Day 25 September – the initiation of Mozambique's independence struggle in Chai, Cabo Delgado province

Christmas/Family Day 25 December

Each city and town also has a 'city/town day' commemorating its founding. Maputo Day is 10 November; for the dates of other city/town days, check with the provincial administration in each provincial capital.

The main holidays affecting accommodation availability, especially in the south, are South African school holidays, particularly the December–January holiday break, and around Easter. For exact dates, see www.saschools.co.za/sas/calendar.htm.

INSURANCE

A travel-insurance policy to cover theft, loss and medical problems is essential. Before choosing a policy spend time shopping around, as those designed for short package tours in Europe won't be suitable for Mozambique. Also be sure to read the fine print, as some policies specifically exclude 'dangerous activities', which can include scuba diving, motorcycling and more. At a minimum, check that the policy covers emergency medical evacuation to Johannesburg and/or an emergency flight home. For more, see p196 and p193.

INTERNET ACCESS

Internet access is easy and fast in Maputo, where there are numerous internet cafés. Elsewhere, there are internet cafés in most provincial capitals and some larger towns – often at the local Telecomunicações de Moçambique (TDM) office. Rates average US$2 per hour

and connections range from reasonable to good.

With your own laptop, you can get on line at top-end hotels in Maputo, and at a few other hotels elsewhere in the country. Wireless-access points are rare, though this is likely to change rapidly, so ask around.

For a small sampling of internet resources on Mozambique, see p15.

LEGAL MATTERS

The use or possession of recreational drugs is illegal in Mozambique. However, grass and more are readily available in several places along the coast where an influx of travellers has created demand. If you're offered any thing, it is invariably part of a set up, usually involving the police, and if you're caught, penalties are very stiff. At the least, expect to pay a large bribe to avoid arrest or imprisonment (which is a very real risk).

If you're arrested for more 'legitimate' reasons, you have the right to talk with someone from your embassy, as well as a lawyer, though don't expect this to help you out of your situation with any rapidity. Driving on the beach, driving without a seatbelt (for driver and front-seat passengers), exceeding speed limits and driving without a red hazard triangle in the boot are common ways of attracting police attention and demands for a bribe or fine. For more on what to do if you're stopped by the police, see p172.

MAPS

The most readily available and user-friendly country map is put out by Ravenstein and is best purchased before arriving in Mozambique. It shows many smaller towns, has inset maps for central Maputo and Beira, and the road network is generally accurate, although it's gradually becoming outdated. Cartographia publishes essentially the same map, which is sometimes available in Maputo. Futur puts out the good Mozambique Tourist Map with city inserts, available at their Maputo office (p57) and some hotels and bookshops.

InfoMap (www.infomap.co.za) puts out a Mozambique map with GPS coordinates for the southern part of the country, although the road network in the north is more accurate on the Ravenstein map. Globetrotter also puts out a Mozambique map, with numerous town inserts. If you'll be self-drive touring off main

DIRECTORY

roads, check out www.tracks4africa.co.za for downloads of GPS maps.

Coastal and maritime maps (cartas náuticas) are available from the **Instituto Nacional de Hidrografia e Navegação** (Inahina; ☎ 21-429240, 21-429108; Rua Marques de Pombal) in Maputo for a negotiable US$12 apiece. Inahina is at the capitanía (maritime office), behind the white Safmar building near the port. Inahina also sells a tide table (tabela de marés) for the country (US$5).

For detailed topographical maps, contact the **Direcção Nacional de Geografia e Cadastro** (Dinageca; ☎ 21-302555; www.dinageca.gov.mz; 537 Avenida Josina Machel, Maputo).

If you'll be combining travels in Mozambique with elsewhere in the region, look for Lonely Planet's Southern Africa Road Atlas.

There is an excellent series of city maps for several of Mozambique's provincial capitals put out by Coopération Française together with the local municipal councils. They cover Maputo, Beira, Quelimane, Nampula and Pemba, but can be difficult to find – check at bookstores and hotel bookshops, or at the local municipal council.

MONEY

Mozambique's currency is the metical (plural meticais, pronounced 'meticaish'), abbreviated Mtc. As of July 2006, the 'metical nova família' (new family metical) was introduced, at a rate of 1000 old meticais to one metical nova família. Only nova família metical notes and coins will be accepted now. In theory, prices throughout the country are to remain the same, just minus the final three zeros. So, something priced at Mtc25,000 under the old system will be Mtc25 under the metical nova família system. Metical nova família note and coin denominations are notes of Mtc20, Mtc50, Mtc100, Mtc200, Mtc500 and Mtc1000, and coins of Mtc1, Mtc2, Mtc5 and Mtc10. One metical nova família is equivalent to 100 centavos (Ct), and there will also be coins of Ct1, Ct5, Ct10, Ct20 and Ct50. For exchange rates, see inside the front cover. For an overview of costs, see p13. Metical prices mentioned in this book are for the nova família metical.

Under the old system, a unit of Mtc1000 was called a conto or, occasionally in street slang, a pão, and it's likely this terminology may continue. Thus a nova família price of Mtc5 may still be quoted as 'cinco contos', or sometimes 'cinco pão'.

Outside of Maputo, the best way to travel is with a good supply of cash in a mixture of US dollars (or South African rand, especially in the south) and meticais (including a good supply of small denomination notes, as nobody ever has change). Supplement this with a Visa card for withdrawing meticais at ATMs (the best way of accessing money); and a supply of travellers cheques for emergencies (though they are difficult to change). Away from major towns and ATMs, cash is the only option.

ATMs

All larger towns have ATMs for accessing cash meticais. Most accept Visa card only and many have a limit of Mtc3,000,000 (US$120) per transaction. There are none in rural areas.

Black Market

Due to currency deregulation, exchange rates are 'free', so banks and the privately owned foreign-exchange bureaus can offer current market rates and the black market is hardly an issue. You may be offered 5% or 10% more than bank or bureau rates by shady-looking characters on the street, but the risks are much higher than any potential gain and you can assume it's a set up.

Cash

US dollars are easily exchanged anywhere in the country, and – together with South African rand (which are especially useful in southern Mozambique) – are the best currency to carry. Note that only new-design US dollar bills will be accepted, and some vendors may be reluctant to accept US$50s and US$100s (though this is less of a problem than it used to be since the introduction of the new-design US bills). Other major currencies can be changed in Maputo, but usually at less favourable rates.

Most banks don't charge commission for changing cash, and together with foreign-exchange bureaus, these are the best places to change money, although some banks (especially in smaller towns and many BIM branches) will only let you change cash if you have an account.

In Maputo and a few other cities there are also private foreign-exchange bureaus, which usually give a rate equivalent to or slightly higher than the banks and are open longer hours. Shops selling imported goods will often change cash dollars or rand into meticais at a rate about 5% higher than the bank rate and can be helpful outside of banking hours. Changing money on the street isn't safe anywhere and is illegal – asking shopkeepers is a much better bet. If you do try, be discreet, watch out for set ups involving the police, and count and recount before handing over your cash.

Credit Cards

Credit cards are accepted at most top-end hotels, a few midrange places, at most car-hire agencies, and by a few dive operators, but otherwise are of only limited use in Mozambique. Visa is by far the most useful, and is also the main (often only) card for accessing money from ATMs. MasterCard, while generally accepted by major hotels and car-hire agencies, does not work in many ATMs.

It's possible in theory to use credit cards for cash advances (in meticais, or in dollars with a high commission) at several banks in Maputo and major towns, although few are willing to do this now that ATMs are in place. Commissions for meticais withdrawals average 1%. Unlike at the ATMs, there is no maximum limit (other than whatever your card company imposes) placed on withdrawals.

International Transfers

With time (allow at least several days) and patience, it's possible to organise international bank transfers in Maputo and sometimes you may have the choice of getting your money in dollars or rand rather than meticais. If you do request a transfer, arrange for the forwarding bank to send separate confirmation with full details. In the event of problems, you can then go into the local bank with the proof that your money has been sent. For all transfers, you'll need details of your home bank account, including account number, branch and routing numbers, address and telephone number.

Security

Because of the lack of ATMs outside of major centres and the near impossibility of changing travellers cheques upcountry, you may find yourself needing to carry a fair amount of cash. It's well worth taking the time to divide this into several stashes and sew a few inner pockets into your clothes – in addition to an internal money belt – to hide it away. We know several travellers who have been saved

by a 'decoy' wallet that is easily accessible and can be handed over if you have the bad luck to be robbed, while the main part of your funds and passport remain safely hidden. Decoy wallet or not, it's also a good idea to keep a small amount of cash handy and separate from your other money so that you do not need to pull out a large wad of bills for making purchases.

Wear loose-fitting clothing so your internal money belt isn't visible. Wearing an external money pouch is just asking for trouble, as is keeping money in your back pocket.

Safes are available at top-end hotels and at some midrange establishments. However, many hotels in Mozambique don't offer this service. Leaving your valuables in your room is risky, though depending on the circumstances, it may be less risky than carrying them with you on the street.

Tipping & Bargaining

In low-budget bars and restaurants tipping is generally not expected, and locals usually don't tip unless they're out to impress. At anywhere upscale or catering to tourists, tipping is customary. About 10% is usually appropriate, assuming service has been good. Tips are also warranted, and always appreciated, if someone has gone out of their way to do something for you.

Bargaining over prices is part of everyday life in Mozambique. However, apart from craft markets and other tourist-oriented places – where initial prices will almost always be wildly exaggerated – don't assume that every price quoted is inflated. In markets, especially in smaller towns, the first price is often the 'real' price (the same price locals pay). A bit of good-natured negotiating is never out of place, but if the seller refuses to budge, you can assume that their initial price was at a level they feel is fair. If you've just arrived in Mozambique, take time to become familiar with standard prices for basic items, keeping in mind that prices can vary depending on location and season: fruit and vegetables are generally more expensive in cities, whereas tinned goods cost more in remote areas, as transport costs must be paid.

Travellers Cheques

Regulations on travellers cheques change frequently, but when this book was researched, cheques could only be changed in Maputo,

Beira and a few other provincial capitals, only at Standard Bank, and only with high commissions (minimum US$35 per transaction, original purchase receipt required). Only a small handful of hotels accept travellers cheques as direct payment, and then usually with a 5% surcharge to cover their banking costs. The bottom line: while it's a good idea to bring some along as an emergency standby, travellers cheques shouldn't be relied on as a source of funds in Mozambique.

PHOTOGRAPHY & VIDEO
Film & Equipment
Print film is available in Maputo, Beira and larger towns. In Maputo, a reasonably good range of brands and types are available, generally in speeds of ASA100, 200 and 400, but elsewhere selection is limited. Slide film is only occasionally available in Maputo.

There are several fairly reliable processing shops in Maputo for print film, though it's generally best to wait until you get home. Upcountry, developing is erratic and often of inferior quality. Slide film can only be processed in Maputo.

A small selection of camera batteries is available in Maputo, as is a limited selection of digital photographic equipment. While most internet cafés don't do CD burning, you can print digital photos or burn CDs at photo shops in major cities.

For film, ASA100 is good for most situations and lighting conditions in Mozambique. For shots of birds and wildlife (if you're lucky enough to spot any), try a lens between 210mm and 300mm, or a 70mm to 300mm zoom. Zoom lenses are good as you can frame your shot easily to get the best composition; a 200mm lens is the minimum you will need to get good close-up shots. Telephoto (fixed focal-length) lenses give better results than zoom lenses, though you will be limited by having to carry separate lenses for various focal lengths. For photographing people, a 50mm lens should be fine. If you are using zoom or telephoto lenses, bring some ASA200 or ASA400 film with you from home.

Whatever equipment you take, carry it in a bag that will protect it from dust and knocks, and that ideally is waterproof. Also make sure your travel-insurance policy covers your camera. For more tips, look for a copy of *Travel Photography* by Richard I'Anson.

Restrictions
Photographing government buildings, ports, airports, or anything connected with the police or military – including parades and other official gatherings – is not permitted. If you try anyway, it may result in your film being confiscated, or, as happened to us, being delivered a swift kick in the heels by a policeman who was obviously taking his job seriously.

Technical Tips
The best times to take photographs are in the early morning and in the late afternoon, when the rising and setting sun optimally illuminates the country's rich panorama of colour. Mornings also have the advantage that the streets are not as busy, and there tends to be less dust in the air. To avoid underexposure in shots of people and animals, take light readings on the subject rather than on the background.

POST
International mail from Maputo takes about 10 days to Europe and costs about US$1.20 per letter. Domestic mail is more sporadic, with letters taking between one week and one month to reach their destinations.

Major post offices have poste restante. Letters are generally held for one month, sometimes longer, and cost US$0.15 to receive.

SHOPPING
Mozambique is known for its beautiful and highly stylised woodcarvings and turned wood items, as well as for its paintings, pottery and basketware. Other crafts include jewellery (particularly silverwork), leatherwork and textiles.

For Makonde woodcarvings, Pemba, Nampula and Maputo are the best places to start your search. The widest selection of sandalwood carvings is in Maputo. Inhambane province is known for its baskets, and Cabo Delgado for its attractive woven mats. The etched clay pots made by Makonde women and sold in Nampula, Pemba and Maputo make beautiful but heavy souvenirs. Some of the best silver artisanship in the region comes from Ilha do Ibo in the Archipélago das Quirimbas. While the silver itself is often not of high quality, the craftsmanship is highly refined. The colourful cloths (*capulanas*) worn by women around their waist can be found at markets everywhere and make practical souvenirs – useful as tablecloths, wraps, wall hangings and more. *Capulanas* are more colourful in the north, where shades of yellow and orange dominate.

When buying woodcarvings, remember that many of the pieces marketed as ebony may be simply blackened with shoe polish or dye. Rubbing the piece with a wet finger, or smelling it, should tip you off. Higher-quality pieces are those where more attention has been given to detail and craftsmanship. If you're using this book as an armchair reader, and won't have the chance to get to Mozambique, you can contact Artes Maconde (see p157) and Shanty Craft (p69), who both take orders for local carvings and crafts, and will mail or ship internationally. Finely crafted wood products are also available online at www.allanschwarz.com/bracelet.php.

For some tips on shopping responsibly (and on what souvenirs to avoid), see boxed text, p42. For more on bargaining, see p177.

SOLO TRAVELLERS

While you may be a minor curiosity in rural areas, especially solo women travellers, there are no particular problems with travelling alone in Mozambique, whether you're male or female. Times when it is advantageous to join a group are for car hire, dhow safaris and organised excursions (when teaming up can be a significant cost-saver); when going out at night (travelling solo can be limiting on the nightlife); and if you're interested in hiking (it's always wise to travel at least in pairs in the bush). If you do go out alone at night, take taxis and use extra caution, especially in urban and tourist areas. Also, it's generally assumed that everyone in bars – male and female – is looking to pick up, unless you already have an escort.

Whatever the time of day or location, avoid isolating situations, including isolated stretches of beach. Women, especially, shouldn't hitch alone. For bus journeys, get to the bus stand early to try to get a seat up front, and if you're getting dropped off at a bus stand in the pre-dawn hours, arrange for your taxi to wait with you until you can board the bus or until other people are around. If you are driving, avoid solo night travel. Also see Women Travellers, p181.

TELEPHONE

Mozambique's telephone system is efficient, though there aren't enough lines to meet demand. For international calls, all larger towns have telecom (Telecomunicações de Moçambique or TDM) offices open at least during business hours Monday through Saturday, and daily in cities. There are also card phones which can be used for international calls, with cards sold at TDM offices and nearby shops. The TDM Bla-Bla Fixo card is a pre-paid card for fixed lines (including at TDM offices and card phones), and is cheaper for international dialling than if you call from TDM directly. Collect (reverse charge) calls are only possible to Portugal.

Domestic calls cost about US$0.10 per impulse; most short calls won't use more than two or three impulses. Calls to Europe, the USA and Australia cost about US$6 for the first three minutes (minimum), plus US$2 for each additional minute. Regional calls cost about US$3 for the first three minutes. Rates are slightly cheaper on weekends and evenings.

If you are looking for a number: the Mozambique telephone directory (*Lista Telefónica*) is online (www.tdm.mz and www.paginasamarelas.co.mz).

In 2005, all Mozambique telephone numbers changed from five or six digits to eight digits, including provincial area codes. The provincial codes (which must always be dialled, no matter where you are calling) are listed inside the front cover of this book, and at the start of each town listing. No initial zero is required.

Cell Phones

Cell phones (GSM900 system) are widely used; the numbers are seven digits, preceded by ☎ 82 for **mCel** (www.mcel.co.mz) or ☎ 84 for **Vodacom** (www.vm.co.mz). The dialling networks were recently changed, so now – as with landline numbers – no initial zero is required. If you see an old-style Mozambique cell number listed as '082-XXX XXX', just move the initial zero to the end of the old six-digit number before dialling. Otherwise, assume that seven-digit cell numbers listed with zero at the outset are in South Africa; these must be preceded by the South Africa country code (☎ 27).

The cell network is expanding, and now covers provincial capitals, although many rural areas are still out of reach. Check the mCel and Vodacom websites for coverage (*cobertura*) maps. The main provider, mCel, has a massive advertising campaign, with outlets (look for the bright yellow shops) everywhere around the country where you can buy SIM card starter packs (US$2) and get linked into the network. Vodacom also has shops in major towns, with similar services.

Telephone Codes

When calling Mozambique from abroad, dial the international-access number (☎ 09 from South Africa), then the international code for Mozambique (☎ 258), followed by the provincial or city code (no zero) and the number. For cell numbers, dial the international-access number, followed by the international code, the cell prefix (no zero) and the seven-digit number.

TIME

Time in Mozambique is GMT/UTC plus two hours. There is no daylight savings. Because the country is so large, and parts of it so far east in relation to other countries in this time zone, it gets light very early in some areas, with daybreak at about 4am in parts of Cabo Delgado province.

TOILETS

Toilets in Mozambique are either sit-down style with a toilet bowl and (sometimes) a seat, or squat style, with a hole in the ground, often rimmed by a tile frame with rests for the feet. For the uninitiated, the keys to a successful outcome with the squat toilets are positioning the feet well, and ensuring that odds and ends from your pockets don't fall down into the hole.

Running water is a luxury in many areas. With public toilets, if you have a choice, go for a squat-style toilet, as these usually come equipped with a bucket of water and tend to be more sanitary than flush toilets, which are often clogged. Public toilets almost never have toilet paper. For those that do, the custom is to dispose of the paper in the nearby basket, rather than into the toilet itself.

Bidets are a ubiquitous feature of many bathrooms in Mozambique, left over from colonial days, though most don't have running water, except those in upscale hotels.

TOURIST INFORMATION

The national tourist organisation, **Fundo Nacional de Turismo** (Futur; www.futur.org.mz) is primarily geared to advertising and tourism promotion, but its English-language website is a good introduction to the country, with a comprehensive overview of tourism developments and some helpful links. Most Mozambique embassies also have a supply of tourist brochures and general information.

TRAVELLERS WITH DISABILITIES

While there are few facilities specifically for the disabled, Mozambicans tend to be very accommodating and helpful to disabled people. Those who are mobility impaired are especially likely to meet with understanding, as there are hundreds, if not thousands, of amputees throughout the country – victims of land mines set during the war.

The most accessible and easily negotiable area of the country is Maputo. Many of the upscale hotels have wheelchair access and/or lifts, and taxis and hire cars are readily available (though taxis don't have wheelchair access, and most are small). While most sidewalks have kerbs, often fairly high, the road network is tarmac and in good condition.

For travel upcountry, getting around on public transport usually means lots of crowds, heat and jostling. Travelling by hired car is the best option, though expensive. Along the coast you'll rarely need to deal with long flights of steps – just soft, deep sand – although chalets at some resorts are built on stilts.

The squat-style toilet facilities, common throughout Mozambique outside tourist hotels, can put a strain on anyone's knees, no matter what their physical condition. Except at top-end hotels in Maputo, there are never hand grips on the walls, and few bathrooms large enough for manoeuvring a wheelchair. As far as we know, there are no facilities anywhere in the country specifically targeted at deaf or blind visitors.

Useful contacts include the following:
Access-Able Travel Source (www.access-able.com) Has lists of tour operators offering tours for travellers with disabilities.
Disability Online (www.disabilityonline.com) A large data base of links and resources for disabled travellers.
Endeavour Safaris (www.endeavour-safaris.com) Focuses on South Africa and other areas of the region, and may be able to help with Mozambique itineraries as well.
Epic-Enabled (www.epic-enabled.com) More of the same.

VISAS

Visas are required by all visitors except citizens of South Africa, Swaziland, Zambia and Botswana. They are currently available at most major land and air entry points (US$25 for a one-month, single-entry visa). However, regulations change frequently and queues at busy borders are often long, meaning that it's best (and often cheaper) to arrange your visa in advance. This is especially true if you're arriving in Maputo via bus from Johannesburg, as most buses won't wait for you to arrange your visa.

Fees vary according to where you buy your visa. Outside Africa, it costs anywhere from US$20 to US$70 for a one-month single-entry tourist visa, and from US$40 to US$125 for a one- to three-month multiple-entry visa. Within the region, fees are cheaper, although you'll need to pay about double for express service (usually anything faster than one week). Same-day visa service is available at several places including Johannesburg and Nelspruit (South Africa). The Mozambican representations in South Africa and Swaziland are the cheapest places in the region to get visas, charging US$13 for same-day service; for getting a visa in Swaziland, you'll need at least three blank pages in your passport. Also note that for getting a visa in Johannesburg, you'll need to go first to a branch of Nedbank and make a cash deposit of the visa fee. Then, take the deposit slip with you to the embassy and make your visa application. Call the embassy (p173) for bank account details. No matter where you get your visa, your passport must be valid for at least six months from the dates of intended travel, and have at least two blank pages.

For South Africans and citizens of other countries not requiring visas, visits are limited to 30 days from the date of entry, after which you'll need to exit Mozambique and re-enter. Note that the length of each stay for multiple-entry visas is determined when the visa is issued, and varies from embassy to embassy; only single-entry and transit visas are available at Mozambique's borders.

While in Mozambique, you may hear talk of a 'univisa' – planned to be implemented by 2010 by Mozambique and the other Southern African Development Community (SADC) countries. Once in effect, the same visa will be good for Mozambique and many of its neighbours.

Visa Extensions

Visas can be extended at the immigration office *(migração)* in all provincial capitals provided you haven't exceeded the three-

month maximum stay. Processing takes one to three days and is usually fairly straightforward. Don't wait until the visa has expired, as hefty fines (US$100 per day) are levied for overstays.

WOMEN TRAVELLERS
Status of Local Women

To understand the reception that you're likely to receive as a woman travelling in Mozambique, it's worth taking a look at the status of local women. The country is notable for holding a place among the top twenty countries worldwide for its percentage of female parliamentarians. Currently, over 30% of deputies in Mozambique's parliament are women, ranking it as number two in Africa. The prime minister is a woman, and there are several female cabinet ministers (including the Minister of Foreign Affairs) and vice-ministers, and a small but influential group of highly educated Mozambican women in the private sector. The national women's organisation, Organização das Mulheres Moçambicanas (OMM), although politicised, is well established and enjoys a high profile throughout the country. In the heady post-independence days of the early 1970s, Frelimo declared women's emancipation to be an integral aspect of Mozambique's revolutionary struggle.

In contrast with this encouraging picture is the fact that in many areas, especially among the country's large rural population, women are frequently marginalised. The difference in male and female literacy rates (33% for women versus 64% for men), and the education gender gap at the secondary and tertiary levels, are just two indicators. And, the realities can be seen simply by looking around: one of your most lasting impressions of travel in Mozambique is likely to be how hard the women work.

Despite a progressive land law, women still struggle for land rights. Polygamy, which is common in many areas, is another factor, as is migrant labour. Thanks to the high percentage of men (especially in southern Mozambique) who are migrant workers in South African mines, many women are left to raise their families alone. When their husbands return home, they bring back better salaries from the mines, and potentially AIDS. Economic realities and limited job opportunities also force many women to turn to sex for survival. About 55% of Mozambican AIDS sufferers are women.

DIRECTORY

Attitudes towards Foreign Women

It's rare to find a Mozambican woman travelling alone for no apparent purpose and lone foreign women seen to be idly wandering around the country may be viewed as something of a curiosity, especially in remote areas. Apart from this, attitudes in Mozambique towards foreign women travelling alone tend to be fairly liberal. Although you'll still get questions about what you are doing, and where your husband and children are, reactions are usually matter-of-fact. In tourist areas, if you're backpacking, locals may assume you are a Peace Corps volunteer, and if you're in a vehicle, the assumption will be that you're either a South African on holidays, or one of Mozambique's large brigade of aid workers.

It's a great help both in explaining yourself, and in getting to know local women, if you are able to surmount the language barrier – either by learning Portuguese or by working with a translator.

Sexual hassles rarely go beyond the verbal. However, to avoid problems getting started, things like dressing conservatively, wearing a ring, and having a husband or boyfriend (fictitious or not) somewhere nearby all seem to help, as do heeding the precautions outlined under the next section. Going to a bar on your own is seen as an open invitation.

Safety

As far as safety is concerned, the best maxim is, 'An ounce of prevention is worth a pound of cure.'

Common-sense precautions are well worth heeding: don't wander around alone anywhere at night, and during the daytime avoid anywhere that's isolated, including streets, beaches and parks. A few extra meticais spent on a taxi are well worth it. Be cautious about opening your door to a knock if you're alone in your hotel room/house, and never let anyone unknown in with you. Especially away from the coastal resorts, dress modestly, and ideally with clothing that's not skintight. Be wary of anyone who tries to draw you into an isolated situation. Also be wary of accepting certain invitations and of the signals your behaviour may be giving off. Avoid hitching alone and if you do hitch, avoid getting in cars with only men.

Many budget hotels double as brothels and are best avoided if you're travelling solo.

WORK

It isn't permitted to work in Mozambique if you enter on a tourist visa. In order to get the required residency (*Documento de Identificação e Residência para Estrangeiros* or DIRE) and work permits, you need an offer of employment. Your employer will also be required to pay various fees, including one equalling a month or two of your salary.

Apart from resorts (where there are the occasional jobs with dive operators) and tourism-related establishments, the majority of positions are with international aid organisations. However, as most of these hire through their headquarter offices, it's better to start your research before leaving home.

Most volunteer work is in teaching, health care and school construction. Good initial contacts include **InterAction** (www.interaction.org), whose excellent twice-monthly subscriber newsletter advertises both paid and volunteer positions internationally, including in Mozambique; and the Mozambique page of **Volunteer Abroad** (www.volunteerabroad.com/Mozam bique.cfm), with links to volunteer opportunities in the country. There is extensive missionary work in Mozambique, so another possibility would be to make inquiries through your local church.

Transport

GETTING THERE & AWAY

ENTERING THE COUNTRY

Mozambique is straightforward to enter, but you should expect the occasional bureaucratic hassles and – for popular border posts such as South Africa and Swaziland – long lines at the visa counter during peak periods (a good reason to arrange your visa in advance, p180).

Only a valid passport and visa are required to enter, plus the necessary vehicle paperwork if you are driving.

AIR
Airports

Maputo's **Mavalane International** (MPM; ☎ 21-465827/8; www.aeroportos.co.mz) is the main airport, with a modest collection of souvenir shops, ATM (Visa cards only), post office, telephone centre, and a branch of **Linhas Aéreas de Moçambique** (LAM; ⏲ 6am-10.30pm) and **Cotacambios** (foreign exchange bureau; ⏲ 6am-9.30pm Mon-Thu, 6am-10pm Fri, 7am-10pm Sat & 11.30am-10.30pm Sun). Airports with regularly scheduled regional flights include **Vilankulo** (☎ 223-82207), **Beira** (BEW; ☎ 23-301071/2), **Nampula** (APL; ☎ 26-213100, 26-213133) and **Pemba** (POL; ☎ 272-20312).

Airlines

Mozambique's national carrier is **Linhas Aéreas de Moçambique** (LAM; code TM; ☎ 21-468 0000, 21-490590; www.lam.co.mz; hub Mavalane International, Maputo). In addition to its domestic network (p190), flights connect Johannesburg with Maputo (daily), Vilankulo and Beira (both twice weekly); Dar es Salaam with Pemba (five weekly); and Lisbon (Portugal, five weekly) with Maputo. Other airlines flying into Mozambique:

Kenya Airways (code KQ; www.kenya-airways.com; hub Jomo Kenyatta International, Nairobi) Twice weekly between Maputo and Nairobi.

Pelican Air Services (code 7V; www.pelicanair.co.za; hub Johannesburg International) Daily between Johannesburg and Vilankulo via Kruger Mpumalanga International Airport, with connections to the Bazaruto archipelago.

SAAirlink (code SA; www.saairlink.co.za; hub Johannesburg International) Three times weekly between Beira and Johannesburg, and between Maputo and Durban.

South African Airways (SAA; code SA; www.flysaa.com; hub Johannesburg International) Daily between Maputo and Johannesburg.

Swazi Express (code Q4; www.swaziexpress.com; hub Durban) Two to three flights weekly between Durban, Matsapha (Swaziland), Maputo and Vilankulo.

TAP Air Portugal (code TP; www.tap-airportugal.pt) Five flights weekly between Maputo and Lisbon.

Tickets

LAM and TAP Air Portugal run occasional specials between Lisbon and Maputo. SAA has good deals on intercontinental through tickets; if you fly with them intercontinentally to Johannesburg, it's often only marginally more expensive to connect on to Maputo.

THINGS CHANGE…

The information in this chapter is particularly vulnerable to change. Check with the airline or a travel agent to make sure you understand how a fare or ticket works, and be aware of the security requirements for international travel. The details given in this chapter should be regarded as pointers and are not a substitute for your own careful, up-to-date research.

TRANSPORT

ARRIVAL & DEPARTURE TAXES

There's an arrival tax of US$2. Departure tax is US$20 for intercontinental and regional flights, payable in meticais, US dollars or South African rand.

Otherwise, the best way to save money on your Mozambique ticket is to look for good deals on fares into Johannesburg or other regional capitals, and then travel overland or get an onward ticket from there. Also check fares into Nairobi, from where you can connect on Kenya Airways direct to Maputo. For northern Mozambique, look at fares into Dar es Salaam, with connections from there to Pemba.

Online ticket sellers include:

Cheapflights (www.cheapflights.co.uk)

Cheap Tickets (www.cheaptickets.com)

Expedia (www.expedia.com, www.expedia.co.uk, www.expedia.ca)

Flight Centre (www.flightcentre.com)

LowestFare.com (www.lowestfare.com)

OneTravel.com (www.onetravel.com)

STA Travel (www.statravel.com)

Travel.com.au (www.travel.com.au) Bookings from Australia.

Travelocity (www.travelocity.com, www.travelocity.ca)

Africa

For regional connections, see Airlines (p183) and Indian Ocean Islands (opposite).

Several Maputo hotels, notably Hotel Polana and Hotel Pestana Rovuma, offer package deals between Johannesburg and Maputo that also include airfare. Good deals are also offered out of Johannesburg by most of the lodges on Archipélago de Bazaruto, and by the beach resorts at Barra (p92) and south of Inhambane (p88).

Ticket discounters include **Rennies Travel** (www.renniestravel.com) and **STA Travel** (www.statravel.co.za), both with offices throughout Southern Africa. **Flight Centre** (☎ 0860 400 727, 011-778 1720; www.flightcentre.co.za) has offices in Johannesburg, Cape Town and several other cities.

Asia

Most routes go via Johannesburg. Possibilities include direct from Singapore on **Singapore Airlines** (www.singaporeair.com), from Hong Kong on **Cathay Pacific** (www.cathaypacific.com) and from Kuala Lumpur on **Malaysia Airlines** (www.malaysiaairlines.com). From Mumbai, you can fly to Nairobi or Dar es Salaam, and connect to Pemba or Maputo, or alternatively go via Mauritius and Johannesburg on **Air Mauritius** (www.airmauritius.com).

CLIMATE CHANGE & TRAVEL

Climate change is a serious threat to the ecosystems that humans rely upon, and air travel is the fastest-growing contributor to the problem. Lonely Planet regards travel, overall, as a global benefit, but believes we all have a responsibility to limit our personal impact on global warming.

Flying & Climate Change

Pretty much every form of motor transport generates CO_2 (the main cause of human-induced climate change) but planes are far and away the worst offenders, not just because of the sheer distances they allow us to travel, but because they release greenhouse gases high into the atmosphere. The statistics are frightening: two people taking a return flight between Europe and the US will contribute as much to climate change as an average household's gas and electricity consumption over a whole year.

Carbon Offset Schemes

Climatecare.org and other websites use 'carbon calculators' that allow travellers to offset the greenhouse gases they are responsible for with contributions to energy-saving projects and other climate-friendly initiatives in the developing world – including projects in India, Honduras, Kazakhstan and Uganda.

Lonely Planet, together with Rough Guides and other concerned partners in the travel industry, supports the carbon offset scheme run by climatecare.org. Lonely Planet offsets all of its staff and author travel.

For more information check out our website: www.lonelyplanet.com.

Singapore, Hong Kong and Bangkok are the best places to shop for tickets. Discounters include **STA Travel** (Thailand ☎ 0 2236 0262; www .statravel.co.th; Singapore ☎ 6737 7188; www.statravel.com .sg; Hong Kong ☎ 2736 1618; www.statravel.com.hk; Japan ☎ 0353-912 922; www.statravel.co.jp). Also try **No 1 Travel** (☎ 0332-056 073; www.no1-travel.com) in Japan, and **Four Seas Tours** (☎ 2200 7760; www.fourseastravel .com/english) in Hong Kong. **STIC Travels** (www .stictravel.com) has offices throughout India. Another agency is **Transway International** (www .transwayinternational.com).

Australia & New Zealand

There are direct flights to Johannesburg (with connections to Maputo) from Sydney and Perth on **Qantas** (www.qantas.com.au), and from Perth on SAA. Alternatively, connect to Johannesburg on Air Mauritius from Perth, or via Singapore, Hong Kong or Mumbai (Bombay).

Discounters include **Flight Centre** (☎ 133 133; www.flightcentre.com.au) and **STA Travel** (☎ 1300-733 035; www.statravel.com.au). For online bookings, try www.travel.com.au.

From New Zealand, the best options are via Australia, Singapore, Hong Kong or Malaysia to Johannesburg and on to Maputo. Another option is **Emirates** (www.emirates.com) via Dubai, with connections to Dar es Salaam, and then on LAM to Pemba or Maputo. **Flight Centre** (☎ 0800-243 544; www.flightcentre.co.nz) and **STA Travel** (☎ 0508-782 872; www.statravel.co.nz) have branches throughout the country. For online bookings, try www.travel.co.nz.

Continental Europe

LAM and TAP Air Portugal fly between Lisbon and Maputo. From other European capitals, the best routings are via Johannesburg, or via Nairobi on Kenya Airways. Hubs include Paris, Amsterdam, Frankfurt and Zurich.

For northern Mozambique, try looking for a good fare to Nairobi, Blantyre or Dar es Salaam, and then continue overland or via air from there. Ticket agencies include:

Airfair (☎ 0206-20 51 21; www.airfair.nl) Netherlands.

Anyway (☎ 08 92 89 38 92; www.anyway.fr) France.

Barcelo Viajes (☎ 902 11 62 26; www.barceloviajes .com) Spain.

CTS Viaggi (☎ 064 62 04 31; www.cts.it) Italy; specialising in student and youth travel.

Just Travel (☎ 089-747 33 30; www.justtravel.de) Germany.

Lastminute (www.lastminute.fr, www.lastminute.de) France; Germany.

Nouvelles Frontières (www.nouvelles-frontieres.fr, www.nouvelles-frontieres.es) France; Spain.

OTU Voyages (www.otu.fr) France; for students and youth.

STA Travel (☎ 0180 545 64 22; www.statravel.de) Germany; for travellers under the age of 26.

Voyageurs du Monde (☎ 01 40 15 11 15; www.vdm .com) France.

Indian Ocean Islands

From Madagascar, connections are either via Johannesburg or Nairobi on **Air Madagascar** (www .airmadagascar.mg), or via Johannesburg on SAA and SAAirlink. **Air Tanzania** (www.airtanzania.com) flies between Moroni (Comoros) and Dar es Salaam, from where you can connect to Pemba.

Mauritius is something of a hub, with connections from Asia (Singapore, Hong Kong and Mumbai) on Air Mauritius, and then to Johannesburg, Nairobi or Dar es Salaam and on to Mozambique.

For the Seychelles, connect via Johannesburg on **Air Seychelles** (www.airseychelles.com) or via Nairobi on Air Kenya.

Middle East

The best connections are from Cairo to Nairobi and on to Maputo on Kenya Airways or from Dubai to Dar es Salaam on Emirates, connecting to Pemba.

Agencies to try include **Al Rais Travels** (www .alrais.com) in Dubai; **Egypt Panorama Tours** (☎ 023-590 200; www.eptours.com) in Cairo; the Israel Student Travel Association (ISTA;026-257257) in Jerusalem; and **Orion-Tour** (www.oriontour.com) in Istanbul.

South America

SAA and **Varig** (www.varig.com.br) link São Paulo and Johannesburg. Malaysia Airlines flies between Buenos Aires, Cape Town and Johannesburg. Discounters include **ASATEJ** (☎ 54-011 4114-7595; www.asatej.com) in Argentina; the Student Travel Bureau (☎ 3038 1555; www.ividiomas.com) in Brazil; and **IVI Tours** (☎ 0212-993 6082; www.ividiomas .com) in Venezuela.

UK & Ireland

Airlines flying between London and Southern Africa include **British Airways** (www.britishairways .com), **Virgin Atlantic** (www.virgin-atlantic.com) and SAA, all to Johannesburg. Otherwise, hunt for a cheap fare to Nairobi or Dar es Salaam, and continue from there to Mozambique. Kenya Airways does the London to Maputo route via

TRANSPORT

Nairobi. From Ireland, connect via London or a continental European capital.

Advertisements for many discounters appear in the travel pages of the weekend broadsheet newspapers, in *Time Out*, the *Evening Standard*, in the free online magazine **TNT** (www.tntmagazine.com) and in the free *SA Times*, which is aimed at South Africans in the UK and sometimes advertises good deals to the region. Recommended agencies include:

Bridge the World (☎ 087-0444 7474; www.b-t-w.co.uk)
Flightbookers (☎ 087-0814 4001; www.ebookers.com)
Flight Centre (☎ 087-0890 8099; flightcentre.co.uk)
North-South Travel (☎ 012-4560 8291; www.northsouthtravel.co.uk) North-South Travel donate part of their profit to projects in the developing world.
Quest Travel (☎ 087-0442 3542; www.questtravel.com)
STA Travel (☎ 087-0160 0599; www.statravel.co.uk) For travellers under the age of 26.
Trailfinders (www.trailfinders.co.uk)
Travel Bag (☎ 087-0890 1456; www.travelbag.co.uk)

USA & Canada

The only direct flights from North America are on SAA from New York and Atlanta via Johannesburg to Maputo. Another inexpensive option is flying to London on a discounted transatlantic ticket, where you can then purchase a separate ticket to Johannesburg or Nairobi, then to Maputo. Alternatively, watch for specials to Lisbon, with direct connections on to Maputo.

From the US west coast, Malaysia Airlines flies from Los Angeles to Kuala Lumpur, from where you can connect to Johannesburg and on to Maputo.

San Francisco is the ticket consolidator (discounter) capital of America, although some deals can be found in Los Angeles, New York and other big cities. See p183 for online booking agencies. Another to try: **STA** (☎ 800-781-4040; www.sta.com), for travellers under 26.

LAND

Everyone entering Mozambique overland needs to pay an immigration tax of US$2 or the equivalent in meticais, rand or the local currency of the country from which you're arriving. Have exact change, and get a receipt. For additional fees for drivers, see p192.

Border Crossings

There are almost two dozen official land entry points into Mozambique. Except as noted, most borders are open from 6am to 6pm.

MALAWI

The busiest crossing is Zóbuè, on the Tete Corridor route linking Blantyre (Malawi) and Harare (Zimbabwe). Others include at Dedza (85km southwest of Lilongwe), Milange (120km southeast of Blantyre), Entre Lagos (southwest of Cuamba), Mandimba (northwest of Cuamba), Vila Nova da Fronteira (at Malawi's southern tip), and Cóbuè (Lago Niassa).

SOUTH AFRICA

The busiest crossing is at **Komatipoort/Ressano Garcia** (⏱ 6am-10pm), northwest of Maputo. Others include **Kosi Bay/Ponta d'Ouro** (⏱ 8am-4pm), 11km south of Ponta d'Ouro; **Pafuri** (⏱ 8am-4pm), in Kruger park's northeastern corner; and **Giriyondo** (⏱ 8am-4pm Oct-Mar, 8am-3pm Apr-Sep), west of Massingir.

SWAZILAND

The main crossing is at **Lomahasha/Namaacha** (⏱ 7am-8pm) in Swaziland's extreme northeast corner, with another, quieter post at **Goba/Mhlumeni** (⏱ 7am-6pm).

TANZANIA

The main crossing is at Namiranga, 130km north of Moçimboa da Praia. You can also get your passport stamped (but no visas) at the village of Moçimboa do Rovuma, and there are border and customs officials at Palma and Moçimboa da Praia for those arriving from Tanzania by boat. It's also reportedly possible to get stamped in at the Rio Rovuma crossing between Lichinga and Songea (Tanzania).

ZAMBIA

The main crossing is at **Cassacatiza** (⏱ 7am-5pm), 290km northwest of Tete. There's another crossing at **Zumbo** (⏱ 7am-5pm), at the western end of Lago Cahora Bassa.

ZIMBABWE

The main crossing points are at Nyamapanda on the Tete Corridor, linking Harare with Tete and Lilongwe (Malawi), and at Machipanda on the Beira Corridor linking Harare with the sea. Other crossings: at Espungabera, in the Chimanimani mountains, and at **Mukumbura** (⏱ 7am-5pm), west of Tete.

Malawi

TO/FROM BLANTYRE

The Zóbuè crossing has good roads and public transport connections on both sides. There are daily vehicles from Blantyre to the border via Mwanza (US$4). Once on the Mozambique side (the border posts are separated by about 5km of no-man's-land, although a new single-stop border post is planned), there are daily chapas to Tete. Buses between Blantyre and Harare via Zóbuè can drop you at Tete.

The Vila Nova da Fronteira crossing sees a reasonable amount of traffic, although it's still an off-the-track journey on mostly unpaved but decent roads on the Mozambique side. There are daily minibuses from Blantyre to Nsanje and on to the border. Once across, you can find chapas along a reasonable road via Mutarara to Sena, and from there on to Caia on the main north–south road.

The Milange crossing is convenient if you want to go to Quelimane or Gurúè, or on to Ilha de Moçambique. There are regular buses from Blantyre via Mulanje to the border. Once across, there are several vehicles daily to Mocuba, and then frequent transport on to both Quelimane and Nampula.

The crossing at Entre Lagos (for Cuamba and northern Mozambique) is possible with your own 4WD, or on one of the chapas that run between the border and Cuamba. On the Malawi side, there are minibuses from the border to Liwonde. Another option is the Malawi train that runs weekly, currently on Monday, to the border (on Tuesday in the opposite direction), from where you'll need to take a chapa to Cuamba. There's basic accommodation in Entre Lagos.

Most travellers use the more northerly crossing by Mandimba. There's frequent transport on the Malawi side to Mangochi, from where you can get minibuses to Namwera, and on to the border at Chiponde. Once in Mozambique, there are daily vehicles from Mandimba to both Cuamba and Lichinga.

TO/FROM LILONGWE

The Dedza border is convenient for Lilongwe, and is linked with the EN103 to/from Tete by a scenic tarmac road. From Tete, there's usually at least one chapa daily to Vila Ulongwé and on to Dedza. Otherwise, go in stages from Tete via Moatize and the junction about 15km southwest of Zóbuè. Once across the border, it's easy to find transport for the final 85km to Lilongwe. We've had several reports about travellers having difficulty getting a Mozambique visa at Dedza, so arrange one in Lilongwe beforehand.

South Africa

TO/FROM NELSPRUIT & JOHANNESBURG

Bus & Chapa

There are daily minibuses and chapas to Maputo from Ressano Garcia (US$3.50, two hours, 120km), Nelspruit (US$10, three hours, 230km) and on to Johannesburg (nine hours, 590km), with the best connections in the early morning. Much better is to use one of the large 'luxury' buses that do the route daily (US$30 to US$38 one-way, eight to nine hours), listed on p69. All lines also service Pretoria. You can also travel in each direction on the following lines between Maputo and Nelspruit but not between Nelspruit and Johannesburg. Organise your Mozambique visa in advance, as lines are long at Ressano Garcia and most buses won't wait. The following phone numbers are all dialled within South Africa:

Greyhound (☎ 011-276 8500; www.greyhound.co.za) Daily from Johannesburg's Park City Station at 6.45am and from Maputo at 7.30am.

InterCape Mainliner (☎ 021-380 4400; www.inter cape.co.za) Daily from Johannesburg's Park City Station at 8am and from Maputo at 7.45am.

Panthera Azul (☎ 011-618 8811/3; www.pantherazul .co.za) Daily from Johannesburg (34 Bezuidenhout Ave, Troyville) at 7am; from Maputo at 6.45am Monday, Wednesday and Friday, at 4am on Tuesday, Thursday and Saturday, and at 7am on Sunday.

Translux (☎ 011-774 3333; www.translux.co.za) Daily from Johannesburg at 8.45am; from Maputo at 7.45am.

Car

There's a good road connecting Maputo with Johannesburg via Ressano Garcia, with tolls in Mozambique at Matola and Moamba, and in South Africa between Middelburg and Witbank, at Machadadorp, and west of Malelane.

Train

South Africa's **Komati line** (☎ 011-774 4555; www .spoornet.co.za) travels between Johannesburg and the Komatipoort border post daily (13 hours). Once across, it's possible in theory to continue to Maputo by rail. However, service in Mozambique is slow and connections times often don't coincide, so it's much faster to take a chapa. If you decide to stick with the rails, see p70 for schedules and fares between Ressano Garcia and Maputo.

TO/FROM KRUGER NATIONAL PARK

There are two border points between Mozambique and South Africa's Kruger park, neither

TRANSPORT

accessible via public transport and both requiring 4WD on the Mozambique side.

Giriyondo sees a small but steady stream of 4WD adventurers looking for an alternate route to the Mozambican coast. See p84 for more on this crossing.

Pafuri can be used to access the rough tracks across Gaza and Inhambane provinces to Mapinhane (at the junction with the EN1) and the coast, or to go southeast into Parque Nacional do Limpopo, or towards Chokwé and the EN1 – all 4WD territory. There's also a 4WD track sponsored by **Sanparks** (www .sanparks.org) and **Parque Nacional do Limpopo** (www .dolimpopo.com) that uses this crossing. The Rio Limpopo is unbridged and crossable only in the dry season. Mozambique visas are not issued at Pafuri, so arrange one in advance. There are no fuel points anywhere along the route to Vilankulo until the EN1.

OTHER ROUTES

Between Durban and Maputo, **Panthera Azul** (☎ in Durban 031-309 7798) has buses via Namaacha and Big Bend in Swaziland (US$35, 8½ hours) departing Maputo at 7am Tuesday, Thursday and Saturday, and Durban at 7am Wednesday, Friday and Sunday.

For travel via the Kosi Bay border post, see p79.

Swaziland

BUS & CHAPA

Minibuses depart Maputo throughout the day for Namaacha (US$2, 1½ hours), with some continuing on to Manzini (US$5, 3½ hours).

Bill's Bus runs an occasional shuttle between Manzini and Maputo, with connections to Tofo; get details through **Grifter's Lodge** (www.grifterslodge.com) in Swaziland or Diversity Scuba in Tofo (p90). Maputo Backpackers (p64) and **Sobantu Guest Farm** (www.swaziplace .com/sobantu) also have a shuttle between Maputo and various points in Swaziland, connecting to Tofo. Prices for both: about US$23 one-way between Swaziland and Maputo, and US$55 from Swaziland to Tofo.

CAR

The road is fairly good tarmac the entire way and easily negotiated with 2WD. The Namaacha border is notoriously slow on holiday weekends; the quiet border at Goba (Goba Fronteira) – reached via a scenic, winding road on the Mozambique side – is a good alterna-tive. The new road from Swaziland's Mananga border, connecting north to Komatipoort-Ressano Garcia, is another option.

Tanzania

BUS & CHAPA

For all Mozambique–Tanzania posts, arrange your Mozambique visa in advance. Pick-ups depart Mtwara (Tanzania) daily between 6.30am and 8am to the Kilambo border post (US$2.50, one hour), and on to the Rovuma, which is crossed via dugout canoe (US$2, 10 minutes to over an hour, depending on water levels). On the Mozambique side, there are usually two pickups daily to the Mozambique border post (4km further) and on to Palma and Moçimboa da Praia (US$10, four hours). The last one leaves around noon, so it's worth getting an early start from Mtwara. If you get stuck overnight at the Rovuma, there's a bedbug-ridden guesthouse on one of the sandbanks in the middle of the river. Camping on the river bank on the Mozambique side is a better option. Also see p165.

The Rovuma crossing is notorious for pick-pockets. Keep an eye on your belongings, especially when getting into and out of the boats, and keep up with the crowd when walking to/from the river bank.

The crossing north of Moçimboa do Rovuma is rarely used and entails long walks on both sides (up to 25km in Tanzania, and at least 10km in Mozambique). The first Tanzanian town is Newala, from where there are daily buses to Mtwara. In Mozambique, there's a daily chapa between Moçimboa do Rovuma and Mueda, departing Moçimboa do Rovuma by midmorning.

In the west, there is a truck every other day from Lichinga via Macaloge and Nova Madeira to the Rovuma. Once at the river, cross by dugout canoe and then make your way (first on foot, then via sporadic transport on a rough road) to Songea. We've heard that you can get your passport stamped at the border; otherwise, there's an immigration office in Songea.

CAR

The road from Mtwara (Tanzania) to the border is mostly unpaved but in good condition. There's a **vehicle ferry** (☎ in Tanzania 0744-869357; per vehicle US$50) at Kilambo which operates at high tide. It generally runs daily during peak travel seasons (December-January, around Easter, and July-August), though this can't be counted on. To avoid long waits, call to let the captain know when you're coming. In Mozambique, get an update at Russell's Place (p155), Pemba. In Tanzania, if you can't get through on the ferry number, ask at **Ten Degrees South** (www.eco2.com) or The Old Boma (www.mikindani.com), both in Mikindani.

On the Mozambique side, the road is unpaved but in fair condition during the dry season from the border to Palma, a mix of tarmac and good graded dirt from Palma to Moçimboa da Praia, and tarmac from there to Pemba.

Work has started on the Unity Bridge over the Rovuma, well southwest of Kilambo, near the confluence of the Rio Lugenda, and accessed from Mozambique via Mueda. Once completed (likely not within the lifetime of this book – the cornerstone was laid in late 2005), it should make all this easier, albeit somewhat longer.

Zambia

The roads of the Cassacatiza–Chanida border crossing are reasonably good, but the crossing is seldom used as most travellers combining Mozambique and Zambia go via Malawi. Chapas go daily from Tete to Matema, from where there's sporadic transport to the border. On the other side, there are daily vehicles to Katete (Zambia), and then on to Lusaka or Chipata.

The rarely used crossing at Zumbo is difficult to access from Mozambique, and of interest primarily to anglers and bird watchers heading to the western reaches of Lago Cahora Bassa; see p122.

Zimbabwe
TO/FROM HARARE

Both the Nyamapanda and Machipanda border crossings have reasonably good tarmac access roads, are heavily travelled by private vehicles, and are easy to cross using public transport or hitching.

From Tete, there are frequent vehicles to Changara (US$3, 1½ hours) and on to the border at Nyamapanda, where you can get transport to Harare. Through buses between Blantyre and Harare are another option, though schedules have been erratic due to fuel shortages in Zimbabwe.

From Chimoio, there is frequent transport to Machipanda and on to the border, from where you'll need to take a taxi for the 12km to Mutare, and then get Zimbabwe transport or the night train to Harare. In theory, this departs Mutare at 9pm, arriving in Harare at 5.30am the next morning, although schedules have been interrupted in recent times.

The seldom-used route via the orderly little border town of Espungabera is slow and scenic, and an interesting dry-season alternative for those with a 4WD. Public transport on the Mozambique side is scarce.

Mukumbura, best done with 4WD, is of interest mainly to anglers heading to Cahora Bassa dam. There is no public transport on the Mozambique side.

SEA & LAKE
Malawi

The *Ilala* ferry services several Mozambican ports on its way up and down Lago Niassa, departing Monkey Bay (Malawi) at 10am Friday, arriving in Metangula (via Chipoka and Nkhotakota in Malawi) at 6am Saturday, reaching Cóbuè around noon, Likoma Island (Malawi) at 1.30pm, and Nkhata Bay (Malawi) at 1am Sunday morning. Southbound, departures are at 8pm Monday from Nkhata Bay and at 6.30am Tuesday from Likoma Island, reaching Cóbuè at 7am and Metangula at midday. The schedule changes frequently; get an update from **Malawi Lake Services** (ilala@malawi .net). Fares are about US$20/US$40 for economy class/1st-class cabin between Nkhata Bay and Cóbuè. There are immigration posts in Metangula and Cóbuè (and on Likoma Island and in Nkhata Bay, for Malawi). You can get a Mozambique visa at Cóbuè, but not at Metangula. Slow sailing boats also go between Likoma Island, Cóbuè and Metangula; see p149.

Meponda was formerly linked with Malawi's Senga Bay via the weekly MV *Mtendere*. It's currently not running but it's worth asking around to see if services have resumed. Local boats travel frequently between Meponda and Senga Bay but the crossing is risky due to sudden squalls and not recommended. The closest immigration office is in Lichinga.

South Africa

There are no regularly scheduled passenger ships between South African and Mozambican ports, other than luxury cruise liners. One to try: **Starlight Lines** (www.starlight.co.za), which runs luxury liners from Durban that call at Ilha de Inhaca, Barra, the Archipélago de Bazaruto and Ilha de Moçambique. Otherwise, the best bet is to ask around at boating clubs in Durban to see whether any boats are looking for additional crew.

Cargo ships rarely take passengers, but if you want to try your luck, a good initial contact is **Tall Ships** (www.tallships.co.za), which has cargo ships between Durban and various Mozambican ports.

TOURS

All of the following organise travel to Mozambique, as well as in-country itineraries. Many top-end hotels and lodges in Maputo and Pemba also offer fly-in packages from Johannesburg. The Mozambique pages in the South African travel magazine **Getaway** (www.getawaytoafrica.com) are a good source of information on package tours and cruises.

Dana Tours (www.danatours.net) A recommended Maputo-based operator covering most areas of the country, and also doing Mozambique–South Africa combination itineraries.

Makomo Safaris (www.makomo.com) Combination itineraries for northern Mozambique, southern Tanzania, Zambia and Malawi.

Mozaic Travel (www.mozaictravel.com) Coastal Mozambique, and dhow trips around the Archipélago de Bazaruto.

Mozambique Connection (www.mozambiquecon nection.|co.za) A comprehensive and long-established operator, covering most of the country. All price ranges.

Mozambique Tours (www.mozambiquetravel.co.za) Fly-in packages to the Archipélago de Bazaruto and other southern Mozambique destinations.

Ocean Island Safaris (www.oceanislandsafari.com) Luxury travel to the Archipélago das Quirimbas, and itineraries combining Mozambique and other Indian Ocean islands.

Wildlife Adventures (www.wildlifeadventures.co.za) Coastal Mozambique, and itineraries combining Mozambique with elsewhere in southern and East Africa.

Zambezia Travels (www.zambezia.ch) Quelimane-based, and recommended for central Mozambique, Gurúè, Monte Namúli, Cuamba, Lichinga and other points north; also good for exploring away from established routes.

GETTING AROUND

AIR
Airlines in Mozambique

The national airline is **Linhas Aéreas de Moçambique** (LAM; ☎ 21-468000; www.lam.co.mz) which, with Moçambique Expresso (Mex), runs most non-

---

DOMESTIC DEPARTURE TAX

Departure tax on domestic flights is US$8, payable in dollars, meticais or rand.

---

charter flights within Mozambique, linking Maputo with Inhambane, Vilankulo, Beira, Chimoio, Quelimane, Tete, Nampula, Lichinga and Pemba. Service has improved markedly in recent years and flights are generally reliable. Baggage handling has also improved, but don't check anything of value. More problematic are overbookings; always reconfirm your ticket and check in well in advance. Flights can be paid for in local currency, dollars or rand, and in Maputo, Beira and Nampula by Visa or Master-Card. Sample one-way fares and flight frequencies include: Maputo to Pemba (US$392, daily), Maputo to Beira (US$236, daily), Maputo to Lichinga (US$368, three per week), Tete to Quelimane (US$296, one per week) and Maputo to Vilankulo (US$216, four per week).

LAM offers frequent specials; watch for advertisements in the daily newspaper, *Notícias*. You can also save by asking for one of their *Jacto Popular* fares, which require three to five days advance purchase.

Other domestic carriers and routes include:

Air Corridor (☎ 21-311582, 26-213333; aircorridor@teledata.mz) The single Air Corridor plane does a daily run up and down the coast, stopping at Maputo, Beira, Quelimane, Nampula and Pemba; cheaper than LAM.

Moçambique Expresso (Mex; ☎ 21-466008; mex@mex.co.mz) A LAM subsidiary, flying LAM routings.

Serviço Aéreo Regional (SAR; ☎ 26-212401, sargaw@teledata.mz) Twice weekly between Nampula and Cuamba.

TransAirways (☎ 21-465108; transairways@virconn .com) Daily between Maputo and Ilha de Inhaca.

TTA (☎ 21-465484, 21-465015, 282-82348) Daily between Vilankulo and the Bazaruto Archipelago, together with Pelican Air Services (see p183).

Most of the above also do charters. Others include **Rani Aviation** (Pemba Beach Resort Hotel, ☎ 272-21770, in South Africa 011-465 6904; www.pembabeachresort .com) and **Quirimbas Aviation** (☎ 272-21808; aircharters -quirimbas@plexusmoz.com), both between Pemba and the Archipélago das Quirimbas, and **Unique Air Charter** (☎ 01-465992; Maputo Airport).

BICYCLE

Cycling is a good way to see the 'real' Mozambique, but you'll need plenty of time to cover the long distances. You'll also need to plan the legs of your trip fairly carefully and to carry almost everything with you, including all spares, as there are long stretches with little or nothing en route. Avoid cycling in Maputo and along main roads whenever possible, as there's often no shoulder, traffic is fast and drivers have little respect for cyclists. A cross-terrain bike is best for secondary and tertiary roads, and for the many sandy beach access roads.

The most pleasant hours for cycling are between dawn and midmorning to avoid the heat and the worst of the traffic, and to have plenty of time in the afternoon to relax on the beach. Carrying a tent is essential. However, because of land mines, the odd chance of encountering roaming wildlife (especially in the north), and general security, it's not a good idea to free camp (plus it's illegal). It's much better to arrange something with villagers, who will invariably warmly welcome you.

A good lock is also essential. And even when locked, it's worth keeping the bike in view. You're bound to be the greatest novelty that's rolled into most towns, and anything removable, such as tyre pumps and water bottles, is likely to make its way into the hands of local souvenir hunters and entrepreneurs. Bicycles can be transported on buses; expect to pay from US$2 to US$5 depending on the journey.

Rental & Purchase

Heavy, Chinese-made single-speeds can be easily rented for the day in most towns. Ask around by the market or at bicycle repair stands. In Maputo and other places with large numbers of expatriate residents, you can sometimes find decent mountain bikes for sale. Embassy notice boards are a good place to start. A better option is to buy a bicycle in South Africa and then try to sell it in Mozambique before you leave, although the market is limited. Spares for Western-made bicycles are not available in Mozambique. However, you may be able to pick up some useful parts from stolen bicycles at Maputo's Mercado de Xipamanine (p62), and bicycle repair stands everywhere are excellent at improvisation.

BOAT

There is no regular passenger service between major coastal towns. However, it's worth asking at ports and harbours, as there is frequent cargo traffic along the coast and captains are sometimes willing to take passengers. Chances improve the further north you go. Possibilities include small freighters running between Quelimane, Nacala and Pemba, and regular ferries between Beira and small towns along the Sofala coastline. On larger ships, once you find a captain willing to take you, the price generally includes meals and a cabin. On Lago Niassa, there is passenger service between Metangula and Cóbuè (p189).

If you've brought your own boat into Mozambique, beach launching requires a permit from the local maritime office (*administração marítima or capitania*). Most southern coastal resorts can also help you sort this out.

For information on dhow safaris, see p169.

DHOW TRAVEL

Dhows (*barcos a vela* in Portuguese) have played a major role in Mozambican coastal life for centuries, and are still the main form of transport and means of livelihood for many coastal dwellers, especially in the north.

If the wind is with you and the water calm, a dhow trip can be enjoyable, and will give you a better sense of the centuries of trade that shaped Mozambique's history. However, if you're becalmed miles from your destination, if seas turn rough, if the boat is leaking or overloaded, if it's raining, or if the sun is strong, the experience will be much less pleasant.

The best way is to try dhow travel arrange a dhow safari with one of the operators listed on p169. Some things to keep in mind if you decide to do things on your own:

- Travel with the winds, which blow from south to north from approximately April/May to August/September and north to south from November/December through February.

- Be prepared for rough conditions. There are no facilities on board, except possibly a toilet hanging off the stern. As sailings are wind and tide dependent, departures are often during the predawn hours.

- Journeys often take much longer than anticipated; bring plenty of extra water, food and sun protection plus waterproofing for your luggage and a rain jacket.

- Boats capsize and people are killed each year as a result. Avoid overloaded boats, and don't set sail in bad weather.

BUS

As long as you're fortified with nerves of steel (for the high speeds), plenty of patience (for the many stops en route), and lots of time (for the huge distances) bus travel is the most straightforward and economical way to get around Mozambique. Good services connect all major towns at least daily.

A large bus is called a *machibombo*, and sometimes also *autocarro*. The main companies are: the declining Transportes Oliveiras, with an extensive but slow route network in southern and central Mozambique; the buses that formerly belonged to the now-defunct TSL, and which operate on the southern routes; and the good Grupo Mecula, which has reasonably comfortable buses and an extensive network in northern Mozambique. Many lines run both express and stopping services. If there's a choice, it's worth paying the small difference between the two, as express is significantly faster, and you'll have fewer problems with overcrowding and squawking chickens.

Most towns don't have central bus stations. Rather, transport usually leaves from the bus company garage, or from the start of the road towards the destination (which often involves a short hike from the centre of town). Long-distance transport in general, and all transport in the north, leaves early – between 3.30am and 7am. Outside of southern Mozambique and along the Beira corridor, it's often difficult to get a vehicle anywhere after midmorning. And unlike many countries where you spend interminable periods waiting for vehicles to fill, Mozambican transport usually leaves quickly and close to the stated departure time. If a driver tells you they will be departing at 4.30am, get there by 4.15am, latest. Sample journey fares and times: Maputo to Inhambane (US$9, seven hours); Nampula to Pemba (US$7, seven hours); Maputo to Beira (US$30, 18 hours).

Classes & Reservations

All buses have just one class. For some routes it's possible – but seldom essential – to buy a ticket a day in advance. Generally, showing up on the morning of travel (about an hour prior to departure for heavily travelled routes) is enough to ensure you get a place. If you are choosy about your seat, get to the departure point a bit earlier. To avoid the crowds at the ticket window, especially in Maputo, it's easier to simply board and buy the ticket from the conductor. If a bus has baggage on the roof, chances are that it's not an express bus (most of which have luggage compartments underneath).

CAR & MOTORCYCLE

If you have your own vehicle in the region, or can afford rental and fuel costs, Mozambique is an adventurous but highly satisfying destination to tour as self-drive. Road savvy helps, as does experience driving elsewhere in Africa.

Bringing Your Own Vehicle

In addition to a passport and driving licence, drivers need third-party insurance, a temporary import permit, the original vehicle registration papers and an authorisation document from the rental agency or registered vehicle owner, plus two red hazard triangles in the boot. If you're towing a trailer or boat, a hazard triangle needs to be displayed on your front bumper and at the back of the trailer, and trailers also require reflective tape. You'll also need a sticker on the back of the vehicle (or at the end of the trailer) showing the country of registration (eg ZA for South Africa).

Temporary import permits (TIP, about US$2) and third-party insurance (US$23 to US$31 for 30 days; trailers from US$12) are available at most land borders, and you'll be need to show the paperwork at all checkpoints (and will be fined if you can't produce it). Fees can be paid in meticais, dollars or the local currency of the country you are leaving. As some smaller border posts don't always issue third-party insurance, it's worth arranging this with your local automobile association if planning to enter Mozambique via an out-of-the way routing. If you find yourself in Mozambique without it, try contacting **Hollard Seguros** (☎ 21-313114; www.hollard.co.za) to help you sort it out.

Driving Licence

You'll need either a South African or international drivers licence to drive in Mozambique. Those staying longer than six months will need to get a Mozambique drivers licence.

Fuel & Spare Parts

Petrol is a scarce commodity off main roads, especially in the north. Diesel supplies are cheaper and more reliable. Always carry an extra jerry can or two and tank up at every opportunity, as filling stations run out with some frequency or, if there's a power outage, fuel may not be accessible. In some places, the only choice will

ROAD DISTANCES (KM)

	Beira	Chimoio	Inhambane	Lichinga	Maputo	Nampula	Pemba	Ponta d'Ouro	Quelimane	Tete	Vilankulo	Xai-Xai
Beira	---											
Chimoio	162	---										
Inhambane	707	664	---									
Lichinga	1184	1308	1938	---								
Maputo	1080	1037	406	2311	---							
Nampula	928	978	1608	688	1981	---						
Pemba	1355	1405	2035	746	2408	427	---					
Ponta d'Ouro	1190	1147	516	2421	110	2091	2518	---				
Quelimane	481	531	1161	814	1534	484	911	1644	---			
Tete	555	371	1035	560	1408	840	1267	1518	902	---		
Vilankulo	481	438	280	1712	620	1382	1809	730	935	809	---	
Xai-Xai	906	863	235	2137	174	1807	2234	284	1360	1234	449	---

TRANSPORT

be petrol sold from roadside *barracas* (stalls); watch for petrol mixed with water or kerosene. Unleaded fuel (*gasolina sem chumbo*) is available in major centres, but not elsewhere. Fuel prices in Mozambique average about US$1 per litre for petrol, somewhat less for diesel.

A limited supply of spare parts is available in Maputo and in major towns upcountry. Otherwise, they'll need to be special-ordered from South Africa.

Hire
There are rental agencies in Maputo, Beira, Nampula and Pemba. Elsewhere, you can usually arrange something with upscale hotels. Rates start at US$100 per day for 4WD, excluding fuel. At the moment, no rental agencies offer unlimited kilometres. Rental cars from Mozambique can be brought across the borders into South Africa and Swaziland only. Let the rental agency know in advance so that they can prepare the necessary paperwork.

Insurance
All private vehicles entering Mozambique are required to purchase third-party insurance at the border, which covers you to some degree in the event of hitting a pedestrian or another Mozambican vehicle. Given the relatively high incidence of vehicle thefts and break-ins in Mozambique, it's also advisable to take out good insurance coverage at home or (for rental vehicles) with the rental agency to cover damage to the vehicle, yourself and your possessions. Car rental agencies in Mozambique have wildly differing policies (some offer no insurance at all and those that do often have high deductibles that won't cover off-road driving) so inquire before signing any agreements. If renting in South Africa, ask whether Mozambique is included in the coverage.

Purchase
High duties and associated costs, as well as problems with stolen cars, make it not really worth considering purchasing a vehicle in Mozambique for most travellers. If you will be in Mozambique for an extended period, embassy notice boards are the best place to check for ads for used vehicles. As many of these will have been imported under the special tax

TRANSPORT

NIGHT DRIVING

Night driving is particularly hazardous in Mozambique and should be avoided. Apart from road hazards (such as pedestrians, potholes and unmarked construction sites), many vehicles have no lights. Numerous accidents result when a broken-down vehicle is left in the roadway – without lights or other markers – and another vehicle slams into it in the dark.

Safety is also a concern, as there are long stretches of road with nothing along them – not ideal should you have a breakdown or otherwise need assistance. Armed robberies and car hijackings are a risk in some areas, especially near the South African border. If you do need to drive at night, use appropriate speeds, watch for pedestrians and obstacles in the road and keep the doors locked and windows up.

The same applies to public transport; try to get an early enough start so that you reach your destination before nightfall and avoid night routes whenever possible.

---

provisions applicable to diplomats, check out the fees and taxes you'll need to pay in addition to the selling price.

Road Conditions

Mozambique's road network is steadily improving and most southern coastal areas between Maputo and Vilankulo are reachable with 2WD, with the exception of some sandy resort access roads. A 2WD vehicle is also fine for the roads connecting Nampula, Nacala, Ilha de Moçambique and Pemba, for the Beira corridor, and for the Tete corridor between Harare (Zimbabwe) and Tete. For most other routes, you'll need 4WD with high clearance. However, all it takes is a heavy rainstorm or some flooding to change the road map so if you're driving ask around to get the latest updates.

As of now, most of the main north–south highway is tarmac and in reasonable shape except for the stretches between the Rio Save and Beira (under construction), from Caia north to Quelimane and on to Nampula (also under construction), and from Palma north to the Rio Rovuma. The Beira corridor (EN6) is ashpalt and in generally good condition, especially from Chimoio westwards. The road from Chimoio to Tete and Zóbuè is generally good tarmac, as is that from Tete to Harare.

From Lichinga to Cuamba and on to Nampula, the road is reasonably good to Mandimba, good from there into Cuamba, and in rough but reasonable condition from there on to Nampula. Milange to Mocuba is unpaved but fine during the dry season.

A road distances chart is included (p193). However, it's usually senseless to calculate driving times based on distance without taking road conditions into account. A very rough average along the EN1 and other main routes would be 50km to 70km per hour, and 30km per hour off main routes. A few examples: the 500km from Vilankulo to Beira (a combination of good and bad roads, and currently under construction) takes about nine hours by car and somewhat longer by bus, while the 300km between Lichinga and Cuamba takes six to seven hours. An exception is the new and excellent highway between Inchope (west of Beira) and Caia.

Road Hazards

Drunk driving is common, as are excessive speeds. Both together mean that there are many road accidents. To minimise encounters with drunk drivers (or, if you are on public transport, to minimise the chances of your own driver being drunk), travel as early in the day as possible.

If you are not used to driving in Africa, watch out for pedestrians, children and animals on the road or running into the road. Many locals have not driven themselves, especially in rural areas, and are not aware of concepts such as necessary braking distances. Night driving should also be avoided and always choose to take buses rather than chapas. Tree branches in the road are the local version of flares or hazard lights, and mean there's a stopped vehicle, crater-sized pothole or similar calamity ahead. The difficulty of spotting the branches after dusk is yet another reason not to drive at night.

Road Rules

In theory, traffic in Mozambique drives on the left. At roundabouts, traffic in the roundabout has the right of way (again, in theory). There's a seatbelt requirement for the driver and front-seat passenger. Speed limits (usually 80km/h on main roads, and 50km/h or less when passing through towns) are enforced by radar and should be strictly adhered to as controls are frequent. Fines for speeding, seatbelt and other traffic infringements vary and should always be negotiated (in a polite, friendly way), keeping in mind that the standard speeding fine is about US$20. In addition to avoiding fines, another reason to limit your speed is to escape the axle-shattering potholes that can appear out of nowhere, or children or livestock running unexpectedly into the road.

Driving on the beach is illegal (fines are about US$80), and driving off-road isn't recommended because of the risk of landmines.

HITCHING

As anywhere in the world, hitching is never entirely safe, and we don't recommend it. Travellers who decide to hitch should understand that they are taking a small but potentially serious risk. This said, in parts of rural Mozambique, your only transport option will be hitching a lift. In general, hitching is not particularly difficult, though it's often slow off main routes. Going to/from beaches and resort areas is easiest on weekends. Payment for lifts is usually not expected, though it's best to clarify before getting in, and a small token of thanks, such as paying for a meal or making a contribution for petrol is always appreciated. If you do need to pay, it is usually equivalent to what you would pay on a bus or chapa for the same journey. To flag a vehicle down, hold your hand out at about waist level and wave it up and down; the Western gesture of holding out the thumb is not used. The best place to wait is always outside town at the head of the road leading to your destination. Hitching in pairs is safer, and women should avoid hitching alone. In urban areas, hitching through less salubrious suburbs, especially at night, is asking for trouble. Throughout the country, the prevalence of drunk drivers makes it worth trying to assess the driver's condition before getting into a vehicle.

LOCAL TRANSPORT
Chapa

The main form of local transport is the chapa, the name given to any public transport that runs within a town or between towns, and isn't a bus or truck. They're usually a converted pickup or minivan, and are notorious for careening wildly through the streets, packed to bursting point. On some longer routes, your only option will be a *camião* (truck). Many have open backs, and on long journeys the sun and dust can be brutal unless you get a seat upfront in the cab.

Prices for chapa transport are fixed. Intra-city fares average US$0.20; long-haul fares are usually slightly higher than the bus fare for the same route. The most comfortable seat is up front with the driver, on the window side, though you'll have to make arrangements early and sometimes pay more.

Chapa drivers aren't known for their safe driving and there are many accidents. If you have a choice, bus is always a better option. Patience, combined with a sense of humour, also helps when taking local transport.

Like buses, chapas in Mozambique tend to depart early in the day and relatively promptly, although drivers will cruise for passengers before finally leaving town. City chapas run throughout the day, and can be hailed down almost anywhere.

Taxi

Maputo, Beira, Nampula and Pemba have taxi services and there are a few private taxis in Quelimane. Apart from airport arrivals, taxis don't cruise for business, so you'll need to seek them out. In Maputo, Nampula and Pemba, some taxis have meters. Otherwise, you'll need to negotiate a price. Town trips cost from US$2.

TOURS

All of the tour companies listed on p190 can organise itineraries within Mozambique as well.

TRAIN

Mozambique has a straggling rail network. The only passenger train regularly used by tourists is the slow line between Nampula and Cuamba (see p145). For more on the slow line between Maputo and the South African border, see p187. For information on other local lines from Maputo – all slow and prone to breakdowns – see p70.

There are vendors at all the train stations, but it's a good idea to bring along some food and drink to supplement what's available en route. Second class, when available, is not in the least plush, but is reasonably comfortable, with windows that open. Third class is hot and crowded. Bookings for all routes can be made the morning of travel.

TRANSPORT

Health Dr Caroline Evans

A long as you stay up to date with your vaccinations and take basic preventive measures, you're unlikely to succumb to most of the health hazards covered in this chapter. While Mozambique has an impressive selection of tropical diseases on offer, it's more likely you'll get a bout of diarrhoea or a cold than a more exotic malady. The main exception to this is malaria, which is a real risk throughout the country.

BEFORE YOU GO

A little pre-departure planning will save you trouble later. Get a check-up from your dentist and from your doctor if you have any regular medication or chronic illness (eg high blood pressure and asthma). You should also organise spare contact lenses and glasses (and take your optical prescription with you); get a first-aid and medical kit together; and arrange necessary vaccinations.

Travellers can register with the **International Association for Medical Advice to Travellers** (IMAT; www .iamat.org), which provides directories of certified doctors. If you'll be spending much time in remote areas (ie anywhere away from Maputo), consider doing a first-aid course (contact the Red Cross or St John's Ambulance), or attending a remote-medicine first-aid course, such as that offered by the **Royal Geographical Society** (www.wildernessmedicaltraining.co.uk).

If you bring medications with you, carry them in their original (labelled) containers. A signed and dated letter from your physician describing all medical conditions and medications, including generic names, is also a good idea. If carrying syringes or needles, be sure to have a physician's letter documenting their medical necessity.

INSURANCE

Find out in advance whether your insurance plan will make payments directly to providers or will reimburse you later for overseas health expenditures. Most doctors and clinics in Mozambique expect up-front payment in cash. It's vital to ensure that your travel insurance will cover the emergency transport required to get you at least to Johannesburg (South Africa), or all the way home, by air and with a medical attendant if necessary.

If your policy requires you to pay first and claim later for medical treatment, be sure to keep all documentation. Some policies ask you to call back (reverse charges) to a centre in your home country where an immediate assessment of your problem is made. Since reverse-charge calls aren't possible in Mozambique (except to Portugal), contact the insurance company before setting off to confirm how best to contact them in an emergency.

RECOMMENDED VACCINATIONS

The **World Health Organization** (www.who.int/en/) recommends that all travellers be covered for diphtheria, tetanus, measles, mumps, rubella and polio, as well as for hepatitis B, regardless of their destination. The consequences of these diseases can be severe, and outbreaks of them do occur.

According to the **Centers for Disease Control and Prevention** (www.cdc.gov), the following vaccinations are recommended for Mozambique: hepatitis A, hepatitis B, rabies and typhoid, and boosters for tetanus, diphtheria and measles. While a yellow fever–vaccination certificate is not officially required to enter the country unless you are entering from a yellow fever–infected area, carrying one is advised; check with your doctor before travelling, and also see p201.

MEDICAL CHECKLIST

It's a very good idea to carry a medical and first-aid kit with you, to help yourself in the case of minor illness or injury. Following is a list of items to consider packing.

- Antibiotics (prescription only), eg ciprofloxacin (Ciproxin) or norfloxacin (Utinor)
- Antidiarrhoeal drugs (eg loperamide)
- Acetaminophen (paracetamol) or aspirin
- Anti-inflammatory drugs (eg ibuprofen)
- Antihistamines (for hayfever and allergic reactions)
- Antibacterial ointment (eg Bactroban) for cuts and abrasions (prescription only)
- Antimalaria pills
- Bandages, gauze, gauze rolls and tape
- Scissors, safety pins, tweezers
- Pocket knife
- DEET-containing insect repellent for the skin
- Permethrin-containing insect spray for clothing, tents, and bed nets
- Sun block
- Oral rehydration salts
- Iodine tablets (for water purification)
- Sterile needles, syringes and fluids if travelling to remote areas
- Acetazolamide (Diamox) for altitude sickness (prescription only)
- Self-diagnosis kit that can identify malaria in the blood from a finger prick.

INTERNET RESOURCES

A good place to start is the Lonely Planet website at www.lonelyplanet.com. The World Health Organization publishes the helpful *International Travel and Health*, available free at www.who.int/ith/. Other useful websites include **MD Travel Health** (www.mdtravelhealth.com), and **Fit for Travel** (www.fitfortravel.scot.nhs.uk).

Government travel-health websites include the following:

Australia www.dfat.gov.au/travel/
Canada http://www.hc-sc.gc.ca/english/index.html
UK www.doh.gov.uk/traveladvice/index.htm
USA www.cdc.gov/travel/

FURTHER READING

A Comprehensive Guide to Wilderness and Travel Medicine by Eric A Weiss (1998)
Healthy Travel by Jane Wilson-Howarth (1999)
Healthy Travel Africa by Isabelle Young (2000)
How to Stay Healthy Abroad by Richard Dawood (2002)

Travel in Health by Graham Fry (1994)
Travel with Children by Cathy Lanigan (2004)

IN TRANSIT

DEEP VEIN THROMBOSIS (DVT)

Prolonged immobility during flights can cause deep vein thrombosis (DVT) – the formation of blood clots in the legs. The longer the flight, the greater the risk. Although most blood clots are reabsorbed uneventfully, some might break off and travel through the blood vessels to the lungs, where they could cause life-threatening complications.

The chief symptom is swelling or pain of the foot, ankle or calf, usually but not always on just one side. When a blood clot travels to the lungs, it may cause chest pain and breathing difficulty. Travellers with any of these symptoms should immediately seek medical attention. To prevent DVT, walk about the cabin, perform isometric compressions of the leg muscles (ie contract the leg muscles while sitting), drink plenty of fluids and avoid alcohol.

JET LAG

If you're crossing more than five time zones you could suffer jet lag, resulting in insomnia, fatigue, malaise or nausea. To avoid jet lag try drinking plenty of fluids (nonalcoholic) and eating light meals. Upon arrival, get exposure to natural sunlight and readjust your schedule (for meals, sleep, etc) as soon as possible.

IN MOZAMBIQUE

AVAILABILITY & COST OF HEALTH CARE

Maputo is the only place in the country with good emergency medical service, although for Western standards, expect to pay Western prices. Elsewhere, facilities range from limited to non-existent. All provincial capitals have a hospital that can test for malaria. These tests are very cheap (usually about US$1) and well worth getting if you have even the slightest suspicion that you may have become infected. In smaller towns, the only facility will often be a local health post. If you become seriously ill, the best thing to do is to seek treatment in South Africa, return home or at least try to make your way to Maputo.

HEALTH

If you fall ill in an unfamiliar area, ask staff at a top-end hotel or resident expatriates where the best nearby medical facilities are, and in an emergency contact your embassy.

There are numerous well-stocked pharmacies in Maputo; upcountry, all provincial capitals have at least one or two. These will invariably carry chloroquine and sometimes Fansidar (both for malaria) and other basics, though it's best to bring whatever you think you may need from home. Always check the expiry date before buying medications, especially in smaller towns. We've given some suggested dosages in this section, but they are for emergency use only. Correct diagnosis is vital.

There is a high risk of contracting HIV from infected blood transfusions. The **BloodCare Foundation** (www.bloodcare.org.uk) is a useful source of safe, screened blood, which can be transported to any part of the world within 24 hours.

INFECTIOUS DISEASES

Following are some of the diseases that are found in Mozambique, though with a few basic preventative measures, it's unlikely that you'll succumb to any.

Cholera

Cholera is usually only a problem during natural or artificial disasters (eg war, floods or earthquakes), although small outbreaks can possibly occur at other times. Travellers are rarely affected. Cholera is caused by a bacteria and spread via contaminated drinking water. The main symptom is profuse watery diarrhoea, which causes debilitation if fluids are not replaced quickly. An oral cholera vaccine is available in the USA, but it is not particularly effective. Most cases of cholera could be avoided by careful selection of good drinking water and by avoiding potentially contaminated food. Treatment is by fluid replacement (orally or via a drip), but sometimes antibiotics are needed. Self-treatment is not advised.

Dengue Fever (Break-bone Fever)

Dengue fever is spread through the bite of the mosquito. It causes a feverish illness with headache and muscle pains similar to those experienced with a bad, prolonged attack of influenza. There might be a rash. Self-treatment: paracetamol and rest.

Diphtheria

Diphtheria is spread through close respiratory contact. It usually causes a temperature and a severe sore throat. Sometimes a membrane forms across the throat and a tracheostomy is needed to prevent suffocation. Vaccination is recommended for those likely to be in close contact with the local population in infected areas. More important for long stays than for short-term trips. The vaccine is given as an injection alone or with tetanus and lasts 10 years.

Filariasis

Tiny worms migrating in the lymphatic system cause filariasis. The bite from an infected mosquito spreads the infection. Symptoms include localised itching and swelling of the legs and/or genitalia. Treatment is available.

Hepatitis A

Hepatitis A is spread through contaminated food (particularly shellfish) and water. It causes jaundice and, although it is rarely fatal, it can cause prolonged lethargy and delayed recovery. If you've had hepatitis A, you shouldn't drink alcohol for up to six months afterwards, but once you've recovered, there won't be any long-term problems. The first symptoms include dark urine and a yellow colour to the whites of the eyes. Sometimes a fever and abdominal pain might be present. Hepatitis A vaccine (Avaxim, VAQTA, Havrix) is given as an injection: a single dose will give protection for up to a year, and a booster after a year gives 10-year protection. Hepatitis A and typhoid vaccines can also be given as a single dose vaccine, hepatyrix or viatim.

Hepatitis B

Hepatitis B is spread through infected blood, contaminated needles and sexual intercourse. It can also be spread from an infected mother to the baby during childbirth. It affects the liver, causing jaundice and occasionally liver failure. Most people recover completely, but some people might be chronic carriers of the virus, which could lead eventually to cirrhosis or liver cancer. Those visiting high-risk areas for long periods or those with increased social or occupational risk should be immunised. Many countries now routinely give hepatitis B as part of the routine childhood vaccination.

It is given singly or can be given at the same time as hepatitis A (hepatyrix).

A course will give protection for at least five years. It can be given over four weeks or six months.

HIV

Human immuno-deficiency virus (HIV), the virus that causes acquired immune deficiency syndrome (AIDS), is a major problem in Mozambique, with infection rates averaging about 16% nationwide, but much higher – well over 20% – in some areas. The virus is spread through infected blood and blood products, by sexual intercourse with an infected partner and from an infected mother to her baby during childbirth and breastfeeding. It can be spread through 'blood to blood' contacts, such as with contaminated instruments during medical, dental, acupuncture and other body-piercing procedures, and through sharing used intravenous needles. At present there is no cure; medication that might keep the disease under control is available, but these drugs are too expensive for the overwhelming majority of Mozambicans and are not readily available for travellers either. If you think you might have been infected with HIV, a blood test is necessary; a three-month gap after exposure and before testing is required to allow antibodies to appear in the blood.

Malaria

This is the most serious risk in Mozambique. There are thriving populations of malaria-carrying mosquitoes throughout the country, and taking prophylaxis or otherwise protecting yourself from bites is highly important. Infection rates are higher during the rainy season, but the risk exists year-round and it is extremely important to take preventative measures, even if you will just be in the country for a short time.

Malaria is caused by a parasite in the bloodstream spread via the bite of the female Anopheles mosquito. There are several types of malaria, falciparum malaria being the most dangerous type and the predominant form in Mozambique. Infection rates vary with season and climate, so check out the situation before departure. Unlike most other diseases regularly encountered by travellers, there is no vaccination against malaria. However, several different drugs are used to prevent malaria and new ones are in the pipeline. Up-to-date advice from a travel-health clinic is essential as some medication is more suitable for some travellers than others. The pattern of drug-resistant malaria is changing rapidly, so what was advised several years ago might no longer be the case.

Malaria can present in several ways. The early stages include headaches, fevers,

---

ANTIMALARIAL A TO D

A Awareness of the risk. No medication is totally effective, but protection of up to 95% is achievable with most drugs, as long as other measures have been taken.

B Bites – avoid at all costs:

- Sleep in a screened room, use a mosquito spray or coils and sleep under a permethrin-impregnated net at night. Light-weight travel-style nets are not available in Mozambique, so buy one before leaving home.
- Cover up in the evenings and at night with long trousers and long sleeves, preferably with permethrin-treated clothing. Light-coloured clothing is best.
- Apply appropriate repellent to all areas of exposed skin in the evenings. While prolonged overuse of DEET-containing repellents may be harmful, especially to children, its use is considered preferable to being bitten by disease-transmitting mosquitoes.
- Avoid perfumes, aftershave and heavily-scented soaps.

C Chemical prevention (ie antimalarial drugs) is usually needed in malarial areas. Expert advice is needed as resistance patterns can change, and new drugs are in development. Not all antimalarial drugs are suitable for everyone. Most antimalarial drugs need to be started at least a week in advance and continued for four weeks after the last possible exposure to malaria.

D Diagnosis. If you have a fever or flu-like illness within a year of travel to a malarial area, malaria is a possibility, and immediate medical attention is necessary.

generalized aches and pains, and malaise, which could be mistaken for flu. Other symptoms can include abdominal pain, diarrhoea and a cough. Anyone who develops a fever in a malarial area should assume malarial infection until a blood test proves negative, even if you have been taking antimalarial medication. If not treated, the next stage could develop within 24 hours, particularly if falciparum malaria is the parasite: jaundice, then reduced consciousness and coma (also known as cerebral malaria) followed by death. Treatment in hospital is essential and the death rate might still be as high as 10% even in the best intensive-care facilities.

Many travellers are under the impression that malaria is a mild illness, that treatment is always easy and successful and that taking antimalarial drugs causes more illness through side effects than actually getting malaria. In Mozambique and elsewhere in the region, this is unfortunately not true. Side effects of the medication depend on the drug being taken. Doxycycline can cause heartburn and indigestion; mefloquine (Larium) can cause anxiety attacks, insomnia and nightmares, and (rarely) severe psychiatric disorders; chloroquine can cause nausea and hair loss; and proguanil can cause mouth ulcers. These side effects are not universal and can be minimized by taking medication correctly (eg with food). Also, some people should not take a particular antimalarial drug (eg people with epilepsy should avoid mefloquine, and doxycycline should not be taken by pregnant women or children younger than 12).

If you decide that you really do not wish to take antimalarial drugs, you must understand the risks and be obsessive about avoiding mosquito bites. Use nets and insect repellent, and report any fever or flu-like symptoms to a doctor as soon as possible. Some people advocate homeopathic preparations against malaria, such as Demal200, but as yet there is no conclusive evidence that this is effective and many homeopaths do not recommend their use.

People of all ages can contract malaria and falciparum causes the most severe illness. Repeated infections might result eventually in less serious illness. Malaria in pregnancy frequently results in miscarriage or premature labour. Adults who have survived childhood malaria have developed immunity and usually only develop mild cases of malaria; most Western travellers have no immunity at all.

Immunity wanes after 18 months of non-exposure, so even if you have had malaria in the past and used to live in a malaria-prone area, you might no longer be immune.

If you will be away from major towns, it's worth considering taking standby treatment, although this should be seen as emergency treatment only and not as routine self-medication. It should be used only if you will be far from medical facilities and have been advised about the symptoms of malaria and how to use the medication. If you do resort to emergency self-treatment, medical advice should be sought as soon as possible to confirm whether the treatment has been successful. In particular you want to avoid contracting cerebral malaria, which can be fatal in 24 hours. As mentioned on p197, self-diagnostic kits, which can identify malaria in the blood from a finger prick, are available in the West and a worthwhile investment.

The risks from malaria to both mother and foetus during pregnancy are considerable. Unless good medical care can be guaranteed, travel in Mozambique while pregnant should be discouraged unless essential.

Meningococcal Meningitis

Meningococcal infection is spread through close respiratory contact and is more likely in crowded situations, such as dormitories, buses and clubs. Infection is uncommon in travellers. Vaccination is recommended for long stays and is especially important towards the end of the dry season, see p171. Symptoms include a fever, severe headache, neck stiffness and a red rash. Immediate medical treatment is necessary.

The ACWY vaccine is recommended for all travellers in sub-Saharan Africa. This vaccine is different from the meningococcal meningitis C vaccine given to children and adolescents in some countries; it is safe to be given both types of vaccine.

Poliomyelitis

Generally spread through contaminated food and water. It is one of the vaccines given in childhood and should be boosted every 10 years, either orally (a drop on the tongue) or as an injection. Polio can be carried asymptomatically (ie showing no symptoms) and could cause a transient fever. In rare cases it causes weakness or paralysis of one or more muscles, which might be permanent.

Rabies

Rabies is spread by receiving the bites or licks of an infected animal on broken skin. It is always fatal once the clinical symptoms start (which might be up to several months after an infected bite), so post-bite vaccination should be given as soon as possible. Post-bite vaccination (whether or not you've been vaccinated before the bite) prevents the virus from spreading to the central nervous system. Animal handlers should be vaccinated, as should those travelling to remote areas where a reliable source of post-bite vaccine is not available within 24 hours. Three preventive injections are needed over a month. If you have not been vaccinated you will need a course of five injections starting 24 hours, or as soon as possible, after the injury. If you have been vaccinated, you will need fewer post-bite injections and have more time to seek medical help.

Schistosomiasis (Bilharzia)

This disease is spread by flukes (minute worms) that are carried by a species of freshwater snail. The flukes are carried inside the snail, which then sheds them into slow-moving or still water. The parasites penetrate human skin during paddling or swimming and then migrate to the bladder or bowel. They are passed out via stool or urine and could contaminate fresh water, where the cycle starts again. Paddling or swimming in suspect freshwater lakes (including many parts of Lago Niassa) or slow-running rivers should be avoided. There might be no symptoms. There might be a transient fever and rash, and advanced cases might have blood in the stool or urine. A blood test can detect antibodies if you might have been exposed and treatment is then possible in specialist travel or infectious-disease clinics. If not treated the infection can cause kidney failure or permanent bowel damage. It is not possible for you to directly infect others.

Trypanosomiasis (Sleeping Sickness)

Spread via the bite of the tsetse fly. It causes a headache, fever and eventually coma. There is an effective treatment.

Tuberculosis (TB)

Tuberculosis is spread through close respiratory contact and occasionally through infected milk or milk products. BCG vaccination is recommended for those likely to be mixing closely with the local population, although it gives only moderate protection against TB. It is more important for long stays than for short-term stays. Inoculation with the BCG vaccine is not available in all countries. It is given routinely to many children in developing countries. The vaccination causes a small permanent scar at the site of injection, and is usually given in a specialist chest clinic. It is a live vaccine and should not be given to pregnant women or immuno-compromised individuals.

TB can be asymptomatic, only being picked up on a routine chest X-ray. Alternatively, it can cause a cough, weight loss or fever, sometimes months or even years after exposure.

Typhoid

This is spread through food or water contaminated by infected human faeces. The first symptom is usually a fever or a pink rash on the abdomen. Sometimes septicaemia (blood poisoning) can occur. A typhoid vaccine (ty-phim Vi, typherix) will give protection for three years. In some countries, the oral vaccine Vivotif is also available. Antibiotics are usually given as treatment and death is rare unless septicaemia occurs.

Yellow Fever

Although Mozambique does not require you to carry a certificate of yellow-fever vaccination unless you're arriving from an infected area (which includes neighbouring Tanzania),

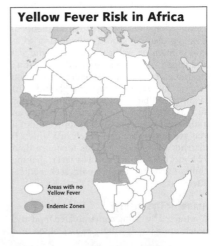

Yellow Fever Risk in Africa

Areas with no Yellow Fever

Endemic Zones

HEALTH

it is recommended for almost all visitors by the **Centers for Disease Control and Prevention** (www .cdc.gov/travel/yb/outline.htm£2).

Yellow fever is spread by infected mosquitoes. Symptoms range from a flu-like illness to severe hepatitis (liver inflammation) jaundice and death. The yellow-fever vaccination must be given at a designated clinic and is valid for 10 years. It is a live vaccine and must not be given to immuno-compromised or pregnant travellers.

TRAVELLERS' DIARRHOEA

Although it's not inevitable that you will get diarrhoea while travelling in Mozambique, it's certainly very likely. Diarrhoea is the most common travel-related illness and sometimes can be triggered by simple dietary changes. To help prevent diarrhoea, avoid tap water, only eat fresh fruits and vegetables if cooked or peeled, and be wary of dairy products that might contain unpasteurised milk. The small plastic bags of water sold on street corners are best avoided. Also take care with fruit juice, particularly if water may have been added. Milk in many up-country restaurants is made from reconstituted milk powder, which is safe if it's been made with boiled or mineral water.

With its excellent fruits and fresh produce, and seafood-based cuisine, Mozambique can be quite healthy, as far as diet is concerned. Yet while freshly cooked food can often be a safe option, plates or serving utensils might be dirty, so be selective when eating food from street vendors (make sure that cooked food is piping hot all the way through). If you develop diarrhoea, be sure to drink plenty of fluids, preferably an oral rehydration solution containing water (lots), and some salt and sugar. A few loose stools don't require treatment, but if you start having more than four or five stools a day, you should start taking an antibiotic (usually a quinoline drug, such as ciprofloxacin or norfloxacin) and an antidiarrhoeal agent (such as loperamide) if you are not within easy reach of a toilet. If diarrhoea is bloody, persists for more than 72 hours or is accompanied by fever, shaking chills or severe abdominal pain, seek medical attention.

Amoebic Dysentery

Contracted by eating contaminated food and water, amoebic dysentery causes blood and mucus in the faeces. It can be relatively mild and tends to come on gradually, but seek medical advice if you think you have the illness as it won't clear up without treatment (which is with specific antibiotics).

Giardiasis

This, like amoebic dysentery, is caused by ingesting contaminated food or water. The illness usually appears a week or more after exposure to the offending parasite. It might cause only a short-lived bout of typical travellers' diarrhoea, but it can also cause persistent diarrhoea. Ideally, seek medical advice if you suspect you have giardiasis, but if you are in a remote area you could start a course of antibiotics.

ENVIRONMENTAL HAZARDS
Heat Exhaustion

This condition occurs following heavy sweating and excessive fluid loss with inadequate replacement of fluids and salt, and is particularly common in hot climates when taking unaccustomed exercise before full acclimatisation. Symptoms include headache, dizziness and tiredness. Dehydration is already happening by the time you feel thirsty – aim to drink sufficient water to produce pale, diluted urine. Self-treatment: fluid replacement with water and/or fruit juice, and cooling by cold water and fans. The treatment of the salt-loss component consists of consuming salty fluids as in soup and adding a little more table salt to foods than usual.

Heatstroke

Heat exhaustion is a precursor to the much more serious condition of heatstroke. In this case there is damage to the sweating mechanism resulting in an excessive rise in body temperature, irrational and hyperactive behaviour, and eventually loss of consciousness and death. Rapid cooling by spraying the body with water and fanning is ideal. Emergency fluid and electrolyte replacement is usually also required by intravenous drip.

Insect Bites & Stings

Mosquitoes might not always carry malaria or dengue fever, but they (and other insects) can cause irritation and infected bites. To avoid these, take the same precautions as you would for avoiding malaria (see p199). Use DEET-based insect repellents. Excellent clothing treatments are also available; mosquitos that land on treated clothing will die.

Bee and wasp stings cause real problems only to those who have a severe allergy to the stings (anaphylaxis.) If you are one of these people, carry an 'epipen' – an adrenaline (epinephrine) injection, which you can give yourself. This could save your life.

Sandflies are found in some areas. They usually only cause a nasty itchy bite, but they can carry a rare skin disorder called cutaneous leishmaniasis. Prevention of bites with DEET-based repellents is sensible.

Scorpions are frequently found in arid areas. They can cause a painful bite that is sometimes life-threatening. If bitten by a scorpion, take a painkiller. Medical treatment should be sought if collapse occurs.

Bed bugs are often found in hostels and cheap hotels. They lead to very itchy, lumpy bites. Spraying the mattress with crawling-insect killer after changing bedding will get rid of them.

Scabies is also frequently found in cheap accommodation. These tiny mites live in the skin, particularly between the fingers. They cause an intensely itchy rash. The itch is easily treated with malathion and permethrin lotion from a pharmacy; other members of the household also need treating to avoid spreading scabies, even if they do not show any symptoms.

Snake Bites

Do not walk barefoot, or stick your hand into holes or cracks. However, 50% of people bitten by venomous snakes are not actually injected with poison (envenomed). If bitten by a snake, do not panic. Immobilise the bitten limb with a splint (such as a stick) and apply a bandage over the site, with firm pressure – similar to bandaging a sprain. Do not apply a tourniquet, or cut or suck the bite. Get medical help as soon as possible so antivenom can be given if needed.

Water

Avoid drinking tap water in Mozambique unless it has been boiled, filtered or chemi-cally disinfected (such as with iodine tablets). Never drink from streams, rivers and lakes. It's also best to avoid drinking from pumps and wells – some do bring pure water to the surface, but the presence of animals can still contaminate supplies.

Traditional Medicine

More than 80% of Mozambicans rely on traditional medicine, often because conventional Western-style medicine is too expensive, or because of prevailing cultural attitudes and beliefs. It might also be because there's no other choice: a World Health Organization survey found that although there was only one medical doctor for every 50,000 people in Mozambique, there was a traditional healer (*curandeiro*) for every 200 people.

Although some traditional remedies seem to work on malaria, sickle cell anaemia, high blood pressure and some AIDS symptoms, most healers learn their art by apprenticeship, so education (and consequently application of knowledge) is inconsistent and unregulated.

Rather than attempting to stamp out traditional practices, or simply pretend they aren't happening, a positive step has been an attempt to regulate traditional medicine by creating healers' associations, such as the Associaça o dos Médicos Tradicionais de Moçambique (Ametramo; see boxed text 'Feeling under the weather?', p31). Among other things, Ametramo is working to obtain more formalised education for its members, and training them in HIV/AIDS prevention and treatment in ways that are compatible with Western medicine. Yet, in the short term, it remains unlikely that even a basic level of conventional Western-style medicine will be made available to all Mozambicans. Traditional medicine, on the other hand, will almost certainly continue to be widely practised.

HEALTH

Language

CONTENTS

Portuguese is the official language of Mozambique. It is widely spoken in larger towns, less so in rural areas. Mozambique's numerous African languages, all of which belong to the Bantu family, can be divided into three groups: Makua-Lomwe languages, spoken by more than 33% of the population, primarily in the north; Sena-Nyanja languages in the centre and near Lago Niassa; and Tsonga languages in the south. The exact number of independent languages spoken in Mozambique has not been established, although it is estimated that there are at least nine, and perhaps as many as 16. Outside southern resorts and the areas bordering Zimbabwe and Malawi, English is not widely spoken. In northern Cabo Delgado and Niassa provinces near the Tanzanian border, Swahili is frequently heard and is often more useful than Portuguese. See p205 for a few Swahili greetings and essentials.

PORTUGUESE

PRONUNCIATION

The pronunciation guides included with the words and phrases below should make things a lot easier for the uninitiated. Word stress is indicasted by the italicised syllable.

LOCAL GREETINGS

While learning some Portuguese will greatly facilitate your travels in Mozambique, learning a few words of one of the local languages is even better. Grammar books and the like are difficult to find. Bookstores in Maputo have the best selection, though even there the choice is limited. Your best bet is to arrange a tutor, but in the meantime, a few greetings and basic phrases will be warmly received.

One of the most useful languages in Maputo and southern Mozambique is Shangana:

Good morning.	*lixile* (li-*shee*-le)
Good afternoon.	*lipelile*
Thank you.	*kanimambo*
Goodbye.	*salani*

In the far north near Lago Niassa, most people speak Nyanja:

Good morning.	*mwaka bwanji*
Good afternoon.	*mwalongedza*
Thank you very much.	*zikomo kwambile*
Goodbye.	*ine de likupita*

The main languages in central Mozambique are Sena and N'Dau. To greet someone in Sena, say *magerwa*. In N'Dau, it's *mawata*. In and around Chimoio, you will also hear Manica, and the greeting, *mangwanani* .

In much of Nampula and Cabo Delgado provinces, where major languages include Makonde, Makua, the most useful greeting is *salaam'a*. In northern Cabo Delgado Swahili is useful (see p205).

A characteristic feature of Portuguese is the use of nasal vowels and diphthongs (vowel combinations). Pronounce them as if you're trying to make the sound through your nose rather than your mouth. In the pronunciation guides, 'ng' is used to indicate a nasal sound.

GENDER

Portuguese has masculine and feminine forms of nouns and adjectives. Alternative endings appear in this language guide separated by a slash with the masculine form first. Generally, a word that ends in **o** is masculine and one ending in **a** is feminine, with a few exceptions.

ACCOMMODATION

I'm looking for a ...
Procuro ...   proo-*koo*-roo-...
Where's a ...?
Onde é ...?   ongd e ...
  camping ground
  um parque de campismo   oong park-de kang-*peezh*-moo
  guesthouse
  uma pensão   oo-ma peng-*sowng*
  hotel
  um hotel   oong oo-*tel*
  room
  um quarto   oong *kwarr*-too

I'd like a ... room.
Queria um quarto de ...   kree-a oong *kwarr*-too de ...
Do you have a ... room?
Tem um quarto de ...?   teng oong *kwarr*-too de ...
  double
  casal   ka-*zal*
  single
  individual   Ing-dee-vee-*dwal*
  twin
  duplo   doo-ploo

Do you have ...?
Tem ...?   teng ...
  a room with a private bathroom
  um quartro com casa   oong kwar-too kom ka-za
  de banho privativo   de ba-nyoo pree-va-*tee*-voo
  a safety deposit box
  uma caixa de segurança oo-ma ka-sha de se-goo-*rang*-sa

For (three) nights.
Para (três) noites.   pa-ra (trezh) noytsh
Does it include breakfast?
Inclui pequeno   eeng-kloo-*ee* pee-*ke*-noo
almoço?   al-*mo*-soo
May I see it?
Posso ver?   po-soo verr

How much is it per ...?
Quanto custa por ...?   kwang-too koos-ta porr ...
  night
  uma noite   oo-ma *noy*-te
  person
  pessoa   pso-a
  week
  uma semana   oo-ma se-*ma*-na

CONVERSATION & ESSENTIALS
Hello.
Bom dia.   bong dee-a

Hi.
  Olá.   o-*la*
Good day.
  Bom dia.   bong dee-a
Good evening.
  Boa noite.   bo-a noy-te
See you later.
  Até logo.   a-te lo-goo
Goodbye.
  Adeus.   a-*dyoos*
How are you?
  Como está?   ko-moo shta
Fine, and you?
  Tudo bem, e tu?   too-doo beng e too
Pleased to meet you.
  Prazer.   pra-*zerr*
Yes.
  Sim.   seeng
No.
  Não.   nowng
Please.
  Por favor.   poor fa-*vorr*
Thank you (very much).
  (Muito) Obrigado/a.   (mweeng-too) o-bree-*ga*-doo/da
You're welcome.
  De nada.   de na-da
May I?
  Da licensa.   da lee-*seng*-sa

EMERGENCIES

Help!
Socorro! — soo·ko·rroo
It's an emergency.
É uma emergência. — e oo·ma e·merr·zheng·sya
I'm lost.
Estou perdido/a. — shto perr·dee·doo/da
Where are the toilets?
Onde ficam os — ong·de fee·kam oos
lavabos? — la·va·boos
Go away!
Vai-te embora! — vai·te eng·bo·ra

Call ...!
Chame ...! — sham ...
 a doctor
 um médico — oong me·dee·koo
 an ambulance
 uma ambulância — oo·ma am·boo·lan·sya
 the police
 a polícia — a poo·lee·see·a

Excuse me. (to get past or requesting help)
Com licença. — kong lee·seng·sa
I'm sorry. (to apologise)
Desculpe. — desh·kool·pe
What's your name?
Como se chama? — ko·moo se sha·ma
My name is ...
Chamo-me ... — sha·moo·me ...
Where are you from?
De onde é? — de ong·de e
I'm from ...
Sou (da/do/de) ... — so (da/do/de) ...
May I take a photo (of you)?
Posso tirar(-lhe) uma — po·soo tee·rarr(·lye) oo·ma
foto? — fo·too

DIRECTIONS

Where's ...?
Onde fica ...? — ong·de fee·ka ...
Can you show me (on the map)?
Pode mostrar-me — pod moos·trarr·me
(no mapa)? — (noo ma·pa)
How far is it?
Qual a distância daqui? — kwal a dees·tan·see·a da·kee
How do I get there?
Como é que eu — ko·moo e ke e·oo
chego aí? — she·goo a·ee
Turn left/right.
Vire à esquerda/direita. — veer a skerr·da/dee·ray·ta

near ... — *perto ...* — perr·too ...
straight ahead — *em frente* — eng frengt

north — *norte* — nort
south — *sul* — sool
east — *este* — esht
west — *oeste* — oo·esht

HEALTH

I'm ill.
Estou doente. — shto doo·eng·te
I need a doctor (who speaks English).
Preciso de um médico — pre·see·zoo de oong me·dee·koo
(que fale inglês). — (ke fal eeng·glesh)
I've been vomiting.
Tenho estado a vomitar. — ta·nyo shta·doo a voo·mee·tarr

Where's the — *Onde fica ...* — on·de fee·ka ...
nearest ...? — *mais perto?* — ma·ees perr·to
 dentist — *o dentista* — oo deng·teesh·ta
 doctor — *o médico* — oo me·dee·koo
 hospital — *o hospital* — oo osh·pee·tal
 medical centre — *a clínica médica* — a klee·nee·ka me·dee·ka

I feel ... — *Estou ...* — shto ...
 dizzy — *com tonturas* — kong tong·too·ras
 nauseous — *com naúseas* — kong now·shas

antiseptic — *antiséptico* — an·tee·sep·tee·koo
asthma — *asma* — azh·ma
contraceptives — *anticoncepcional* — an·tee·kon·sep·syoo·nal
diarrhoea — *diarréia* — dee·a·ray·a
fever — *febre* — febr
malaria — *malaria* — ma·la·ree·a
pain — *dores* — dorsh
painkillers — *analgésicos* — a·nal·zhe·zee·koos

I'm allergic — *Sou alérgico/a* — so a·lerr·zhee·
to ... — *à ...* — koo/ka a ...
 antibiotics — *antibióticos* — ang·tee·byo·tee·koos
 aspirin — *aspirina* — ash·pee·ree·na
 bees — *abelhas* — a·be·lyas
 peanuts — *amendoins* — a·meng·doyngs
 penicillin — *penicilina* — pnee·see·lee·na

LANGUAGE DIFFICULTIES

Do you speak English?
Fala inglês? — fa·la eeng·glesh
Does anyone here speak English?
Alguém aqui fala inglês? — al·geng a·kee fa·la eeng·glesh
I (don't) understand.
(Não) Entendo. — (nowng) eng·teng·doo
Could you please write it down?
Pode por favor escrever — po·de·porr fa·vorr es·kre·verr
num papel? — noom pa·pel

NUMBERS

0	zero	ze·roo
1	um/uma (m/f)	oong/oo·ma
2	dois/duas (m/f)	doys/dwash
3	três	tresh
4	quatro	kwa·troo
5	cinco	seeng·koo
6	seis	saysh
7	sete	set
8	oito	oy·too
9	nove	nov
10	dez	desh
11	onze	onqz
12	doze	doz
13	treze	trez
14	quatorze	ka·torrz
15	quinze	keengz
16	dezesseis	dze·saysh
17	dezesete	dze·set
18	dezoito	dzoy·too
19	dezenove	dze·nov
20	vinte	veengt
21	vinte e um	veengt e oong
22	vinte e dois	veengt e doysh
30	trinta	treeng·ta
40	quarenta	kwa·reng·ta
50	cinquenta	seeng·kweng·ta
60	sessenta	se·seng·ta
70	setenta	steng·ta
80	oitenta	oy·teng·ta
90	noventa	noo·veng·ta
100	cem	sang
200	duzentos	doo·zeng·toosh
1000	mil	meel

SHOPPING & SERVICES

What time does ... open?
A que horas abre ...?   a ke o·ras a·bre ...
I'd like to buy ...
Queria comprar ...   kree·rya kom·prarr ...
How much is it?
Quanto custa?   kwang·too koosh·ta
That's too expensive.
É muito caro.   e mweeng·too ka·roo

Where is ...?
Onde fica ...?   ong·de fee·ka ...
  an ATM
um multibanco   oom mool·tee·bang·koo
  a bank
um banco   oom ban·koo
  the ... embassy
a embaixada do/da ...   a eng·bai·sha·da doo/da ...
  a foreign-exchange office
uma loja de câmbio   oo·ma lo·zha de kam·byoo

  a market
um mercado   oom merr·ka·doo
  a pharmacy/chemist
uma farmácia   oo·ma far·ma·sya
  the police station
o posto de polícia   oo pos·too·de poo·lee·see·a
  the post office
o correio   oo coo·ray·oo

Can I pay ...?
Posso pagar com ...?   po·soo pa·garr kom ...
  by credit card
cartão de crédito   karr·towng de kre·dee·too
  by travellers cheque
cheque de viagem   she·kee de vee·ya·zheng

I want to buy ...
Quero comprar ...   ke·roo kom·prarr ...
  a phone card
um cartão telefónico   oong kar·towng te·le·fo·nee·koo
  stamps
selos   se·loosh

Where can I ...?
Onde posso ...?   on·de po·soo ...
  change a travellers cheque
trocar traveler cheques   troo·karr tra·ve·ler she·kes
  change money
trocar dinheiro   troo·kar dee·nyay·roo
  check my email
ver o meu e-mail   ver oo me·oo e·mail
  get Internet access
aceder à internet   a·se·der a een·terr·net

TIME & DATES

What time is it?
Que horas são?   ke o·ras sowng
It's (ten) o'clock.
São (dez) horas.   sowng (desh) o·ras

now	agora	a·go·ra
this morning	esta manhã	esh·ta ma·nyang
this afternoon	esta tarde	esh·ta tard
today	hoje	ozh
tonight	esta noite	esh·ta noyt
tomorrow	amanhã	a·ma·nyang
yesterday	ontem	ong·teng

Monday	segunda-feira	sgoon·da·fay·ra
Tuesday	terça-feira	terr·sa·fay·ra
Wednesday	quarta-feira	kwarr·ta·fay·ra
Thursday	quinta-feira	keeng·ta·fay·ra
Friday	sexta-feira	saysh·ta·fay·ra
Saturday	sábado	sa·ba·doo
Sunday	domingo	doo·meeng·goo

TRANSPORT
Public Transport
Which ... goes to ...?
Qual o ... que vai para ...?   kwal oo ... ke vai *pa*·ra ...
(ferry) boat
barco (de travessia)   *barr*·koo (de tra·*ve*·sya)
bus
autocarro/   ow·too·*kaa*·rroo/
  machibombo   ma·shee·*bom*·bo
converted passenger truck
chapa(-cem)   *sha*·pa(·seng)
train
comboio   kom·*boy*·oo

When's the ...	*Quando sai o ...*	*kwang*·doo sai oo
... (bus)?	*(autocarro)?*	(ow·too·*ka*·rroo)
first	*primeiro*	pree·*may*·roo
next	*próximo*	pro·*see*·moo
last	*último*	*ool*·tee·moo

What time does it get to ...?
Que horas chega a ...?   ke *o*·ras *she*·ga a ...
A ... ticket to (...)
Um bilhete para (...)   oong bee·*lyet* pa·ra (...)
Please take me to (this address).
Leve-me para (esta morada), por favor.
le·ve·me *pa*·ra (*esh*·ta moo·*ra*·da) porr fa·*vorr*

(bus) stop	*paragem*	pa·*roo*·zheng
customs	*alfândega*	al·*fang*·de·ga
immigration	*imigração*	ee·mee·gra·*sowng*
visa	*visto*	*veesh*·to

Private Transport
I'd like to hire a/an ...
Queria alugar ...
ke·rya a·loo·*garr* ...
4WD
um quatro por quatro   oom *kwa*·troo por *kwa*·troo
bicycle
uma bicicleta   *oo*·ma bee·see·*kle*·ta

Also available from Lonely Planet:
Portuguese Phrasebook

car
um carro   oong *ka*·rroo
motorbike
uma motocicleta   *oo*·ma mo·too·see·*kle*·ta

Is this the road to ...?
Esta é a estrada para ...?
esh·ta e a es·*tra*·da *pa*·ra ...
Where's a gas/petrol station?
Onde fica um posto de gasolina?
on·de *fee*·ka oong *pos*·too de ga·zoo·*lee*·na
Please fill it up.
Enche o depósito, por favor.
en·she oo de·*po*·see·too porr fa·*vorr*
I'd like ... litres.
Meta ... litros.
me·ta ... *lee*·troosh

avenue	*avenida*	a·ve·*nee*·da
beach	*praia*	*prai*·a
beach road	*marginal*	mar·zhee·*nal*
bush (countryside)	*mato*	*ma*·to
diesel	*diesel*	*dee*·sel
documents	*documentos*	do·koo·*meng*·toosh
(passport, drivers licence, car registration papers, etc)		
fine (penalty)	*multa*	*mool*·ta
a lift/ride	*uma boleia*	*oo*·ma bo·*lai*·a
petrol	*combustível*	kom·boo·*stee*·vel
(unleaded)	*(sem chumbo)*	(seng *shoom*·boo)
roadside stall	*barraca*	ba·*ra*·ka
street	*rua*	*roo*·a
tar/asphalt	*alcatrão*	al·ka·*trowng*
track	*pista*	*pee*·sta

The (car/motorbike) has broken down at ...
(O carro/A motocicleta) avariou em ...
(oo *ka*·rroo/a moo·too·see·*kle*·ta) a·*va*·ryo eng ...
The car won't start.
O carro não pega.   o *ka*·ho nowng *pe*·ga
I need a mechanic.
Preciso de um mecânico.   pre·*see*·soo de oong
                            me·*ka*·nee·koo
I have a puncture/flat.
Tenho um furo no   *ta*·nyoo oong *foo*·roo noo
  pneu.   pe·*ne*·oor
Where can I get this repaired?
Onde posso consertar   *on*·dee *po*·soo kon·ser·*tar*
  isto?   *eesh*·too
I've run out of petrol/gas.
Fiquei sem gasolina.   fee·*kay* seng ga·zoo·*lee*·na
I've had an accident.
Sofri um acidente.   soo·*free* oong a·see·*deng*·te

Glossary

See the food glossary on p52 for culinary terms and Mozambican dishes.

ablutions block – a building containing a toilet, shower and washing facilities, found mainly in camping grounds and caravan parks
aldeamentos   village complexes
alfaiataria – tailor's shop
ANC – African National Congress
animist – various definitions, but the most useful seems to be: 'beliefs based on the existence of the human soul, and on spirits that inhabit or are represented by natural objects and phenomena, which have the power to influence human life for good or ill'
assimilados – a colonial-era population classification, referring to those Mozambicans who adopted Portuguese customs and ways
autocarro – see machibombo
Av (Avenida) – Avenue

baía – bay
bairro – neighbourhood, area or section of town
baixa – the lower-lying area of a city or town. Since in coastal Mozambique this often means the part of the city near the port, the baixa is frequently synonymous with 'commercial district'.
baixar – to reduce or decrease (as in price)
barraca – market stall or food stall
barragem – dam
BIM – Banco Internacional de Moçambique
buleia – lift (ie, in a vehicle) – a very useful word in Mozambique
buraco – hole, pothole

cabines públicas – public telephone booths
caipirinha – A (traditionally Brazilian) cocktail made from lime juice, sugar and ice mixed with cachaça, vodka or rum
Caixa Postal (CP) – post office box (in addresses)
camião, camiões – truck(s)
capitania – port authority
capulana – a colourful cloth worn by women around their waist
casa de cultura – literally, 'house of culture'; cultural centre found in each provincial capital. The casas de cultura exist to promote traditional culture and are good sources of information on traditional music and dance performances in the area.
casal – room with a double bed
cascata – waterfall

casita – bungalow
cerveja – beer
chapa (from chapa cem) – any public transport that is not a bus or truck; usually refers to converted minivans or pick-ups (chapa cem means 'tin 100', in reference to the original price for a ride – Mtc100, in the days of the old metical)
chegar – arrive (hora de chegada – time of arrival)
comida – food
correios – post office

dhow – traditional Swahili Arabic sailing boat
dia da cidade – city or town day; a holiday commemorating the town's founding, often celebrated with parades and song and dance performances
duplo – room with two twin beds; see also casal

EN1 – Estrada Nacional 1; the main south–north highway
EN6 – Estrada Nacional 6; the highway running from Beira west towards Chimoio and the Zimbabwe border
estrada – road, highway

feira – trading fair
feticeiros – witch doctors
fortaleza – fort
Frelimo (Frente da Libertação de Moçambique) – Mozambique Liberation Front

ilha – island
indígenas – literally, 'indigenous people', refers to a colonial-era population classification
inselbergs – isolated rocky hills common to parts of Southern Africa; literally means 'island mountains'

já – meaning 'already', 'yet', 'now', 'right now/at once/ right away'. If you inquire when your meal will be ready, waiters may tell you 'vem já', which means it's coming right up (although in reality it will likely be a while). 'Até já', also frequently used, means 'goodbye' (said with the expectation that you will see the other person in the near future).

LAM – Linhas Aéreas de Moçambique; the national airline
lobola – bride price or dowry
lago – lake

machamba – small farm plot
machibombo – bus
makwaela – a type of dance popular in the south, characterised by a cappella singing accompanied by foot percussion

mapiko – a ritual dance of the Makonde in northern Mozambique; mapiko also refers to the wooden masks worn by the dancer

marginal – beach road

marimba – African xylophone, made from strips of resonant wood with various-sized gourds for sound boxes

marrabenta – Mozambique's national music, with an upbeat style and distinctive beat

mata bicho – literally, 'kill the beast', a common expression for breakfast (the official translation for breakfast is pequeno almoço)

mato – bush (é muito mato, meaning 'it's really remote' – ie when speaking of an area or locale)

mercado – market

metical, meticais – Mozambican currency

migração – immigration

minas (minas de terra) – land mines

monte(s) – mountain(s)

nyanga – panpipes; also the name of a dance in which the dancer plays the panpipes

paragem – stop (ie, bus or transport stop)

parque nacional – national park

pastelaria – shop selling pastries, cakes and often light meals as well

pensão, pensões – inexpensive hotel(s)

piri-piri – hot pepper (a common addition to food in many parts of the country)

pousada – hotel or inn, usually a step up from a pensão

praça – square

praia – beach

prazeiro – prazo holder

prazo – privately owned agricultural estates allocated by the Portuguese crown; the prazo system was used by the Portuguese between the 17th and early 20th centuries in an attempt to strengthen their control in Mozambique

pregos – steak and egg sandwich

pronto/a – ready (estamos prontos para sair – we're ready to leave)

quente – hot (as in água quente, hot water)

refresco – soda, soft drink

régulo – chief, traditional leader

Renamo – Resistência Nacional Moçambicana/ Mozambican National Resistance (the main opposition party)

reserva – reserve

rondavel – round African-style huts or buildings

rua – street

sair – depart (hora de saída – the time of departure)

salão de cha – teahouse, cafe

tabacaria – small shop selling magazines, tobacco etc

tabela de marés – tide table

TDM (Telecomunicações de Moçambique) – the national telecommunications company

timbila (plural of mbila) – type of marimba or xylophone used by the Chopi people

tudo bem – everything's fine (in reply to 'como está'); also, as question ('tudo bem?'), meaning 'everything OK?'

tufo – a dance of Arabic origin, common on Ilha de Moçambique and along the northern coast

vinho – wine

xima – maize- or cassava-based staple, usually served with a sauce of beans, vegetables or fish; also known as upshwa in some areas

Behind the Scenes

THIS BOOK

Both editions of Mozambique have been researched and written by Mary Fitzpatrick. The first edition of this book was based on the Mozambique chapters of Malawi, Mozambique & Zambia, which was written by David Else. The Health chapter was written by Dr Caroline Evans. This guidebook was commissioned in Lonely Planet's Melbourne office and produced by the following:

Commissioning Editors Jessa Boanas-Dewes, Will Gourlay, Lucy Monie
Coordinating Editor Chris Girdler
Coordinating Cartographer Daniel Fennessy
Coordinating Layout Designer Carol Jackson
Managing Editor Imogen Bannister
Managing Cartographer Shahara Ahmed
Assisting Editor Helen Koehne, Phillip Tang
Assisting Cartographers David Connolly, Joshua Geoghegan, Corey Hutchison, Erin McManus, Julie Sheridan
Cover Designer Jane Hart
Project Managers Craig Kilburn, John Shippick
Language Content Coordinator Quentin Frayne

Thanks to Sin Choo, Sally Darmody, Mark Germanchis, Laura Jane, Raphael Richards, Celia Wood

THANKS
MARY FITZPATRICK

Many people assisted me with time, information and logistics for this edition. In particular, I'd like to thank Lesley Sitch and Bart van Straaten in Pemba; Dr Baldeu Chande, Director of the Reserva do Niassa; Luís Carvalho,

Sr Fernando and Phil Gray in Nampula; Chief Park Warden Roberto Zolho, Vasco Galante and Bart Wursten at Parque Nacional de Gorongosa; Helen O'Sullivan in Beira; Joshua Sullivan-Pires in Vilankulo, and the many other PCVs who so generously helped me out, including Fran in Inhambane and Katie in Bilene. In Maputo, special thanks to Argentina Matavel for her generous offers of hospitality; to Sidney Bliss for his ongoing assistance; to Francisco Muianga; to David Ankers; and to Natalie Tenzer-Silva and her colleagues. I am also grateful to all those who wrote in with comments on the previous edition, especially Marta Stolarska, and to those who helped me on a previous unpublished edition of this guidebook, in particular Dr José Dias in Pemba, Robin Mason and John Newstead.

Last but not least, a big thank you to Rick and to Christopher for their enthusiasm, support, patience, company and good humour during the research and writing of this book.

OUR READERS

Many thanks to the travellers who used the last edition and wrote to us with helpful hints, useful advice and interesting anecdotes:

A Gep Aadriaanse, Zournatzi Athena **B** Ami Baker, Lucy Bale, Richard Bartlett, Omar BenYedder, Lars Bergmeyer, Amei Binns, Jane Bode, Carol Bouchard, Ruth Butterworth **C** Diego & Silvia Candida, Lauren Capstick, Catarina & Alex Castro, Francesco Catalano, Maria Cecilia Macatangga, Antoni Cladera, Matthew Coghlan **D** Charles Dawson, Winnie de Rooen **E** Diana en Erwin, **F** Marianne Freire, Kevin Fromme **G** Rob Garner, Lee Gillyon, Rachel Godley,

---

THE LONELY PLANET STORY

The story begins with a classic travel adventure: Tony and Maureen Wheeler's 1972 journey across Europe and Asia to Australia. There was no useful information about the overland trail then, so Tony and Maureen published the first Lonely Planet guidebook to meet a growing need.

From a kitchen table, Lonely Planet has grown to become the largest independent travel publisher in the world, with offices in Melbourne (Australia), Oakland (USA) and London (UK). Today Lonely Planet guidebooks cover the globe. There is an ever-growing list of books and information in a variety of media. Some things haven't changed. The main aim is still to make it possible for adventurous travellers to get out there – to explore and better understand the world.

At Lonely Planet we believe travellers can make a positive contribution to the countries they visit – if they respect their host communities and spend their money wisely. Every year 5% of company profit is donated to charities around the world.

Kolby Granville, Alex Guerrero **H** Sue Hall, Andrew Hamling, Ingrid Hansen, Katherine & Christoph Hantel, Gary W Hickman, Gerrie Holtzhausen **I** Christine Ingemorsen, Peter Isaksson **J** Mary Johnson **K** Marius R Karlsen, Raphael Keller, Steven Kennewell, Matt Kenny, Christopher Kitchin, Eddy Kleingeld, Andreas Konieczen, Milena Kraus, Blaz Mojca, Lisa Krhin **L** Chris Lanyon, Johan Le Roux, John Linnemeier, Gary Lowe **M** Brian MacCormaic, Magali Malherbe, Dale Malmskog, Jan Mecklenburg **N** Peter Nauta, Jane Nightingale **O** Erika Olivier, Kjeld Olsen, Amanda Oostendorp, Jenny Orchard **P** Shawn Plummer, Adam Pollock **R** Birgitte Rask, Meloney Retallack, Liz Robertson, **S** Eva Sandberg, Raquel Saraiva, Nicola Scevola, Eva Schneider, Jim Shelley, Julie Silva, Peter Sloth Madsen, Nicole Smith, Paul Spaans, Avi Srebro, Peter Steiner, Ruth C Stoky, Marta Stolarska, Kathy Stroud **T** Ian Tarplee, Sofia Tengvall, Greg Thomas, David Thornforst **V** Edda-Nathalie van den Bergh, Maartje van der Kluit, Teun van Metelen, Alex van Oostenrijk, Paul Venturino, Bostjan Veronik **W** Joseph Winter, Jan Witkiewicz, Manfred Wolfensberger, Alastair Womack **Z** Peter Zaeh

SEND US YOUR FEEDBACK

We love to hear from travellers – your comments keep us on our toes and help make our books better. Our well-travelled team reads every word on what you loved or loathed about this book. Although we cannot reply individually to postal submissions, we always guarantee that your feedback goes straight to the appropriate authors, in time for the next edition. Each person who sends us information is thanked in the next edition – and the most useful submissions are rewarded with a free book.

To send us your updates – and find out about Lonely Planet events, newsletters and travel news – visit our award-winning website: **www.lonelyplanet.com/contact**.

Note: we may edit, reproduce and incorporate your comments in Lonely Planet products such as guidebooks, websites and digital products, so let us know if you don't want your comments reproduced or your name acknowledged. For a copy of our privacy policy visit www.lonelyplanet.com/privacy.

Index

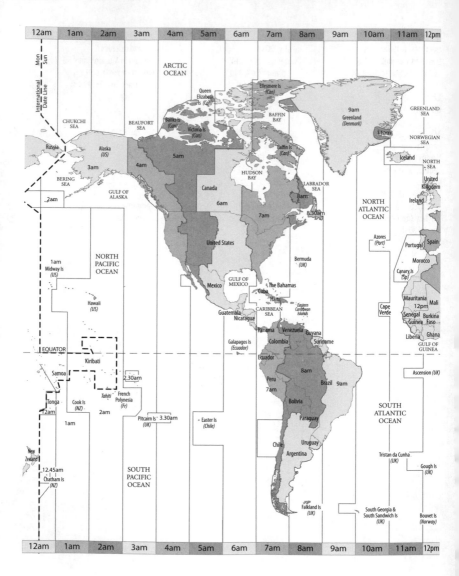

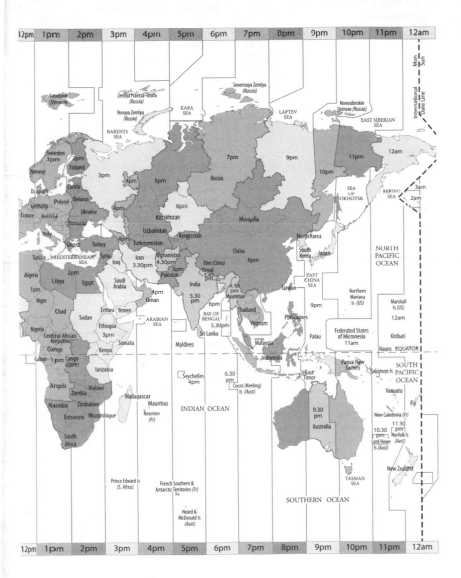

MAP LEGEND

ROUTES

Tollway	Mall/Steps
Freeway	Tunnel
Primary	Pedestrian Overpass
Secondary	Walking Tour
Tertiary	Walking Tour Detour
Lane	Walking Trail
Under Construction	Walking Path
Unsealed Road	Track
One-Way Street	

TRANSPORT

Ferry	Rail
Bus Route	

HYDROGRAPHY

River, Creek	Canal
Intermittent River	Water
Swamp	Lake (Dry)
Mangrove	Lake (Salt)
Reef	Mudflats

BOUNDARIES

International	Regional, Suburb
State, Provincial	Ancient Wall
Disputed	Cliff
Marine Park	

AREA FEATURES

Airport	Land
Area of Interest	Mall
Beach, Desert	Market
Building	Park
Campus	Reservation
Cemetery, Christian	Rocks
Cemetery, Other	Sports
Forest	Urban

POPULATION

CAPITAL (NATIONAL)	CAPITAL (STATE)
Large City	Medium City
Small City	Town, Village

SYMBOLS

Sights/Activities
- Beach
- Castle, Fortress
- Christian
- Hindu
- Islamic
- Museum, Gallery
- Point of Interest
- Pool
- Ruin

Eating
- Eating

Drinking
- Drinking

Entertainment
- Entertainment

Shopping
- Shopping

Sleeping
- Sleeping
- Camping

Transport
- Airport, Airfield
- Border Crossing
- Bus Station
- General Transport
- Parking Area
- Petrol Station
- Taxi Rank

Information
- Bank, ATM
- Embassy/Consulate
- Hospital, Medical
- Information
- Internet Facilities
- Police Station
- Post Office, GPO
- Telephone
- Toilets

Geographic
- Lighthouse
- Lookout
- Mountain, Volcano
- National Park

LONELY PLANET OFFICES

Australia
Head Office
Locked Bag 1, Footscray, Victoria 3011
☎ 03 8379 8000, fax 03 8379 8111
talk2us@lonelyplanet.com.au

USA
150 Linden St, Oakland, CA 94607
☎ 510 893 8555, toll free 800 275 8555
fax 510 893 8572
info@lonelyplanet.com

UK
72–82 Rosebery Ave,
Clerkenwell, London EC1R 4RW
☎ 020 7841 9000, fax 020 7841 9001
go@lonelyplanet.co.uk

Published by Lonely Planet Publications Pty Ltd
ABN 36 005 607 983

© Lonely Planet Publications Pty Ltd 2007

© photographers as indicated 2007

Cover photograph by Getty Images: Mozambique, man carrying basket on head, Penny Tweedie. Many of the images in this guide are available for licensing from Lonely Planet Images: www.lonelyplanetimages.com.

Printed by SNP Security Printing Pte Ltd, Singapore